NO PLACE LEFT TO GO

Why Palestine Matters

Donald E. Wagner

foreword by Rev. Dr. Munther Isaac
preface by Rev. Wendell Griffen

OLIVE BRANCH PRESS

An imprint of Interlink Publishing Group, Inc.
Northampton, Massachusetts

First published in 2026 by

Olive Branch Press
An imprint of Interlink Publishing Group, Inc.
46 Crosby Street, Northampton, MA 01060
www.interlinkbooks.com

Based on the previously published *Glory to God in the Lowest*

Library of Congress Cataloging-in-Publication data available
ISBN-13: 978-1-62371-622-6

Printed and bound in the United States of America

Praise for Donald E. Wagner's *Glory to God in the Lowest*

"A gripping memoir that tells a powerful conversion story of a white evangelical Christian who came to dedicate his life and career for the cause of justice in Palestine with all the ups and downs that comes with such a dedication. A must read for anyone looking for an eyewitness account of major political and religious developments in the modern Middle East and for firsthand insights into the early years of Christian and Human rights advocacy for Palestine in the United States."
— Rev. Prof. Dr. Mitri Raheb, President, Dar. al-Kalima University, Bethlehem, Palestine

"Don Wagner's personal journey on the road to justice for all in the Century-long struggle between Palestine and Israel, and between Arabism and Zionism, is compelling for several reasons. It is a unique combination of personal awakening and the real issues involved that must be resolved. It uncovers the wider forces of ignorance, colonialism, incompetence and brutality by many parties that have allowed the conflict to persist for so long. His own grasp of the truth that powered his battle for justice for all is likely to be a microcosm of what the warring parties and their backers must eventually experience for human dignity, justice for all, and God's love and peace to reign in this tortured land."
— Rami G Khouri, American University of Beirut

"Donald Wagner offers us a memoir that is beautifully written, carefully nuanced, and deeply moving. It is his story about how he grew from a conservative Christian home to become an assertive and engaged advocate for Palestinian rights. Along the way he shows the ways in which Christian Zionism, a legitimator of U.S. policy, skews political realty in 'the holy land,' and the way in which truth-telling, well beyond such beguiling ideology, is an urgent requirement among us."
— Walter Brueggemann, Columbia Seminary

"This memoir is a testimony to the integrity of its author who spent most of his life's journey witnessing for the truth about the Palestinian struggle for justice and liberation. In a lucid account that stimulates and provokes the reader, Don dismantles/critiques the 'heresy' of Christian Zionism and proclaims that God is glorified in the liberation of the 'lowest' … A brave journey anchored in truth and driven by justice for Palestine … This book is inspiring … Readers will find Don's lucid critique about Christian Zionism stimulating and provocative."
— Rev. Dr. Naim Ateek, Co-founder of Sabeel—Jerusalem and author of *Justice and Only Justice*

"A powerful personal testimony and an incisive political history … And like Don Wagner, it embodies compassion, intelligence, conviction and courage. Christians, Jews—or anyone concerned with justice in Israel/Palestine—would do well to read this book."
— Rabbi Brant Rosen, Tzedek Synagogue, Chicago

"Don Wagner has had the courage to listen to Palestinians, and to speak the truth about Palestine at the times and in the places where silence would have been much easier and more advantageous. He has personally borne witness to key events in the history of the Palestinians and the people of the region, especially Israel's horrifying 1982 invasion of Lebanon. Throughout, he has walked unwaveringly by their side. In sharing this journey through these pages, Don gives us the treasured gift of insights from what he has seen and done and true hope that justice is still ours to win, together."
— Ali Abunimah, Co-founder, Electronic Intifada and author of *One Country*

"A profound and deeply moving personal account that embraces faith and justice to fearlessly exit the indoctrination of political Jewish and Christian Zionism. Evangelical Christians beware! This book will shake your understanding of Israel to its foundations—for the better of yourself and us all."
— Sam Bahour, writer, businessperson, activist

"If you have never read a single book about the struggle for justice and peace in Israel and Palestine, this is the one I hope you'll read. If you've read a lot, and are about to give up hope, this is also the book I hope you'll read. It not only helps you understand the situation in the so-called Holy Land; it also helps you feel the pain, the longing, the courage, and the love of good people working, praying, and giving their lives to bend the arc of history toward justice. Don Wagner educates and inspires me, and this book will educate and inspire you too."
— Brian D. McLaren, author of *Faith after Doubt*

"Eye-opening, heart-moving … This is the engrossing story, briskly told, of someone whose experience in the Middle East transformed him from 'an apathetic, conservative evangelical Christian' to an energetic and courageous advocate of justice for the Palestinians, with an embrace of liberation theology in between."
— Nicholas Wolterstorff, Emeritus Professor of Philosophical Theology, Yale University

To my adult kids and grandkids:
Jay, Tracy, Ashley, and Aiden,
Matt, Kristy, Luke, Colin, and Claire
Anna, Dave, Nora, and Lucy,
My sister Karen and her husband Ken,
My beloved wife, Linda

And to my extended family of activists, mentors,
and prophetic voices for justice, peace, and love
for the untold number of Palestinian victims of the Israeli-US
genocide of 2023-6 and innocent Israeli victims of October 7, 2023—
sumud and steadfastness, until justice reigns.

CONTENTS

FOREWORD

by Rev. Dr. Munther Isaac

"Blessed are the peacemakers, for they will be called children of God"

Matthew 5:9

As a Palestinian Christian pastor and theologian, writing during a televised genocide against my people in the Gaza Strip, I keep returning to the wisdom of the lifegiving Beatitudes, which represent the heart of Jesus' teachings. They illustrate how Jesus envisioned the character of his followers and the nature of the movement he started. Jesus describes his followers as the poor in spirit, those who mourn, the meek, those who hunger and thirst for righteousness, the merciful, the pure in heart, the peacemakers, and those who are persecuted for the sake of righteousness.

The conclusion of the Beatitudes is particularly telling and intriguing: "Blessed are those who are persecuted for the sake of righteousness (justice)." Could Jesus be implying the inevitability of persecution for those who seek righteousness and justice? In other words, those who seek peace, hunger and thirst for justice and righteousness, will inevitably face rejection and even persecution?

Jesus touches on another foundational principle in the movement he started: solidarity for the cause of righteousness will inevitably face rejection and even persecution, according to Jesus' teachings, and justice does not come without a cost. Solidarity, by definition, is costly. The world, by some wonder, seems to love peacemakers and boast about justice. The world blesses and even awards peacemakers. But it is the justice of the empire—a justice that comes at the expense of the vulnerable and those deemed unworthy. This type of celebration of "peace" often stems from a shallow and even naïve understanding of peace, or a so-called peace that comes through strength, might, and the elimination of the vulnerable. Many think of peace as diplomacy, and even neutrality.

There are times when peacemaking is actually just that: the art of mediation, taking a middle-ground position, reconciling opposing convictions, and clarifying perceptions. Yet, in many cases, peacemaking is much more than this. In the reality of our fallen humanity, conflicts are seldom just conflicts. Words like "oppression," "domination," and "exploitation" of the vulnerable and marginalized seem to be more accurate descriptions of the world we live in. In such situations, peacemaking becomes a prophetic act of courage, truth-telling, and even speaking truth to power.

Peacemaking entails unavoidably taking sides: standing with the oppressed against the oppressors, the meek against the logic of the empire, and the marginalized against the dominant. It means standing on the side of justice and truth. To do so is to risk positioning oneself against oppressive empires and what they stand for. Solidarity, by definition, is costly. Further, solidarity is an action. It does not stop at mere words. Sometimes, words and statements are important. Many times, however, they are a convenient way of avoiding the need to act and leave one's comfort zone. Solidarity is replaced by "thoughts and prayers" (and usually there is no praying or thinking). But in the way of Jesus, solidarity is always active and even messy. "I was hungry and you gave me food, I was thirsty and you gave me something to drink, I was a stranger and you welcomed me, I was naked and you gave me clothing, I was sick and you took care of me, I was in prison and you visited me." This goes way beyond "thoughts and prayers." It involves actually bringing food and water to those who need it. This is a solidarity that literally takes you to visit prisoners, not merely sending a postcard to prisoners. Associating and identifying with the prisoners, besieged, and marginalized is how Jesus understood and practiced solidarity. To do so, we must confront our own prejudices and presuppositions, in a true act of repentance and transformation, and then step into the world of the perceived "other," allowing their lived experience and often-dismissed perspective to shape and challenge our prejudices and lead us out of our comfort zones and into the space of solidarity.

The case of justice for Palestinians illustrates this principle of costly solidarity. For years, standing for the just cause of Palestinians came with a cost, because it meant standing against the oppressive practices of a powerful state supported by a powerful empire and ruthless lobbies. In my book, *Christ in the Rubble: Faith, the Bible, and the Genocide in Gaza*, I speak of three intertwining factors that enabled the recent genocide in Gaza: coloniality, racism (rendering Palestinians as less human), and theology. These factors have, for seventy-six years, worked hand in hand and enabled the Israeli settler colonialism of Palestine and the systemic oppression of Palestinians.

Israel today, backed by the United States and other superpowers, acts with total impunity based on the logic "might is right." They have crushed the indigenous Palestinians. In this logic of empire, Palestine is a "land without people," not literally, but in terms of people who are equal in worth and dignity in the sight of colonialism. Religion and the Bible are weaponized, using concepts like promised land, election, and covenant to eliminate the rights of Palestinians, rendering international law and human rights inapplicable to Palestinians. By February 2025, US President Donald J. Trump proposed to expel the Palestinians from the Gaza Strip and turn Gaza into a "Middle East Riviera" for tourists and wealthy residents. Israel's extremist politicians and Prime Minister Netanyahu welcomed the proposal. Rather than redress the genocide that Israel had conducted for fifteen months, primarily with US funding, the two million Palestinian survivors would now be expelled to foreign countries in violation of every standard of international law and basic morality. As Don Wagner argues in this second edition of *No Place Left to Go: Why Palestine Matters,*"Palestine may be the last test case for international law and the global world order."

To stand for the cause of justice and liberation for Palestinians, especially in the midst of Western and US Christianity, means not only standing for the humanity of Palestinians but also calling out the colonial oppressive nature of Israel and the fact that it is US money and political support that enables this injustice. It also means challenging ideologies and theologies of supremacy, racism, and entitlement and daring to call zionism and Christian zionism for what they truly are: racist and colonial ideologies.

And it means challenging the dominant Christian zionist theology that still today dominates churches, theology, popular books, and the academy and most seminaries in the United States. It will naturally lead to rejection and persecution. The fate of the students and faculty who protested during the recent genocide against Palestinians during the spring of 2025 is just the latest example of this costly solidarity.

The journey of my good friend Don Wagner is an embodiment of this principle of costly solidarity. Wagner is not the only one, but he was certainly among the first who challenged Christian zionism from within. And as his journey clearly reveals, Wagner's stances for justice and challenging the logic of the empire and the theology of Christian zionism did not come without a cost. There was a price to pay. There was a risk to take. Travels to Palestine and Lebanon in times of war and massacres. Wagner's solidarity was a solidarity of presence and courage. It was a costly solidarity.

Writing the foreword for this book is an acknowledgment and expression of gratitude from a Palestinian theologian, on behalf of the many Palestinian friends Don has gained over the years. We are grateful for this peacemaker, a true child of God.

Rev. Dr. Munther Isaac is a Palestinian Christian pastor, author, and theologian. He is Director of Christ at the Checkpoint, a ministry by and for evangelical Christians. His 2023 Christmas Eve sermon on "Christ in the rubble of Gaza" went viral and serves as the title of his latest book (Eerdmans, 2025). After serving as the Pastor of Christmas Lutheran Church in Bethlehem, he is currently Pastor of the Evangelical Lutheran Church of Hope in Ramallah, Palestine.

PREFACE

by Judge Wendell Griffen

On April 4, 1967, Martin Luther King Jr. delivered a speech at Riverside Church in New York City that called on the United States to end its war in Vietnam and named racism, materialism, and militarism as "giant triplets" that placed the United States on the wrong side of a global revolution against colonialism, imperialism, and tyranny. King's speech was denounced by US President Lyndon Johnson, major news outlets, and even by some supporters of the civil rights movement.

As a Black man from the deep South, I am well acquainted with racism not only as individual discrimination but as a system of oppression. The collective aspect of how Blacks and, for that matter, browns and Asians were kept out of the mainstream in educational opportunities, politics, even some white churches, restaurants, and movie theaters is well known but easily forgotten.

During my first trip to the "unholy land," as Don Wagner calls it, the systemic racism was all too familiar and was in fact worse than the Jim Crow laws in the United States. When Archbishop Desmond Tutu visited the Palestinian areas for the first time, he stated the apartheid system in Palestine was worse than what Black South Africans faced during the white apartheid regimes.

Don Wagner's memoir claims King's warning about the "giant triplets" is consistent with the message of the prophetic faith of the Hebrew prophets and Jesus. Moreover, it can be applied to US and Israeli actions concerning the land known as Palestine. The failure of the United States to heed Dr. King's warning has been in many ways responsible for US-led wars in Iraq and most recently the financing of Israel's genocidal war in the Gaza Strip and now the West Bank. The moral and political blindness of the US-Israeli alliance has for the most part been a tragic failure, leaving Israel alienated from its neighbors and less secure than at any point in recent history. Palestinians have suffered a modern holocaust yet are still standing and demanding justice, equality, the right of return to a state of their own. Neither genocide nor systemic apartheid made Israel secure.

In this revised edition, Wagner has made the point with even more prophetic urgency. Palestine is sacred for Judaism, Christianity, and Islam. Since the Roman expulsion of most Jews in the second century CE, the Arab Christian and Muslim majority and Jewish minority population was ruled by various invading empires. When Britain replaced the Ottoman Turks following World War I under a League of Nations mandate, it favored Jewish colonization of Palestine at the expense of Palestinian efforts to achieve sovereignty. Then the United States replaced Britain as the dominant imperial power in the Middle East. Starting in 1945 with Harry S. Truman, every US president and presidential candidate, whatever their political party, has pledged fealty to Israel's right to exist but denied the same political right of self-determination for the Palestinians.

Wagner's memoir examines how zionist ideology and its stepsister, Christian zionism, have impacted his work as a Christian pastor, a university professor, and an activist. He often met considerable resistance from fellow pastors, academic colleagues, and especially the organized pro-Israel advocacy organizations. His faith, and the firsthand experiences of the severe suffering of his Palestinian friends, made his trial seem rather small.

His transition from Christian zionism to an eventual embrace of liberation theology has provided him with new eyes to see what was previously covered in political religious hypocrisy. Hearing Wagner's apt description of "an unholy land" may be uncomfortable for many of us, but it is precisely this tragedy that beckons us to go join the calling to speak truth to power where injustice still reigns.

As you read this revised second edition, remember that US news outlets distort news reports about the Arab-Israeli dispute. As Wagner shares, the well-known reporter Wolf Blitzer was once on the staff of the pro-Israel lobby AIPAC and defended the 1982 Israeli invasion of Lebanon that resulted in the deaths of scores of Palestinian and Lebanese civilians, including nineteen schoolgirls, a few years before he became the chief political anchor for CNN. In this revised edition, Wagner shares how zionist ideology continues to dominate both US political parties, US national security strategy, academia, and most religious institutions.

Henry David Thoreau said, "A truly good book teaches me better than to just read it. I must soon lay it down, and commence living on its hint … What I began by reading I must finish by acting." When you finish reading *No Place Left to Go,* consider following Thoreau's example. Lay it down. Reflect on what you have read. Then commence living on its hint. Act on it. God willing, a sufficient number of us will do so in liberating ways for besieged people across the region that waits for us to recognize, protect, support, and respect a sovereign state called Palestine, and liberation from zionism for both Palestinians and Israeli Jews.

Rev. Wendell Griffen is pastor of New Millennium Church in Little Rock, Arkansas, and Co-Chair of the Samuel DeWitt Proctor Conference, a Black liberationist interdenominational global movement. Griffen served as a state appellate and trial judge in Arkansas for twenty-five years and is a private consultant on cultural competency and inclusion. He is the author of The Fierce Urgency of Prophetic Hope *(2017) and coauthor (with South African liberation theologian Allan Boesak) of* Parables, Politics, and Prophetic Faith *(2023).*

A NOTE ABOUT SPELLING AND CAPITALIZATION OF TERMS

Throughout the book I have chosen to use the lowercase for several terms, including "evangelical," which should only be capitalized when it refers to a denomination, as in Evangelical Covenant Church.

The term antisemitism is spelled with a lowercase a and s, which is the preferred spelling by scholars in Jewish studies. For details, see the volume *On Antisemitism: Jewish Voice for Peace.*[1]

Likewise, zionism and Christian zionism will be spelled with a lowercase z, as zionism is a political ideology and I am using Christian zionism primarily in a political sense or to describe a false interpretation of the scriptures.

I spell holy land and unholy land in the lowercase as no land is holy, only God is holy. Given the severity of the injustices currently practiced in Palestine and Israel, there is additional reason to maintain a lowercase spelling, at least until historic Palestine is decolonized and the apartheid system and occupation are ended with full justice for all the citizens of this troubled land.

All Arabic, Hebrew, and Greek words will be italicized, with the English translation in parentheses.

INTRODUCTION: NOTHING HAS CHANGED AND EVERYTHING HAS CHANGED

Sam Bahour, the respected Palestinian businessman and political analyst, summarized the Palestinian dilemma after the Hamas attack of October 7, 2023, with a paradox: "Nothing has changed and everything has changed." Bahour went on to paint a grim picture for the people of Gaza and all of Palestine, given Israel's free hand to conduct a genocidal war in the Gaza Strip underwritten by the United States and various European and Arab countries. In the West Bank and East Jerusalem, militant settlers have been given a free hand to conduct pogroms and warn Palestinians everywhere they will be "transferred" (forcibly expelled) to other countries.[2]

"Nothing has changed" means Israel's vicious system of apartheid will only get worse in East Jerusalem, the West Bank, and for Palestinian citizens of Israel. Extremist settlers now work intimately with the Israeli Defense Forces to raid villages, burn homes, conduct pogroms, steal land, kidnap youth, and create a reign of terror with impunity in the colonized territories. On July 19, 2024, the International Court of Justice ruled for the first time that Israel is responsible for a system of apartheid in all the occupied territories. The report confirmed what international human rights agencies such as Amnesty International, Human Rights Watch, the Israeli human rights organization B'Tselem, and three others stated previously.[3]

But far worse is Israel's genocidal war in the Gaza Strip, where 2.4 million Palestinian citizens of Gaza face daily bombardment, massacres, and multiple war crimes from the Israeli army, air force, and navy, including the mass starvation campaign engineered by Israel. Euro-Med updated the projected number of dead, injured, or detained in Gaza in mid-October 2025 to 270,000, which includes those still missing and under the rubble.[4] It now seems clear that as long as the United States continues to underwrite the genocide, the Netanyahu government will use this opportunity to murder as many of the

Gazans as possible and expel the survivors at a later date. The failure of the international community to stop the genocide represents the worse global humanitarian disaster since the Nazi Holocaust.

The Palestinian poet and author Susan Abulhawa said after visiting Gaza in early March 2024: "Nothing can truly prepare you for this dystopia. What reaches the rest of the world is a fraction of what I've seen so far, which is only a fraction of this horror's totality. Gaza is hell. It is an inferno teeming with innocents gasping for air." Abulhawa concluded her powerful report: "Despite Israel cutting power and internet, Palestinians have managed to livestream a picture of their own genocide to a world that allows it to continue. But history will not lie. It will record that Israel perpetrated a holocaust in the 21st century."[5]

If the immediate future for Palestinians is so desperate, then what has changed? One important change is that Palestine and Palestinians were nearly forgotten by the summer of 2023, but are once again at the top of the global agenda. The street protests that began in fall of 2023 were followed by university encampments in the spring of 2024. They represented a new wave of popular resistance, but were brought to a halt by the punitive campaign by the Trump Administration and pro-Israel lobby, which forced campus protests temporarily underground. The protests were often led by a broad coalition of young Jews, Muslims, black, and brown students and other youths.

A second change took place in early October 2023, when the United States, Israel, and Saudi Arabia were to sign a new round of the Abraham Accords, but the effort was canceled indefinitely. The accords were designed to normalize Israel's apartheid strategies in exchange for a US–Israeli security agreement with most Arab governments from Saudi Arabia to Morocco. The Hamas action of October 7 was timed to subvert the agreement.

Due to these dramatic political shifts that have altered the Palestinian case at a global level, I have decided to update my memoir, originally titled *Glory to God in the Lowest: Journeys to an Unholy Land.* This is a defining moment for the Palestine question and at the same time for the global world order. If this genocidal war is allowed to erase 2.4 million Palestinians in Gaza, the consequences will be devastating for other vulnerable populations, starting with the West Bank and East Jerusalem, or in the Congo, Southern Sudan, or wherever authoritarian regimes wish to liquidate their opposition. Little to nothing has changed for Palestinians, yet this is unquestionably a Kairos moment, a decisive period for the question of Palestine—and "everything has changed." The election of Donald J. Trump in 2024 continued the Biden policy of underwriting the genocide in Gaza, expanding it to include the possibility of erasing the entire population of Gaza and turning the enclave into a "Riviera" with condos and hotels that will benefit Trump and billionaire oligarchs in his political orbit.

My hope is that my journey will help readers make the transition I've been through to recognize the beauty, inspiration, and importance of the Palestinian people. I also hope readers will recognize the urgency of the Palestinian case for freedom, liberation, and independence, which has been denied them for at least 120 years and counting. Many of you may be encouraged to take up their struggle and find the rewards and challenge of standing with them and a growing global solidarity movement. You will see they have no place left to go other than historic Palestine, through a negotiated political settlement with Israel that honors the dignity, equality, sovereignty, and security of both people.

I have revised much of the text of the original memoir and given it a new title, *No Place Left to Go: Why Palestine Matters.* The new edition features a new preface, foreword, and introduction, with commentary on the impact of the Gaza genocide throughout the text. The final two chapters have been completely revised in light of the genocide. While "everything has changed," we know the immediate future will only get worse for Palestinians before freedom and liberation come. We cannot and will not allow them to stand alone, challenging the false gods of militarism, racism, and economic exploitation that now dominates Israel and many of the Western powers. Our task as people of faith or no faith is to unmask the false powers and point the way to healing and freedom for all, as if our own survival depends on it. And perhaps it does.

My goals for this second edition had to change in the wake of the genocide in the Gaza Strip. The first goal is to argue as clearly as possible for a comprehensive political solution to the 120-year Palestinian-Israeli struggle and state why Palestine is a key to maintaining the global world order (international law), which has been exposed as toothless and incapable of holding the United States, Israel, and most of Europe accountable. I looked back on my personal experiences such as when I returned from the Israeli invasion of Lebanon in

June 1982, and debated an Israeli general who said, "This (war) is our final solution to the Palestinian problem." I now realize this was a clear sign of what many Israeli zionists and military officials really believed in—the erasure of Palestinians.

I saw it again three months later, when I entered the Palestinian refugee camps Sabra and Shatila and saw the bodies of defenseless children, women, and men slaughtered by Lebanese militias under the watchful eye of the Israeli Defense Forces. The cover-up that followed was another warning of where the Palestinian case was headed. These are the signals and trends I hope to reveal in this edition.

My second goal in writing the memoir is to reflect on my gradual transformation from an apathetic, conservative evangelical Christian to someone with a passion for justice. What factors were behind this dramatic change? Where and why did it occur? It may have started when I was in college and failed to challenge the racism in my fraternity, or perhaps it really hit me when I arrived at Princeton and encountered the anti-Vietnam war protests and the civil rights movement. At the same time, my theological assumptions were challenged by a course on liberation theology, which shocked my understanding of Jesus' mission and my apathetic response to the injustices around me.

The third theme includes my struggle with white privilege and awareness that came thanks to five years serving in an amazing Black congregation. The patience and love of this "beloved community" led me to become an anti-racist, which helped me question the liberal form of Christian zionism I embraced in seminary. My worldview shifted when I learned about the Nakba, the catastrophe in 1948–49 that continues to the present day. A trip to Lebanon, Palestine, and Israel moved me to such a degree that I left the pastorate and began full-time work on Palestinian human rights. The rest of my life has been a rich and challenging time of consciousness raising, advocacy, losing a job or two, yet discovering the fulfillment that comes as a byproduct of truth telling and solidarity with Palestinians and fellow travelers in the justice movement.

A significant part of the third theme entailed coming to terms with the ideology of Christian and Jewish political zionism. This too has been a process of growing into a more critical analysis, recognizing the false gods of exceptionalism, militarism, hyper nationalism, and *hasbara* ("propaganda") that have infected Western culture, politics, the media, and our respective religions.

This has often been a complex challenge as it has infected most aspects of our worldview and is now a global phenomenon. When Rev. Mitri Raheb says, "We as Palestinians are occupied by Israel (zionism) and the Bible," he is also warning us that we are occupied by the same false gods, but in a more subtle and pervasive way.

The memoir is divided into six sections, each including two to four chapters. It opens with a new foreword by Rev. Dr. Munther Isaac and Judge Wendell Griffen. Then my revised narrative begins.

Section I, Beginnings, reviews my childhood growing up in a traditional, white *Leave It to Beaver* family. As a white male influenced by the usual male stereotypes and the post-World War II American colonial ethos, I was also grounded by the rich love of my family. They were committed evangelical Christians with conservative Republican values, shaped by Dwight D. Eisenhower and later Ronald Reagan's conservatism. My dad was a World War II veteran, as were several other family members. Things came to a head during the mid 1960s when I became involved in not only the antiwar movement, but also the civil rights movement. The memoir follows my journey and the inevitable tension with my family and within myself.

Section II: Transformed by the Black Church and Liberating Gospel, follows my journey in the civil rights movement to five exciting years as an associate pastor in a vibrant Black church. This "beloved community" welcomed our family and became a home and source of inspiration, dealing with my white privilege and becoming an anti-racist. I loved these people; they gave me more than I could have imagined, and I am eternally grateful.

Section III, Journeys to an Unholy Land, begins my experience with the Palestinian issue, which would become a political and spiritual calling for the rest of my life. The epigraph for this section provides a window into my journey: "Our greatest form of education is what we unlearn." My first trip to the Middle East planted seeds of change within me, and within three years I left the pastoral ministry and began four decades of work in the Israeli-Palestinian solidarity struggle. The Gaza genocide casts a shadow over this chapter and throughout the rest of my journey.

Section IV, "Doctor, My Eyes Have Seen the Pain," examines a series of devastating political events, including a week under Israel's bombardment of

Lebanon in June 1982. I returned to Chicago for a summer of intensive political advocacy in opposition to the war. In mid-September, I returned to Beirut, arriving in the Sabra and Shatila refugee camps a day after the massacres that foreshadowed the genocide in Gaza. My pledge to the Muslim sheikh became a lifelong reminder of my accountability to the victims: "Just go home and tell the truth."

Section V, Palestine Is Still the Issue, opens with my experiences during the First Palestinian Intifada of December 1987–93. I was fortunate to experience most of the initial year firsthand; as painful as it was at times, it was one of the most unified periods of Palestinian resistance, primarily nonviolent and highly creative. The Intifada forced Israel to negotiate directly with the PLO under the US-supervised Oslo Accords of 1993–99, which were a disaster. This section ends with my fifteen-year journey "in and out of academia."

Section VI: Liberating Your Mind: Zionism, Christian Zionism, and Resistance, is a new chapter analyzing three types of the Christian zionist movement, including my personal experiences and why I changed. The continuing Nakba of 1948–49 casts a pall over how the myths of zionism are sustained and why settler colonial analysis and Palestinian liberation theology are critical tools that offer liberation and justice. The genocidal war of 2023–25 is a reminder of the urgent need to be liberated from these false ideologies.

Conclusion: No Place Left to Go: Why Palestine Matters, argues that the genocide in Gaza and all of Palestine is a test case for the global world order. After the Nazi Holocaust and World War II, the Fourth Geneva Conventions and the International Criminal Court and International Court of Justice stipulated that there will never again be a genocide or holocaust for anyone. How ironic that Israel and even the United States could be convicted of genocide against the indigenous Palestinians in historic Palestine. Now it is Palestine's turn to realize the justice that has been denied them for 125 years and counting.

—Donald E. Wagner, Orland Hills, Illinois; a sojourner in the land of the Algonquin, Miami, Potawatomi, and Ojibwe nations, January 2026

Section I:
Chapters 1–3
Beginnings

"In a time of universal deceit, telling the truth is a revolutionary act."

—Author unknown (often attributed to George Orwell)

Chapter 1
COMING OF AGE IN THE SIXTIES: A JOURNEY TO POLITICAL CONSCIOUSNESS

"I learned that courage was not the absence of fear, but the triumph over it. The brave person is not he who does not feel afraid, but he who conquers that fear."

—Nelson Mandela

Driving home on a desolate stretch of country road after a family visit in Lockport, New York, flames suddenly burst forth from under our car. My mother and I were less than three miles from my grandparents' home. Mom stopped the car on the side of the road and pulled me out. I was two-and-a-half, but this event is etched in my mind. It was a windy and snowy night in midwinter. Staring at the flames, we moved to a safe distance from the fire and felt the howling wind and snow in our faces. Mom held my hand and began to pray, asking God to protect and provide for us.

Our eyes were transfixed on the flames as we stood there for no more than fifteen minutes. Suddenly there came a stillness in the storm and the fire swiftly died out. We waited a few minutes before cautiously moving toward the car. There was no apparent damage to the doors or the outside of the car. Mom opened the passenger door and checked the seats and console, which were untouched by the fire. We got in and sat down on the seats. Mom turned the key a couple of times to start the engine. No luck. On the third or fourth try, the engine started, and finally, with grateful hearts, we were on our way home.

When we arrived at my grandparents' home, Mom asked me to describe what had just happened. As Mom told the story through the years, I said something like, "We were driving home and the car caught fire. We got out and prayed and God put out the fire." My childlike grasp of the event revealed a simple trust in God's presence and care for us, because "God put out the fire." This memorable experience was a simple declaration of faith as I learned it from my parents and grandparents, who lived by this faith every day. Their daily prayers at meals and bedtime taught me at an early age that God is ever-present, and prayer is one way to communicate our joys and concerns to the Creator.

This chapter will examine the interplay among my parental and extended family influences. It will include the post-World War II political environment and my emerging self-awareness, including my theological and political consciousness. The immediate context is set in the final years of World War II, followed immediately by the anxieties of the Cold War era with a touch of racism, conservative politics, and the evangelical Christian influence of my family. These were the primary sources of my childhood values, worldview, religious faith, and political awareness. In many ways these forces collided with a personal need for independence that gradually manifested itself in my teenage years.

Rooted deep within my family was an intimate, loving, and deeply personal relationship with a steadfast God who was guiding our journey. I learned about Jesus, God's "son," who died for our sins and offered us the gift of eternal life. My early sense of the Christian faith was highly personal and focused on my individual salvation through Jesus Christ. I have no recollection of a social consciousness or sense of responsibility for the poor and disenfranchised during these years. I did see glimpses of compassion for the poor from Grandpa Nelson, and they were seeds planted in my consciousness that bloomed later in my journey.

I inherited other values, including a strong sense of patriotism, respect for the military, duty to the country, and the racial prejudices that accompany a sense of white privilege, often overt but usually subtle. By the age of six or seven I was influenced by end-time premillennial dispensationalist theology, complete with the Rapture, Battle of Armageddon, and the role of Israel, God's chosen people.

This chapter seeks to pull together the threads that wove the tapestry of my original worldview, including my belief system, conservative politics, social influences, and racism. My journey reached a climax in the turbulent mid-1960s as a young seminary student, when I ran into the combustible blend of liberation theology, anti-Vietnam War rallies, and the civil rights movement.

Within a matter of six months, my conservative evangelical and Republican worldview began to unravel. At that point I was seeking something deeper, broader, and in touch with the issues of the mid-sixties, in contrast to the assumptions of my childhood. The new patterns were far from a finished product as they continued to change and be redefined with time, events, and my emerging social and political consciousness. I believe God was reshaping my theological journey in a dialogue with global events.

The car fire incident occurred during the winter of 1944 when my dad was based in England with the US Army during World War II. Dad left for Europe when I was six months old, and I did not see him again until I was three and a half. When Dad enlisted and headed for boot camp, Mom and I moved into my grandparent's home. Mom worked two jobs during the war years, as did Grandpa Nelson, who ran a Texaco station in nearby Lockport, New York, and maintained a 100-acre farm in his spare time. Grandma took care of me during the day, and my three caregivers provided a warm and loving environment. The farm always had a special place in my heart as I grew older, and I returned to it every summer to help my grandparents with harvests and simply to spend time with them.

World War II dominated our lives during my early childhood. Letters from my dad and updates on the war were the topics of family conversations and prayer before meals and bedtime. I had several uncles and cousins deployed in Europe or the Pacific theaters and we prayed for them all by name. We also prayed for Norway and Grandpa Nelson's family who were under Nazi occupation. Grandpa's younger brother, Uncle Earling, fought with the Norwegian underground and was captured by the Nazis. After he escaped from prison, he took an extended vacation with us on the farm. He became my favorite uncle, perhaps because he was on the wild side, very independent, and his stories set him apart from the rest of my family.

Another legacy of the war was family patriotism that quickly translated into conservative Republican politics. This political affiliation ran through the entire family on both the Nelson and Wagner sides. To this day, I can't think of a single member of my family who is a member of the Democratic Party aside from my kids, my wife, Linda, and me. I still remember a conversation I overheard at dinner when my Grandpa Wagner said President Franklin D. Roosevelt (a hated Democrat) deliberately led us into World War II by coordinating the bombing of Pearl Harbor with the Japanese government.

Conspiracy theories did not begin with the Trump administration. I was shocked and naively asked how he knew this, and he simply said, "I heard it on the radio." Aside from my question, nobody challenged him.

But stronger than patriotism and Republican Party affiliation was the family's conservative evangelical piety and beliefs. My maternal grandparents, John and Anna Nelson, set the pace in many ways with their passionate love of Jesus, the Bible, and regular prayer. My mother and her brother, my godfather Uncle Norm, were shaped by these commitments throughout their lives. My dad was more reserved, but he spoke through his actions as a very dedicated evangelical, having been raised in conservative Missouri Synod Lutheran churches.

Grandpa and Grandma Nelson were pillars of their independent Bible church down the road in the country hamlet of Cambria, New York. As a child, I heard too many sermons on the rise of the Antichrist, the Rapture, and Battle of Armageddon from our pastor, Rev. Burns. Our family sat in the front pew on the right side of the sanctuary every Sunday morning. When I was about three years old, I was feeling bored with church and left the pew when no one was looking. I moved to a spot behind the choir during their anthem and got on my hands and knees. I made my way through the choir and pinched the soprano soloist in the leg during her solo. She let out a scream and Grandpa rushed up and marched me out of the church for an appropriate scolding. I'm not sure how to interpret this incident other than it was a modest protest against worship on my part and a sign my independent streak could manifest itself in inappropriate ways.

—

My grandparents and parents lived through the Depression, and they never forgot it. We were not a wealthy family and were at peace with our simple lifestyle. If the basic expenses of food and shelter were covered, we were thankful. Other matters such as updating our wardrobes, a new car, and going out to eat were not necessities. Dad saved coupons and did all the grocery shopping with discounts in mind. He also saved us an enormous amount of money with his ability to repair televisions, radios, and major appliances. He could also do plumbing and light carpentry, skills I now regret never learning.

Family vacations were usually spent at my Grandfather Wagner's somewhat run-down cottage on Lake Chautauqua. Mom and Dad loved being there because it was a change of scenery, and free. We rarely went out for dinner, but every other week we splurged at a local restaurant featuring a Friday night fish fry—"All you can eat for $2.99 per person with a coupon." Looking back as an adult with a family of my own, I have no regrets and continue the family tradition of saving coupons and maintaining a frugal lifestyle.

Family visits were our primary means of socializing when we were young, which my sister Karen and I enjoyed until we reached junior high school and preferred to be with our friends. We usually visited family on Sundays, alternating between visits to Grandpa and Grandma Nelson on the farm or driving to nearby Buffalo and visiting the Wagner clan. I still get excited about the thought of my Aunt Marie's German potato salad with diced bacon and vinegar dressing. On special occasions, she added roast beef and the legendary Buffalo special: beef on weck sandwiches.

Dad mastered the beef on weck sandwich, a Buffalo "delicacy" including thinly sliced but rare roast beef piled an inch and a half high on a German-style kummelweck bun (a kaiser roll topped with salt crystals and caraway seeds). Before serving, Dad dipped the roll in au jus sauce and smothered it with fresh horseradish. The only places you can get the authentic beef on weck is at one of the Buffalo area bars or restaurants specializing in it. I have yet to find an acceptable beef on weck outside of western New York State.

After Dad returned from the war, we moved to Lockport, an industrial city about thirty miles north of Buffalo. We lived in a blue-collar neighborhood where the men marched off to work each morning with their lunch pails in hand. Most of them worked at the Harrison Radiator plant, a subsidiary of General Motors, a fifteen-minute walk from our street. Dad worked for the Bell Telephone Company, where he started at an entry-level position as a lineman. He worked his way up the company ladder to become a line foreman and then a regional supervisor.

We lived on an all-white block adjacent to a small African American community, plagued with the usual neglect. Reid Street was unpaved and lacked snow removal, a serious issue in the Buffalo region. Hyde Park Boulevard, our white block, was a nice red-brick street with all the services, including efficient snow removal. It was home to a mixture of second-generation Italians, Germans, Poles, and Irish. The disparities between Hyde Park Blvd. and Reid Street reinforced the not-so-subtle white privilege we took for granted.

There were several kids my age in the two neighborhoods, and we all met on a homemade baseball diamond to play the game I came to love. We tossed the bat and chose teams and everyone got along. I was new to the game when we moved there and was usually among the last chosen. The older boys were the best players, and Keith and Brian Reynolds, Black Americans, were the most skilled. They were always kind to me and helped me learn the basics of hitting and fielding. I do not recall a single incident where someone uttered a racist remark, but racism was omnipresent in the systemic separation of our neighborhoods and attitudes.

At school, Blacks and whites sat next to each other and occasionally visited each other's homes to play after school. However, in reality, we were separated by one block and generations of racial discrimination that gave those of us on the white block several advantages for simply being born white. I recall one incident that did turn ugly in terms of overt racism. I walked home from school a few times with Rosemary Jones, a Black girl in my class who lived in the Reid Street neighborhood. We were only seven or eight years old, but I recall being harassed by older white kids because I was walking with a Black girl. They ridiculed both of us and called Rosemary the N-word and me "a N-lover."

I regret I lacked the courage to call them out for their abusive remarks. For some reason, this incident has remained with me through the years as a missed opportunity. Perhaps worse, I gave in to the taunting and stopped walking home with Rosemary. I wonder if this troubling incident planted a seed in my consciousness concerning the injustice caused by racism.

Grandpa Nelson was a mentor in challenging racism, showing me an alternative model. My loving and reserved grandma and mom would occasionally make racist remarks. Grandpa never allowed a slur to go unchallenged. Sometimes he was gentle and on other occasions he was very direct and forceful. I learned later that Grandpa went out of his way to hire Black and Puerto Rican immigrants on the farm because as an immigrant, he understood how difficult it was for them to find work. He always paid them a fair wage. Mom told me about the time Grandpa and Grandma provided housing for a Black family who had fallen on hard times during the Depression. They provided a bedroom, and the family usually ate dinner with Grandpa, Grandma, Mom, and Uncle Norm. The family stayed with them for several months until they were on their feet again.

Grandpa Nelson's history as an immigrant provided him with life experiences that nurtured his compassion for minorities and the poor. He arrived in this country alone at the age of fifteen, having left Norway for life in the

United States. He became a farm laborer and worked side by side with Black and Puerto Rican laborers. These early experiences allowed him to see his coworkers as equal human beings. He began to understand the racism at work in society. Eventually he saved enough money to purchase the farm and provide a home for his young bride, Anna Kraft. His Christian faith became the foundation of his values and actions. I believe Grandpa served as a model for me, but it took several years before it bore fruit.

Chapter 2

JOURNEY TO ADULTHOOD AND POLITICAL ENGAGEMENT

"When I was a child I spoke like a child, I reasoned like a child, when I became an adult, I put an end to childish ways. For now we see in a mirror, dimly, but then we shall see face to face. Now I know only in part, then I will know fully, as I have been fully known. Now faith, hope, and love abide, these three, and the greatest of these is love."

—I Corinthians 12:11-13

Growing up in post-World War II America meant I absorbed a heavy dose of Cold War politics. The 1950s were dominated by Republican patriotism, including the McCarthy investigations and the accompanying anxieties about Communists infiltrating our communities and family. Mom and Dad were active in local Republican Party politics and staunch supporters of Dwight Eisenhower, Richard Nixon, and Barry Goldwater. As a World War II veteran, Dad believed the country needed a strong military force to protect us from the growing Communist threat, both foreign and domestic, as it lurked within the country and on foreign soil.

One of our favorite television shows as a family was the award-winning *I Led 3 Lives*, starring Richard Carlson as Herbert Philbrick. Philbrick was an advertising executive by day, but evenings and weekends he was a double agent for the FBI, infiltrating the Communist Party and saving the country from the enemy in each dramatic episode. This was high-stakes political theater but based on real events and eminently believable.

The fear factor drove the narrative, and there is nothing like fear to drive home a political message. One could suspect the neighbors next door, your schoolteacher, and even your own sister as possible Communist agents. These fears and values shaped our family's politics, worldview, and even our conservative evangelical faith during the 1950s and early 1960s.[6]

Dad flew the flag in front of the house daily until he and Mom moved into a retirement home about forty years later. By the time I was in high school, Dad was the treasurer of the Western New York Republican Party. Dad and Mom were both strong supporters of Richard Nixon and campaigned for Barry Goldwater in 1964. Later they were regular volunteers for our conservative Republican congressman, Jack Kemp, who they knew on a first-name basis from Hamburg Presbyterian Church, where Jack and his wife, JoAnne, were regular attendees. Jack gained fame as the star quarterback for the Buffalo Bills football team before launching his political career.

My family did not like John F. Kennedy because he was a Roman Catholic and "could not be trusted." They were suspicious because they believed Kennedy would be taking orders from the pope if he were elected president. In those days, many fundamentalist Christians believed the pope was the Antichrist, the emissary of Satan on earth during the last days. Mom and Dad were loyal supporters of Richard Nixon and agreed with his militarism, conservative rhetoric, and perhaps his not-so-covert racism. When Nixon was impeached, my parents thought it was a liberal conspiracy, and they were among the last to admit he violated the Constitution.

Dad's strong anti-Catholic sentiments became personal when I was in high school. My first girlfriend was Nancy Kramer, a terrific friend with a fabulous sense of humor. Nancy's family attended St. Mary's Roman Catholic Church. One day after school, I walked Nancy to her home when it started to snow. Nancy lived in the country, about two miles out of town. We were having a good time at her house when we realized it was the dinner hour and I was supposed to be home by 6 PM. Nancy's dad was delayed by the snow and neither Nancy nor her mom drove. I called home, hoping Mom could come and get me, but she was reluctant to drive in the snow. She said Dad would come and pick me up when he returned home from work. I knew the ride home would not go well.

Dad showed up at around 7 PM and he was angry. He did not get angry often but when he did, look out. As soon as I got in the car he said, "All right, I've told you several times I want you to break off this relationship with the Catholic girlfriend. This is it. I want no back talk from you. I want to see action.

This is the last time you go out with her, understand?"

I said, "No, I do not understand and I'm not breaking it off."

He refused to talk to me the rest of the way home and gave me the silent treatment for about two weeks. It was dad's personal version of the Cold War.

My quest for independence, or what the psychoanalyst Abraham Maslow called "self-actualization," seemed to be awakening during this phase of my life. I began to test the rigid norms of my family for the first time. I was beginning to see a wider world than our narrow evangelical values and restrictions. I thought I was old enough to decide who I wanted to date, and my conservative father's fierce anti-Catholic views would not limit my choices. In the case of dating Nancy, I was surprised my mother took my side. This incident was one of the first in a long series of differences I had to negotiate with my parents, and my peers, but my insistence on dating a Catholic gave me confidence to continue the struggle for independence.

Another sign of my emerging independence came when I received a letter from the Selective Service. I responded by filing for "conscientious objector" status without telling my parents. In fact, I did not discuss it with anyone and in hindsight that was a mistake. I needed some guidance in the process, and I based my appeal on my Christian faith, claiming Jesus never endorsed war and counseled against "raising the sword." My request for the C-O status was rejected and I did not pursue it. Other than my religious motivations, I have no idea where this initiative came from as it did not come from my parents or the preaching I heard at church.

As I approached my senior year in high school in 1960, I realized it would be wise to select a college some distance from home. The decision would give me the opportunity to be on my own and increase my personal freedom. It was time to figure things out for myself and take the next step toward a broader education in life. It wasn't a decision based on an unhappy childhood or dislike of my parents. On the contrary, I had a loving and very happy childhood. But I was getting in touch with my need for independence.

I decided to attend Westminster College in Pennsylvania, about fifty miles north of Pittsburgh and over 200 miles from the front door of our home. I never visited Westminster prior to my arrival for freshman week but did enough research to know it was the right choice. First, it was far enough from home that I would be totally away from parental controls yet close enough to hitchhike home for a long weekend. Second, and perhaps most important, it was an athletic powerhouse and ranked in the top ten nationally in football, basketball, and baseball for small colleges. I planned to play basketball and baseball. Third, it was a Christian college with an evangelical tradition but affiliated with the mainline Presbyterian denomination. My parents preferred that I attend college in Buffalo and commute from home, but I never applied to universities in the Buffalo area.

Westminster College's religious orientation was evangelical but far from strict and rigid. We had to take two "Bible courses" our freshman year and no other religion courses were required. We had to attend chapel services three days per week, but half the students slept through it in our comfortable new chapel seats. We were free to study, believe, date, and make our own lifestyle choices, some of which were wayward to say the least. According to the lifestyle regulations, there were "no drugs or alcohol" on campus but the rule was rarely enforced. The beer, wine, and mixed drinks flowed freely at the fraternity and sorority houses, where campus social life was thriving.

When my parents helped me move into Russell Hall for my freshman year, I felt an immediate burst of freedom when they drove off. I was on my own and it fully agreed with me. It was time for me to break free from their narrow lifestyle, but I was not about to go off the deep end. I was careful in my use of alcohol and only tried marijuana once or twice. I was never homesick like some of my neighbors in the dorm. It was simply time for a fresh start, a type of coming of age, leaving home and being on my own.

One of the first things I did was go down to the field house and scrimmage with some of the freshman recruits for the basketball team. I was a decent basketball player and was a starter on my high school team, but I was not an elite player. Within five minutes I could see there were six or seven guys who were in the elite class. They were taller, faster, more accurate shooters, and generally more talented than me. I was as good or better than the rest of the guys, and I could have made the freshman team. But this experience was humbling and a good wake-up call. I would not be playing much and I couldn't see myself "riding the bench." I decided to concentrate on baseball, my studies, and having a good time. Actually, concentrating on my studies came last.

I joined a fraternity (Sigma Nu) the second semester of my freshman year. In the early sixties, the Greek system was thriving at Westminster and it was the primary social vehicle. Our freshman fraternity class at Sigma Nu was one of the largest pledge classes in the school's recent history and I was excited to be part of it. Unfortunately, I learned about the fraternity's restrictive religious and racial clauses after I made the commitment. In hindsight, I should have quit the fraternity on the spot as an act of resistance but lacked the moral fortitude and political awareness. I was too interested in having a good time with the guys and too politically immature to take a stand against racism.

Our Sigma Nu chapter did take an honorable step by ignoring the religious/ethnic clause and offered full membership to Jewish brothers, a move we all celebrated. This decision triggered a reaction from Sigma Nu's national headquarters and we were placed on probation, which we also celebrated. But we did not go far enough. Some of us raised the issue of challenging the racism clause to grant full membership to our Black brothers. We were told by upperclassmen not to move so fast as it was complicated. I wanted to invite my friends Larry Pugh and Tony Jackson, star football and baseball players respectively, but there was little support.

I knew we let down Larry, Tony, and all Black students. Larry was a talented and fascinating person who happened to be an All-American (small college) defensive lineman. He was later elected to the College Football Hall of Fame and drafted by the Cleveland Browns, but a serious knee injury curtailed his profession career.

Larry was much more than a talented athlete. He was sharp intellectually with a warm and engaging personality. He was very mature for his age, far more than I was, and grounded in who he was as a human being. He was not the least bit cocky or arrogant and was respectful of others. He was supremely confident, and no one was about to push him around.

When I realized Larry, Tony, and others were denied membership in Sigma Nu simply because of the color of their skin, it made me angry. Larry and Tony had more to offer our Sigma Nu chapter than 90 percent of the current members, myself included. I began to recognize my failure and our collective mistake as symbolic of what was going on in this country. Unfortunately, I took the comfortable way out of this dilemma with the rest of my fraternity brothers. This was a missed opportunity for all of us, one that could have been an important statement for justice on our campus and perhaps beyond. In my case, everything was about to change.

Chapter 3
A CHANGE IS GONNA COME

"Education consists mainly of what we have unlearned."

—Mark Twain

I began my senior year in college facing a number of major decisions. First, I had no idea what I would do after graduation, and suddenly it was the fall semester of my senior year. I considered playing professional baseball and had the opportunity to sign a contract to play in the lower minor leagues in the St. Louis Cardinals system. After a couple of strong years of college baseball with solid statistics for batting average and pitching, I was tempted to sign.

I ranked in the top ten nationally for earned run average (small college) and my batting average was .429 my junior year and around .300 my senior year. We played a competitive schedule in college, facing Division I schools like the University of Pittsburgh, Duquesne, and St. Francis. At the same time, I knew deep down I lacked the ability to succeed at the professional level. Playing in the major leagues was a childhood fantasy since I was ten years old. Now it was time to abandon the fantasy and get serious about my vocational plans.

A second option was to obtain a teaching certificate and pursue a career in teaching and coaching. I had plenty of coaching experience and loved working with kids. My four years as a recreation director for the park district back home was very rewarding, but it seemed like a step backward. I started to get serious about academics by the second half of my junior year and hit my academic stride during my senior year, which may seem unusual to some people. I was a late bloomer in this regard, but I never regretted the fabulous experiences of my college years. It was a simple matter of moving on from my fraternity and sports phase to finding fulfillment in academics.

A third decision involved my relationship with my girlfriend Karen Beecher. We started dating in the fall of my junior year, but she dropped out of school and moved back home to Erie, Pennsylvania, midway through the year. I spent several weekends hitchhiking up to Erie to visit her and we fell in love. By the fall of my senior year we began to talk about marriage, as it seemed like most of our friends were getting married. Why not us? Karen was tired of living at home and we both thought we were ready for married life. Little did I realize how immature I was and how attached I remained to the crazy lifestyle of college life.

My fourth decision was whether I should consider giving theological seminary a trial year. Seminary had been an option since my freshman year of college, but I always resisted it. The thought of becoming a pastor never appealed to me because I did not wish to live under the microscope of a congregation's expectations. I remembered the gossip around our Sunday dinner table about the pastor and the pastor's family. The criticisms seemed petty and unfair. On the other hand, I had just taken two courses in theology and philosophy that stimulated my academic interests more than any other classes in college.

The course on the Hebrew prophets—Isaiah, Jeremiah, Ezekiel, Amos, Micah, and Jonah—had a particular impact on me. It was taught by a new professor, Bob Cochenauer, a creative and inspired teacher who applied the prophets' messages to the political issues of our time. This was my first opportunity to study the Bible and reflect on its direct relevance to modern events like war, race, poverty, and materialism. The class gave me a hunger for more courses like it. I felt as if I was waking up academically after wasting three years of academic opportunities.

My good friend and fraternity brother Dave Schieber and his wife, Linda, were planning to attend Louisville Presbyterian Theological Seminary. I considered Princeton Seminary but decided on Louisville because this was an experimental year for me, and Louisville Seminary seemed to be more nurturing. Moreover, I wasn't sure God was calling me to this type of vocation.

After graduation from Westminster College, Dave and Linda were married and I was Dave's best man. A month later, Dave was my best man when Karen and I decided to get married. We moved to Louisville, Kentucky, without having visited the campus prior to arriving for classes. It was then that we quickly realized we were ill prepared for the financial pressures, the annoying habits we found in each other, and the clash of values. I was missing the freedom and carefree fraternity life, yet I was ready to immerse myself in academics. Moreover, I needed to bring in some income for us to pay the bills, so I took a job in a church on weekends. It meant driving at least two hours to Cincinnati on Saturday mornings and returning late Sunday evening giving Karen and me less time together.

Louisville Seminary offered a strong academic program of theological study with a small student body and caring faculty. It was an excellent environment for me to evaluate whether the academic study of theology was right for me. I was stimulated by the rigor of a full course load with fascinating subjects like church history, theology, and a challenging class in New Testament exegesis with the inspiring professor, George Edwards. I was intrigued by his random comments revealing his anti-war and civil rights sentiments perhaps more than his exegesis of the Greek text of the Gospel of Mark.

I had serious remedial work to pursue, unlike most of the students, because I did not take a pre-theological curriculum in college. As a psychology major, I added random electives in such fields as astronomy and geology because they were easy. However, by the spring of my first year at Louisville I was convinced the decision to attend seminary was correct, as long as I could avoid pastoral ministry.

By Easter of that year I started to explore the possibility of transferring to Princeton. Princeton offered a more diverse array of faculty and a much larger student body. Karen was excited about a fresh start as she hated her job and liked the idea of being in a community like Princeton. We were struggling with our marriage, and we were hoping a change of scenery would help our relationship.

We started packing as soon as I received the letter of acceptance to Princeton. This would be our second major move in a year, but we were excited about it. I wanted to pursue more courses in theology, and Princeton offered a wide range of coursework from traditional Calvin scholars to liberal Niebuhrian ethicists and radical liberation theologians. I wanted to try them all. In addition, the seminary was a block or two from Princeton University, and we could cross-register and take courses. Simply being in a larger stimulating academic environment had significant appeal. By late August 1965, we headed east in our Volkswagen bug, pulling a small U-Haul trailer after shipping thirty-five boxes of our possessions to Princeton via Greyhound. (Only twenty-two boxes arrived, but we never missed what was lost.)

The move to Princeton presented an unexpected political and theological challenge. The year was 1965 and the United States was in the throes of rising tensions over racism and protests against an unpopular war. Both issues were on full display at Princeton University, and the actions spilled over to the seminary. It was relatively easy for seminary students and faculty to become engaged in the political and cultural issues at the university, and I decided to get involved. The Vietnam War was the hot-button issue at Princeton, and various perspectives were available on campus, including those of pro-war speakers from the faculty and the Johnson administration. I decided to attend both pro-war and anti-war lectures so I could make up my own mind.

The more I listened to the different viewpoints, the more I found myself slowly pulled toward the anti-war position. Initially, I was confused as I was supportive of the war when I arrived at Princeton. My dad's arguments mirrored those of the Republican nominee in the 1964 presidential election, Barry Goldwater, who subscribed to the domino theory, i.e., if Vietnam falls to Communism, most of Southeast Asia will follow; next will be the Middle East, Africa, and parts of Europe. Literally, all of my family and friends from high school supported the war, and several paid a heavy price—dying, being traumatized, or being seriously wounded in Vietnam. I was so apolitical I failed to vote in the 1964 election. But "the times were a-changin'" and I was open to changing with them.

While I was attending lectures and teach-ins at the university, the academic course load at Princeton Seminary was inspiring and at the same time very demanding. I took a rigorous, upper-level theology course from Edward Dowey on the history and theology of the Protestant Reformation. I surprised myself and a few classmates when I received an A on a difficult midterm exam. The average grade in the class of seventy-five students was a C-. My grade on the exam was a real confidence booster, and I realized I could manage the academic demands with hard work and preparation. I was convinced the decision to study at Princeton was right for me, and this was the right time to be there.[7]

One of my other courses brought a serious challenge to my evangelical theology, my conservative political perspective, and my worldview. It was a course on liberation theology taught by Richard Shaull, a self-proclaimed Marxist theologian and one of the first liberation theologians in the United States. Shaull's theology was shaped by his work in the barrios of Colombia as a missionary in the 1950s. He was part of the emerging liberation theology movement among Latin American priests and theologians who brought a radical critique to both the political and ecclesiastical structures.

In some ways there was nothing new about liberation theology as it followed Jesus' method of going to the poor and living in solidarity with those at the margins of society. However, its message and method focused on the poor and marginalized. Liberation theologians claimed the focus of our ministry and education must begin with the impoverished masses. This is "God's preferential option for the poor." The liberation theologians challenged the traditional top-down hierarchical approach to education, which I found interesting as the criticism applied to Princeton's preferential option for the traditional lecture model.

The new breed of Latin American theologians practiced a bottom-up approach, where priests and laity were equal partners in small-group learning modules called "base communities." A major feature of the new educational model was "praxis" or critical reflection and analysis of the biblical texts while giving serious consideration to the oppressive political situation. Praxis and several themes of liberation theology were borrowed from Marxist ideology, which added a significant dimension of controversy to Latin American liberation theology.[8]

Professor Shaull was a radical thinker and advocated what he called "revolutionary liberation theology." Those of us who were new to his thinking discovered both inspiration and a number of theological "surprises" that commenced when he passed out the course syllabus. I recall my shock when I looked at the reading assignments, which ranged from selected biblical passages, Chairman Mao's Little Red Book, the writings of Marx and Engels, *The Autobiography of Malcolm X*, Frantz Fanon's *The Wretched of the Earth*, Martin Luther King Jr.'s "Letter from a Birmingham Jail," and Paulo Freire's *Pedagogy of the Oppressed*.

Shaull incorporated lectures by Rubem Alves, his young Brazilian doctoral student who was an emerging liberation theologian. Alves's lectures, adapted from his doctoral dissertation, were eventually published as *A Theology of Human Hope*. Their lectures and the assigned readings combined to shatter most of my evangelical theological assumptions as well as my conservative political values. My world was turned upside down in one semester.

Shaull also challenged how theology was being taught in other courses I was taking, like the theology of John Calvin and the above-mentioned class on the Protestant Reformation. Most of the instruction was the traditional top-down lecture approach. While I was eager to embrace the challenges to my views on militarism, race, capitalism, and pedagogy, I reached a point where I was in over my head. It was too much to absorb, and I needed help.

I talked it over with Karen who listened attentively and tried to assist me, but she admitted the theological issues were unfamiliar to her. I also processed the issues with fellow evangelical students, but they were having the same difficulties. I spoke to a grad student who recommended I spend some time with the Princeton director of Young Life. I was familiar with the Young Life movement from volunteer work I did in college and appreciated its evangelical theology and progressive approach to engaging youth. The director's name escapes me, but he knew exactly what I was going through, having had a similar transition as an evangelical when he entered Princeton ten years earlier.

His wise counsel was to keep questioning everything, whether from Professor Shaull, the Marxist political narratives I was reading, or even John Calvin and the Bible. He said, "By all means, question your evangelical assumptions about God, Jesus' divinity, the Resurrection, the Bible, and everything else." He said this is a good problem to have. "Take this opportunity to see what you really believe and why you believe it. Eventually, a new theological framework will emerge.

"Don't rush this process," he counseled. "It should become a lifelong practice of critical thinking." He assured me, from his personal experience, that I would come through this with a different theological orientation and worldview. He said, "You will be a different person from who you were a few months ago when you entered seminary."

I'll always remember a phrase he added: "God, Jesus, and the Bible can take all the challenges that modern scholarship or Professor Shaull can throw at them. The question is, can you take it? Relax, reflect, grow wiser, and, by all means, trust the process." His advice was exactly what I needed. Mark Twain's quote was already beginning to take effect: "Education consists mainly in what we have unlearned."

Next on my reeducation project was one of the most formative events of my first year at Princeton. In March 1967, I joined several Princeton University and seminary students and drove to Washington, DC, for the Clergy and Laity

Concerned (CALC) anti-war conference. The conference was cosponsored by a broad coalition of religious and secular anti-war organizations with CALC as the primary organizer. Clergy and Laity Concerned was established by the National Council of Churches in 1965. Among its founders were the Catholic theologian and activist Daniel Berrigan; Abraham Joshua Heschel, perhaps the leading Jewish theologian in the United States; John C. Bennett, president of Union Theological Seminary; and William Sloane Coffin, the chaplain at Yale University.

The conference gave me the political and theological analysis I needed to move to the next level of political consciousness and eventual activism. One prominent speaker after another presented their analyses of why the Vietnam War was illegal, immoral, and politically dangerous. In addition to the founders of CALC, the list of speakers included Andrew Young of the Southern Christian Leadership Conference, CALC Director Richard Fernandez, and Martin Luther King Jr.

Dr. King's lecture was a highlight. This was when he made his first public statement connecting the civil rights movement to the anti-war movement. The Washington conference was a trial balloon for him prior to his major address at Riverside Church a month later.

When the final speaker ended his talk, the participants were sky-high with enthusiasm and ready to march. We gathered outside the church and were joined by approximately two hundred anti-war demonstrators who had not attended the conference. Leading the march in the front row were the keynote speakers with Dr. King at the center. I was able to position myself three rows behind him throughout the march. We started walking the ten blocks toward the White House. As we walked, a small crowd stopped to watch the procession, and most of the people applauded and cheered for us.

We also heard the occasional negative remarks about our lack of patriotism and failure to support the troops. We passed a small group chanting "Communists go home" and "If you don't like it here, try Moscow." Their signs and buttons identified them as supporters of Carl McIntyre's breakaway Bible Presbyterian Church. McIntyre had a radio broadcast and was president of the American Council of Churches, a small network of fundamentalist churches. He supported the Vietnam War and was a close ally of the white apartheid regime in South Africa. He was also a supporter of Ian Paisley, the Northern Ireland nationalist who opposed Ireland's struggle for independence from England.

Looking back on the anti-war protests in the late sixties, I see several parallels but also marked differences. Student protests and the anti-war movement were beginning to have a significant impact on both the country and Congress in 1967. Congress was still resisting the calls to end the war, as it is today in 2025. The current opposition to the genocide in Gaza has been significant on university campuses and in the streets, often led by young Jewish and Muslim activists.

Like the late 1960s and 70s, it is largely the youth who are leading the protests on the Palestine question. We are beginning to see this trend today with young evangelicals who are resisting the Christian zionist and Trumpian rhetoric on the Middle East. The protests against the Democratic Party's convention in the summer of 2025—exposing the gap between the youth and moderate gatekeepers of the party—were a direct parallel to the pro-war Johnson Democrats of 1968. Moreover, the intersectional nature of the youth in today's protests are a reminder of the anti-racist claims of the Black Panthers and the progressive wing of the civil rights movement. It took another five years for the Vietnam War to be declared a failure and mistake. I wonder how long it will take for the United States to end the genocide in Palestine and honor international law, including self-determination and the right of return for Palestinians.

I stepped out of the march and started talking with a few students in the McIntyre group, forgetting we were advised to ignore such tempting opportunities. The students were fiercely anti-communist and argued with slogans and canned talking points such as the domino theory, which I challenged immediately. Within five minutes, I realized my conversation was falling on deaf ears, even when I referenced the Sermon on the Mount and the need to follow Jesus rather than the war texts in the Book of Joshua. I realized they followed a different Jesus and bowed to the "god" of hyper-nationalism (today we would call it Christian nationalism). It wasn't long before I sensed I was getting angry. I politely wished them God's peace and ran to catch up with the march, assuming my position three rows behind Dr. King.

We arrived at the White House, and Dr. King gave a brief speech. He was joined by John Bennett and Rabbi Heschel, and the three walked up to the White House to deliver a statement demanding that President Lyndon Johnson bring an immediate end to the war in Vietnam. Thanks to Dr. King, the march received modest coverage in the media, but President Johnson never responded.[9]

I became a committed disciple of Dr. King after the Washington march and followed his career closely. I read everything he wrote and watched his campaigns and speeches through the media. King was "a mentor to me from afar" as I embraced his theology and philosophy of nonviolent resistance. His analysis of the Vietnam War and its connection to the civil rights movement was a brilliant moral and tactical move.

King addressed the three major evils in his speech: racism, poverty, and militarism. He said they could only be challenged by a mass movement uniting the civil rights and anti-war movements. He hoped others would follow their lead. I am struck by the relevance of Dr. King's analysis of the three major evils, which remain unresolved and continue to haunt the body politic as much in 2025 as they did in 1967. The excessive levels of US military and economic support to underwrite over 80 percent of Israel's genocide in Gaza confirm the fact that the three evils King addressed are alive and well in both political parties, and most of the Senate and House of Representatives. Until they are addressed with significant policy changes and political accountability, we will be witnessing the decline and fall of the American empire in our lifetime, which may be a blessing.

The Washington conference inspired me to become active in the civil rights movement and study King's faith-based approach to nonviolent resistance. The experience initiated my preparation for my first vocational assignment, but at the time I was completely unaware of it.

Reading Malcolm X's autobiography for Professor Shaull's course also had an impact on me. Shaull's lectures on Malcolm raised the importance of his revolutionary approach to end racism by turning to Black power. Malcolm's hard-hitting analysis of systemic racism challenged me to go deeper in my analysis of power and systemic racism than I had initially considered. It also challenged me to examine my white privilege and my personal contribution to racism.

Malcolm's life story was profound, inspiring, tragic, and very important for the left wing of the civil rights movement. His autobiography and the biography *The Dead Are Arising* by Les and Tamara Payne bring new information to what we knew of Malcolm's life and teachings.[10] Malcolm was a courageous warrior for justice who was hunted by J. Edgar Hoover and the FBI as well as the disciples of Elijah Muhammad once Malcolm broke with his former mentor.

From my initial study of liberation theology, I could see how Malcolm's and Martin Luther King's messages complemented each other. Both messages were necessary for a thoroughgoing critique of racism and the corrupt systems in the United States. Dr. King and Malcolm were laser focused on their call to end the plague of racism since the origins of the United States and running through every dimension of the country. The claim that "racism is America's original sin" is true at every level of government, religion, and society at large.

Dr. King's approach was grounded more in the message of Jesus, the prophets, and the New Testament, incorporating Gandhi's philosophy of nonviolent resistance. Dr. King's consistent critique of the racist systems in the United States is often sanitized by white interpreters who miss the radical dimension of his message. Malcolm's critique of the white power structure was more confrontational and raised the need for Black power and Black independence in the struggle. By 1967–68, Malcolm had more appeal among young Blacks, who were growing impatient with Martin and the nonviolent wing of the civil rights movement. Moreover, Malcolm did not dismiss armed struggle, something I rejected for myself, although I could see its value for others.

Two years later, when I looked back on what prepared me to be a pastor in the Black community, I could see how Martin and Malcolm inspired different trajectories. Dr. King prepared me for the Black church, with a critical analysis of racism, the demands of faith, and the need to proclaim a Jesus-centered, anti-racist Gospel of nonviolent resistance. His powerful "Letter from a Birmingham Jail" warned his movement of several obstacles, including his warning to beware of the false narratives of white liberals.

Malcolm pushed me to be more critical of the white establishment in other ways. He was one of the first to call us to be an anti-racist, and not be content with assimilation. I did not grasp this difference at first, and it took me a few years to incorporate the analysis. In many ways Malcolm's analysis was at the heart of the Black power movement and was a necessary correction to the white liberal "trickle-down theory" and the assimilationist approach.

Malcolm also prepared me for future meetings with members of the Black Panther Party in Newark and East Orange, a movement I would have dismissed without his message. As challenging and uncomfortable as it was, I knew I had to listen to the Black Panthers and take their analysis seriously. Malcolm's message ran through the programs and the speeches of their leaders, however without his initial commitment to Elijah Muhammad's unusual interpretation of Islam.

By the end of my first year at Princeton I was a different person. I was finding my academic stride and was able to make theological and political adjustments to meet the academic challenges. My critical thinking skills were enhanced in my theological and political analysis. My life, worldview, politics, theology, and my vocational direction were rapidly evolving with a focus on justice. My political and theological world shifted a full 180 degrees from who I was ten months earlier when we arrived in Princeton. I'm not sure I was fully aware of how much I had changed, but a visit to our families served as a barometer.

After a visit with Karen's family in Pennsylvania, we drove to Buffalo to visit with my family. I wasn't really thinking about my appearance, which had changed gradually through the year. My hair was longer than it was on my previous visit home, and I was wearing John Lennon-type sunglasses. We pulled into the driveway of the house where I grew up and I stepped out of our Volkswagen bug, anticipating the warm welcome we always received from my family.

As soon as I stepped out of the car, the joy evaporated. I saw my beloved mother's countenance drop when she laid eyes on me, and her long anticipated warm reception turned as cold as a Buffalo winter. Mom was angry and on the verge of tears. My sister Karen and Dad were right behind her, and both were upset. When my mother saw me, she yelled, "What has happened to you? You are not my son!" She ripped off my Lennon sunglasses and crushed them under her foot. She repeated, "You are not my son," and ran into the house crying.

I was devastated. I had never seen her do anything like that. I followed Mom to her bedroom, where she was sitting on her bed sobbing. I put my arm around her, searching for the right words. Finally, I said something like, "Look, Mom, I love you and this is just a minor conflict between us. We can work it out. This is only about outward appearances and what really matters is God's love in our hearts. Let's pray together for God's guidance." Holding her hands, I prayed, "Dear God, grant us understanding and renew our love for each other, which has always been the center of our family. Take us deeper into your presence and renew us with the reconciling presence of your love, in Jesus' name. Amen."

Mom stopped crying and said a prayer of her own, asking God to help her understand what was going on between us. We gave each other a hug and

I breathed a sigh of relief. I realized I should have been more sensitive about how my family would react to my outward appearance. I should have had a haircut and removed the sunglasses before exiting the car. On the other hand, my appearance represented who I was at that time. Was I correct in forcing the issue with my family or should I have been more sensitive about my family's conservative values?

Given what did happen, Mom, Dad, and I were forced to recognize that I was no longer the high school boy living at home and abiding by the house rules. In spite of the insensitivity on my part, this incident did establish a new way for our family to begin processing the changes I was undergoing. The visit broke the ice and paved the way for future conversations and experiences that did touch on the deeper changes in my beliefs and values.

The rest of the weekend was peaceful and free of the initial hostilities. One conversation involved a final attempt by my mother to suggest a change in where I was studying. Mom said, "I wish you could transfer from that liberal Princeton to a more evangelical seminary like Dallas." I simply replied, "Well, I'm finding Princeton to be exactly what I need at this time and honestly believe this is where God has led me." Mom and Dad accepted my answer, and surprisingly, there were no arguments.

All things considered, this was a milestone weekend for me and my family. I did not realize how important the weekend was until I thought it through on the way home. We were learning to love each other despite our significant differences. We had crossed a bridge, leaving behind parental controls and moving into a world of more mature and respectful relationships. The bridge was still fragile and could easily be shaken by the winds of controversy. Eventually we would need to deal with my new views on the Vietnam War, the civil rights movement, and the impact of liberation theology.

I can't recall who said it, but it rang true for this visit: "Every battle does not need to be Armageddon." The potentially explosive issues like race, Jesus the liberator, and my anti-war advocacy could wait. We drove out of our beautiful, lily-white suburb, and I was more aware than ever that I was on a journey. While I could go home again, I could never settle down and live in the village I loved. It was no longer my current home.

Section II:
Chapters 4–7

Transformed by the Black Church and Liberating Gospel

"It was very difficult to become a Christian if you were a Black man on a slave ship, and the slave ship was called The Good Ship Jesus."

—James Baldwin

Chapter 4

OUT OF THE IVY TOWER: TIME TO WALK THE TALK

"Tell me and I forget. Teach me and I remember. Involve me and I learn."

—Benjamin Franklin

A friend who was finishing his doctorate at Princeton University warned me, "Princeton can become a womb if you aren't careful. Once you settle in and get comfortable with the academic grind, you may find it difficult to leave the womb. I suggest you take a break from Princeton and get a job in the real world. You can always return and do the PhD in three or four years." His warning resonated with me as I could sense I was getting too comfortable in the womb.

Karen and I loved the Princeton community. I was finding academic life meaningful. After I received my Master of Divinity degree, I enrolled in the Master of Theology program and found a job on campus and worked weekends in a wonderful Black church in East Orange, New Jersey. In the spring of 1968, I started working on my application for the PhD program at Princeton University and remembered my friend's warning.

As I reflected on my future, a colleague at Presbyterian headquarters in New York called to suggest I consider applying for a new position in South Africa under the direction of the World Council and South African Council of Churches. It was an intriguing opportunity to work undercover in the anti-apartheid movement. He said there would be some risk as I would be working with a variety of anti-apartheid movements that were considered illegal by the white apartheid regime in South Africa. Most of the organizations were closely connected to the outlawed African National Congress.

I prayed for clarity about the opportunity. The position required a three-year commitment to live in South Africa, but Karen wasn't interested in moving out of the country. I called my friend and gave him a reluctant but realistic "no." At this point, with the PhD program looking like our best option, we assumed Princeton would be our home for the next three to five years. During the fall semester, I explored the option of taking a church position and applied for three separate job openings. We visited all three, and two of them offered me the position, one in Detroit and another near Pittsburgh. I turned down both job opportunities as they were not a good fit for my gifts or interests.

About a week before Easter I received a call from Rev. Joe Roberts, who was the pastor of Elmwood Presbyterian Church in East Orange, New Jersey, where I had worked on Sundays for nearly two years. Joe said the governing body in Presbyterian congregations, known as the session, spent the past year exploring the possibility of hiring their first full-time assistant pastor. The congregation had doubled in size under Joe's charismatic leadership the past five years and now his workload was unmanageable.

Joe caught me off-guard when he said, "We are excited to offer you the position of becoming our first assistant pastor." I had no clue Elmwood was ready to hire a full-time assistant let alone consider hiring me, a white guy, with limited experience. I had to sit down and reflect on Joe's amazing offer and discuss it with Karen.

My response to Joe was something like, "Joe, this is unbelievable. Are you serious? God sure works in mysterious ways. I'm sitting here thinking about starting a PhD program but knew deep down I should be pursuing a full-time job. I love working with you and the friends at Elmwood. Absolutely yes—I am honored, surprised, thrilled. Yes, I accept. But give me a day or two so I can process it with Karen. I know she enjoys Elmwood and will give an enthusiastic 'yes.'"

Joe suggested we take our time and think it through for a couple of days, saying he and the session hoped we would say yes.

I added, "Me too. When does the job begin?"

"I'd say right after your graduation from Princeton, around the middle of June," he said. "That way you two can come up and find housing and assist us with Daily Vacation Bible School that gets underway around June 15."

I was ecstatic. Karen and I went out for dinner to discuss the offer. She said, "Yes, of course. I can't believe Elmwood is making this offer to us." We had several details to work out, such as Joe's one caveat. The church budget was unable to pay the minimum salary required by the Presbyterian denomination of $50,000 per year. The presbytery had granted permission to make us an offer of $40,000 plus a housing allowance, medical insurance, and pension. This was a higher salary than either of us had ever received, and Karen planned to work. The salary was more than acceptable to us. I said, "Let's go home and call Joe right now and accept the offer."

Karen suggested we should sit on the decision overnight and see how we felt in the morning. I was reluctant but said, "Well, OK. I know I won't change my mind. I am absolutely thankful and thrilled." Then she said, "You know what? Let's go home and call him now. Let's do it." We called Joe and I said, "We talked it over and the answer is an enthusiastic yes. We accept." Joe asked if Karen was OK with the financial package, so I put her on the phone. She gave her full support. By the end of the conversation, Joe had her laughing when he offered to celebrate by taking us out to the local White Castle for sliders. What an amazing opportunity it would be to serve full-time in a remarkable Black congregation with the gifted Joe Roberts. This was an answer to my prayers about our uncertain future.

Karen and I started packing in preparation for the move to East Orange the first week of June 1968. Our first decision was to find housing. I was somewhat familiar with the area, having worked at Elmwood on Sundays. I often did research in adjacent Newark for my master's dissertation on the Newark riots of July 1967. People were still talking about the riots and the unresolved problems that remained. One problem I underestimated was the high degree of polarization and blatant racism in the white community. I should have expected it, but due to my brief in-and-out visits and spending most of my time in the Black community, I missed this development.

One Saturday evening, we were staying with friends in the church and decided to go out for dinner at a popular Italian restaurant recommended by some of our Princeton friends. Our hosts were busy that evening, so we drove to Newark's North Ward, a predominantly Italian neighborhood. We crossed the street at the border between East Orange and Newark and saw four or five men armed with automatic weapons, leaning against a black Cadillac. I had never seen civilians walking around with weapons on full display.

This was our introduction to the white vigilante organization called the North Ward Citizens Committee, led by Anthony Imperiale, Newark's outspoken councilman. The committee was a white militia, similar to the Ku Klux Klan minus the white hoods. The group patrolled the border between Newark and East Orange's Black community. Its goal was to prevent any Black people from entering the North Ward.

Anthony Imperiale, an ex-Marine and dues-paying member of the Ku Klux Klan, played his role as leader with an accent on aggression and racism. Representing the North Ward as a member of Newark's City Council, he was an unrepentant white supremacist with rhetoric that stoked the fears and racist tendencies of the North Ward citizenry. He insisted on the right of whites to arm themselves and protect their neighborhoods from the Black community on their doorstep. A *New York Times* interview with Imperiale reflects the growing tension over race:

> "I'm called a bigot, a racist, a night rider, a vigilante, and all the rest," he complained during the early hours yesterday as he completed an uneventful automobile patrol of the North Ward and the outer fringes of the nearby Negro Central Ward. "We're supposed to be night riders, and you might call us vigilantes, but we resent that in a way," he said as he eased his black 1959 Cadillac sedan in front of the Imperiale Association of Judo and Karate, headquarters of the citizens' committee."[11]

New Jersey Governor Richard Hughes eventually called the North Ward Citizens Committee "vigilantes" and "brownshirts," and openly campaigned to shut them down.

I was watching the evening news a few days later and saw a report on two Black teenagers from East Orange who were severely beaten by the members of the North Ward Citizens Committee. The youths had ridden their bikes into the Central Ward to buy an ice cream cone when Imperiale's thugs beat them and damaged their bicycles. One boy was hospitalized from the beating. Tensions escalated immediately in a war of words between the Black Panther Party and the Citizens Committee.

The Panthers demanded the governor shut down the committee immediately as an illegal white supremacist militia. They also threatened an armed confrontation unless Imperiale and his militia issued a public apology and paid the medical bills and other expenses to the families. Within forty-eight hours, the Citizens Committee issued a public apology, covered the medical bills, and purchased new bicycles. The governor's action was not immediate, and the Panthers launched a sustained campaign across the state demanding the governor permanently shut the group down. After several months, Governor Hughes closed the committee's office on the grounds that it constituted an illegal, violent hate group.

Karen and I continued to search for an apartment. I wanted to live in an all-Black neighborhood within walking distance of the church. She preferred to be at least ten to fifteen minutes from the church to ensure our privacy. She knew the high school kids would want to hang out at our house, and while she enjoyed their company, Karen thought a little distance might be in order. I encouraged her to decide on an apartment, saying I would be fine with her decision provided the neighborhood was racially mixed and within ten minutes of the church.

She found an apartment about a ten-minute drive from the church in a racially diverse neighborhood. Karen was excited about the swimming pool, which initially embarrassed me. We visited the apartment and decided to take it. After a week of hot weather and enjoyment in the pool, I dropped my resistance and found the amenity to be a welcomed asset.

My first day on the job at Elmwood provided a surprising learning opportunity. Joe suggested my first official task as the new assistant pastor would be to deliver the welcome and opening prayer at daily vacation Bible school. We expected over 300 children and thirty teachers and staff on the first day. I was excited to begin my new ministry and start working with the teachers and children.

Five minutes before the opening program, Joe knocked on my office door and said, "Sorry man, but the toilet in the men's bathroom just backed up and the janitor didn't show today. Could you go in and clean the bathroom? It's the only one available to boys. I'll do the prayer and welcome." What could I say but "of course"?

The bathroom was worse than I could have imagined. I was literally mopping the floor and shoveling feces for what seemed like two hours (actually it was about forty-five minutes). I could not help but think, "After three years, two master's degrees, and ordination to the ministry, is this what I signed up for?" Then I caught myself and realized: Black folks have been doing these menial jobs for hundreds of years for whites, and it's about time we switched it around. I'm the minority person here, so get over it and do what's asked of you for the benefit of everyone.

Once the bathroom was clean, I took a few minutes to wash up, returned to my office, and reflected on what had just happened. I thought more about my frustration and asked myself, "OK, what can I learn from this disgusting experience?" My mind turned to some of the basic themes of liberation theology, thinking they might provide some insights. I thought about the model Jesus gave to his disciples in washing their feet. The "praxis" process at the heart of liberation theology reminds us to respond with compassion to real-life situations. Today's experience should qualify as "real-life." Praxis also involves reflection on our experiences with an emphasis on solidarity, humility, compassion, and justice. As I was reflecting on these lessons, my phone rang. It was Joe inviting me to lunch at our favorite Jewish deli.

We sat back and laughed at the incongruity of a Princeton Seminary education and my first full day on the job cleaning the boys' bathroom. Joe could not resist making jokes about the situation. He helped me laugh at myself and brought humor into the reflection process. The best hot pastrami on rye in New Jersey also helped. The debriefing with Joe was exactly what I needed to move on and integrate the experience.

One of Joe's funniest ideas was a new metaphor for the ministry that should be used by seminaries. If Jesus washed the feet of his twelve disciples, students should have the experience of shoveling urine and feces while cleaning a bathroom. Could this be a new model for servant ministry?

The "boys' bathroom experience" also served as a reminder to start working to reverse my preference for the traditional top-down teacher/student model of instruction. I could start by rereading Paulo Freire's *Pedagogy of the Oppressed* and implement the bottom-up approach. Elmwood provided the opportunity to experiment with the Freire model at the heart of liberation theology. When I tried it out with the high school youth group, I was pleased with the results.

Finally, I understood that I had to be far more vigilant about any element of paternalism in my attitudes and actions. I needed to operate in complete solidarity and equality with everyone. I had to be careful with the "suffering servant" model and make sure my commitment was sincere and without a trace of self-righteousness. People in the congregation, and young people in particular, would pick up the slightest hint of inauthenticity. I had a lot to learn and implement through trial and error, but Elmwood Church offered me the opportunity to work on these issues in a loving community.

Chapter 5
THE SIN AND SICKNESS OF RACISM: THE CONTEXT FOR SERVICE AND GROWTH

"Racist ideas make people of color think less of themselves, which makes them more vulnerable to racist ideas. Racist ideas make white people think more of themselves, which further attracts them to racist ideas."

—Ibram X. Kendi, *How to Be an Antiracist*

Elmwood United Presbyterian Church was unique in many ways. It was a merger between a dying white congregation in East Orange where whites had fled to the suburbs to escape the arrival of a Black population from Newark's Central Ward. Elmwood's membership had grown to approximately 750 members in five years, 99 percent of whom were Black Americans plus a few African immigrants. The only white members were two retired missionaries, Rev. Robert and Mildred Thompson, and two spouses of mixed marriages. Karen and I made quick friends with several members who invited us over to their homes for dinner. We enjoyed their company and looked forward to reciprocating and enjoying other social events with them.

Since Elmwood's membership had more than tripled in five years, there was a need to increase opportunities for fellowship and building community in small groups. Joe and the session suggested my job would be to build a strong youth group, develop small-group opportunities including adult education courses, organize social justice and advocacy groups, and assist Joe in worship, pastoral calling, and hospital visits.

Elmwood's strongest asset was the Sunday morning worship experience with Joe's inspired preaching and a strong music ministry. Joe was a charismatic preacher who grew up in the Black church. His dad was an African Methodist Episcopal pastor, so Joe knew the riches of the Black gospel tradition, the importance of a strong musical program, and the power of the preached word. As a skilled organist himself, Joe knew what was necessary for a strong music ministry.

Joe did his seminary work at New York's Union Theological Seminary in the liberal theological tradition of Paul Tillich, Reinhold Niebuhr, and the ethicist Paul Lehmann. He had the uncanny ability to preach on complex theological and social justice topics but break it down with personal applications. He successfully blended the personal gospel of Jesus with social justice, drawing from Black theologians like Howard Thurman and Martin Luther King Jr., and the novels of James Baldwin. It was a gift for me to listen and learn from his powerful sermons.

One of Joe's first decisions when he came to Elmwood was to assemble a dynamic music ministry. He found a talented director in Frederick C. Martin, who was trained in gospel, jazz, and classical music. Elmwood had a choir of fifty-five members and recorded three albums based on concerts they performed for the congregation and community. The choir offered two concerts every year featuring gospel and spirituals with classical favorites. Fred was fond of saying, "We do Bach and Beethoven alongside 'Precious Lord' and 'Down By the Riverside,' all in the same evening." The choir was a draw for visitors on Sunday mornings. With the music program and Joe's preaching, the sanctuary was near capacity on most Sunday mornings.

East Orange had been a majority white suburb as late as 1955 when the demography began to shift toward the 70–75 percent Black majority by 1970. The school district was 85 percent Black, and nearly a quarter of the children came from families on public assistance. East Orange was essentially an extension of Newark's Black majority population as it moved from the Central Ward corridor toward East Orange. Black families were seeking better housing, stronger schools, and an escape from Newark's urban blight and violence.

The majority of Elmwood's members were professionals and largely middle-class, with a few in the upper-middle class. At the same time, a significant number of Elmwood's members lived below the poverty line, whether in East Orange or in Newark's economically deprived Central Ward. Newark had been receiving inadequate city services for decades as its population grew and became increasingly impoverished. The jobless rate was 20–25 percent, and unemployment was above 40 percent. The schools and public housing were severely overcrowded. Drug addiction and violent crime were rampant.

On July 14, 1967, the Central Ward exploded when two white Newark policemen arrested and attacked a Black taxi driver. Pent-up violence was unleashed for six days. Department stores were burned and looted as were several businesses throughout Newark's downtown and surrounding neighborhoods. Open warfare between the police and mostly Black civilians shut down the city until the National Guard arrived. Twenty-six people died during the riots, and hundreds were injured. Several blocks of the Central Ward were left in ruins. Newark wasn't the only city to explode that summer. Detroit, LA's Watts neighborhood, New York's Harlem, and several smaller cities erupted within a week of the Newark riots.

In many ways, the same pattern was repeated on October 7, 2023, when after seventy-five years of military occupation and fifteen years of a strict blockade on food and essential goods, the Gaza Strip erupted as Palestinian resistance fighters and attacked the area just east of Gaza in Israel. It was not lost on the Palestinians that these Israeli villages and farms were lost by their parents and grandparents in 1948 when the Palestinians were forcibly transferred into the Gaza Strip and Israelis took their homes and farms without compensation. I condemn Hamas' taking of hostages and killing innocent Israeli citizens, but Palestinians had every right to resist the brutal military rule under international law.

Many analysts predicted Newark would see another round of violence when the National Guard departed. The show of force brought a tense, temporary truce, but the underlying problems were not addressed. The economic blight, lack of jobs, police violence, and systemic impoverishment and racism worsened. The racial polarization intensified as the Black and white communities armed themselves for "the fire next time." The blatant racism emanating from the North Ward Citizens Council and Anthony Imperiale infuriated the Black community and widened the racial divide. Newark was a classic case of urban blight, violence, extreme poverty, and hopelessness. The city was written off by many analysts who predicted it would never recover.

While I was conducting research for my master's dissertation in late 1967 and 1968, I interviewed several pastors and heads of social service agencies in Newark's Central Ward. Looking around at boarded-up buildings, men hanging out on street corners, and the high levels of poverty, I could see why Newark exploded that summer. It was just a matter of time before the frustrations boiled over.

The federal government's Kerner Commission Report, issued in March 1968, arrived just in time for me to summarize my research and dissertation findings. The Kerner Commission was criticized for its controversial but honest conclusion, stating in no uncertain terms, "White racism, not Black anger, was at the heart of the Newark riots." Forty years later, *Smithsonian* magazine ran an insightful article by Alice George titled "The Kerner Commission Got It Right, But Nobody Listened." George points out how the Kerner Report shocked the political establishment by "turning their assumptions upside down." The article summarized the Kerner Report's conclusions:

> Bad policing practices, a flawed justice system, unscrupulous consumer credit practices, poor or inadequate housing, high unemployment, voter suppression, and other culturally embedded forms of racial discrimination all converged to propel violent upheaval on the streets of African-American neighborhoods in American cities, north and south, east and west. And as black unrest arose, inadequately trained police officers and National Guard troops entered affected neighborhoods, often worsening the violence. White society is deeply implicated in the ghetto. White institutions created it, white institutions maintain it, and white society condones it. The United States was poised to fracture into two radically unequal societies—one black, one white, separate and unequal.[12]

My dissertation was not a deep and probing analysis, but I did utilize the Kerner Report as it confirmed what I was hearing from several Black pastors, social workers, and church members. The research and five case studies opened my eyes to the complex problems facing Newark and the surrounding communities like East Orange. The superficial Band-Aid solutions implemented by decades of government policies failed to halt Newark's decline into systemic poverty. Elmwood was a step removed from the epicenter of the Newark riots, but it was by no means immune from the same problems.

A significant number of our members at Elmwood grew up in the Central Ward and were thankful to leave it behind. However, most of Newark's problems were already in East Orange in one form or another, and East Orange had to face that fact. Thankfully, most people saw the dangerous trends and wanted to work proactively to address the issues before they became unwieldy.

As I look back on my introduction to Newark's problems, it strikes me that I failed to utilize the wisdom of liberation theology in my dissertation. I was just getting acquainted with this revolutionary approach to theology, but regrettably I ignored it. Had I utilized the pedagogical framework such as the "preferential option of the poor," my research and analysis would have been different. The focus on liberation theology would have led me to focus on the radical need for a political and economic transformation designed to empower the poor Black and brown populations of Newark in order to lift them out of endless cycles of violence, powerlessness, and death ("Jesus' preferential option for the poor"). Rather than concentrating on traditional leaders, such as clergy, teachers, and social agencies, I could have interviewed people on the streets, especially the poor, who were the primary victims of the racist systems.

My daily experiences as a new pastor in the Black community reminded me of my naivete about how systemic racism functions. A good example of my personal naivete occurred the first time I took holy communion to shut-ins. I liked how Joe organized the session and sent people out in pairs. The elders met for a light lunch after worship, and then we went to Joe's office for our assignments and prayer. Outreach efforts such as this showed how Elmwood Church was striving to be a loving family looking out for "the least of their sisters and brothers."

My assignment was to join Elder Al Jenkins, a middle-aged Black American who grew up in Newark's Central Ward and had been involved in street gangs as a youth. Al was highly personable, with a refreshing sense of humor and a savvy street-wise orientation to Newark. During lunch we discussed my research in Newark and how we both loved Claude Brown's *Manchild in the Promised Land*, which was set in Harlem. Al said it reminded him of his youth growing up in Newark.

Just before we left, Al said, "Hey Don, you should put on a clerical collar before we leave."

"Why?" I asked. "I don't have one and have never worn one."

Al and Joe laughed as Joe pulled out an extra clerical collar from his desk, saying, "Hey man, put it on." Al added, "It's pretty hardcore where we are going. It's just for your protection."

Nodding, I smiled, saying, "OK, I get it." I should have known this myself but was appreciative that my friends were looking out for me.

When Al and I arrived at the high-rise projects, I immediately saw the wisdom of the clerical collar. We were in the heart of the riot zone. Stores were still boarded up, and since it was the middle of winter there were no unemployed men on street corners. We parked and walked over to the housing complexes, where we were warmly greeted by several young men at the entrance. One of them stepped forward and put out his hand to welcome us. We shook hands and he looked me in the eye and said, "Hello, Father. Can we help you?" Al and I explained the purpose of our visit and mentioned the name of the elderly couple we hoped to see. The young man replied, "Follow me, I know exactly where they live." Two of the young men, both in their late teens or early twenties, escorted us to the apartment on the top floor of the building, and we thanked them. They couldn't have been more helpful.

We knocked on the door and were welcomed by the elderly couple. They were living in absolute squalor. The wife was in a wheelchair, the apartment was run-down and very cold. The hallways and stairwells outside the apartment reeked of urine and overflowed with litter. Al noted a bathroom window with bullet holes that had been covered with cardboard. They told us the window had been that way since the riots in July, six months ago. They had been calling for someone to repair it but had gotten no response.

Al used their phone and called some friends on the Elmwood Church Deacon Board and asked one of them to come down as soon as possible and repair the window. We asked them if there was anything else they needed and they said it was increasingly difficult for them to buy groceries. There were no grocery stores within walking distance and their daughter recently moved out of the area. Al asked what they needed and jotted down a list of items and called the deacons again. He said the deacons would be there in a couple of hours, and from now on the Deacon Board would make sure they had fresh groceries every week. They were so appreciative I thought they would cry.

We had a good discussion and offered Holy Communion and a prayer. They were extremely thankful for our visit. We asked if they needed anything else and they said we were like angels to them. Al gave them the name and phone number of the chair of the Deacon Board and encouraged them to make a list of any home repairs, medicine, groceries, or anything else the deacons could do. We told them the tradition of deacons looking out for the needs of church members dated back to the early church.

This visit was an eye-opener for me on multiple levels. During my research, I visited several churches and social service agencies in the neighborhood but had not been inside the projects. This experience showed me another dimension of severe poverty, urban blight, and why people riot when their pleas for help are ignored for years. As we left the projects, we thanked the young men hanging out at the entrance.

If I could do my research again, I would be interviewing people like the elderly couple and others in the projects, especially the young men in the lobby. I was just a few years older than them and wondered what it would be like growing up with no money, no employment opportunities, and no future. Their best option was the gangs that often led to drugs, crime, and a short life expectancy.

My other takeaway was the devastating impact of systemic racism and poverty. The individual cases were one dimension of poverty, but when you looked around, this was a sick and destructive system. It was the result of decades of myopic government policies that failed to address root causes of poverty, and traditional social services were inadequate. The Kerner Report was correct. Newark was proof we were two societies, one Black the other white—separate and unequal.

As I reflect on my experiences in the Black community, it is easy to see how these prepared me for my visits to Beirut and the Palestinian struggle. In Beirut, the West Bank, and Gaza Strip, poverty was the direct result of the settler colonial system. Israel's systemic efforts to displace and replace the Palestinian majority mirrored what the United States did to its indigenous First Nations population.

By 2023, the Israeli military occupation of the Gaza Strip, East Jerusalem, and West Bank had been entrenched for seventy-five years. Six international human rights organizations had officially declared Israel's military rule as systemic apartheid, and war crimes, similar to what the white regime in South Africa had sustained until it was overthrown. South African leaders like Archbishop Desmond Tutu and others said what Israel was doing was actually worse than anything they had to endure. The situation in Newark and most major US cities was similar—a violent, systemic form of racism impoverishing and abusing Black Americans along racial lines, just as Israel was abusing Palestinians.

Each system is dehumanizing and designed to control, if not eliminate, indigenous people whose very existence stood in the way of the colonial powers. I will address both systems of control, systemic racism, and violence throughout this memoir. They are at the heart of my political and religious journey. While I was drawn to the issue of racial injustice at home and the violence in historic Palestine, I continued to be inspired by the message of Jesus, the Hebrew prophets, the centrality of justice in the Qur'an, and the themes of the Universal Declaration of Human Rights. They combine to call us to higher standards and actions based on equality, justice, and compassion for all. Jesus' message on the Last Judgment claims our lives will be reviewed on how we treat those in prison, the hungry, and the poor, and perhaps those facing genocide:

> "For I was hungry and you gave me food, I was thirsty and you gave me drink, I was a stranger and you welcomed me, I was naked and you clothed me, I was sick and you visited me, I was in prison and you came to me." Then the righteous will answer him, saying, "Lord, when did we see you hungry and feed you, or thirsty and give you drink? And when did we see you as a stranger and welcome you, or naked and clothe you? And when did we see you sick or in prison and visit you?" And the King will answer them, "Truly, I say to you, as you did it to one of the least of these my sisters and brothers, you did it to me."[13]

Chapter 6
LEARNING FROM A MASTER TEACHER

"Your best teacher is your last mistake."

—Ralph Nader

On my second Sunday after being installed as Elmwood's assistant pastor, I was waiting for Joe in his office. It was close to 11 AM and a small group of Elders were anxiously waiting with me for our prayer before the 11 AM worship service. Joe was running late, and it was 10:55 AM.

Rufus Howard, one of our hardworking and faithful elders, joked with me, saying, "Well, Don, I hope you have a sermon ready in case Joe doesn't show up." I laughed with Rufus and the others but suddenly wondered what I would do if something happened to Joe. What if he was suddenly taken ill? There was no way I could preach on short notice. Another elder called Joe's home to see if he had left the house. All of a sudden, Joe pulled into the driveway and ran into the office, apologizing profusely for his lateness. No one was more relieved than I was. After a prayer, we walked quickly to the sanctuary where we lined up behind the choir for the processional.

Joe mopped his brow as we started walking up the aisle, singing the opening hymn as we processed. He leaned over about halfway to the front and said, "Hey man, could you take the pastoral prayer this morning? I haven't finished the conclusion to my sermon and need to give the Holy Spirit more time to work with me."

I had never heard the phrase about the Holy Spirit but laughed and replied, "Sure, I'll take it."

Prior to seminary I was comfortable with extemporaneous prayer in public but had lost that ability. The professor of my homiletics (preaching) class insisted on having students write out pastoral prayers in great detail. He graded us on grammar, spelling, syntax, and logic. Presbyterian clergy are prepared to be intellectually rigorous and function "decently and in order," but these methods were a far cry from what was needed in the Black church. It was another case of "unlearning" what I was taught and reworking it for the Black worship experience.

I was nervous and far from inspired, but I managed to offer the pastoral prayer that morning. The experience taught me I didn't need to write out my prayers. An outline in my head and a prayer from the heart and soul was what the people needed. I realized this approach comes from the depths of the soul and a prayerful state prior to and during the worship experience. It wasn't long before I was back to impromptu prayers without a manuscript. The Princeton approach to homiletics was helpful to a point, but it did not prepare me for leadership in Black worship.

As I watched and listened to Joe that morning, I was curious as to whether the Holy Spirit had actually paid him a visit. As the sermon moved toward its climax, I saw Joe reach down and push a button on the lower right side of the pulpit. A light came on in front of Fred Martin on the organ console, and Fred quietly played a familiar spiritual. Within two minutes, the cadence of Joe's preaching reached an elevated inflection as he brought a moving story to its conclusion. The choir had been humming with the organ when Fred lifted his arms, and they stood and started to sing. When Joe reached the end of his sermon, he was shouting his final phrases, filled with emotion. The congregation rose to its feet, hands lifted to the sky and waving, praising God with one of my favorite Black spirituals:

> I want Jesus to walk with me.
> I want Jesus to walk with me.
> All along my pilgrim journey
> Lord I want Jesus to walk with me.
>
> In my sorrows, Lord walk with me.
> In my sorrows, Lord walk with me.
> When my heart is truly aching,
> O Lord, I want Jesus to walk with me.

Many wept in sheer joy. I stood with them, and tears filled my eyes as we sang the last verse. I could not explain why I was crying, but the combination of Joe's moving conclusion, the choir, and the collective joy of the congregation generated an energy that was contagious. It felt like we had been to the mountaintop and had glimpsed the promised land. As they say in the Black church, "The preacher brought us home this morning." And yes, the Holy Spirit was indeed working with Joe. Princeton Seminary did not have this homiletical method in its repertoire.

One of the most inspiring and impressive aspects of the Elmwood congregation was its strong sense of community. The Sunday morning worship service was a highlight of the community, anchored by Joe's preaching, the music, and shared fellowship. Elmwood Church enthusiastically welcomed visitors, encouraged them to return, and urged them to get involved in various programs. My role was to help strengthen the programs to complement outside Sunday morning worship. We started to put more emphasis on Sunday school, and I was building a stronger youth program, starting with the high school youth group. I began to organize small-group fellowship experiences and midweek adult education classes. Then I created a social justice committee, where we studied community issues where we might have an impact.

Martin Luther King Jr. often talked about the "beloved community," where everyone is welcomed and valued for who they are "regardless of race, ethnicity, status, or power." I saw the "beloved community" in action at Elmwood Church. The Sunday morning worship experience was designed to lift up the congregation so they could find inspiration to face the burdens they were carrying during the week. Diana L. Hayes discusses Dr. King's basis for this concept of "beloved community" and reminds us that it originates in Africa:

> African American spirituality was forged in the fiery furnace of slavery in the United States. The core was African in origin, in worldview, in culture, and traditions … There is no life without the community and there is no community without the active participation of all. As a well-known African proverb states, "I am because we are." That is, unlike in Western society, it is not the individual but the community that is of critical importance.[14]

My experiences with Black families, the Elders, the high school youth, and so many other members at Elmwood provided a sense of family and a welcoming spirit to a higher degree than I had experienced in any of the dozens of churches I had attended since I was a child. Karen and I were part of the family and have never found a church as welcoming, friendly, and inclusive as Elmwood.

When Dr. King described the "beloved community," he envisioned a time when Black and white Americans, and other ethnic and religious groups, would be reconciled in a new society where dignity, equality, and justice prevailed. Joe Roberts and several elders stated publicly that Elmwood's social experiment with Karen and me was one attempt to be "a beloved community." We were truly blessed to be part of this experiment. An initiative like this, we believed, was more likely to be initiated by the Black community. (Somewhat later I experienced a similar sense of community in the Middle East where family and the collective experience were emphasized over the individualism of the West. Generous hospitality is a consistent highlight of Arab culture and similar to what we experienced at Elmwood Church.)

Another aspect of Elmwood that stands out was the community's sense of humor and capacity to see joy in all kinds of encounters. I experienced a readiness to laugh at the incongruities of life. It seemed that most Black people had this gift. One weird but memorable experience occurred about a month into my first year of full-time work at Elmwood. I was walking past the altar one morning on my way to a staff meeting when I noticed a group of men wheeling a casket into the sanctuary. I paused to see if this would be an open- or closed-casket funeral.

In seminary we were advised to always have the casket closed for the funeral service. I had not performed a funeral at that point but was told the tradition in the Black church was to keep the casket open until the end of the service. I greeted our custodian, George Roberts (no relation to Joe), who was vacuuming the carpet in preparation for the funeral service.

The men from the funeral home wheeled the casket to the front and opened it. I could see the deceased person down to his waist and assumed the entire service would be held with an open casket. I planned to discuss the issue with Joe to learn if Elmwood always had the open casket, figuring that sooner or later, I would be conducting my first funeral. I arrived at Joe's office and we started our staff meeting. After no more than ten minutes, Mrs. Howard, the chair of the Altar Guild, burst into the office shrieking, "Come quick… something strange just happened in the sanctuary." We had no idea what was happening—whether it was a fire or something worse.

Racing to the sanctuary, we noticed the vacuum cleaner still running with the custodian nowhere in sight. Mrs. Howard turned off the vacuum. Eager to clear up the confusion, she said, "Let me explain what just happened." As she had been fixing the flowers on the altar, she heard Mr. Roberts utter a penetrating howl. He had been vacuuming around the casket when the deceased man suddenly sat straight up. Completely spooked, he ran out of the sanctuary screaming that he would never return to the church.

Looking past Mrs. Howard, we saw she was absolutely correct. The deceased was still in a sitting position. I knew he was not sitting up twenty minutes earlier when I left the sanctuary. Joe went over and lowered the body saying, "I don't think the funeral home put embalming fluid in this guy." Joe laughed and said, "Well, this is Elmwood's version of the raising of Lazarus, but we only got it half right. He rose up, but he's still dead. No resurrection from the dead today, folks."

We had a good laugh and returned to our meeting. Joe called the custodian and told us, "Old Man Roberts quit on the spot." He said, "There is no way in hell he is returning to the church." The experience, while hilarious, was too much for the elderly custodian. Joe had to replace him immediately. He turned to me and chuckled. "I'll bet they never prepared you for something like this at Princeton."

"No way. Does this happen often?"

He laughed and said this was a first. "But be sure to stick around because you never know what's going to happen here."

Months later, I was working on a social justice project that I hoped could involve more of the congregation. I was increasingly aware of how the drug problem in East Orange was getting out of control and could see the evidence in our high school youth group. I called a meeting and formed a group called the Elmwood Drug Education and Rehabilitation Task Force to begin studying the problem.

The task force included medical professionals, educators, parents, and high school students. We met regularly and consulted specialists in the police force, high school social workers, East Orange Hospital, and politicians. One of our physicians from the church who specialized in drug rehabilitation gave us access to other specialists. Everyone involved in the project was convinced something had to be done immediately. There was no question the drug problem was on the verge of becoming an epidemic in East Orange.

After nearly a year of hard work, we collected the best data available on the problem in East Orange and decided to consult experts at the hospitals, police officials, and leading drug rehabilitation centers in Newark. We made site visits to the top three facilities in Newark and talked to former addicts about the problems in East Orange. They all agreed the problem was growing rapidly and it needed immediate attention. We held an informational forum in the church for the community and had top experts on the panel from East Orange, including the director of a treatment center in Newark. One of our key members of the church task force was the president of our high school youth group, a bright and wise young man, who affirmed the need for a center and referenced several friends who were struggling with drugs.

We decided to hold a forum for the church and East Orange community with a panel including the high school principal, social workers, the president of our youth group, and medical professionals. The forum was well attended by church members, parents, neighbors, and youth. The task force then met to review our next steps. We agreed to draft a proposal for action and submit it to the church decision-makers. We summarized our analysis and made a strong case for a drug education and treatment center in East Orange. The most successful treatment program in Newark was willing to work with us to set up a satellite treatment and education center in East Orange.

We proposed the center should be housed at our church. We outlined an educational component and had a signed commitment of cooperation from East Orange High School and most of the city's junior high school principals. We also had endorsement letters from the mayor of East Orange, three city council members, the chief of police, and medical professionals. The most effective treatment center in Newark came with endorsements from local hospitals, the school board, and police. The program we selected employed recovered drug addicts, social workers, and a team of physicians who served as consultants. The treatment involved a carefully monitored methadone maintenance program with several weeks of required psychotherapy with a psychiatric nurse.

We submitted the proposal to Pastor Joe for feedback before taking it to the session for final approval. Joe was impressed by our proposal and the amount of research that went into it. He agreed that such a program was needed in East Orange, but he questioned whether the center should be housed in the church building. Joe thought we were moving too fast on the location and suggested taking a step back and engaging the congregation and immediate neighborhood in an educational process. He did not think the congregation or neighbors were on board with our proposed location.

We countered that time was of the essence, and we had the support of city leadership, several church members, and our neighbors. Joe eventually agreed to take the proposal to the session for its approval but said we should be prepared with a backup plan, perhaps a delay in implementation and doing surveys and more education in the interim.

Two members of the task force and I presented the proposal to the session. When the discussion period arrived, we were surprised that most of the elders were strongly opposed. They agreed with our analysis of the problem but thought our solution was premature and suggested we should look for another location in East Orange.

The elders' opposition to the proposal convinced Joe and some of our task force that we should go back to the mayor and rework the plan. They urged us to find another location for the drug center and also opposed the incorporation of ex-addicts in the program. Neighbors feared that it would attract other addicts to the neighborhood, leading to increased levels of theft and drug use.

The session considered the proposal a month later. After a brief discussion, the proposal was voted down. The sticking point was having the center located in the church. That and the opposition from the neighbors, the use of ex-addicts, and the fact there were viable alternatives elsewhere in East Orange led to a negative vote. We were thanked for our hard work and reminded that nothing has been lost; the idea of the center was absolutely correct, but not in the church building.

All of us on the task force were disappointed with the decision, but most of us were prepared for it. We agreed to turn the project over to the City of East Orange, whose officials had expressed interest in implementing the plan. We were disappointed not to implement it at the church, but we turned the project over to the mayor and City of East Orange. Within a year, a rehabilitation center was established.

I learned a number of lessons from this experience and filed them away for future consideration. My enthusiasm for a solution was commendable, but my enthusiasm was also a problem. I was impatient and rushed the project, and some of my task force members followed my lead. We should have taken the proposal slower and solicited more feedback from the immediate neighbors and church members. We should have talked to the elders and perhaps made adjustments midcourse. We could have solicited feedback through surveys, neighborhood meetings in homes, more educational panels, and hiring a professional research firm. These lessons in consensus building and uniting the community behind a project before implementing it would eventually come into play.

A different learning experience occurred when I reached out to a small group affiliated with the Black Panther Party in East Orange and Newark. The voice of the Black Panthers was not represented in our congregation. I had been reading about them for two years and was familiar with their political views, their programs, and particularly their grass roots work with youth and the poor. I wanted to listen and learn from them. The mainstream media consistently denigrated them as extremists. As for me, anyone J. Edgar Hoover demonized was probably OK in my book. I wanted to cut through the propaganda, meet them for myself, and see their programs in action.

One night, Karen and I attended one of our choir's parties, where I learned two of the women in the choir were married to men affiliated with the Panthers. I made my way over to William, the coach of our highly successful church high school basketball team and reportedly a member of the Black Panther Party. His wife was urging him to leave as they were late for the baby sitter, but he seemed willing to talk. As we chatted about sports, his wife jokingly said, "Don, if you can get him to come to church, I'll forgive you for making us late."

I assured William that I was opposed to pressure tactics on religious issues, and he said, "Don't worry, there is no way you will get me inside a church building on a Sunday morning. I'm simply not a believer in the pie-in-the-sky answers you guys dish out." I replied that I'd heard of his affiliation with the Black Panthers and was interested in learning about their programs for young people. He said, "We provide breakfast for close to 100 children every day before school and have literacy instruction and survival skills training after school. Since the riots and rise of the white racist militias, we believe a showdown is coming, so we are preparing for it. We need to take matters into our own hands and do not expect to be bailed out by racist white systems that could care less about us." I told him I wanted to take a look at their youth programs sometime in the near future.

His wife interrupted, encouraging him to back off. I said, "No, no, I'm very interested in what he's saying, but I don't want to delay you any longer. Let's get together sometime soon and talk about politics."

She apologized and said, "Sorry to be pushy, but we are nearly an hour late. You two need to get together, so I hope it happens." I thanked William and we agreed to have that conversation. We shook hands and off they went.

About a month later, I was walking through the church gym on the way to my office. William was shooting baskets. He yelled across the gym, "Hey man, I hear from the guys that you played a little ball once upon a time." I replied, "Yeah, back in high school, but that was a few years ago. I'm really rusty and haven't played for a couple of months."

"That's OK," he said. "Come on and let's go one-on-one until the team arrives. How about it? We can figure out a time for lunch after we play ball."

I wondered whether this was a good idea. I figured this guy was probably really good, and he would destroy me… but so what? It would be a chance to get to know him on another level. I heard William played basketball in college, and he was bigger than me, about six feet four inches, and solidly built. His Afro made him look even bigger. But I agreed. I retrieved my gym shoes from my car, and after a few practice shots, our contest began.

We agreed to play until the winner reached fifteen points, one point per basket. William was very aggressive. Initially he took me to the basket, overpowering me, dunking the ball twice, and leading three points to none. After a slow beginning, I began to analyze his game. I realized he protected the basket on defense, as he could really jump to cover the key and the rim, but he was not coming out to defend the outside shot. That would be my point of attack. I was able to get into a rhythm and made a couple of long jump shots from outside the key. We went back and forth, and finally I hit the game-winner, enabling me to squeak a 15–14 victory. I thanked him for the game and said I needed to get some work done at the office but suggested we meet for lunch.

As we shook hands, William said, "Damn, man, you've got a nice outside shot. Let's set a date for that lunch." I thanked him for the game and suggested a couple of times to meet the following week. William said he and a friend were going to a lecture by Amiri Baraka, at his center in Newark. He invited me to join them. Baraka, born Leroi Jones, was close to the Panthers. A nationally known Black poet, music critic, and author, Baraka had already drawn comparisons to James Baldwin. I was familiar with his writings and readily agreed to join William and his friend.

I joined them for two events at Baraka's center, where I had the opportunity to meet the poet in person. William told me he worked on a few projects with Baraka, who assisted the Panthers in East Orange with their youth program. I decided to explore an idea with him about an educational program I was considering.

I asked William if he would be willing to lead a discussion group at church on Black power and its implications for Newark and East Orange. He was enthusiastic about the idea and joked, "As long as I don't have to attend worship Sunday morning, we are good." He suggested two books: Eldridge Cleaver's *Soul on Ice* and a collection of Amiri Baraka's poetry and political essays.

William was critical of *Soul on Ice*, despite the fact that Cleaver was the national director of the Black Panther Party. He thought Cleaver was "dumbing down" the real message of Black power in order to sell books to white people, which to him was "a foolish compromise." Then he added, "Since *Soul on Ice* is on the *New York Times* bestseller list, it might build our audience and allow me to provide folks with a critical perspective."

William's suggestion worked. We had excellent attendance and lively discussions. At times the talk was heated, but always respectful, and the participants seemed to enjoy the exchanges with William. He seemed pleased with the evening sessions. I could tell he appreciated the opportunity. I was content to stay in the background and simply facilitate the exchange of viewpoints. He seemed to enjoy challenging people's assumptions; at times he lost people with his radical analysis. But overall this was an excellent educational process. Most of those who attended said the church needed to do more programs like this one.

I never became close friends with William, but we did develop respect for one another. I learned from his political analysis and worldview. I was grateful to have the opportunity to understand his perspective and learn from him. William helped me distinguish between being an assimilationist and an anti-racist, a very important distinction. His basic illustration was this: "It's the difference between Malcolm X and the teachings of Martin Luther King Jr."

The other lesson I learned from my connection with William was the need to establish relationships on other people's terms. Whether it meant risking a game of one-on-one with William on the basketball court or joining him at Baraka's Center in Newark, I needed to step out of my comfort zone. In a way, it was another case of downward mobility based on humility, respect, and equality of persons. I was learning by practicing the power and possibilities of Paulo Freire's principles of praxis and bottom-up learning.

When the Palestine issue captured my attention, I turned back to this lesson, which is to center the voices of those you seek to assist, as they know better than you what is needed for justice. The Israeli and US media strategy is to demonize and marginalize Palestinian voices as illegitimate partners in the discourse about the Israeli-Palestinian political struggle. I have not always been consistent in this project; there have been times when it seemed an outsider voice like mine was helpful, as when I was a witness to Israel's 1982 war in Lebanon. Nevertheless, I have tried to put into practice the value of centering Palestinian voices whenever possible. I believe they are the best equipped to speak on their own behalf and that my role should be one of empowering their legitimacy and visibility whenever possible.

Karen's experience at the church was overwhelmingly positive but quite different. I felt a calling to serve the church and I understood it to be an all-encompassing passion and vocation rolled into one. It was a spiritual, political, economic, and a deeply personal commitment that gave me a profound sense of fulfillment. My problem was that I needed to set clear boundaries so I could carve out enough time for us to work on our relationship.

As for Karen, after two miscarriages in two years, she was pregnant again. We knew we had to be careful, so we checked with Joe Roberts for advice on a gynecologist. Joe put us in touch with a church member who came highly recommended from several women in the church. Ruth Holly was very strict, advising Karen to leave her job at the three-month mark of the pregnancy and limit her activity. Karen didn't mind leaving the job. After all, it meant she would be completely free for unlimited time at the pool through the summer.

Aided immeasurably by the wise counsel of Dr. Holly, Jay Douglas Wagner was born on Groundhog Day, 1970. There was some drama two weeks prior to Jay's birth. Dr. Holly specified Karen should plan on a cesarean section, which was fine with us. When we went in for her final sonogram about ten days prior to the birth, the technician lamented, "I'm sorry, but I can only see one arm, so you should prepare yourselves for that possibility." We prayed about it and knew we were ready to love Jay no matter what, praying, "Just let Jay be a healthy baby."

I paced and prayed all that morning at the hospital. Since it was a cesarean birth, I was not allowed in the operating room. The nurse came out and told me we had a healthy boy. Karen was fine but still under sedation. I hesitated for a second and asked, "How are his arms and legs?"

The nurse unrolled the little blanket and smiled, "Have a look. Both arms and legs are healthy and strong." All I could say was, "Thank God! What a gift!"

Jay and I often joke about how easy it was to recognize him in the viewing room for new babies. He was the only white kid born that week at Newark Hospital. Today, Jay and his wife, Tracy, are the parents of two wonderful children, Ashley and Aiden, our first grandchildren. They are amazing parents and very involved in the children's lives, including sports, music, church, and academics. Jay runs a successful business in Toledo, Ohio, and Tracy manages the medical records, personnel issues, and finances for her sister Susan, who is a physician in charge of twelve retirement homes.

Jay's arrival was a true blessing. The outpouring of love from the church was unbelievably generous. Jay's baptism by Joe at Elmwood Church was a very moving experience for us. The decision to come to Elmwood was a gift in every way. We were happy as a family and I was learning more than I could keep up with—whether growing in my pastoral skills, understanding systemic racism, or becoming more of an anti-racist. However, we were not prepared for the dramatic change that was in the air.

Chapter 7
AN UNEXPECTED TRANSITION

"Don't ask what the world needs. Ask what makes you come alive, and go do it. Because what the world needs is people who have come alive."

—Dr. Howard Thurman

Listening to Joe Roberts deliver sermons every week provided both inspiration and an education on Black history and theology. Joe was drawing on his personal history growing up as a preacher's son in the African Episcopal tradition. His illustrations included courageous Black women and men like Ida B. Wells and Sojourner Truth, Frederick Douglass, Martin Luther King Jr. and Malcolm X. The novels of James Baldwin and quotes from Langston Hughes, Ralph Ellison, and Richard Wright filled a gap in my Eurocentric education.

The person Joe quoted the most was someone I had never heard of prior to serving at Elmwood: Howard Thurman. Thurman was a Black liberation theologian, author, and mystic. Once I started reading Thurman's published works like *Deep Is the Hunger* and *Jesus and the Disinherited,* I recognized the blind spot in my education. I'm sure most universities and seminaries have made the necessary corrections today and include the wisdom of minorities and women in their curriculum. But when I attended seminary, Black preachers, political leaders, and theologians were nowhere in sight—except, that is, in Professor Shaull's courses.

Howard Thurman had the ability to blend the spiritual and social-justice dimensions of the Gospel in a way that spoke to me. There was a gap in my personal and spiritual journey. I tended to be an extroverted, activist, people-oriented person, but I yearned for a more intentional life of solitude and reflection. I prayed regularly, but I was so busy with the demands of the job and my activist tendency that my prayers were just one more facet of my hurried age that occurred on the run. Thurman spoke to that need as one who respected and practiced solitude.

Vincent Harding, a close advisor to Martin Luther King, summarized Thurman's theology with two words: "liberating spirituality."[15] At the outset of *Jesus and the Disinherited,* Thurman identifies his target audience by asking this difficult question: "What does Jesus offer those who have their backs up against the wall?" He was writing to Black students, academics, activists, and lapsed churchgoers who had grown disenchanted with traditional Christianity.

Thurman wanted to address the frustrations and understandable impatience among Blacks who had waited too long for an end to systemic racism and the daily humiliation and oppression people were enduring. By the late 1960s, many were abandoning the church. Young Blacks and those who were well-educated believed the church had abandoned the struggle for justice. As a result, the covert and overt racism still dominant in mainstream Protestant and Roman Catholic denominations was ignored.[16]

Thurman cites the parallels between the decades of the brutal Roman occupation of Palestine in Jesus' day and the equally long history of slavery and systemic racism in the United States. Jesus had to contend with a powerful Roman Empire and the intransigent Jewish religious hierarchy. Both authorities wanted to see him eliminated. Despite this, Jesus gained popularity among the masses and brought an uncompromising message of God's love, radical inclusion, and call for liberation from all forms of injustice and violence.

Thurman made a strong case for Jesus as a disrupter of racialized systems and the status quo in his day. In one of the clearest examples, he invoked the Samaritans as models of compassion and suffering love. The familiar parable of the Good Samaritan has the Samaritan traveler showing compassion and extravagant mercy for the Jew beaten by robbers and left by the roadside to die. In the parable, the religious leadership walked past the victim and did nothing to assist him. However, it was an outcast, a Samaritan who "had pity on him," who took him to an inn and paid for his care and a room. In those days, Jews viewed Samaritans as unclean and avoided contact with them at all costs. Yet in this story, the Samaritan was the hero by demonstrating compassion to a Jewish person in need.

A more graphic example of racism occurs when Jesus goes straight into the center of Samaria and meets a Samaritan woman at the well.[17] Samaritans were not only to be avoided, but it was also forbidden for men to meet single women in public. The territory of the Samaritans was an example of religious and social apartheid in first-century Palestine. Jews who traveled near Samaria had to go out of their way to avoid entering Samaritan territory. Jesus subverted the archaic laws because they were based on racist principles and contrary to life as God intended it to be lived.

Jesus intentionally disrupted the racist practices and showed us how we can challenge such discriminatory systems by choosing normal relationships based on compassion and love. The fact that the text highlights a Samaritan woman is not accidental. The same prohibitions concerning gender existed then as now, and Jesus offers an alternative to gender apartheid. Thurman's message to young Black men and women was liberating and compelling. The story illustrates how far the religious establishment had fallen from God's intentions for communities. The implications for young Black activists and lapsed Christians could not be missed.

But Thurman was not finished. He takes the call to activism and liberation one step further. He shows us how Jesus was consistently practicing a pattern of withdrawal and solitude when he retreated to "a desolate place."[18] Jesus was highly intentional about maintaining a disciplined practice of solitude that included time for silence, prayer, meditation, and reflection. Apparently, this discipline was a high priority for Jesus. His active and demanding public ministry was balanced with his need for solitude.

I was struck by a moving story about Dr. King and Dr. Thurman that relates to the need for rest and renewal. Dr. King was in New York City to promote his book *Strive for Freedom* when a deranged woman attacked him with a sharp bookmark, stabbing him several times and nearly severing vital veins and arteries in his neck. Dr. Thurman visited King in the hospital and urged him to take an additional two weeks in order to fully recover from his wounds. King initially said it was impossible as the demands on his schedule had him booked to speak in several cities. King said he would need to leave the hospital within a couple of days.

Thurman prevailed on him, advising King to rethink his schedule and offering to spend several days with him discussing the use of nonviolent resistance in the civil rights movement. King finally gave in to Thurman's advice, canceling the speaking engagements and spending another week with Thurman. They discussed strategies of nonviolence and how and where the civil rights movement could incorporate more nonviolent direct action in theory and practice. Thurman also urged Dr. King to take more time in prayer, meditation, and reflection in the future.

Once King recovered, he made a serious attempt to incorporate Thurman's wisdom into his backbreaking schedule. From his hospital visit forward, King stayed in close touch with Dr. Thurman, who served as a consultant to King. Dr. King's staff noted their leader took more time in solitude and prayer and urged them to do the same. Several sources, including Andrew Young and Vincent Harding, said King always carried a dog-eared copy of Thurman's *Jesus and the Disinherited* when he traveled. He consulted it again and again when the pressures mounted. If we look closely, we can hear Thurman's ideas in King's sermons and speeches.

It took me several years before I integrated Thurman's advice about solitude and reflection into my life. Perhaps I was too young or simply foolish as I was always busy, particularly when the children were young. I did maintain a morning and evening discipline of prayer, but it was too brief and lacked serious time for reflection. I took solace in a popular book of prayers by Malcolm Boyd, appropriately titled *Are You Running With Me Jesus?*, although Boyd's lifestyle was not what Jesus had in mind for prayer and solitude.

Fifteen years later, I had a serious bike accident that put me in intensive care for forty-eight hours with a concussion, seven broken ribs, a lacerated spleen. I was riding my bicycle at full speed to reach my office for a conference call when I hit a pothole and flew over my handlebars, hitting the street with full force. I was not wearing a helmet. This was long before these things became standard among bike riders. My physician said that had I not brought my arm under my head to cushion the blow, I would have sustained serious brain damage.

When I left the hospital, I had to learn to sleep sitting in a chair. There is little else you can do for broken ribs. In the initial week or two, every time I adjusted my position brought excruciating pain. During the long, sleepless nights and days, I decided to practice meditation and mindfulness. I tried to focus on my broken ribs and lacerated spleen, mentally visualizing their healing as I meditated. It was the first time I tried anything like this, but the process brought a peaceful time of rest that often induced me to fall asleep. My enforced time of silence and meditation became a gift.

After a month of convalescing, I had my checkup with the physician and he surprised me by saying, "I can't believe this. You are healing faster than anyone I have seen. This is amazing." I smiled, because I knew what was happening.

He asked, "What are you doing?"

I told him about my meditation practices.

He replied, "Well, I don't believe in this as a scientist, but it seems to be working for you, so keep doing it." From that point forward, I became a believer in meditation. I was still too busy to practice it daily, but it was a discipline I turned to more frequently. Thurman's "liberating spirituality" was a reminder to make it a daily practice, but I was not sufficiently disciplined to fully commit to it until I retired. I learned a great deal from the speeches and writings of the Vietnamese Buddhist monk Thích Nhất Hạnh, who emphasised mindfulness. He noted how we are so impulsive and action oriented that we instinctively respond to situations with the mindset of "Don't just sit there, do something." Perhaps what we need to do is, "Don't just do something, sit there." In other words, take time to listen to yourself, reflect on your dilemma and what's going on around you. Just sit and perhaps you will be wiser. You might even hear God's voice. Then you will know when and why you should take action.

Early in my third year of full-time ministry at Elmwood Church, we received the shocking news that Joe Roberts was leaving. Joe had received an offer to become an executive with the Southern Presbyterian Church in Atlanta, with a focus on racial reconciliation. The Presbyterian church divided over slavery in 1861, and the northern and southern branches had finally made the decision to reunite. As they were about to enter a period of reconciliation and education, Joe was asked to facilitate the healing process.

We were thrilled for Joe and his family, but it took the rest of us a long time to recover from the shock over his impending departure. We finally faced the facts and accepted that Joe was destined for greater challenges. We needed to move forward as a congregation and prepare for a future without Joe as our leader.[19]

Joe's departure meant my role was about to change. The session worked out an arrangement where I became the interim pastor with more leadership responsibilities, serving with a team of elders to cover the workload. The new plan had me preaching every other week, a challenge I welcomed. On alternate Sundays, we scheduled a number of leading Black preachers on the East Coast to deliver the Sunday sermon. It was a wonderful opportunity for the congregation to hear the best Black preaching in the country. It was gratifying that we were able to maintain the high standards Joe set through his preaching. The congregation was very patient with me as I tried to improve my preaching skills. I knew from the outset there was a clear drop-off when I preached, but the congregation was kind and encouraging.

After a year and a half as the interim pastor, I was convinced this was not the way I could best serve God. I was approaching burnout, working overtime while trying to manage my original responsibilities along with handling most of the demands of the interim pastor. I reached the conclusion that my gifts and skills were not aligned with church administration, fundraising, and various pastoral responsibilities. I was improving as a preacher—I even learned how to close my sermons with the organist and choir, as I had seen Joe implement so effectively. But I could never get accustomed to preaching every week.

My primary concern during this period was meeting our monthly budget, as donations usually decline when a strong leader departs. By the grace of God, and thanks to the diligent efforts of a skilled team of elders, we did not fall behind with the budget. The congregation gave generously. My role as interim pastor lasted longer than I expected, and aside from my fatigue, I found it fulfilling.

When we reached the two-year mark of my service as the interim pastor a surprising question was put to me. A group of elders from the session's search committee for the new pastor asked me to consider becoming a candidate for the senior pastor position. They indicated there was significant support in the congregation for me to assume the position. I had no idea this was the case and simply assumed that at twenty-eight, I was too young, too inexperienced—and too white. In time, I expressed my appreciation for considering me and promised to pray about it and get back to them in a couple of days.

When Karen and I discussed our future options, it was clear she was ready for a move. We had been at Elmwood Church for four years on a full-time basis (plus the additional two years I served as a seminary intern). I knew how demanding the position of senior pastor was, but uppermost in my mind was the conviction that Elmwood needed a Black pastor to take the congregation to the next level.

Elmwood needed to be a beacon of Black leadership in the community and in the Presbyterian church at large. The race questions, poverty, and social justice could be articulated and promoted best by a strong Black pastor. Moreover, the question of vision and cutting-edge advocacy needed a Black senior pastor for the sake of integrity and forcing the white power structures to face the challenges of the 1970s.

Another consideration informing my decision was the opportunity the position of senior pastor at Elmwood Church offered a Black woman or man at that point in history. Joe Roberts had elevated Elmwood's prestige not only in the Newark/East Orange area but across the Presbyterian denomination. How could I, in good conscience, stand in the way of a gifted Black woman or man to have this opportunity? It was easy for me to find employment, whereas there were very few Black churches in the denomination. There were also very few white congregations hiring Black pastors. I decided to remove my name as a candidate.

This was not a magnanimous decision. It was common sense. I tried to be racially and morally conscious about my decision. My prayer time and reflection led me to be at peace with the process. The more I thought about it, the principles of liberation theology were an added factor that convinced me to say no to the kind offer. The need to challenge the white community to rise to the values articulated in Black liberation theology needed to be articulated by a Black leader. The prophetic mission of the church in combating racism, undoing white privilege, in making decisions based on the "preferential option for the poor," would have more impact if it came from a Black leader. As a white man I was still a symbol of the problem called racism.

As my ministry at Elmwood Church drew to a close, the congregation was effusive with gratitude, love, and good wishes for our family. I was acutely aware of how much I had learned from them and what an honor it had been to serve these people. I had grown in my awareness in matters of racism and white privilege, and still had plenty of room for growth. The years at Elmwood were destined to be the most concentrated and significant period of racial awareness and growth in my life.

I told the session I was committed to staying in my position until a replacement was hired. I suggested I would leave Elmwood immediately after they found a new senior pastor so he or she could hire their own assistant. I updated my dossier (the church's version of a curriculum vitae) and was fortunate to interview for an associate pastor position with a large congregation in Ridgewood, New Jersey. I was offered a position with responsibilities in adult education, youth ministry, and church and social concerns.

Ridgewood is an overwhelmingly white, wealthy, and an elite suburb of New York City, about twenty miles west of the George Washington Bridge. It was just an hour north of East Orange but represented a dramatic demographic change. Karen was excited about the opportunity, and while I would have preferred another predominantly Black community, it was her turn to decide where we lived. The church provided a three-bedroom house in a residential area, just two blocks from the church. We moved when Jay was about a year old.

The time at Elmwood seemed to fly by too quickly. Looking back on the experience, I realized how much I had learned about myself, both my gifts and my limitations, and what a profound experience it had been on the race question. I had improved on my public speaking, including the capacity for impromptu prayers and presentations. I also gained leadership skills in leading a congregation and in an urban community with important training in race relations and Black culture and spirituality. My commitment to liberation theology was enhanced.

In addition, I developed a strong youth ministry and implemented service projects. I learned from my failure with the drug rehabilitation project and what it takes to implement something of that magnitude. I also learned how to multitask with multiple agendas running simultaneously. My sense of confidence was strong, but I knew my limitations—particularly those related to my administrative ability and being the lead pastor in a congregation.

Karen and I knew our worship experience was about to be dramatically different. We were leaving a community that had surrounded us with love and grace. We did not know if the next community and church would be as warm and hospitable. Elmwood provided a glimpse into what Dietrich Bonhoeffer and Dr. King called the "beloved community." The effusive love and joy Elmwood gave so freely inspired me and provided a base for racial reconciliation that was priceless. I have always valued the fact that this was where our son Jay was born, baptized, and welcomed into a truly loving and warm fellowship of believers—regardless of race.

Our experience at West Side Presbyterian Church proved to be another beloved community with loving friendships and interesting challenges. While the Ridgewood years deserve another chapter or two, I must hasten to introduce the next major theme of my vocational life: the trials and tribulations of the Middle East conflict, to which I now turn.

Section III: Chapters 8–12

Journeys to an Unholy Land

"Ah, you who make iniquitous decrees, who write oppressive statues, to turn aside the needy from justice and to rob the poor of my people of their rights, that widows may be your spoil, and that you may make the orphans your prey! What will you do on the day of punishment, in the calamity that will come from far away? To whom will you flee for help and where will you leave your wealth?"

—Isaiah 10: 1-3

Chapter 8
MIDDLE EAST CALLING

"When faithfulness is our standard, we are more likely to sustain our engagement with tasks that will never end: doing justice, loving mercy, and calling the beloved community into being."

—Parker Palmer

Israel was under attack as we drove from New Jersey to our new home in the Chicago area in early October 1973. The Arab-Israeli War (also known as the Ramadan War or Yom Kippur War) began on October 6, 1973, with a surprise attack on Israel by Egypt and Syria with limited support from other Arab armies. Their main goal was to regain territory lost to Israel in the war of 1967, including the Golan Heights, West Bank, Gaza Strip, East Jerusalem, and the Sinai Peninsula. I remember pausing to pray for Israel when I heard it was losing the initial phase of the war. I was a Christian supporter of Israel, but at this point I was a liberal Protestant and a "post-Holocaust" supporter of zionism, having jettisoned the evangelical/fundamentalist narrative.

Fifty years later, almost to the day, on October 7, 2023, Israel again seemed unprepared for another surprise attack, this time as Hamas broke out of the "open-air prison" called the Gaza Strip. The Hamas fighters attacked military installations, Israeli villages, and civilians who were attending a music festival. While Palestinians had a right under international law to attack military personnel and facilities, that right did not extend to innocent Israeli civilians and must be condemned as a war crime.

The attack threw Israel into a panic. It was quickly revealed that Israel had relaxed its military presence in the region, moving troops to the West Bank at the request of far-right Knesset members Ben-Gvir and Smotrich, who demanded military protection for ultra-Orthodox religious festivals in the

West Bank. The Israeli Defense Forces immediately launched a brutal assault on Gaza as military spokesmen called for Gaza to be completely leveled and every civilian and noncombatant in Gaza to be treated as Hamas or a military target. Israel proceeded to conduct what was termed a "probable genocide" by the International Court of Justice.

Shortly after the 1973 October War ended, we heard news reports indicating that the war had shifted in Israel's favor. News analysts said the reason for the change was a significant infusion of weapons and military intelligence from the United States. After the dust settled, both the Arab and Israeli sides reflected on the impact of the war. Israeli military officials came under fire for their lack of preparedness while the Egyptian and Syrian people wondered why they lost the war after winning the first phase.

A few weeks after the war, OPEC (Organization of Petroleum Exporting Countries) launched an oil embargo on the countries that supported Israel in the war. Beginning on October 29, 1973, the boycott hit Americans where it hurt—in the wallet and gas tank. The embargo brought about a period marked by long lines at gas stations. Cutting oil production also meant the price of a gallon of gas skyrocketed. Several stocks crashed. Americans blamed the "greedy Arabs." The oil boycott and gas station lines lasted through the winter, finally ending in late March 1974.

While Israel continued its mop-up operation and won the war, Karen, Jay, and I settled into our new home. I started my new ministry at First Presbyterian Church in downtown Evanston, Illinois, in mid-November 1973. Located in a few blocks from Northwestern University, the church had a robust congregation of 1,800 members. Evanston is a city of approximately 80,000, Chicago's closest suburb on the north shore of Lake Michigan. Driving north on Sheridan Road along the lake, one hardly notices where Chicago ends and Evanston begins, but within a few blocks, it becomes clear that you are in a more expensive real estate bracket.

I knew the First Presbyterian Church's senior pastor, Ernie Lewis, and his associate Paul Suzuki from my year at Louisville Seminary when I worked as a seminary student in Cincinnati. They reached out to me in Ridgewood and persuaded me to join the staff they were building in Evanston. Ernie and Paul were dedicated evangelicals, but the First Presbyterian Church staff and congregation had a variety of theological perspectives. A third member of the staff was Rev. Gary Skinner, a gifted colleague with a liberal theological perspective.

Also on staff part-time was Rev. Dr. Bud Ogle, a brilliant theologian and campus pastor at Northwestern University. Bud and I spent our first year of seminary at Louisville. Bud transferred to Yale Divinity School where he became a leader of the anti-war movement with William Sloane Coffin, Yale's chaplain. I welcomed the opportunity to serve a congregation and staff with this theological diversity, and while Ernie promoted me as an evangelical, he learned later that my views were more eclectic than they were while I was at Louisville.

My first official assignment at the church involved a joint meeting with the Adult Education and Church and Society committees. I was assigned to these committees as part of my job description, which also included youth ministry. I was welcomed as the new pastor for the two committees, and, after introductions, the person chairing the meeting suggested we consider cosponsoring an educational series on some topic of social concern. Everyone agreed with the suggestion, and we began to explore possible topics.

Bill Cline, an active layperson at the church and a fundraiser for Northwestern University, proposed a course on the Arab-Israeli conflict. The issue was on everyone's minds thanks to our mutual frustration with the long gas lines. Bill suggested the topic in order to examine the complicated issues beneath the surface of media coverage. He said there was significant confusion about the recent October war, and a great deal of misinformation was circulating in the media. We adopted the theme and Bill added a caveat.

He suggested we offer something different from the typical pro-Israel bias we hear all the time in the mainstream media and US politicians. "It's time we had the courage to hear the other side," he said. "We are not getting the full story, and the church should be a place where we explore all sides of major issues. We are long overdue to listen to the Palestinian and Arab side of the conflict." Some committee members agreed while others seemed puzzled.

My reaction to Bill's proposal was visceral. I spoke up immediately, saying, "If we organize a class on the Arab-Israeli conflict, I suggest we strive for balance and hear from both sides equally." Most of the group agreed with me. Someone said, "Let's hear the facts on both sides and let people make up their own minds."

Bill seemed frustrated by my comments. "Look," he said, "the Israeli perspective is all we hear from our media and elected officials. I don't know why we need to keep repeating this perspective when it dominates the media day and night. It is no coincidence that most people have a pro-Israel bias. Let's hear another viewpoint for a change. As a church, we should provide it."

I was feeling uneasy with the direction the conversation was going and pushed back, emphasizing the need for "balance and transparency." After a few rounds of lively debate, we decided to hold the course by alternating speakers from each perspective. Bill and another committee member offered to book the Arab and Palestinian speakers and listed several Arabic names that were unfamiliar to me. No one stepped up to invite the pro-Israel speakers. I hesitated as I was unfamiliar with candidates in the Chicago area having just moved here. Cynthia Swarner, the chair of the Church and Society Committee, suggested I should take the lead with the pro-Israel speakers. I finally agreed on the condition that she would work with me.

On the drive home, I reflected on the intense discussion with the two committees and was still troubled by Bill's strong support for the Palestinian cause. His critique of the US media and government being dominated by the "pro-Israel" narrative seemed paranoid and overstated. I took some comfort in knowing other committee members shared my reservations. We had reached a fair compromise in the committee; now I had to figure out how to come up with the pro-Israel speakers. At that point, my approach to Middle East issues reflected my belief in what I would later see as "the myth of balance." The myth ignores the imbalance of power, including economic, military, and political factors that surround the Arab/Israeli issue. This perspective was about to unravel.

The more I thought about it, the more I began to wonder if Bill had a point about the pro-Israel perspective dominating the US media. I had been following the issues in the Middle East since the Six-Day War, when Israel defeated all of the Arab armies in six days. My sympathies were with Israel, heavily influenced by my study of the Holocaust during seminary, which led me to believe Israel provided a safe haven for the Jewish people after the Nazi genocide. I was unaware of the Palestinian issue other than the notion that Yasser Arafat and the PLO were terrorists, and the dark cloud of the attacks at the 1972 Munich Olympics haunted the Palestinian case.

My pro-Israel views were strengthened during my years in the Black church when our congregation twinned with a Newark synagogue. I heard the rabbi make convincing arguments as to why we needed to close ranks in solidarity between Jews and the Black churches after the Holocaust. Tensions had increased in Newark after the riots as Jewish businesses were accused of exploiting the impoverished Black community. I was dedicated to fighting antisemitism and would never abandon that commitment. My visits to Auschwitz and Terezin concentration camps with the West Side youth group reinforced my commitment to the Jewish people.

The Middle East course in Evanston began in January 1974. It was a brutally cold morning with snow, a typical wintry Sunday in Chicago. I arranged the first lecture in our series to be delivered by the Israeli Consul General of the Midwest, the Hon. Shaul Ramati. I was pleased with his passionate and convincing defense of Israel, including his statement concerning the importance of US support for Israel, the only democracy in the Middle East and our "strategic ally."

Mr. Ramati also emphasized why the Middle East "neighborhood" was so dangerous for "little" Israel, reminding us that "Israel's very existence was at risk during the 1973 war." His use of the David and Goliath metaphor was a compelling depiction of Israel as being surrounded by hostile Arab regimes that wanted to destroy "the only Jewish state." His arguments were persuasive and consistent with what I believed. Other than the relatively low attendance of about twenty people, I was very pleased. The participants seemed to appreciate the presentation, although Bill Cline and a few others were not happy.

On the following Sunday, Bill brought in Ibrahim Abu-Lughod, a Palestinian scholar and chair of the political science department at Northwestern University. The professor began his presentation with the story of his family's forced expulsion from Jaffa by Jewish militias during the spring of 1948. Jaffa was the largest Palestinian city, a major economic hub known for its oranges and other citrus products exported to Europe and the Middle East. Its population was 80,000 with an additional 40,000 in the surrounding villages. The zionist militias expelled approximately 95 percent of the Palestinians from Jaffa and its environs, including the Abu-Lughod family, leaving fewer than 3,000 Palestinians behind.

The expelled Palestinians became refugees and were settled in tents by the United Nations and various humanitarian agencies. The refugees took the keys from their homes thinking they would return within a few weeks or at most a couple of months. Some zionist militias promised them they could return once hostilities settled, but as the months went by, they were not allowed to go home. Two years later, it was clear they were permanent refugees when the Jewish state passed laws preventing their return. To this day they remain refugees, hundreds of thousands in congested camps with three and four generations living as stateless refugees.

Professor Abu-Lughod added several disturbing aspects to the story, all of which were new for me. He said the zionist forces destroyed over 515 villages, and the number of Palestinians expelled was literally half the Palestinian population in 1948: 750,000–800,000 as recorded by the United Nations. If their homes were not destroyed by the militias, Israel gave their original homes to Jewish refugees fleeing Europe. Once the new laws were adopted, Palestinian refugees attempting to return were shot on the spot or arrested and jailed.

Professor Abu-Lughod said, "I am still prevented from returning to my home in Jaffa, the city of my birth, where I still hold the property deed to the family home." He told the group, "Each one of you could visit Jaffa tomorrow if you wanted to purchase an airline ticket, but Israel would deny me entry at the airport if I tried to return with you." He added, "If you are Jewish, not only can you visit but you can move there and receive subsidies for your housing. Many Jews make what they call 'Aliyah' to live in Israel or even in the occupied Palestinian territories although they have never before lived in Israel. Yet I was born there and I cannot return despite the United Nations Resolution 194 supporting my 'right of return.'"

He concluded the session by expressing his disappointment at how the world, including several Arab countries, have ignored the Palestinian plight in favor of Israel. He had little hope the OPEC oil embargo would bring any political resolution to the Palestinian case. The professor indicated the Arab countries are usually very good at making bold statements, but they are poor at follow-through concerning justice for the Palestinians. Professor Abu-Lughod's insights raised a number of questions that jarred my pro-Israel narrative. Why had I not heard about these grave injustices? Were they true or were they just Arab propaganda?

Bill Cline stood and thanked the professor for his presentation and the audience applauded. Bill told the class he was a young seminary student in 1949 when he volunteered to go to Lebanon. He stayed there for several months, settling Palestinian refugees in tents. Bill's firsthand account provided further confirmation of the Nakba and the high number of Palestinian refugees who were expelled when Israel became a nation.

This was the first time I heard a clear, passionate, and compelling Palestinian narrative about the events of 1948. I had been following the Israeli-Palestinian struggle off and on since the late 1960s, but this history was completely different from what I had been reading in the *New York Times*. I questioned parts of the professor's presentation, such as his claims about Jewish terrorist groups massacring Palestinians and destroying over 500 villages. The warm reception he received after the lecture indicated the people attending the class found his lecture to be moving and challenging. We had to cut off discussion, which left people wanting more—always a sign the morning was successful.

I walked into my office the Monday morning after our Middle East class, and my first caller identified himself as a Jewish resident of Skokie, a suburb immediately to the west of Evanston. He said he survived the Holocaust and was active in Jewish affairs in Chicago. He had a colleague next to him and put the man on the phone. He was very angry. "We understand you allowed Dr. Abu-Lughod to speak at your church yesterday."

I replied, "Yes, that's correct."

He shouted, "Do you realize you dignified a PLO terrorist yesterday in your church? Shame on you. Abu-Lughod is a friend of Yasser Arafat and is on the Palestine National Council, the PLO's terrorist parliament in exile. He is a horrible antisemite and a PLO terrorist. If this shameful course is not stopped immediately, our organization will be picketing your church next Sunday. I'll give you until Wednesday to cancel the course and we'll be checking to be sure this is done."

I said, "I can't do this without consulting two committees. This is a program of our church and we do not ask outside organizations to authorize our programming. I can't cancel the class. But I invite you to join us at 11 AM next Sunday and hear our speaker from the American Jewish Committee. You are welcome to attend the rest of the series and participate like everyone else. You will be free to ask any questions you wish after the presentation."

He grumbled, "No, you need to tell me by Wednesday the course has been canceled. If not, we will picket your church on Sunday morning and go to the media to expose what you are doing." Then he hung up on me. I was shocked.

From my limited experience as a pastor, the church was an institution where we could have open and free discussions on controversial topics. In Ridgewood (my pastorate after Elmwood) I showed films on the Holocaust and took my students to Nazi concentration camps. We had no threats or opposition from Arab groups or anyone else. This was my first in a series of difficult encounters with organized Jewish and Christian Zionist organizations, which proved to be very effective in controlling the discourse on Israel and Palestine in the media, the churches, academia, and in the body politic. I had a similar experience when we hosted the Black Panther Party, former drug addicts, and other controversial participants.

When the rabbis preached from the pulpit on Sunday mornings, there were no calls of protest. We listened and discussed different viewpoints and gained better analysis as a result. To me, the PLO reminded me of the Black Panthers as several white people and some Blacks considered them terrorists, though they were not. It was clear that accusation was used to delegitimize them. I wondered if the same thing was happening in this case. Isn't free speech protected under the First Amendment to the Constitution?

After the phone call, I thought it would be wise to go downstairs and have a chat with my new boss. The door to the senior pastor's office was open, and I walked in and described the conversation I had just had with the Jewish neighbors from Skokie. Ernie Lewis smiled and half-jokingly said, "OK, Wagner, you've only been here about two weeks and already we have a controversy." We laughed, and started to explore what we could do in the event there were pickets on Sunday morning. We summoned the pastoral staff, Paul Suzuki and Gary Skinner, to the office and discussed how to handle the threat.

Gary was very supportive of standing firm on our First Amendment rights and said by all means we should continue the Sunday morning course. He had attended both sessions and thought we had an excellent lineup of speakers and were offering both sides of the conflict. Everyone agreed the Middle East series should continue. If there were pickets during Sunday's services, we could reiterate our position to the congregation and invite them to attend the 11 AM Middle East class.

There were no pickets, boycotts, or marchers outside our church the following Sunday morning. Apparently, it was just a verbal threat. Our scheduled speaker, a rabbi from the American Jewish Committee, provided another strong pro-Israeli perspective with an appeal for Christians to stand against antisemitism. Word got around the church about the controversy, and it actually boosted our attendance to over fifty participants. The rabbi addressed the long history of Christian antisemitism, dating back to the Bible and running through the Middle Ages, Spain's Inquisition, the Reformation, the Russian pogroms, and the Nazi Holocaust. He said it was incumbent on Christians to stand with Jews and defend Israel.

Then he proceeded to condemn Professor Abu-Lughod as a known antisemite and advised us to check with his organization before we booked Arab speakers in the future. I found this suggestion to be insulting and told him so after the class. He responded, "You have a responsibility as a Christian to allow us, the victims, to guide you in this matter." I failed to tell him the Jews were not the only victims, but I was firm in reiterating our need for independent decision-making regarding church programs. On some occasions we might call for recommendations, but we were not about to adopt a policy of allowing any organization to tell us what we could or could not do.

The next Middle Eastern speaker was Hassan Haddad, a Syrian American and professor of history at St. Xavier University on the south side of Chicago. Professor Haddad was another brilliant speaker who put the 1973 war in historical and political context. He addressed the rise of political zionism at the turn of the last century and how it was supported by England, enabling Jews to settle in the predominantly Arab territory called Palestine. He mentioned the Balfour Declaration of 1917 as one of the most dangerous decisions in the history of the Middle East. He asserted it gave the tiny zionist movement license to increase exclusive Jewish settlements on Palestinian land. This was news to me as I thought the Balfour Declaration was a wonderful document and a gift to the Jewish people. Evidently, it was a gift to the zionist movement and brought disaster to the Palestinians.

Professor Haddad concluded the class by introducing a topic of significant interest to me. He explained how conservative Christian theology and certain pro-zionist interpretations of the Bible were being used to justify Israel's illegal actions, including the theft of Palestinian land and construction of illegal Jewish settlements. He cited several Bible verses to illustrate his points. Then he declared, "I was raised in the church and my father was a Presbyterian pastor in Syria. I have read the Bible since my childhood but believe the way zionists are interpreting the Bible to be a terrible distortion. They are justifying theft and even murder in God's name."

This was another first for me. Professor Haddad was using strong language and making a serious accusation. I was familiar with the verses he referred to but never thought they could be used for political goals at the expense of other people. How could I be sure he wasn't exaggerating or even making this up? Since his statement was within the field of theology, I knew I had to do more research before I was willing to accept his statements.

My mind was spinning after Professor Haddad's lecture. Professor Abu Lughod's historical and political analysis was troubling enough, and now these theological issues on top of the political points Professor Haddad raised were deeply problematic and challenging. I approached him after class and asked for suggested readings about Israel taking Palestinian land and Christians providing biblical justification for the confiscation of land. He could tell I was suspicious of these points, but he was very kind and wrote down titles of several books. He urged me to subscribe to *The Link*, a publication of Americans for Middle East Understanding, and said the group offered discounts on books dealing with this false interpretation of the Bible. He also encouraged me to contact an organization Abu Lughod had referenced in his lecture, the Association of Arab-American University Graduates (AAUG), and ask about its next convention.

The following Monday morning I received another call from what I assumed was the same Jewish group in Skokie. The caller threatened, "We told you to stop this course and you did not listen to us. You are asking for trouble. Be careful. If you continue to bring in these antisemitic speakers, we will be taking action against you personally." Then he hung up.

This time I got angry. We were careful to organize a balanced educational program with 50 percent pro-Israel speakers. It sounded like the caller and his associates were opposed to any Palestinian or Arab speaker who suggested the Palestinians had a case. What was he afraid of? I found the bullying tactics irritating and out of place. I began to wonder about the hostile calls from the pro-Israel groups and why they refused to join the discussion Sunday mornings. It seemed as if a balanced discussion was not acceptable if Palestinians were allowed to make their own case. I resented their harassment and had never seen anything like it in the church.

This was my first experience with the pressure people face when attempting to have a "balanced" and fair discussion about the Israeli-Palestinian struggle. In my case, I was a committed zionist, but the pressure encouraged me to examine the Palestinian side of the arguments. The zionist callers actually weakened their position in my eyes. I decided to do more research on both sides of the struggle.

My journey into the troubled waters of the Israeli-Palestinian struggle had begun. It was no accident that the challenges to my pro-Israel narrative came from two Arab professors. I was grateful for what they shared but still confused about what I believed. The threatening phone calls got my attention but didn't stifle my desire to look more closely at the Palestinian perspective. There seemed to be a parallel between my experience with the Black Panthers in New Jersey and what I was experiencing in Evanston with the Palestinians.

Several years later I heard a remarkable story of Palestinian steadfastness (*sumud* in Arabic) involving the Ibrahim Abu-Lughod. During the last decade of his career, he was teaching at Birzeit University in the West Bank and living in Ramallah. He became seriously ill in 2001 and told faculty colleagues at the university that his dying wish was to be buried in Jaffa at the family gravesite. When he died, the university appealed to the Israeli authorities requesting permission to transport him to Jaffa so he could be buried there. As expected, the request was denied.

For the Birzeit professors, Israel's no was not an acceptable answer. They contacted some Israeli friends, hired an Israeli taxi driver with Israeli license plates, and carefully put the professor's body in the back seat, sunglasses and trademark beret still in place. They belted him in and carefully pinned his coat to the seat. When the taxi driver was interrogated at Israeli checkpoints, the driver and Israeli passengers said, "The old man was sleeping." They showed the professor's US passport at each of the checkpoints, and perhaps because all the passengers were Israelis, they were waved through at every stop. In some cases they were not even checked; the soldiers merely waved the car through with other Israeli cars. Eventually, they reached Jaffa and the professor was laid to rest in the family gravesite.

Professor Abu-Lughod's dying request was granted thanks to his creative friends. Sadly, he never returned to Jaffa during his lifetime. He was buried in the city of his birth thanks to his colleagues and sympathetic Israeli friends who outmaneuvered the military occupation. We were able to share this story at

Northwestern University a few weeks later. I was honored when his wife, Janet Abu-Lughod, asked me to help organize a memorial service at Northwestern's Alice Millar Chapel. Friends came from both coasts, and the chapel was filled with his former students and scholars in a moving service. The professor's defiant spirit was honored as a model of resistance.

After this memoir was published, my wife, Linda, and I visited our good friends Hanna and Tanya Nasir in Birzeit, Palestine. Hanna, the former president of Birzeit University, had hired Professor Abu-Lughod to develop the school's graduate programs. He told me he loved reading my memoir but began to laugh, saying, "But I have a minor correction." He said he absolutely loved my discussion of the professors trip back to Jaffa to be buried, but while it was a dramatic story, they had actually been able to hire an Israeli taxi and had driven directly to Jaffa. He added, "I almost want you to keep the story you told as it is far more creative than what actually happened."

I was embarrassed and noted that the story I had heard was delivered by Palestinians at his memorial service at Northwestern University. Both Hanna and Tanya were laughing; they said it was my choice, and I should feel free to keep the fictional story. I have chosen to share both stories, but with the corrected version in this edition.

Chapter 9

STEPPING INTO THE TROUBLED WATERS OF THE MIDDLE EAST

"A mind that is stretched by a new experience can never go back to its old dimensions."

—Oliver Wendell Holmes

I started to pursue my research on the Israeli-Palestinian struggle before the conclusion of our Sunday morning seminar series at the church. I was advised to use the term "struggle" rather than "conflict," which often implies two equal parties. Since I was the one who insisted on "balance" in the presentations, this was another new insight. The Israeli-Palestinian struggle is not balanced—one side holds most of the cards. Israel has the strongest army, air force, and navy in the Middle East as well as nuclear weapons. The Palestinians have no air force or navy, no airplanes, no nuclear weapons, and today it has a police force but no army. The Islamic parties in Gaza make home-made missiles, but they are inaccurate and have limited range.

As I gathered books and monographs, I started to see the struggle was worse than imbalanced. Not only did the zionist movement and Israel have an overwhelming military advantage, but they had the big powers on their side. Initially, the zionists had the British Empire facilitating their political agenda by supporting the settlement of hundreds of thousands of Jews in historic Palestine (the land area was called Palestine until 1948 when the British Mandate ended and Israel became a state). The Balfour Declaration was actually written into the peace treaties ending World War I, giving the tiny zionist movement additional legitimacy and wedding England more deeply to the zionist agenda. The Palestinians were more than 90 percent of the population, yet were not mentioned and were denied political rights by the declaration.

Themes from Professor Abu-Lughod's and Professor Haddad's lectures haunted me. I read several historical accounts by Jewish, Arab, and American scholars documenting Professor Abu-Lughod's personal story of the family's flight from Jaffa and the statistics he provided in his lecture. The Nakba ("catastrophe") of 1948–49 saw 750,000–800,000 Palestinians driven from their homes. Others who stayed behind or attempted to return were murdered or imprisoned, despite having legal deeds to their property and keys to their homes. Perhaps worse, the zionist militias committed massacres, such as in the village just west of Jerusalem, Deir Yassin. Missionaries living in the area described the massacres and how the zionist militias created panic by driving through neighborhoods warning people to flee or they would be the next "Deir Yassin massacre."[20] The Nakba is not a single event but an ongoing process of ethnic cleansing as we are witnessing today with the genocide in the Gaza Strip that has spread to the West Bank while the world stands by and watches on their televisions.

The Bible was being used to justify the theft of land and murder. I read articles in *The Link* that pointed out how biblical texts were being twisted to claim the modern state of Israel had a right to settle and seize land anywhere in historic Palestine. This meant the Palestinians did not have human rights. They were losing their land and homes to Jewish settlers and half their population had been expelled to other countries in 1948–49. These were among the stories we were not hearing in the mainstream US media.

I decided to phone Professor Abu-Lughod because I wanted to talk to a scholar and ask questions that were not being answered in what I was reading. I did not understand why the United States had become so one-sided on this issue. I wondered about a point made by Jewish writers claiming the Palestinians left in 1948–49 because Arab countries issued radio broadcasts telling them to leave. Was this true? I also wondered why I could find little documentation in the mainstream Western press or scholarship about the 500 destroyed villages? I phoned the professor, hoping he would be willing to sit down and answer these and other questions, but I feared he might be too busy.

I was surprised when he picked up the phone and remembered me from his morning at our church. I told him I had several lingering questions as I had begun to read the materials he and Professor Haddad recommended. He suggested we get together for lunch within a few days at a restaurant within walking distance of the church and his office. He encouraged me to bring my questions and he would do his best to answer them. I was amazed he was available and willing to meet with me.

When we met three days later, I found him to be very personable and down-to-earth. I had not seen the warm and personable side of him when he lectured as he exuded an air of stoic intellectual brilliance. I was struck immediately by how he maintained eye contact when he spoke. He was a handsome man with olive skin, bright green eyes, and a full head of white hair. He was very engaging, sincere, and convincing. I could imagine him being a stimulating professor, challenging the students and inspiring their learning.

He wanted to know about my background before he addressed my questions. He asked me about the factors that shaped my views on the Middle East and Israel. I quickly summarized my conservative Republican upbringing and the influence of evangelical churches. Then I mentioned how I rejected the conservative influences and spoke about my conversion to progressive causes such as my involvement in the anti-war movement and study of the Holocaust in seminary. I added my years in the Black community and our relationship with the Newark synagogue. I noted my strong opposition to antisemitism including my work with youth at another church in Ridgewood, New Jersey, and the groups of youth I led to the Auschwitz and Terezin concentration camps. He listened carefully and then asked how the rest of the Middle East course went at the church.

I shared my experience with the two threatening calls from the Jewish community demanding that I cancel the course or face a picket during Sunday worship. He laughed, saying, "I'm not surprised. What did you do?" Before answering, I had to mention their main complaint, that we had "dignified the presence of a PLO terrorist."

He chuckled and said, "This is not the first time this has happened. But you didn't cancel, did you?"

"No, of course not," I replied. I told him about my background at the Black church and similar experiences at the Ridgewood church prior to moving to Evanston, where we were free to debate any issue. I told him about the series of conversations with the Black Panthers on racism and Black power. He liked my analogy to the Black Panthers being delegitimized as terrorists and the Palestinians having the same experience. He nodded in approval and asked me to share more about my experience with racism and what I had learned.

I turned to what I was reading and asked if he could fill in some of the gaps in my knowledge. I asked him about the pro-Israel literature claiming the Arab countries had radio broadcasts in 1948–49 urging Palestinians to come and live in their countries, which suggested the Palestinians had not been driven out by zionist militias. I asked if he had any hard evidence to challenge these claims.

He was eager to respond. "There were no such broadcasts from Arab countries." He encouraged me to purchase *The Transformation of Palestine*, a volume he'd recently edited. He apologized that he could not give me the volume because he only had his own marked-up personal copy. He assured me I could purchase it at the Northwestern University bookstore across the street after lunch.

He went on to suggest I start with the chapter by the Irish journalist Erskine Childers, who demolished the Israeli myth that Palestinians left their homes in 1948 due to broadcasts from Arab radio stations. Childers researched all the broadcasts from all Arab stations during the period in question, nearly all of which were monitored by the BBC. Having examined every transcript, Childers could not find a single broadcast urging the Palestinians to flee to Arab countries. In fact, there were several broadcasts telling Palestinians to stay in Palestine.

Since the publication of this research, he added, most pro-Israel groups have stopped using the argument. He said such broadcasts simply did not exist. He suggested, "After you read the chapter by Childers, read the introduction by the great historian Arnold Toynbee. Toynbee says in effect, 'These essays shed light on similar Israeli myths that were wrongly promoted as truth in recent years.'"

After our lunch, Professor Abu-Lughod walked over to the bookstore and showed me where the volume was located. When I went to purchase it, he tried to pay for it, but I stopped him. He also recommended a helpful introduction to the conflict, titled *Our Roots Are Still Alive*, which offered an accurate and readable orientation to the Palestine question. I returned to my office and ordered the book. That evening, I read the essay by Erskine Childers and the Toynbee introduction and found them convincing.

—

By the fall of 1974 I was somewhat familiar with the Palestinian perspective and continued my reading and study of the issues. My reading list was growing, with books and articles from both the Israeli and Palestinian perspectives. I received an invitation to attend a meeting at McCormick Theological Seminary to hear a report by seminary students and faculty who had just returned from the Middle East. The students were part of a "traveling seminar" course designed by Bruce Rigdon, a professor of church history at McCormick.

Professor Rigdon opened the meeting with prayer and welcomed the audience, explaining the goals of the "traveling seminar on Eastern Orthodoxy." He said the trip included meetings with various Eastern Orthodox church leaders plus visits to churches, monasteries, and social service agencies in four Middle Eastern countries—Lebanon, Israel and the occupied Palestinian territories, Jordan, and Egypt. Rigdon turned the rest of the program over to students who gave commentary and presented slides that raised several important issues, both theological and political. I signed a list indicating I would be interested in a follow-up meeting.

Two weeks later I received a call from John Lindner, one of the McCormick students, who was a presenter at the recent program. John invited me to attend a follow-up meeting for people who wanted to continue studying the issues. I drove down to McCormick and attended the initial meeting led by John and his wife, Eileen. When I was introduced to Professor Rigdon, I expressed my gratitude for his trip and wished I had been on it. He said he hoped I would join the next one. John and Eileen suggested we become a study group and meet once a month. Eileen said one option was for us to focus on the pre-trip study documents Professor Rigdon prepared for their orientation. She said, "Most of us did not read the material prior to the trip because we were busy with our regular coursework. This group will give us a chance to study the documents and discuss the readings with a wider audience."

A few weeks later, we held our first discussion. Six or so McCormick students, two faculty members, and a handful of clergy and laity from the Chicago area showed up. The study group and its timing aligned perfectly with my personal study plans, and I was eager to discuss issues with an open-minded group. The readings Professor. Rigdon selected focused on Christianity in the Middle East and the political situations in Lebanon, Israel/Palestine, and Egypt. After two meetings at the seminary, we decided to move to a central location, Agape House, on the campus of the University of Illinois Chicago (UIC).

Rev. Dave McGowan, the campus minister at UIC, served as the host of our study group. I was impressed when he welcomed us with a selection of delicious Italian submarine sandwiches. We were in the heart of Chicago's Little Italy neighborhood, just west of the Loop in downtown Chicago, where the Italian delis were plentiful. Dave suggested our group should file papers with the Presbytery of Chicago and become an official "mission task force." If we were accepted, we would have a degree of legitimacy as an official body of the presbytery. We wrote a mission statement, listed our goals, and Dave submitted the document to the presbytery's Church and Society Committee. Within a month we were approved as the Middle East Task Force of the Chicago presbytery. Dave was an amazing organizer and a very astute thinker on social justice issues.

Now that we had a sense of organizational legitimacy, we thought it was time to begin acting like an official organization, despite the fact that we were only ten committed people. Our mission statement read as follows: "On the basis of an understanding of the great evangelical theme of reconciliation, it is an ethical imperative for the United Presbyterian Church in the USA to be reconciled to the conflicting peoples of the Middle East and become an agent of reconciliation." Dave drafted most of the text as he knew what the presbytery needed to hear in a mission statement.[21]

The challenge before us was how we could elevate our activities so as to have some influence in Presbyterian churches in the greater Chicago area. We considered various options including setting up a speakers' bureau, telephoning clergy, requesting adult education classes, and developing a bibliography of readings. We began to implement these projects and realized we needed to do more. By the spring of 1975, we decided to organize a conference focused on Middle Eastern Christians and the Israeli-Palestinian struggle.

In 1974, there were few churches in the United States studying the Middle East and the religious, political, and historical dimensions of the issues. As far as we know, we were among the first official organization affiliated with a Protestant denomination to organize and address these concerns. We were certainly among the first to embrace the Israeli-Palestinian struggle. We learned later that we had a sister group in the Los Angeles area led by Rev. Darrel Meyers, a Presbyterian pastor, who would become a close friend.

The Los Angeles-based group, the Middle East Fellowship of Southern California, began in 1969. The difference in the two groups was that the L.A. group was not affiliated with a denomination. The Middle East Fellowship was a broad ecumenical group from several denominations and they were quite impressive. The group included several clergy, laity, and professors, including the nationally known scholars of the Dead Sea Scrolls, William Brownlee and John C. Trevor.

The Middle East Task Force decided to expand its efforts beyond educational events in local churches. We were searching for a broader venue that could appeal to the Chicago region. We decided to hold a conference for clergy and laity and bring Middle Eastern leaders to Chicago. Professor Rigdon offered to contact leadership at Presbyterian headquarters, then located at 475 Riverside Drive in New York City (affectionately known as "the God Box" or more sarcastically as "Hell on the Hudson").

Bruce spoke to Oscar McCloud, director of the Program Agency, the powerful oversight body for national and international programs. Assisting Dr. McCloud were Syngman Rhee, director of the Middle East and North Africa Desk, and Ed Huenemann, a church theologian. Ed became our point person at the national level as he had close connections with leaders in the Middle East. Ed's daughter Kathy was working in Beirut as a Presbyterian mission advocate and was engaged to Gabriel Habib, the new general secretary of the Middle East Council of Churches.

The Program Agency offered us sponsorship and generous financial support to cover travel, housing, and other expenses for four Middle Eastern Christian leaders. The endorsement from the Program Agency provided additional legitimacy for our new task force by providing credibility from the highest body in the Presbyterian denomination. Once this was in place, it led to endorsements from other local and regional Christian organizations. With these important endorsements, we began to promote the conference in a four-state radius including Illinois, Wisconsin, Indiana, and Michigan.

I was asked to chair the task force because nobody else wanted the job. The original chair was moving out of Chicago, and I urged Dave McGowan to take the job. He in turn said he was too busy and suggested I should do it. I was among the least informed on the issues, but I agreed to take the job temporarily until someone more qualified came forward.

Our initial tasks were to work on an accurate mailing list, develop a conference announcement, confirm a program, and find a conference site. I volunteered to work on the conference site and narrowed it down to three options. I presented the three and the Task Force liked the Christian Life Center in LaGrange, a western suburb of Chicago, run by the Sisters of Nazareth, which implied a Middle East theme. When I visited, representatives of the group asked about the theme of the conference. I told them the focus would be on the Christians in the Middle East including Egypt, Lebanon, and the Palestinians in the Holy Land. They were thrilled and wondered if they could attend the meetings and invite Roman Catholics. "Of course," I responded. "The conference will be open to any and all interested persons." One woman said she had recently traveled to the holy land with a Catholic group. She said she loved seeing the biblical sites but did not speak to any Palestinian Christians. I said they would have the opportunity to host and meet Middle Eastern Christians from Egypt, Lebanon, and Palestinian Christians "right here in your chapel."

The Middle East conference began on Thursday, December 9, 1976, and concluded on Saturday afternoon, December 11. The Christian Life chapel was a perfect setting for our group of approximately 100 participants. We had a good mixture of clergy and laity, primarily Presbyterians, but a variety of Protestants plus Roman Catholics, Eastern Orthodox, secular friends, a few Jews, and Muslims. I was hoping for a larger turnout, but at that point in history, an event on Middle Eastern Christians had limited drawing power.

The four keynote speakers offered timely insights on the history and current status of Christians in the Middle East. I was eager to hear from our speakers because I needed more theological clarity on why justice for Palestinians was important. I still had some lingering guilt about the antisemitism critique. The theological issues were somewhat unclear for me concerning issues like the land and what the Bible teaches about the covenant with Abraham. Does God give the covenant and the land to the Jewish people as implied by certain texts in Genesis? Or is there another way to interpret these texts? I understood why the settlements were illegal from a political and legal analysis, but I needed more input on the theological perspectives.

Our first speaker was Bishop Samuel, the Ecumenical Bishop for the Coptic Orthodox Church, followed by Coptic Orthodox theologian George Bebawi. I think it was Bruce Rigdon who recommended we begin with the Coptic Orthodox speakers as they represented the oldest church in Christendom (some argue the Orthodox Church in Jerusalem was first). Both Coptic speakers referenced St. Mark, the author of the second Gospel who is credited with bringing Christianity to Egypt in 42 CE. He became the first bishop of Alexandria, and his successors are called popes or patriarchs.

In 1976, Pope Shenouda was the Coptic Orthodox patriarch and the 117th successor to St. Mark in an unbroken chain. Pope Shenouda died in 2012. His successor is Tawadros II, the 118th Coptic pope. Bishop Samuel and Professor Bebawi reminded us that Jesus, Mary, and Joseph fled King Herod's persecution in Palestine after Jesus' birth and were welcomed in Egypt as refugees.

Bishop Samuel spent many years as a monk in Egypt's western desert where he lived in solitude as a hermit. He knew Pope Shenouda, who was also a hermit and monk in the same region. The Coptic Church developed the earliest monastic tradition around 250 CE, long before Roman Catholics started monasteries. Bishop Samuel told us there was a renewal of monasticism underway in Egypt and the monasteries were full.[22]

Professor Bebawi challenged the audience with a series of provocative statements. A brilliant, young scholar with a PhD in history from Cambridge University, Professor Bebawi shocked most of us with his critique of the famous Council of Chalcedon (451 CE) as "an unmitigated disaster for the Christians of the Middle East." I assumed the Council of Chalcedon was one of the most important councils in history. All the church history books and professors I had read during seminary praised Chalcedon as one of the most successful councils. We studied how Chalcedon clarified the nature of Christ ("fully human and fully divine"), a necessary doctrinal formula. But we never discussed the impact the council's decisions had on the majority of Christians in the Middle East.

Professor Bebawi said what we had been taught in the West was a "biased and erroneous Western interpretation of the facts." Today we would call this an Orientalist bias. He said the Council of Chalcedon excommunicated the majority of Middle Eastern Christians on faulty theological analysis. There were also political issues at play in their decision. The Western Byzantine Orthodox theologians enjoyed the favor of the emperor, who wanted to control the unruly land of Egypt.

Moreover, Bebawi said, the leading theologians at Chalcedon spoke Greek and were not familiar with the Coptic language and the theological nuances of Coptic Orthodox theology. He claimed the Coptic Church never rejected the human and divine natures of Christ. As a result, the Byzantine (Greek) theologians condemned the Oriental Orthodox Churches (Coptic, Syrian, and Armenian Orthodox) as heretics. These churches were accused of holding the "monophysite" heresy. (Jesus was primarily of a divine nature, not "fully human and fully divine.")

Even more disturbing was the fact the Coptic theologians did not have an opportunity to defend themselves and clarify the subtle theological misunderstandings. The Copts were delayed due to a storm on the Mediterranean Sea and arrived after the decisions were made. Between the linguistic confusion and the failure to hear the Coptic theologians, a tragic mistake was made. The division between Eastern or Oriental Orthodox Christianity and Western Christians could have been reconciled. Bebawi said a reconciliation is underway between Eastern and Western Christians through the new Middle East Council of Churches, where all the churches of the Middle East are full members.

This healing between the Oriental Eastern Orthodox Churches and the rest of Christendom began in 1954 when the Coptic Orthodox Church was invited to participate in the World Council of Churches assembly in Evanston. Bishop Samuel represented the Coptic Orthodox Church as the first Oriental Eastern Orthodox official to meet with the Western churches in 1,500 years. What we learned from Bishop Samuel and Professor Bebawi challenged what was being taught at Western seminaries and graduate schools. The reconciliation between the two branches of Christianity was a matter for our task force to examine and follow-up in the Chicago area.

After lunch, Gabriel Habib was welcomed as the new general secretary of the Middle East Council of Churches. MECC was still in the process of organizing itself, but the official vote to authorize it took place in May 1974. MECC was already the most inclusive Christian ecumenical body in the world. Gaby repeated an important statement from Pope Shenouda on this matter: "We are proud that the Middle East is the place where Christianity is most united after centuries of the worst divisions in church history." The Coptic, Syriac, and Armenian Orthodox Churches were full members and very involved in the Council's committees and leadership."[23] Gaby emphasized the importance of Christian unity given that Christians are a minority in the Islamic world, and it is from this unity that they will be a witness to the world based on the love and justice taught by Jesus Christ.

Paul Tarazi was the next keynote speaker. He addressed the issue of Christian missions and the many problems Middle Eastern Christians have experienced with Roman Catholic and Protestant missionary movements. Professor Tarazi claimed Western missionaries weakened the indigenous churches, usually bringing Western colonial politics, military, and economic interests with them. The British, Dutch, Belgian, Italians, Portuguese, Spanish, and French rulers often used the church to advance their colonial projects, including taking land and resources while subjecting the local population to a military occupation.

The Vatican's support for these imperial interests was stated in the "Doctrine of Discovery," based on a papal bull in the fourteenth century. This unfortunate European legacy of colonial wars, conquest, genocide, and domination continued through the Soviet Union, China, the United States, and other countries. Israel inherited this legacy in the Middle East. Sadly, the Western churches provided a false theology to justify colonization and one of the most obvious examples is what happened in Palestine.

Missionaries were rarely successful in their attempts to convert Muslims or Jews, Tarazi said. In order to justify their benefactors they "stole sheep" from the local churches. The missionaries and priests often told the indigenous Christians they were not "authentic" Christians and needed to convert and be rebaptized into the Roman Catholic or Protestant churches. The Catholics said when you become a baptized Catholic, you will be assured of heaven, sometimes with a brief detour to purgatory. When the Protestants arrived a century later, they said you had to be "born again" and believe in Jesus the way Presbyterians, Lutherans, Baptists, and Methodists believe, and you will go directly to heaven, with no delay in purgatory.

Fr. Paul raised the serious concern Middle Eastern Christians share about the new wave of evangelicals and fundamentalist Christians invading the Middle East with their end-time theology and Christian zionist interpretations of the Bible. Their radio and television programs are already having a major impact in the region, and he saw it as a dangerous trend. Christians in the Middle East needed our help with this problem, as they originate in the United States or Europe and "do not understand these evangelicals let alone how to control them." I found this problem to be of significant personal interest having grown up in such an evangelical church.

Fr. Paul offered a solution to the problem by proposing Western churches could adopt the Eastern Orthodox concept called "peregrination," a theology of pilgrimage. In this approach, Western Christians come to visit, and in certain cases to live, and support local Christian communities in the Middle East. They do not come to replace the historic churches but to respect them, learn from them, and assist their life and witness.

In other words, rather than coming to the Middle East with attitudes of superiority or seeing the local Christians as inferior, these Christians would come as full partners and friends. Middle Eastern Christians are not "targets for missionaries" but sisters and brothers in Christ. Some denominations were beginning to adopt this approach. Western Christians had many gifts to bring such as innovative approaches to Bible study, medical skills, educational tools, technology, and much more. "All of these gifts will be welcomed if the bearers of the gifts come to work with us as equal partners," he added. He said in closing, "Some might even come to the region with one-way tickets and stay with us indefinitely. This is true 'peregrination.'" His biblical reference was from Jesus. "Once the hand is laid on the plow, no one who looks back is fit for the Kingdom of God."[24]

The conference gave me the theological, political, and historical analysis I needed to move to the next level of awareness on the Middle East as a whole, and the Palestine question in particular. The Middle Eastern theologians, historians, and church leaders provided guidance to my unresolved theological questions. I had not asked Professor Bebawi for clarification concerning his remarks on the Council of Chalcedon or the search for unity among the Christians of the Middle East addressed by Gabriel Habib.

I was convinced after the conference it was time for me to travel to the Middle East and see the people and the issues firsthand. Gaby Habib and George Bebawi stayed with me for a week after the conference to see Chicago and to do some Christmas shopping before returning to their families. I thoroughly enjoyed showing off our city, and we had a great time exploring Chicago together. We ate fabulous meals and came back and drank wine around the fireplace as we talked late into the evening. Gaby could only stay four days, but George stayed nearly ten days

We went out for pizza the night before I took Gaby to the airport and he asked me directly, "OK, Don, when are you coming to the Middle East? Let's consider September for your visit. We will have several committee meetings for the MECC in Beirut at that time, and you will be able to meet a number of Christian leaders from around the region. You will find it interesting, and you will be our guest. All you need to do is get there. We will take care of you."

He said Beirut was not safe at that time, but they were hoping for a realistic and lasting ceasefire by late summer or early fall. Gaby said he would monitor the situation and let me know when to come. He offered to organize a program for me, including Beirut and other visits in Lebanon, Jerusalem and the West Bank, to see their work with Palestinians, and finally fly to Egypt where George would host me in Cairo.

I responded immediately: "I am ready and will be awaiting your call. Let's stay in touch. I hope to see you in September. *Inshallah*" ("God willing").

Chapter 10
DIVING INTO THE MIDDLE EAST: FIRST AND LASTING IMPRESSIONS

"Everything changed with the First World War. The Middle East was reorganized, redefined, and the seeds were planted for a century of bloodshed."

—Richard Engel, MSNBC reporter

The pilot on the Middle East Airlines flight announced we were about to land in Beirut. It was September 14, 1977, and I had immersed myself in months of preparation for the trip. This was my first international trip other than the occasional visit to Canada, just a thirty-minute drive over the Peace Bridge from my home in a suburb of Buffalo, New York. I had just celebrated my thirty-fifth birthday and was ready for a new and exciting adventure. A difficult divorce was behind me, and my new interest in the Middle East was taking me to a different world. But was it wise to visit Beirut?

Several friends asked me, "Why would anyone in their right mind go to Beirut for their vacation?" Beirut was characterized by the news media as a once beautiful "Paris of the Middle East" that had descended into endless kidnappings, massacres, and hopeless violence. Just a week prior to my trip, the nightly news ran a segment featuring a car driving through the streets of Beirut dragging behind it a decapitated body as a warning to the opposition. My friends in Beirut said there was a hopeful new truce and encouraged me to come as soon as possible.

Stepping out of the Middle East Airlines plane after twenty-eight hours of travel from Chicago, with two layovers, left me exhausted but slightly revived as I finally reached my destination. I had no idea what to expect as this new adventure awaited me. After long lines at passport control and securing a visa, I collected my suitcase and found a pay phone to call Gaby, the one person I knew in Beirut.

I was eager to hear his voice, but no one picked up the phone. It was approximately 10 in the evening, and I assumed he would be home by now. Checking the number, I dialed again, allowing the phone to ring about twenty times with no answer. I called his office phone in case he was working late. Still no answer. I had no backup plan—Gaby had assured me just two days ago he would be waiting for my call. I wondered if I should consider a hotel. I decided to try one last time. I called the office number and let the phone ring thirty times. Finally, an unfamiliar male voice answered, sounding annoyed. I thanked him for taking the call and told him I was a friend of Gaby Habib's from the United States and that I was at the airport. He said Gaby should be home in an hour and suggested I take a taxi. He said the apartment was in the Ras Beirut area near American University of Beirut. Then he abruptly hung up.

As I walked out of the airport, I was amazed at the energy and party atmosphere outside. It seemed like a giant celebration was underway, with Arabic music, horns honking, friends and families welcoming loved ones with bouquets of flowers. I asked a young man where I might find a taxi and he pointed to the left, "Over there," he said. "Ask for a driver who speaks English and you should have no problem." I headed for the taxis, and after a couple of inquiries I found a driver with a friend in the passenger seat. Both men were conversant in English.

"Get in, my friend! Where are you going?" the driver asked. "I am Muhammad and this is my friend Ahmad."

I told them "Ras Beirut near AUB."

"No problem. We will take you there."

I jumped in the back seat with my suitcase and the cab sped off, driving at breakneck speed down the long airport entry road. Suddenly we came to a checkpoint. A uniformed man with an automatic weapon asked each of us for our passport. I handed him mine and he shined his flashlight on my face and checked the photo of my passport. He handed back all three of our passports and waved us through. I asked the driver and his friend about the checkpoint, and they said, "This is the Lebanese Army. They control the airport, but just wait. We have at least two more checkpoints, possibly three before we can get moving."

I wondered why there were so many checkpoints within a few blocks. I looked to my right and saw a very poor area with tiny cinder block homes. It reminded me of photos I saw of Palestinian refugee camps. Ahmad said this was Bourj el-Barajneh, one of the main Palestinian refugee camps south of Beirut. We turned left and within a couple of blocks arrived at another checkpoint. Muhammad said, "This is the Syrian Army. They can be rough. Give me your passport. They may have a few questions."

The Syrian official scowled and put the flashlight on my face, asking me if I was born in the United States. I thought that was obvious from the data on the passport and simply said, "Yes." Muhammad told him in Arabic I was a graduate student at American University and he was driving me to AUB. Most Americans arriving that week were students attending the university. Flattered to be considered a university student, I was fine with the little white lie as the guard waved us through.

As we drove away, Muhammad apologized, "Sorry I lied, but it will save time. I used the American University excuse as it usually works with the Syrians, especially with American students arriving this week for the fall semester."

Ahmad added, "We have one more checkpoint, but don't worry. The next one is very friendly." It looked like we were passing another refugee camp and I asked about it.

Muhammad said, "This is where we live—Sabra and Shatila refugee camps. Ahmad and I are both from Shatila." I had recently read Fawaz Turki's *The Disinherited*, an account of growing up in one of Beirut's Palestinian refugee camps. Knowing something about the odds against the residents, I had immediate respect for Muhammad and Ahmad.

At the third checkpoint, I recognized the Palestinian flag flying above the booth. A young man stepped out and greeted the driver with a handshake and big smile. He appeared to be about nineteen or twenty and was dressed in army fatigues with a military T-shirt and a maroon beret on his head. I handed him my passport. He studied it for a couple of seconds, smiled and said, "So you are from the United States? *Ahlan wa sahlan* ("You are welcome")."

Then he leaned in and asked, "Tell me, what city are you from in America?"

I replied with great pride, "Chicago."

The young military man pulled back from the car in shock and exclaimed, "Oh my God, Chicago?" Muhammad and Ahmad laughed as Ahmad explained, "We have never met anyone from Chicago. It must be very dangerous there! We saw movies about the mob and Al Capone."

Muhammad laughed and repeated, "Wow, Chicago? Yeah, Al Capone—bang bang, shoot 'em up." They all had a good laugh. I had to laugh with them, considering the irony of the situation. Here we were in the middle of a violent civil war that had taken some ten thousand lives, and they thought Chicago was dangerous! We just stopped at three military checkpoints whose armies were trying to kill each other a few days ago. This place is crazy.

We waved goodbye to our Palestinian military friend and sped off, turning onto the coastal road as the Mediterranean Sea came into view. The corniche, as they call it, was a divided highway along the coast. The neighborhood changed, and several hotels and tall apartment buildings came into view. We passed a large Ferris wheel and small amusement park. Despite the late hour, families were walking along the beach. The street was lined with palm trees; below them were a series of small shops selling souvenirs, shawarma, and falafel sandwiches. People seemed to be enjoying a warm Mediterranean evening thanks to the recent ceasefire. Muhammad remarked, "Things are coming back to normal. We have had so many ceasefires that didn't last. We hope this one will hold."

We were speeding along the corniche for about ten minutes when we turned right and entered a different residential area. Ahmad announced, "Look to your left. This is the famous American University of Beirut with all the red tile roofs." I had read several articles about this famous university, a political hotbed and perhaps the finest university in the Middle East. AUB boasted several famous graduates including the prime minister of Lebanon at that time, Salim al-Hoss; Druze leader Walid Jumblatt; Palestinian academic Hanan Ashrawi; PLO spokesman and author Kamal Nasser; and George Habash, the founder of the Popular Front for the Liberation of Palestine. The driver said we were getting close to our destination.

We pulled up in front of Gaby's apartment, and I thanked the driver and his friend for the wonderful ride and introduction to Beirut. I pulled out my wallet and Muhammad said, "No, no, no. This is our welcome gift to you. Your ride is on us."

I replied, "Thank you but no way. This time with you was a perfect welcome to Beirut after my long flight. You guys were great tour guides." I put a $20 bill in his hand and urged, "Please take this. It's a small token of my gratitude for your company and warm hospitality. Thank you so much for your friendship." He smiled and made one more attempt to return the money before finally accepting it.

We said goodbye, and there was Gaby standing by the taxi to welcome me. I jumped out and hugged him and he kissed me on each cheek and, adding a third, saying, "And one more for the Trinity." I was revitalized despite the long day's journey into the night. Gaby said we would go upstairs for a few minutes and have a drink before he took me to my room. He had a friend upstairs and wanted me to meet him. I said goodbye again to my new Palestinian friends and off they drove into the night.

Gaby's apartment was on the sixth floor of the building. The fourth and fifth floors were set aside as offices for the newly established Middle East Council of Churches. He apologized for missing me at the airport, explaining that he had just finished a tense meeting regarding negotiations between Eastern Orthodox, Catholics, and Protestant leaders. We walked out onto his balcony where a beautiful panorama of Beirut opened up in front of us.

Gaby introduced me to Fr. Yousef, the priest at the Antiochian Orthodox Church Gaby and his wife, Kathy, attended. He was a slender and intellectual looking young man, perhaps in his mid-thirties with a well-trimmed dark beard and wire-rimmed glasses. His black pants and shirt with a clerical collar and cross around his neck identified him as a priest. Fr. Yousef said he wanted to meet me but would have to leave very soon as it was getting late. We sat down and toasted each other. Gaby said Kathy was visiting her family in the United States and passed on her greetings.

I took in the expansive view of Beirut looking south over the Hamra shopping district and noticed rocket fire in the distance. I asked about it, wondering if the ceasefire had suddenly been canceled. Gaby explained, "These are tracer bullets the armies use to check on the positions of their opponents. They are making sure there are no violations to the boundaries agreed upon in last week's ceasefire. Fortunately, everyone seemed to be respecting the agreement, but we have had countless ceasefires that failed since the war started in 1974." I asked them for a quick update on where things stood with the civil war at the moment.

Fr. Yousef added, "This is a big topic, but let me make a few quick observations. You may know about the unwritten 'gentleman's agreement' or 'the national pact' that the different religious communities in Lebanon signed in 1943, when Lebanon received its independence from France. The seeds of the civil war were sown at that time, perhaps even before then. Thanks to this sectarian colonial arrangement, Lebanon's future government would be based on an old census the French conducted in 1932. According to the census, Maronite Christians were approximately 30 percent of the population, Suni Muslims were 22 percent and Shi'ite Muslims around 21 percent, Orthodox Christians 11 percent, Druze 7 percent, Melkites 6 percent, and Protestants 3 percent.

"The Parliament would be constituted as a power-sharing arrangement based on these ratios. The Maronites were the majority and the 'agreement' stipulated the president must be a Maronite Christian, the prime minister a Sunni Muslim, speaker of the house a Shi'ite, and so on down the line of apportionment. This agreement also favored France's colonial designs on Lebanon.

"Each community had representation in the Parliament based on these percentages, so the Maronites had considerable power. Simply put, Lebanon continued to operate with the colonial system established by the French who were aligned with the Maronites. As the population ratios changed in the 1950s and again in the 1970s, the Muslims demanded a new census and redrawing of the power sharing structure. The Maronites resisted as they had benefited financially and politically from the old formula."

Gaby interjected, "It's important to note that in the mid 1950s, the Sunni and Shi'ite Muslims were the largest communities and they demanded a new constitution. You also had nearly 300,000 Palestinians in refugee camps demanding assistance. The Palestinians were mainly Sunni Muslims with about 15–20 percent Orthodox or Catholic Christians. In 1958 there were large demonstrations and some violence erupted that threatened to topple the Parliament. Some call this the first civil war in Lebanon but it didn't last long because the United States sent the Marines here to uphold the old colonial order. The protests became more vigorous in the early 1970s and something had to give. By then another 100,000 Palestinians were pushed out of Jordan and settled here. The Shi'ites grew significantly, and they were opposed to the colonial system."

"The Maronites have a powerful militia trained and financed by Israel, the United States, and France called the Phalangists," added Fr. Yousef. "Their primary role was to maintain the old political arrangement with the Maronites in control. The Muslims, Druze, and most Antiochian Christians demanded change and formed a coalition called the Lebanese National Movement. They are primarily secular and a mixed Christian and Muslim alignment. It's completely wrong to characterize the civil war as a religious war. It's a political and economic challenge to European colonialism that cuts across religious lines."

"What started the civil war?" I asked. "Was there a single incident or was it a culmination of this frustration from those left out of the power sharing?"

"Tensions had been simmering," said Fr. Yousef. "Several incidents could have started the war. Most of us say the spark occurred on April 13, 1975, when a group of Phalangist soldiers shot up a Palestinian bus in the predominantly Maronite suburb of Ain el-Remmaneh."

We stood and they pointed to this area and gave me binoculars. "You should be able to see a large church there. This was the location of the flash point." He added, "The Phalangists and Palestinians had a history of hostility prior to this incident including kidnappings, assassinations, and extreme rhetoric in the media."

The attack occurred when a busload of Palestinians returning from a soccer match passed in front of the Maronite church where a large political wedding was taking place. One member of the Phalangist militias guarding the church fired at the bus, thinking there could be an attack. Someone on the bus fired back, and then all hell broke loose. The Phalangists killed all twenty-seven passengers on the bus. The incident set off a series of revenge killings by Palestinians, and within days it turned into this ugly civil war with massacres and nearly two years of agony.[25]

Fr. Yousef stood and announced, "We are just getting started, but we will continue this discussion another evening, perhaps tomorrow, if our host invites me. We live and breathe politics here, and we love to tell our stories. But I regret that I must leave and get some sleep."

Gaby added, "Yes, we will have dinner here tomorrow evening and continue this discussion. Fr. Yousef should tell you why he needs a good night's sleep."

The priest said that every morning when he gets up to retrieve the newspaper, he might find two or three dead bodies at his door. "This delays the morning coffee and breakfast," he joked. "Various militias drop the bodies at the church because they know I will give them a decent burial. They seem to give me the Christians while the mosque down the street receives the Muslims. Sometimes they leave identification papers and I do my best to track down the families and let them know what happened. When there is no identification, I have to bury them as nameless."

The priest continued, "For me, this has been one of the tragic aspects of the civil war. The militias often kidnap people and try to extort large sums of money from families. This is one of the ways they finance the war. When it doesn't work, they kill the victims and leave their bodies at churches or mosques. We have become a very sick society."

I thanked Fr. Yousef for his summary of the situation and the grim news about his problematic mornings. We wished him a good night's rest and a peaceful breakfast tomorrow, without any funerals. Gaby and I talked a bit longer, but I was also beginning to fade. He walked me to the Near East School of Theology, the Protestant seminary just two blocks away, where I was staying.

As we walked, Gaby apologized for not being home when I arrived at the airport. I told him that I had called several times and finally spoke with a man who answered in a rather gruff voice and told me to take a taxi to the apartment.

Gaby was puzzled. "Someone answered? That is strange because no one was in the office this evening." He asked what number I had dialed, and said I tried both the home and the office phone numbers he had provided. I said eventually a man answered the office phone.

"Very strange," said Gaby. "The only person with a key to the office other than me was Rev. Albert Isteero, the former director of the Near East Council of Churches. He was supposed to be at our meeting tonight and turn in the office keys. He may be the one who answered the phone. This leads me to wonder if he was removing the files we agreed should remain in the office." I thought about this incident as it highlighted the difficulties the MECC faced in building Christian unity after 1,500 years of division in the Middle East.

Gaby said one of the final negotiating points in the meeting with the church leaders was an agreement whereby the Protestant NECC leaders would turn over all of their financial records and correspondence from the previous ten years. "We all agreed these files should be MECC property."

Gaby continued, "Since Rev. Isteero was the only person with a key to the office, he could have been the one who answered the phone. You said it was around 10 PM. I did not reach home until after 11, just before you arrived. When I return to the office now, I will be able to tell if there are any missing files. Get a good night's sleep and I'll let you know what happened when I see you at breakfast. Sleep in a bit and come over at 9 AM. It's great to finally have you with us."

I was thankful Gaby proposed a 9 AM breakfast as I slept a solid eight hours and almost missed our appointment. When I rang the bell at Gaby's apartment, he announced, "Come in. I have a surprise for you."

I entered the apartment, and there was George Bebawi, who had just arrived from Cairo. We greeted each other warmly, and George said he could not wait to take me around Lebanon to meet some of his friends. He said, "Wait until tomorrow. What I am going to show you will be a real eye-opener!" Gaby said he had just started to tell George about what happened in the office late last night.

"The mystery is nearly solved," he said. "It appears Rev. Isteero and possibly his secretary violated our agreement and came into the office last night and removed several files. He may have taken important financial documents including several years of records dealing with donations. We need these statements to assess the financial obligations of the Protestant churches. This is troubling but we will get to the bottom of it. I have turned the matter over to the police who are in the office now getting fingerprints. They will give me a report tomorrow." Gaby added that my call to the office between 10 and 10:30 PM allowed him to provide a timeframe to the police, which was helpful.

George asked Gaby what he planned to do about the violation. Gaby responded, "We will try to resolve this in a way that does not make a big issue out of the theft so our relationships with the Protestants will have a chance to heal. But we will insist on having all the documents returned and the funds turned over to the MECC."

I admired how he looked at the big picture and kept reconciliation and the priority of Christian unity as his goal. The church is not that different from society at large, yet it is called to a higher standard. Someone once mused, "Humankind keeps advancing but humans remain the same." This is the eternal struggle, whether in politics, the church, or in our personal lives. I remembered hearing a quote from television's Mister Rogers, who told the children watching his program, "The greatest gift you ever give is your honest self." I know this was also Gaby Habib's hope for the future. If only it could be applied to Lebanon's political crisis.

Chapter 11
IF YOU HAVE EYES TO SEE: THE BEAUTY AND THE BRUTALITY

"The only true voyage, the only bath in the 'fountain of youth,' would be not to visit strange lands but to possess other eyes, to see the universe through the eyes of another, of a hundred others, to see the hundred universes that each of them sees, that each of them is; and this we will do, with great artists; with artists like these we do really fly from star to star."

—Marcel Proust, *La Prisonnière*

There were no activities set for the following day, so George Bebawi and I left early to see some of his Palestinian and Lebanese friends. George said little else. He told me we would create the itinerary as the day unfolded. I figured the day would be full of surprises and that I needed to trust George, which meant I had to be prepared for a series of risks that challenged my comfort zone.

With a driver provided by MECC at the wheel, we started our journey by crossing the notorious Fouad Chehab Bridge connecting East and West Beirut, also known in Lebanon as Death Alley. When we reached the bridge, George cautioned, "Duck your head below the window and we'll hope the snipers are not here today." The driver floored the vehicle and must have been going close to 100 miles an hour. George laughed and said, "This is how we go from West to East Beirut. There have been hundreds of assassinations on this bridge, and you never know if snipers might be shooting at you today." George was trying to reduce the tension with a joke, but I didn't see the humor in his remark.

We reached the other side in a few seconds and sat back up again. George told us about the fate of Gaby's father who was murdered on the bridge last year by snipers in a case of mistaken identity. He was an elderly shopkeeper who insisted on walking to work over the bridge every day, a pattern he had followed for over forty years. Gaby urged him to change his routine, but he was stubborn and his daily route was a matter of pride. The family still does not know who killed Gaby's father, but police think it was one of the Muslim militias. Thousands of Lebanese families have similar stories involving assassins from various factions in the civil war.

About twenty minutes after we left the bridge, we reached a large, open area where George told the driver to stop, saying, "Let's get out here and I'll explain where we are." He told the driver to return in forty-five minutes. George said it was illegal for us to be in this area as it was a closed military zone. We needed to keep checking the road because if we were caught, the Syrian army and Phalangist militias would arrest us and both were ruthless. George said we were walking over the burial grounds of Tel al-Zaatar (Hill of Thyme), a large Palestinian refugee camp whose residents were massacred. For the past year, the Syrian and Phalangist armies were trying to cover up the tragedy in order to avoid being charged with war crimes. After the massacre the entire camp was bulldozed, leaving the bodies under the rubble.

The massacre occurred roughly a year before my visit, between mid-June and August 1976. We were standing on top of what had once been a thriving city. Nobody knows the exact number of bodies buried beneath the sand dunes where we were walked. At its peak, the camp had 50,000–60,000 poor Lebanese and Palestinian refugees as residents, but many residents fled when the Phalangists attacked. The Lebanese government estimates 5,000–7,000 were killed in the massacre, but other human rights groups say it was at least 10,000. No one will ever know the final body count as the camp was bulldozed and the bodies were beneath our feet.

Flash forward to 2023–25 and we see the same pattern in Israel's genocidal campaign in the Gaza Strip. The Syrian and Lebanese Phalangist militias were never prosecuted for their war crimes in the Tel al-Zaatar massacre. And this was not the first significant massacre of Palestinians; to put this issue in context, the massacres and genocide began in 1948 when Zionist militias conducted a series of massacres that have continued to the present day. One might assume they will continue until there are convictions by the International Court of Justice (ICJ) and the International Criminal Court (ICC). The colonial powers have been able to manipulate the courts until now, avoiding convictions against themselves and their allied militias and surrogate armies, including Israel.

~

George gave a brief history of the hostilities at the camp. The Palestinians arrived in 1948–49 during the *Nakba,* when Israel became a state. Tel al-Zaatar was the largest Palestinian refugee camp in Beirut by 1975. The Phalangist militias campaigned to have the residents moved from East Beirut as they claimed it was too close to their Maronite stronghold. In early January, the Phalangists attacked a poor Palestinian district a few miles from where we stood, also in East Beirut. Over 1,500 Palestinians were killed in the Quarantina operation. A week later, Palestinian militias retaliated and killed a number of Maronite Christians in the city of Damour, just south of Beirut. The Phalangists claimed the killers came from Tel al-Zaatar, and in June they laid siege to the refugee camp.

The fighting was intermittent at first, and by early July the Phalangists invited the Syrian Army to help them defeat the stubborn resistance they met from Tel al-Zaatar. The Syrian army and the Phalangists shelled Tel al-Zaatar for fifty-two consecutive days, preventing food and weapons from entering. Many people starved to death while others died from the shelling. Finally, the Syrians and Phalangists bulldozed the entire camp, burying many alive while covering up evidence of the untold thousands of deceased.

As George told the tragic story, I kept my eyes on the perimeter road, watching for military vehicles. After forty-five minutes I had seen enough, and said, "Let's get back to the taxi." It was a weird sensation knowing we were standing on top of a city that was once home to more than 50,000 residents, with restaurants, community centers, mosques, businesses, and schools. The attempt to whitewash history was likely to succeed, not that different from what Israel accomplished with the Nakba or the history of slavery in the US and its Native American nations. However, in the case of Tel al-Zaatar, it was "brother Arabs" who performed the ethnic cleansing. George said, "And now you are a witness, if not a witness to the actual massacre, you have walked across the remains of the victims."

At the time, I confess the true meaning of the Tel al-Zaatar massacre did not register fully. Most of the residents of Tel al-Zaatar and the other refugee camps in Lebanon arrived there as a result of the continuing Nakba, whether

1948, 1967, or the purge from Jordan in the early 1970s. The fact that none of these massacres or war crimes were prosecuted meant Palestinians were vulnerable to future massacres. Palestinians had no protection or security under the law wherever they lived and certainly not by the United Nations or the international courts that were established after the Nazi Holocaust to protect future victims from the crime of genocide. The Tel al-Zataar massacre was never prosecuted, establishing a pattern of neglect we will see repeated across the next fifty years.

I was relieved to leave Tel al-Zaatar before the militias caught up with us. Walking over the burial grounds of a massacre was challenging, but being arrested by the perpetrators of the slaughter could have been worse. This little adventure was mind-boggling. I wondered what else George had planned for the day.[26]

We traveled north on the coastal road to Jounieh, the center of the Maronite Christians and the headquarters of the Phalangist militia. Jounieh is a picturesque village about twenty miles northeast of Beirut, built on a mountainside overlooking a bay in the Mediterranean Sea. We stopped for a moment to watch the men and women water-ski, a remarkable contrast from where we had walked a half hour earlier. The contrasts in Lebanon are as sharp as anywhere in the world; it's a place where you can see beauty and opulence within minutes of slums and a massacre.

George pointed to the Casino du Liban just south of the bay, the gambling playground for wealthy Saudis, Gulf Arabs, Lebanese elite, and European tourists. To say we were entering a different world was an understatement.

As we drove up the mountainside, we stopped at the towering Our Lady of Lebanon statue. Our Lady was the destination of Maronite pilgrims and the spot where Phalangist militias prayed for victory before their battles. No doubt they came here for a blessing prior to the massacre at Tel al-Zaatar. Most brides and grooms make a brief visit to Our Lady for a priest's blessing after their wedding ceremony. Our Lady is the protector and guiding spirit of the Maronite community. For some Maronites, but not all, the Phalangist ideology had politicized Our Lady as a political and military patron. It was not always like this, but since the civil war began, sentiments had changed. George said that on our return to Gaby's apartment he would show me photos of Phalangist militias sporting pictures of Our Lady on their guns and tanks during the civil war.

We drove to a Maronite seminary where George arranged for us to meet a Maronite monk who was a professor at the seminary. George said some of the monks and priests fight with the Phalangist militias and have no problem taking up arms. We walked to the faculty office of Brother George, a professor of history and theology. Brother George greeted his namesake George (Bebawi) with sincere affection, and then George Bebawi introduced me to the professor. George said I was eager to hear about the Maronites as this was my first visit to the Middle East.

The monk proceeded to deliver a quick overview of Maronite history, beginning with its origins in the fourth century CE after a monk named St. Maroun fled the Taurus Mountains in Syria and settled in the Lebanese mountains, a few miles from where we were sitting. He described the growth of the Maronites through the centuries, including their alliance with France during the Crusades, a relationship that has continued to bring protection and strong cultural and economic relations. The Maronites faced hostilities from some Muslim communities in the 1860s but learned to protect themselves and developed a strong military tradition.

He spoke with pride about their prominence in Lebanon since independence and cited how all Lebanon's presidents have been Maronites. He said I could see how the Maronite villages and cities have prospered in recent years and they wanted to keep it that way. Then he said something that puzzled me. "You may be aware that Maronites are not Arabs. We are the direct descendants of the ancient Phoenicians," he added with pride.

I asked in all innocence, "How do you make the distinction between Maronites as Phoenicians, and the rest of the Lebanese population who say they are Arabs? Aren't you all Lebanese and isn't Lebanon part of the Arab world? I'm confused."

Brother George insisted, "No, we are not Arabs. We were in Lebanon long before the Arabs arrived here, whether Sunni or Shi'ite, and long before the Palestinians. We have lived in the mountains in the eastern and northern part of the country since the fifth century. Islam did not arrive here until the sixth century, so we were established here 100 years before Islam. We can trace our lineage back to the ancient Phoenicians as many scholars have done. Our culture, history, and religion are different. All the other Arab communities lack this heritage, culture, and the rich history we have in this land. Our scholarship is unparalleled. There is really no comparison between us and the Arabs or Muslims."

I said to Professor Bebawi, "You are a Coptic Christian from Egypt. Are you an Arab?"

"Yes," he replied. "I am an Arab Christian with a long history that actually dates back to the Pharaonic period, long before we became Christians in the first century CE. We know from the Coptic language that we have a direct link to the ancient Egyptians of the Pharaonic Era. But we consider Coptic Christians to be an integral part of Egypt and the Arab world. I self-identify as Coptic Arab Christian." Brother George disagreed, arguing the Coptic Christians had a similar history to the Maronites and should consider themselves separate and distinct from the Arabs. Professor Bebawi contradicted this, stating his native language, culture, and history are all interconnected with the Arab world including Islam. The Copts have no problem claiming they are Arab and Christian. Eventually, the two professors agreed to disagree. Their debate was a useful learning experience for me.

The distinction claimed by some Maronites, like Brother George, seemed to be very important to him, but it was clearly a form of exceptionalism with a touch of racism and islamophobia. The claim denies the reality that all the other communities in Lebanon identify as Arab in their ethnicity, with the possible exception of the Armenians, who found a haven in Lebanon after the Turkish genocide of 1915. Their case is unique and very different compared to the Maronites.

I could see on the surface how the Maronite towns and villages seemed more like France than part of Lebanon. Many of the shops we passed had signs in French and English, but not Arabic. The Maronites were enjoying their prosperity and political advantages and wanted to keep it that way. But the problem was that the poorer Muslims and Palestinians were demanding a power-sharing agreement and more of the economic advantages the Maronite areas enjoyed.

I asked Brother George about the future of Lebanon and if he thought the Maronites might set up their own state in alliance with France or Israel. He said some arrangement like this might be necessary, but they would prefer to keep the status quo in Lebanon. He said the Maronites have a strong relationship with Israel, and as they are a major power in the region, the Maronites would welcome a military alliance if the status quo does not work in their favor.

George Bebawi told me later that Israel has been promoting a Coptic ministate in Egypt to complement the Maronite ministate in Lebanon. They had also discussed splitting Iraq into Sunni, Shi'ite, Kurdish, and Assyrian Christian ministates. These plans would, of course, benefit Israel and justify its existence as zionist state in the midst of an Arab majority. It was also a divide-and-conquer formula that would balkanize the Middle East and keep Israel in the driver's seat as the regional superpower.

We thanked Brother George for the lively discussion and drove back to Beirut via the coastal road, avoiding the Fouad Shehab Bridge. The road took us by the old downtown area of Beirut that was utterly destroyed. We drove by block after block of boarded-up businesses, including the luxury Phoenicia Intercontinental Hotel that was a shell of its original self. The notorious Battle of the Hotels destroyed the Phoenicia Hotel and the adjacent Holiday Inn. The destruction was unbelievable; it reminded me of my visit to Dresden after its destruction in World War II.

We passed Ras Beirut and the turnoff to American University and headed toward the airport, turning into Bourj el-Barajneh refugee camp. George said the camp was set up by the United Nations in 1948–49 when Israel drove the Palestinians out of the Galilee. He explained that the one square mile of land of the camp was donated by Lebanese Christian families. Originally designed for 5,000 refugees in tents, it was now filled with tiny cement block units and had a population of 25,000–30,000 refugees. The churches and mosques had worked together since the late 1940s to support the United Nations efforts to provide education and human services to the poor population. George indicated we would see a project of the MECC, working with women and young girls in the camp.

As we walked, we saw children playing everywhere, some working on their soccer skills in the wider streets, others returning home from school in their uniforms, probably from the late shift in their overcrowded but efficient schools administered by UNRWA (United Nations Relief and Works Administration). We reached our destination, a small shop with the MECC logo out front and a sign George translated from Arabic: "Palestinian Embroidery Workshop." We entered and were greeted warmly by Sister Adelle, an Italian nun who had been working in the camp since the mid-1950s.

Sister Adelle was enthusiastic about the support of the Middle East Council of Churches, calling MECC "indispensable." Without the MECC and a few Muslim charities, the women in the camp would not have these opportunities. The goal of the handicraft store and workshop was to bring hope and skills to the residents by focusing on the women and teenage girls in an effort to provide hope where they faced a bleak future. Unemployment was high, nearly 40 percent among men, and underemployment was even higher.

George explained that the high unemployment rate was partially due to the Lebanese government preventing Palestinians from obtaining jobs in most sectors of the economy. Some menial jobs were available, but other than driving taxis and owning small restaurants, they were banned from most professions. A rare few had become professors at Lebanon's universities. The PLO—the major employer—was doing its best to employ an increasing number of mostly men. The women, however, were an afterthought; the traditional culture assumed their role was in the home. Sister Adelle described the work of her store.

"The embroidery workshop achieves several goals at once. First, it helps women generate income for very poor families, especially where the men are unemployed. Second, it helps Palestinians maintain their embroidery craft, truly an art form, that the refugees brought with them from Palestine thirty years ago. We are working to prevent this beautiful art form from disappearing. Each village or city in Palestine has its own unique embroidery pattern called *tatreez*.[27] Third, the workshop provides an educational component where the older women teach the history of Palestine and tell the story of their villages to the next generation. If I had young girls here right now, they could tell you about the village their parents or grandparents fled in 1948, including the families that lived on their street and who lived where on the grandparents' block. Yet they were born here in Beirut and have never visited the village."

She went on to tell us how their work on embroidery helped the teenage girls and the older women gain a sense of pride and identity as they embrace their history. "They already have so much against them as women, as very poor Palestinians, and as people who are marginalized in Lebanese society. They already have these three things against them."

As Sister Adelle described the goals, I could see several themes from liberation theology at work in the embroidery workshop. One of the basic principles is the "preferential option of the poor," a staple in Jesus' ministry. The workshop was serving a marginalized population and emphasizing the forgotten women and young girls, who were the poorest of the poor and most marginalized throughout Lebanon.

The focus on women and young girls was another aspect of Jesus' ministry and a key dimension of liberation theology. Feminist theologians like

Rosemary Ruether and many others made this connection. The philosophy behind the workshop reminded me of Freire's *Pedagogy of the Oppressed*, where we are called to engage with the fringes of society in the process of discovery and liberation. This is precisely what Sr. Adelle was doing by working in small groups and inspiring the teenagers and older women to recover their history and identity. The process inspires learning, motivation, and hope for the difficult future they will face.

George and I saw the sun was beginning to set, so we had to cut the visit short and return to Gaby's apartment for dinner. We thanked Sr. Adelle, and I purchased a tablecloth for my mother, a beautiful, embroidered work of art created by the women of the refugee camp. We arrived at Gaby's apartment, and George and I were glad to settle down on the balcony with a beer and appetizers as we looked out at Beirut in the distance. What a remarkable day! We had seen so much and I had learned about the complexities of Lebanese society, the history and present challenges of Palestinian refugees, as well as the extreme political divides between the Maronite Phalangists, the Palestinians, and the Lebanese Muslims. The polarization was so extreme due to the civil war that I wondered if there was any hope for reconciliation.

I asked Gaby and George, "How will these political divides ever be reconciled?" There was no easy answer, but they seemed to think Lebanon could find its way out of the conflicts if the regional and colonial powers would stay out of its politics. They blamed Israel, Syria, and the Saudis for playing their political games on Lebanese soil. And they weren't alone—the Soviet Union, European powers like France, and the United States also played significant roles. They hoped the United Nations might step up and assist Lebanon with a negotiated settlement and a peace that could provide lasting stability.

"The most difficult issue will be a resolution for the Palestinians," George remarked. "The only solution is for the right of return to be granted to the Palestinians, just as every Jew in the world has it. The United Nations has affirmed the Palestinian right of return, but Israel has rejected it with support from the United States. It has not been enforced. With so many Palestinian refugees in Lebanon (approximately 450,000 by the late 1970s), they represented a significant problem with no solutions on the horizon. The only realistic answer is for the United Nations Resolution 194 of 1949 to be fully implemented so Palestinians can return home or receive reparations. The other essential element will be a Palestinian state with all the rights of self-determination and international legitimacy that were granted Israel by the United Nations in UN Resolution 181.

Gaby said he had been thinking about an idea that would enable me to experience another conflict in the region. He mentioned that MECC, would be sponsoring a youth conference starting tomorrow in Cyprus. "We would hate to see you leave us," he said, "but this is an interesting opportunity for you. We have a young man leaving in the morning and you could fly with him, and then travel to Palestine. Cyprus is another conflict that has similarities to the Israeli-Palestinian struggle. What do you think?"

It sounded like an interesting plan, and I was agreeable, "How can we make it work?" Gaby called his travel agent whose office was near his home. An hour later, he brought tickets to the apartment. My only disappointment was having to leave Lebanon so soon, but I knew I would return.

Gaby called the MECC office and asked Marwan Webbieh to join us. He was a young seminary intern working there part-time. Gaby said I could travel with Marwan and he would introduce me to Palestinians at the Cyprus conference. It was a small conference of around fifty youths from around the Middle East. He said that I could fly from Cyprus to Amman and then cross the bridge to Jerusalem. He added, "George Bebawi and Bishop Samuel's office will host you in Egypt." Suddenly the rest of my Middle East sojourn was arranged with hosts in each country.

This was my last dinner with Gaby, George, and Fr. Yousef, and I had a question for them. I prefaced it by saying I was just thinking out loud but wanted to run an idea past them. I said I was suddenly free to consider a vocational change and was finding myself interested in exploring work on some aspect of the Middle East. While Palestine was a major concern, I was also interested in the future of Middle Eastern Christians. I admitted this was a new idea and I needed to spend time praying and thinking about it before making a final decision.

I then asked them, "What do you think about me considering a move to Beirut or Jerusalem and working for the MECC?" Gaby said they could work with me on this decision and there might be opportunities in Beirut or Jerusalem. George agreed with Gaby, but both added, "'You will need to learn

Arabic and it would be best to be very conversant before you come, but we can help with this."

Fr. Yousef did not agree. "Of course it would be wonderful having you here in Beirut," he said, "but I think you should consider staying in the United States. We need more people over there telling the truth about the Palestinians, Middle Eastern Christians, and Lebanon. Unless you are proficient in languages, it could take you two to three years to be conversant in Arabic. Meanwhile, your country is the biggest problem for justice and peace in the Middle East. At the moment, most US churches support Israel and the zionist movement. This has to change. I think people like you need to stay and organize others to work on these justice and peace issues. Your country is one of our biggest problems."

I was disappointed by Fr. Yousef's answer, but it also hit home. I had a hunch he was correct but had no idea how to act on his suggestions. Where would I begin? I was new to these issues; it might be best to slow down and file this idea away for future consideration. A decision like this would take a great deal of prayer, reflection, and wise counsel from others. I needed to stay in the present moment and allow this idea more time to play out in my subconscious. Winston Churchill once reflected, "It is always wise to look ahead, but difficult to look further than you can see."

As I look back on this decision to focus on Palestine, I now can see that it was the culmination of a process that may have begun at Princeton Seminary when I encountered the anti-Vietnam War movement, civil rights, and a theological transformation that left me confused and questioning what I truly believed. I was gradually discovering a new and different worldview that encompassed my core theological beliefs with a new view of Jesus' call to the poor and marginalized. My five years in the Black church and being loved as a white pastor working through his white privilege, my theology, personal faith, vocational orientation, and values were all shifting in preparation for my encounter with the Palestinian issue. In a sense, I was being prepared for this challenging global issue that was to redirect my life for the next fifty years. It would bring me ridicule, personal threats, job loss, and financial distress, but at the same time it provided me with the sense that I was faithfully following God's will, where my heart was leading me, and the conviction this was the right path to follow. And when considering what the Palestinians have suffered, my modest losses were minuscule in comparison to their losses. My life was being redefined in ways I could not imagine, but in hindsight, "it's a wonderful life," and I simply thank God and the friends, including Palestinians who have encouraged me along the way. All I can say is, it's all about gratitude for these experiences which are gifts from the Almighty and from these generous but suffering people who I hope will one day be free.

Ultimately, this whole process was not about me. Of course it involved me as an average person who was being introduced to a bigger world and significant issues. The Palestinians became the focal point for my particular vocational journey, but it could have been Black liberation, gender equality, Native American justice, or climate justice, but it was and still is Palestine. It's about the Palestinians. It's also about saving the global world order of international law and democracy. My modest role is simply a tiny part of the big picture, so it's wise to keep it all in perspective.

Chapter 12

LEBANON, CYPRUS, ISRAEL/PALESTINE, EGYPT: CAUGHT IN THE GAP BETWEEN JUSTICE AND RESIGNATION

"This land is mine with its multiple cultures: Canaanite, Hebraic, Greek, Roman, Persian, Egyptian, Arab, Ottoman, English, and French. I want to live in all of these cultures. It is my right to identify with all of these voices that have echoed on this land. For I am not an intruder, nor a passer-by... The Palestinian perspective is the opposite of exclusivity. It is about being more than one thing and reflects a readiness to accept the other."

—Mahmoud Darwish

The next morning Gaby and George saw Marwan and me off to the airport from the office in a taxi. I thanked them for the amazing introduction to Lebanon and told George I would see him in Cairo. Gaby said he knew I would return to Beirut fairly soon and we would stay in touch. Marwan and I sat next to each other on the flight to Cyprus with time to get to know each other. Marwan, a student at Near East School of Theology, was having a first year in seminary that was experimental like mine had been.

Marwan's mother was Palestinian and his father Lebanese. He commented on the difficulty he faced growing up with dual nationalities in Lebanon, particularly when one side was Palestinian. His Palestinian grandparents left Haifa during the Nakba in 1948, and his mother was born in a Palestinian refugee camp near Beirut that no longer exists. His problems always surfaced when conservative Christian Lebanese friends or teachers learned about his Palestinian background.

Our conversation turned to the Cyprus conflict as he wanted to brief me prior to landing. I was clueless about the Turkish/Greek Cypriot war other than having heard of Archbishop Makarios, the Greek Orthodox patriarch of Cyprus and the first president of the Greek side of occupied Cyprus. Marwan pointed out several parallels to the Israeli-Palestinian struggle, particularly concerning issues like land, refugees, and outside powers (Greece and Turkey) playing out their problems in another territory. Cyprus was partitioned in 1974 and, like Palestine, it was a divided land with two peoples claiming rights to it. The case of the Greek Cypriots from the north of the island seemed to be another uninvestigated war crime with many similarities to the Palestinian situation.

We arrived around noon, in plenty of time for the opening session of the conference. The youth conference was held on the Greek side of Nicosia, the divided capital city. I learned the concept of "youth" in the Middle East includes people up to the age of forty, so I qualified. The first two speakers provided an overview of the recent civil war in Cyprus, emphasizing the illegality of the Turkish invasion and military occupation of approximately 40–45 percent of the northern side of the island. Turkey expelled most of the Greek Cypriots to the south and set up a Turkish state in the north. Again, religion played an indirect role as the Greeks were Eastern Orthodox Christians and the Turkish Cypriots were Muslims. Like Lebanon and Palestine, the conflict was primarily political and economic, and both elements were needed for a just and lasting peace. Neither Palestine nor Cyprus were at their core religious conflicts.

Like Palestine, Turkish citizens were settled in the north, replacing the Greek Cypriots who were living there. The Greeks became refugees fleeing to the southern side of the island. There was no compensation given to the refugees for their loss of land, and many died in the civil war. Marwan whispered, "We are hearing the Greek Cypriot version of the conflict because we are meeting on the Greek side of the partition. The Turks have a different version, but you won't hear it on this side."

The United Nations brokered a truce in July 1974 that left the capital city of Nicosia divided into two districts, not unlike Beirut and Jerusalem. From our hotel's rooftop bar and pool, we could see the Turkish side of Nicosia with Turkish flags, the checkpoint, and barbed wire at the border crossing, just three blocks from where we stood.

During the afternoon coffee break, we went to the hotel snack shop and I made a serious blunder. After Marwan received his coffee, I stepped up to order, "I'll have a Turkish coffee." I had ordered several coffees in Beirut just a few days earlier by that name. To my surprise, the waiter was highly offended. "Do you know where you are?" he barked. "This is Cyprus coffee. We do not serve Turkish coffee here. They are terrorists. What's wrong with you? Where are you from?" I stepped back and apologized. "Please forgive me, sir. This is my first day in Cyprus and I'm learning. Thank you for correcting me." I'm sure he thought I was another dumb American tourist.

Marwan laughed at my faux pas. As we sat down with our Cyprus coffee, he explained, "The war is still very raw in people's minds. You never know what the waiter and his family suffered during the civil war. It's the same for my mom and her family, who lost everything when the Israelis invaded Haifa and seized their home in 1948. They still hold bitterness toward the Israelis, and I've inherited those feelings. And it's been thirty years since the Nakba for my mother's trauma to heal."

Our afternoon session included a tour of Nicosia with a stop at the checkpoint. From there we traveled to the mountains, which towered nearly 9,000 feet high and offered skiing in the winter. We stopped for a tea break at a hotel with a beautiful view at the top of Mount Olympus. We drove through several picturesque Cypriot farm villages surrounded by vineyards and olive groves. Marwan said, "You will need to try Cypriot wine, some of the best in the region. Some French vineyards buy vines from Cyprus to take home and restore their vineyards."

We arrived in the port city of Larnaca and had dinner on a beautiful Mediterranean beach with outstanding seafood and wine. The wine was fabulous, and a bottle was incredibly inexpensive. I thought about shipping a case of wine home, but regretfully never did. The seafood was fresh, and the calamari appetizers were the best I ever had. Cyprus was like Lebanon, with stunning mountain views and gorgeous beaches, but beneath the beauty, injustices simmered. I filed away my experiences in Cyprus hoping to return someday for a longer visit.

After two days in Cyprus and a very informative conference, it was time to catch our flight to Amman, Jordan. Marwan made sure I met Nader, a Palestinian from Bethlehem. He was pleased to accompany me on the flight to Amman, and from there we would cross the Allenby Bridge and take a taxi to Jerusalem. When we arrived in Amman, I assumed we would leave the airport and take a taxi directly to the bridge and cross to the West Bank and

Jerusalem. I learned the Jordanian government required us to spend 48 hours in the country before crossing the bridge.

We used the time for meetings with MECC staff who suggested we visit the Baqa'a refugee camp, the largest in the Middle East, with over 100,000 residents. We reached Baqa'a by taxi in forty-five minutes as it was close to Amman. The camp was a sprawling city of tiny concrete block homes similar to what I had seen in Beirut, but the camp was twice the size of those in Lebanon. We met with a UNRWA staff member who spoke to us about the history and demographics of the camp. He said the camp had 110,000 residents and expanding every year. After the visit, we took a taxi to the nearby Roman ruins at Jerash, arriving around the dinner with the sun sinking in the western sky.

Tourists were leaving as we entered, and we had the entire site to ourselves. We walked down the main street with various ruins on either side and entered the amphitheater. Nader said it was the best-preserved Roman stadium in the world. It reminded me of pictures of the Coliseum in Rome but on a smaller scale. Nader asked if I would be willing to participate in a little experiment in which I would run up the stairs to the top of the stadium. I gamely cooperated.

Once I'd reached the top, he yelled up to me, "I want you to turn around and look out over Jerash, and then raise your hand when you hear a coin hit the floor." I thought to myself there is no way I will hear it this far away. Nader quipped, "There is a good chance you will hear it. This will be a good hearing test. Let's see if you need a hearing aid. Get ready and listen carefully."

I continued to doubt that I'd be able to hear a coin hit the ground from this height. We were the only people in the theater, so there was no noise, but the stadium's capacity was 35,000, almost the same size as Chicago's Wrigley Field or Fenway Park in Boston. I looked out over the beautiful ruins and noticed the sun was creating a beautiful rose-colored glow on the stone ruins of Jerash. About three or four seconds later, I heard the distinct ring of a coin hitting the stone at Nader's feet. I raised my hand, turned around, and simply said, "Wow. Is that amazing!"

The Roman engineering of the amphitheater was impeccable. The acoustics were brilliant. Nader said Jerash was using the stadium for concerts throughout the summer and fall. It seemed like a perfect venue. I wished I could return and hear a concert there. We left Jerash as dusk illuminated the stones with a calming beauty that underscored my gratitude for another wondrous day.

Marwan and I got up early the next morning and took a taxi down the winding road to the Allenby Bridge, just north of the Dead Sea—the lowest spot on Earth. I could see the city of Jericho off to the right, the oldest city on the planet. Nader briefed me on the procedures. "The Jordanian side will be easy. We will move through customs and passport control quickly on this side. They will stamp our passports and a Jordanian bus will drive us over the Allenby Bridge. Then we have to deal with the Israelis, which is an entirely different matter."

Nader said he had to take a separate bus for Palestinians because they are usually strip searched and must endure a rigorous interrogation. They take Palestinians to a different building from the rest of the tourists. He said they will take every single thing out of his suitcase and inspect it. Nader added, "From this point, we do not know each other. Be sure you do not mention we are friends. It will delay you. Just tell them you are traveling alone. I'll look for you on the benches where you clear customs. Good luck, and make sure you take a look at the mighty Jordan River as we go over the bridge. You will be surprised by how vast it is."

I got on the non-Palestinian bus, and when we reached the Allenby Bridge, all I could see was a dirty little creek. I stood up and wondered aloud, "Is that the Jordan River?"

Someone behind me replied, "Yep, that's the Jordan River, one of the heaviest guarded borders in the world."

Nader had advised me on what to expect from the Israelis at customs. He cautioned again, "Remember, you are traveling alone and this is your first trip to the so-called holy land. Be sure to play up the fact you are a Christian tourist. Don't tell them you will be seeing Palestinians and if asked about the visits in Lebanon and Cyprus, you were attending church conferences. You don't have to give them any information, so play dumb. You are just an American Christian tourist making your first visit here. You want to see the biblical sites in the holy land. Don't lie, but don't give them any additional information. If they ask about your hotel, you will be staying at the YMCA in East Jerusalem. If they ask why, just say because it is cheap. I'll see you outside customs."

When I arrived at customs, I waited in line for about twenty minutes and finally had my opportunity. I was thoroughly questioned about my visits to Lebanon and Cyprus. "Who did I meet in Beirut? What was the purpose of my trip? Who arranged and paid for my tickets? Why did you go to Cyprus?

Who will you see in Israel? Where will you be staying? Why are you visiting Israel? Did anyone give you anything to carry in your luggage?" Following Nader's guidelines, I gave them little information. With the questioning finished, I waited for Nader on the bench outside baggage; thankfully, I had a book to read.

Two hours later, Nader appeared outside customs, shaking his head in apology and saying, "Let's get out of here and catch a taxi." We took a "service" (Palestinian group taxi pronounced "serveese" in Arabic) up the winding road to Jerusalem. The taxi dropped us off at the East Jerusalem YMCA. We had a quick sandwich in the cafe and Nader introduced me to three of his friends who worked there as cooks and waiters. After he left for his home in Bethlehem, the new friends invited me to come back for a drink once I settled in my room.

I bought a bottle of wine to share with them. Two of the three were Muslims, so they declined the wine and had cola instead. They told me to avoid Israeli wine and buy wine from the Cremisan monastery in Beit Jala. We had a great evening. I asked endless questions, and they were happy to educate me. We talked late into the night. I asked about the political situation, their views on the history of Palestine, and if they had any hope for a peaceful future. I asked about their personal lives and if they had family and children. They were all single, hoping to earn enough money so they could get married. One was already engaged.

They answered every question thoroughly and honestly. I was struck by their frankness and how pessimistic they were about their future as Palestinians living under the Israeli occupation. They thought there was little hope Israel would make peace with the PLO and assumed the occupation was permanent. I thought about the occupation as temporary, but they shed new light on that assumption.

Israeli elections had taken place in June 1977, just a few months prior to my trip, and the right-wing Likud government, led by Menachem Begin, were in power. My new Palestinian friends reminded me that Begin was the leader of the zionist militia that massacred over 225 Palestinians at the village of Deir Yassin, just west of Jerusalem. They said the massacre was confirmed by the Red Cross, which discovered the bodies the next day, many stuffed down the village well. One said Begin was wanted for terrorism in England and could not travel there until the British dropped his terrorism status. My friends expected the Likud government would take more land and be more aggressive against the PLO in Lebanon, possibly attacking them in Beirut.

They added, "The United States and Europe have military interests in mind for Israel and will use Israel to protect oil and other economic and political interests in the region." Another goal of the West was "to keep the USSR out of the region, or at least minimize their role." They said none of these factors were favorable for Palestinians. "It is highly unlikely Israel will withdraw from the West Bank, East Jerusalem, and Gaza Strip as long as they are a key player protecting US interests."

Their assessment was very pessimistic but perhaps realistic. After all, they were the ones living under military occupation. I asked if there was anything that gave them hope. They said the Palestinians would not go away, and perhaps in fifty to one hundred years Israel will decline, but for the immediate future, life will be very difficult.

The three young men returned to the speculation about Israel launching a war against the PLO in Lebanon in the near future. They lamented that with the extremist Likud government and Begin now in control of the Knesset, Israel will be much more aggressive. Life would get much worse for Palestinians "both here and in Lebanon." In the meantime, Israel was escalating the theft of Palestinian land and building illegal settlements. "No one can stop them, not even the United States. Most of your political officials support Israel no matter what they do," one said. I thanked these generous young people for their time, their honesty, and how well they educated this American tourist. Since I drank most of the wine, I was having difficulty staying awake and it was very late. We said goodbye and I again expressed my gratitude.

My original plan in Jerusalem was to meet two MECC staff whose offices were next door to the YMCA. I phoned for an appointment and the secretary said the staff were on vacation for another week. As a result, I had two full days on my own to see Jerusalem. I decided to get maps for walking tours so I could make the most of my time. I started my adventure at the Church of the Holy Sepulchre, having read about the different chapels and denominations represented in the historic basilica. My time there was the biggest disappointment of the trip. Perhaps my expectations were too high as I thought it would be an inspirational, spiritual, and educational experience. It turned out to be a chaotic waste of time dominated by insensitive and noisy tourists.

My visit to the Dome of the Rock and Al-Aqsa Mosque were far more satisfying as I was awed by the simplistic beauty of the dome, which is actually a shrine and not a mosque. It commemorates the place where Prophet Muhammad arrived in Jerusalem in his historic night ride and was elevated to the seventh heaven. From the Dome of the Rock I made my way to the nearby Al-Aqsa Mosque, the third-holiest site in Islam. I spent about thirty minutes praying and meditating there, and it was a beautiful time of solitude. Today it is very difficult to gain access to Al-Aqsa in part due to the threats from extremist Jewish settlers. With dinner time approaching, my friends at the YMCA recommended the Philadelphia restaurant, not far from Damascus Gate and three blocks from my hotel. The meal was traditional Palestinian cuisine and truly spectacular. I returned to the hotel and turned in early.

The next morning I greeted my friends on the staff, had breakfast, and headed for the Old City and some shopping. Most of the shops were beginning to open so I made my way to Jaffa Gate and found the art store they recommended for old prints by the British artist David Roberts of nineteenth-century Palestine. The store was owned by an Armenian family, and I purchased two prints they claimed were published at the turn of the century. I took their word for it and was shocked I actually paid $150 for the two. I still have these prints hanging in my bedroom forty-four years later. I asked him about Palestinian pottery, and he said I should avoid the shops in the Old City as they had cheap imitations. If I wanted the authentic pottery, he recommended the Palestinian Pottery factory near the YMCA. I learned later the Armenian owners were friends of his family, but it really is the most authentic Palestinian pottery in Palestine.

I was bored with shopping after ninety minutes, which is usually my limit. I considered another visit to the Holy Sepulchre but thought better of it and visited the Lutheran Church of the Redeemer instead. I found a quiet corner in the sanctuary and spent a welcome thirty minutes in solitude and prayer. I was in a mellow and joyful spirit after that peaceful interlude and adjourned to an outdoor cafe where I could have lunch. Pulling out my journal, I began to write my reflections on the previous days because I had fallen behind on my entries.

As I started to write, a strange feeling came over me. I had the sensation I had been in Jerusalem and the Holy Land on a previous visit. The sensation was very strong, and I could visualize walking into the Dome of the Rock and strolling down the Via Dolorosa. It did not make sense as I had never been off the North American continent prior to this trip. But the sensation stayed with me, and I began to write about it in an attempt to analyze the source of this unusual feeling.

I have a friend who was involved in a form of psychotherapy to heal trauma who swore she was raped and abused by a husband in colonial Philadelphia in the 1770s. It never made sense to me, but she swore it was true, and by working back to the memory, she experienced healing. I do not believe in prior lifetimes or the Hindu Samsara cycle of previous incarnations. But the sensation of having been in Jerusalem was strong and it stayed with me.

I concluded the sensation was in part based on my intensive reading, films, and pictures I had immersed myself in the previous year. Also, I thought the wonderful hospitality of Lebanese and Palestinian friends may have been a factor. Or was it my readiness to move here and find a job in Beirut or Jerusalem? No doubt all of these factors could have triggered the sensation but whatever it was, I needed to pay attention to my growing interest in the Middle East. Perhaps more important, I needed to slow down, pray, reflect, and take these matters with considerable caution and wisdom. I remember the wisdom of Lao Tzu, the Chinese philosopher: "The longest journey begins with a single step." Perhaps I was in the midst of the first step.

As I was writing in my journal, a young woman stopped to ask me how to find the Church of the Holy Sepulchre. I gave her directions, and she asked me if I would be willing to show her the way as she was directionally challenged. I said yes, but asked if she would first allow me to share my experience about my previous day at the Church of the Holy Sepulchre. I told her about the tourists and chaos and asked her to consider what her expectations were about the visit. If she simply wanted a tourist site she might be satisfied, but if she was looking for a peaceful, spiritual experience, she should avoid it at crowded times like this.

Fiona was a graduate student in anthropology at the London School of Economics. She had left the tour group she traveled with as the visits were not satisfying her interests. She said, "They were too evangelical and were trying to convert me… I wasn't interested." She left the group that morning and was starting out on her own with a travel guidebook but was completely lost. She had three days and marked several sites she wanted to see. I told her this was my first time in Jerusalem, and I knew very little, but I did find the Dome of the Rock and Al-Aqsa Mosque to be wonderful visits. I offered to show her how to get there if she was interested.

I invited her to sit down as I was about to have lunch. We ended up having a falafel sandwich and a great discussion about religion, particularly a comparison of Islam and Christianity. She was very interested in Islam and planned to study it when she returned to London. I could tell she had a strong spiritual side to her as she said she meditated each day. She told me about her studies and how she wanted to teach at the university level and get a PhD in anthropology. I told her what I was doing and how I was being drawn to work in the Middle East. We went on to visit the Dome of the Rock and Al-Aqsa and we both spent time in meditation at the mosque, which I found just as rewarding as my time there the previous day.

We left the mosque and returned to the Via Dolorosa, and she invited me to come to her hotel for a drink as she had a bottle of wine in her room. I found myself in a quandary. Fiona was very engaging and beautiful, and I was drawn to her keen mind. We seemed to have good chemistry together. I was attracted to her but thought I should be careful. My emotions urged, "Don't miss this opportunity; this is a beautiful woman… and who knows where it could lead." But I had made a personal vow six months earlier that I would not get involved in any romantic liaisons for a year. I wanted to heal completely from the divorce so I could avoid the rebound phenomenon.

I politely declined, saying I was leaving for Egypt early the next morning and needed to pack and get a good night's sleep. She said she was sorry and understood. We exchanged phone numbers and addresses. I gave her a hug and left. My emotions and libido were firing on all cylinders as I walked away, wondering what I was missing. But I took some satisfaction in keeping my vow. I thought of several friends who jumped into relationships and even marriage on the rebound after a difficult divorce or breakup. None of those relationships went well and simply delayed the healing process.

As I left for Cairo the next morning, I was still thinking about Fiona. Was it a missed opportunity or a wise decision? The gruff instructions from a rude official at Ben Gurion Airport shook me out of my reverie. I bit my tongue, took deep breaths, and said a few prayers to remain peaceful. The key was to stay in the present moment, reminding myself, "These clowns have no power over me. Relax and don't give them any information." I could not help but compare the warm hospitality and humor of the Palestinians with the boorish behavior of the Israeli officials. Still, I realized it was unfair to judge all Israelis based on the behavior of three security officials.

I finally boarded the plane. The short flight from Tel Aviv to Cairo was a reminder of how close these countries were in terms of geography. Lebanon, Syria, Jordan, Israel/Palestine, and Egypt were all within driving distance from Jerusalem—that is, if you could drive directly from Jerusalem to Beirut, Egypt, or Amman without checkpoints and long waits at the borders. The trip was comparable to driving from Chicago to Madison, Wisconsin, or to Indianapolis, Indiana. However, in the Middle East it was impossible to drive from one country to the other due to the impenetrable borders.

As I looked down from the plane's 30,000-foot altitude, I found the proximity of the countries truly remarkable. I could see our flight was leaving the southern coast of Israel and the Gaza Strip, and within minutes I could see the Sinai Peninsula and the Nile Delta off in the distance. After arriving in Cairo's chaotic airport and securing my visa, I headed toward baggage claim and was excited to see a sign with my name on it. Holding the sign was Sonia Mitri, secretary to Bishop Samuel, the person I was hoping to see. My friends in Chicago who visited Egypt with Bruce Rigdon told me to make sure to meet Sonia and secure her as a guide. She was an upbeat and welcoming young woman in her late twenties, with a beautiful smile and warm disposition.

I insisted on taking her to dinner so we could review my schedule and plan the next few days. Sonia was a devout Coptic Orthodox Christian, committed to full-time work for her church. With a passion for serving Jesus and especially the poor, she said her friend Miriam would guide me tomorrow due to a conflict she had at work but that she would be my guide the rest of my time in Egypt. She said Professor Bebawi had to travel to England and apologized for missing me. Our last day would be spent with the poorest of the poor, where the Coptic Orthodox Church has made a long-term commitment with the *Zabbaleen*, the "garbage workers." After dinner we caught another cab to the British hostel where I was staying. Sonia arranged three meetings for me the next day and I was eager to get a good night's sleep. I collapsed into bed, falling asleep in my street clothes.

Late that night, I was awakened by a man screaming at the top of his lungs, seemingly from the hallway. I jumped out of bed, half awake, and went to the door to see what was happening, but no one was there. Then I realized it was the first call to prayer, prior to sunrise, coming from a mosque. I looked out my window and sure enough, my room was twenty-five feet from a large loudspeaker on the nearby minaret. In Beirut and Jerusalem I had heard the call to prayer in the distance and enjoyed the beautiful rhythmic greeting five times a day. But at this hour, it was too much. Fortunately, I had no problem going back to sleep as soon as the message was finished. Before embarking on the day's activities, I managed to change my room to the back of the building.

Sonia arranged for her friend Miriam to meet me in the morning and walk with me over one of the Nile River bridges to the Egyptian Museum. I had a delightful visit in the museum and was amazed at the number of priceless artifacts from the Pharaonic period. I needed a week to do justice to the museum but perhaps on another visit. I met Miriam at noon and we walked across Tahrir Square, where I paused to photograph the largest traffic jam in the world. It looked like eight to ten major streets converged on the square and cars were maneuvering from one lane to the other at a snail's pace. There were trucks, buses, cars, people on bicycles, several motorcycles, and the occasional donkey- or horse-drawn wagon, all trying to negotiate the circle.

Miriam said, "A few months ago, Tahrir Square was filled with thousands of demonstrators who stopped traffic, demanding the Sadat government reinstate subsidies it had cut on flour, rice, bread, and cooking oil." The protesters were victorious, a rare concession by the government. I followed her down the stairs to the Cairo Metro. There were people everywhere. When the train arrived, the cars were jammed with people standing in the aisles and passengers riding on the roofs of cars.

Miriam warned, "You have to run alongside the train and young men will reach out and pull you up. Let's go!" Miriam was a fast runner and I barely kept up with her. We reached up and several strong hands pulled us on board as the train was departing the station. Once on board, the people welcomed us, celebrating our arrival. "It's kind of a thrill ride," I said. We went about three stops and got off at the stop for the historic St. Mark's Coptic Orthodox Cathedral.

The cathedral was a majestic structure. In the twenty or so minutes before our meeting with Bishop Samuel, Miriam took me to the shrines of St. Mark, the first patriarch of the Coptic Church, and St. Athanasius, one of the heroes of the early church era. Athanasius was known for challenging and defeating the Arian heresy at the Council of Nicaea in 325 CE. Then Miriam took me up to Bishop Samuel's office and said she had to go back to work, but she insisted we attend the Wednesday evening service at the cathedral with Sonia. I agreed and expressed my gratitude for her hospitality, noting we could meet before the service and I would take them to dinner. I asked her to select a restaurant close to the church and let me know.

When we met for dinner the following evening, I was eager to learn more from Sonia and Miriam about their backgrounds and hopes for the future. They were close friends, both in their late twenties and working for Bishop Samuel while studying to become deaconesses. The "order of the deaconess" was one of two vocational options for women in the church; the other was to become a nun. Their love of Jesus and the church were at the center of their lives. Both had a strong dedication to serve the poor. They lived at home with their parents and younger siblings, all of whom supported their vocational choices.

After dinner, we entered the massive cathedral, where the large sanctuary was already filling with people settling into their seats. They told me the sanctuary had a capacity of 8,000–9,000. The worship service began with a procession of priests and bishops, striding majestically to the accompaniment of beautiful Coptic hymns that included people playing miniature brass cymbals similar to castanets. Incense filled the cathedral as the bishops marched behind the choir and took their places on the altar. Once they were seated and the hymn concluded, Pope Shenouda walked to the center of the altar. He offered a prayer followed by readings from the scriptures, another hymn, and a brief meditation based on Jesus' Beatitudes (Matthew 5:3–12).

After the meditation, the pope took his seat in the center of the altar and one of the bishops read questions submitted in writing prior to the service. Sonia and Miriam took turns translating for me. The questions ranged from interpretations of Bible verses to advice on marriage and dating. Most of the questions concerned practical issues including sex before marriage, a wife's financial security in marriage, and dating people of other religions. There were no political questions. The pope's answers were conservative to a Western ear, but Egypt is a very conservative culture and religious society, for both Muslims and Christians. Sonia said his advice is received like a word from God, and people follow it. I had never seen anything quite like this. The estimated attendance that evening was in the range of 9,500 people.

The next day, my last full day in Cairo, proved to be one of the highlights of my trip. Sonia took me to the Zabbaleen ("garbage workers") district, a remote part of the city where the poorest of the poor lived. I was surprised to learn 90 percent of Cairo's garbage workers were Coptic Orthodox Christians.

At that time, this capital city of Egypt had not developed a modern system of garbage collection despite being home to 15–16 million people in 1977. For several decades, poor Coptic Christians settled in the Zabbaleen district and tried to eke out a meager living by recycling the paper, cardboard, bottles, cans, and other garbage. Generations of Copts were garbage collectors who went door to door collecting garbage and trash, dumping the garbage into their donkey-drawn carts, and bringing it home to be recycled. Sonia and Miriam volunteered in the district with a literacy and hygiene project under the auspices of Bishop Samuel's office.

Sonia told how the church was putting significant resources, personnel, and construction projects into the Zabbaleen district to provide better housing, community centers, and places for worship. The church was creating jobs and introducing modern methods of sorting and marketing the recycled products. Of significant concern among the Zabbaleen was hygiene, and the church was responding. There were plans for a hospital and more clinics and social service centers. Several physicians were donating a day each week to provide free medical care in the stationary and mobile clinics. Literacy classes and tutoring were available and new schools were being built. The government had abandoned the Zabbaleen, and the church was stepping in big time.

I asked if they were trying to relocate people into better housing. She said most of the Zabbaleen wanted to stay here as this was their community. What the church did in these cases was to build housing and create jobs adjacent to where they were living. They removed most of the garbage around the new housing due to the rats and hygiene issues. Gradually they were moving the people out of the shacks on top of the garbage they used to live.

As we were leaving, Sonia pointed to a hillside at the edge of the district and said the Coptic Church was beginning to construct a large church projected to seat 15,000 people. The new church would open within two years. There were already Coptic masses held in various locations throughout the Zabbaleen district, and weekly Bible studies were very popular. Friday was the day of worship as Egyptian Christians and Muslims worshipped on the same day.

Time was fleeting, and we had to rush to the airport. While the visit to the Zabbaleen district was depressing in some ways, it was also inspiring to see how the church was transforming the lives of the poorest of the poor. This was liberation theology and the message of Jesus at work in profound ways. We caught a taxi to the airport, Sonia having insisted on staying with me all the way. I gave her a book of prayers and a memento from Chicago and invited her to come and speak to our churches. I mentioned some of our mutual friends in the Middle East Task Force like Bruce Rigdon, Frank Baldwin, Carolyn Gifford, and the Lindners, and she asked me to greet each one. I thanked Sonia for everything she taught me and the remarkable people and ministries she shared.

"You must come back and spend more time with us," she said with a smile. "There is so much more to see here; we barely scratched the surface." I assured her I would return, hopefully within a year or two. Sonia made Egypt come alive for me. I truly appreciated the emphasis on the poor and initiatives like what we just saw in the Zabbaleen district. Her personal commitment to follow Jesus and serve the poor was inspiring. She gave me a small book on the history of the Coptic Orthodox Church and an English translation of the Coptic Mass of St. Basil, which I still treasure.

As I flew back to Chicago, overwhelmed by the insights I'd gained during this wonderful trip, I began to page through two journals packed with my trip reflections. More than the politics, culture, and religious aspects of the Middle East, all of which were very important, what I treasured most was the warm hospitality and the conversations with the fine people I'd met. From Gaby Habib, George Bebawi, and Fr. Youssef to Sister Adelle and the women in the refugee camp, the people in Cyprus—including Marwan and the angry waiter—the Palestinians who stayed up half the night to educate me, and finally Sonia, Miriam, and Bishop Samuel in Egypt. I made several new friends I felt sure I would see again in the near future.

What were my takeaways from this remarkable three-week sojourn in the Middle East? The first was the abundant hospitality and love of the people who received me in each country. Each stop of my journey introduced me to people who generously took me in and gave of their time. Arab hospitality and generosity reminded me of what I experienced in the Black church for nearly five years. The personal care inspired me to improve my own practice of hospitality whenever I had the opportunity to host guests in my home.

Second, I gained theological inspiration from liberation theology and saw it in action throughout my trip. I saw it in the women like Sister Adelle, who was serving in Bourj al-Barajneh refugee camp. I heard it in discussions with Gaby Habib and George Bebawi about theological issues at the heart of the Middle East conflicts. I saw it at work in a profound way in the Zabbaleen district with the poorest of the poor. Miriam and Sonia were living examples of liberation theology. Among the themes of this theology I saw were the centrality of justice, the preferential option of the poor, honoring the poor who were God's children created in the image of God. These humble servants were all confronting systemic poverty, racial and political injustice, and the legacy of colonialism and settler colonialism.

Third, I could see fundamentalism rising among Jews, Christians, and Muslims from Lebanon to Palestine/Israel and Egypt. In Israel, the right-wing extremist Menachem Begin had been elected prime minister in June 1977. Begin was a leader of the Irgun terrorist group that claimed responsibility for blowing up the King David Hotel in 1947 and was still wanted by Scotland Yard when he took power. He was popular with fundamentalist Christians in the United States. Could the United States play an independent and honorable role in resolving the Palestinian crisis in a manner that was consistent with international law and justice for Palestinians and Israelis? This was a dangerous mixture of religion and politics that blossomed into a political gold mine for Israel. My haunting experience walking over the remains of the Tel al-Zaatar massacre was a foretaste of future massacres, or what Palestinians call "the continuing Nakba."

Fourth, the newly established Middle East Council of Churches promised to bring unity to the divided Christians and their churches in the Middle East. Christians are a small minority of 15 million among over 200 million Muslims. Their only hope was to unite and work closely with Muslim partners who would stand with them when problems arose. Some Christian leaders feared Christian communities were already at risk and could disappear in the coming years, whether in Palestine, Lebanon, Iraq, Syria, or Jordan. I heard this theme in every place I visited, and while it was understated, it was an issue to watch. Christian unity was an existential necessity for Christian survival. Christian unity is echoed in Jesus' great prayer for unity, recorded in John's Gospel: "The glory that you [God] have given me I have given them [the church], so that they may be one, as we are one." (John 17:22).

Fifth, and perhaps most problematic, was the grim reality that my country, the United States, was the most serious obstacle to justice and lasting peace throughout the Middle East. US policies were undermining the future of Christians in the Middle East with political policies that advanced US interests with no consideration of the Christians, or the Muslims for that matter. Christians will vanish in Lebanon, Syria, Iraq, and Palestine if the United States fails to practice justice for all citizens of the region. It will be important to monitor the future of Christians in the Middle East as part of my personal responsibility.

Sixth, the future of Lebanon was a major concern that raised many questions about the role of the US. What would be the consequences of the US and Israel taking sides with the Maronites and Israel in a civil war? Would this lead to the division of Lebanon into smaller and less viable cantons? What will happen to the Palestinians, and why did the US avoid the Palestinian refugee problem? What would happen to the fragile balance of the different Christian and Muslim communities? While the US justified its approach with the rhetoric of Cold War politics (keep the Soviets out), how did this square with the rule of law? It seemed myopic and could easily backfire.

Finally, I was increasingly drawn to a career change, and the Middle East seemed to be where I was feeling God was leading me. I still needed to sort this out through prayer, reflection, and careful research. Whether it would mean moving to the Middle East or staying in the United States, as Fr. Yousef recommended, I did not know. I needed to take this monumental decision slowly, with significant discernment. After this visit, I realized how complex the region was and saw the many political, economic, and religious dynamics that were at play.

This trip was a turning point for me, nudging me closer to a vocational change. The experiences during this month in the Middle East had an emotional, spiritual, moral, and intellectual impact that would take a couple of years but the seeds of change were planted in Lebanon, Cyprus, Jordan, Palestine and Israel in September 1977.

The words of the Chinese philosopher Lao Tzu confirmed my decision. "The journey of a thousand miles begins with a single step."

Section IV: Chapters 13–16

Doctor, My Eyes Have Seen the Pain

Doctor, my eyes have seen the years
And the slow parade of fears without crying
Now I want to understand
I have done all that I could
To see the evil and the good without hiding
You must help me if you can
Doctor, my eyes
Tell me what is wrong
Was I unwise to leave them open for so long?

—Jackson Browne

Chapter 13
BEGIN THE PILGRIMAGE TO PALESTINE

"Life is like riding a bicycle. To keep your balance, you must keep moving."

—Albert Einstein

When I returned home from my travels to my position as an associate pastor at First Presbyterian Church in Evanston, IL, I could sense the uneasiness in my heart, soul, and mind. I was no longer at peace, nor was I fulfilled as a pastor in this congregation. Something had changed in me and I had to figure out if it was of God or just fleeting emotions. I was growing impatient with the constraints of the pastoral ministry and wondered if it was time to move on.

Serving on a staff of a large downtown congregation had its blessings and limitations, and one of them was speaking prophetically on social justice issues. I had seen too much injustice in the Middle East, and this particular church wasn't the most receptive place to raise controversial issues. At one time it had seemed open, but the theological orientation of the church was becoming more conservative. Jackson Browne's song spoke to me because he wasn't talking about his physical eyes, but rather the pain of acknowledging the world's great injustices .

On my first Sunday morning worship service after the trip to the Middle East, I was asked to offer the pastoral prayer, which is a five-minute prayer that touches on various issues and events impacting church members and the local community. It often includes prayers for the sick, comfort for families who recently lost a loved one, and issues impacting the larger community like homelessness and poverty. World missions and pressing global issues can be included. When I was praying that Sunday morning and reached the last section of social concerns, I was suddenly moved to pray for the Israeli-Palestinian struggle, including the painful case of millions of Palestinian refugees mired in impoverished camps with no future. I had not planned to do this, but it was on my heart, and I believe the Holy Spirit prompted me to articulate the truth of the matter.

Following the service, the clergy and lay leaders went to the exit doors to greet the congregation as they left. It was unusual to receive comments on a pastoral prayer, but on this occasion three people took exception to my prayer for the Palestinians, including a prominent elder. He accused me of inserting a political statement into the prayer and let me know it was completely out of place in Christian worship.

A few minutes later, as I was hanging up my robe in the office, one of our new clergy on staff approached me, fuming with anger. He said my prayer was an affront to God and insensitive to the congregation. "How could you pray for PLO terrorists in a Christian worship service?" I was not surprised by his response. He was a very conservative evangelical who subscribed to the Christian zionist interpretations of the Bible. I said it was a sincere prayer from my heart and came from the desperate conditions I witnessed on my trip. I offered to take him to lunch and share my experiences. I also reminded him that my prayer focused on the refugees mired in extreme poverty and hopelessness. Clearly, he could not see Palestinians as humans, only as PLO terrorists.

He sneered and said, "I'm not the least bit interested. From now on I'm going to call you the PLO pastor. I'll be monitoring you closely."

"If you are monitoring me," I suggested, "then you might be interested in hearing more about these issues. They are on the hearts and minds of millions of Christians in the Middle East." He stormed out of the office.

I later learned from a colleague that he was advocating a plan to prevent me from participating in worship. When I eventually confronted him about it, he agreed to drop the idea.

As I reflected on these exchanges, I wondered if this was a signal from God and from the people to rethink my future at the church. I was aware of my growing impatience with the narrow viewpoints I continued to encounter from my colleagues at church. When I arrived at the church a few years ago and assumed my position it was a different staff as most of the progressives had moved and the current staff were very conservative.

It felt as if I was operating out of an entirely different theological, spiritual, and political model than the others. It seemed as though I needed to conform to their conservative silence on these critical issues or get out of the church.

I discussed my confusion with my spiritual partner Bud Ogle and he encouraged me to listen to my passion for the Middle East, pray, and struggle with my sense of God's calling.

Wes Granberg-Michaelson's insightful book *Without Oars* offers wisdom for people in dilemmas such as the one I was facing. He explores the concept of pilgrimage as a metaphor of faith and a journey into the unknown. In the early church and Middle Ages, the practice of pilgrimage was a method of spiritual discernment. The pilgrim was one who left on a risky journey and did not know what she or he would encounter on the way.

The pilgrim left most possessions behind and was completely vulnerable and dependent on God. The journey was long, arduous, and stripped the pilgrim of all pretense. It was a type of downward mobility toward humility and vulnerability before God and others. As the pilgrim progressed on the journey, several insights were revealed as the pilgrim faced his or her limitations and utter dependence on God. Wes calls the insights "liberating grace," a deeper and more intimate relationship with God that sheds light on one's life.

This analogy speaks to me as I think back to this period in my life. My pilgrimage to the Middle East was the first major step leading to a career change. Running through my mind were questions like: should I leave a well-paying position in the church that brought financial stability and a clear career path for the future? What should I do if this position becomes unfulfilling and those around me were offered no support or pledged to undermine me? Was this new passion simply a fantasy, a passing interest after a trip, or was it an authentic calling to serve God in a different way?

As I reflected on my next steps, I wrote in my journal and proposed three possible options to consider as my "first steps in the thousand-mile journey." I had not dismissed moving to the Middle East, but Fr. Yousef's suggestion to stay in the United States remained prominent in my thinking. Another option was to explore church positions in the US that would enable me to work on Middle East issues in the US context. Still another option was working with secular peace and justice organizations in the US.

I contacted friends at Presbyterian headquarters to explore opportunities available in the Middle East. They invited me to attend a conference in New York City hosted by the Presbyterian denomination's Program Agency for about sixty clergy from across the country. The conference was organized around a Middle East theme and gave me the opportunity to meet others in the denomination who shared my interests. I met pastors like Rev. Darrel Meyers from Los Angeles, who became a lifelong friend.

Between sessions I had a chance to talk privately with two denominational executives about Middle East work in the denomination, on the Palestinian struggle or Middle Eastern Christians. They said my best option was to apply for one of the jobs in the Middle East; positions were open in Egypt, but they would not include a focus on Palestine. When I asked about working in the United States on the Palestinian issue, I was warned to be careful. They said there were no such positions, and if they did exist, I would be advised to avoid them. They said advocating for Palestinians was a kiss of death to a career in the church and elsewhere. I would face consistent opposition and never again get a job in the denomination including the local church if I went down that road. I said I was already familiar with the opposition.

My options were quickly narrowing to secular organizations working on Middle East issues which, in 1979, were limited to number of Arab American organizations in the US, all led by Arabs, including the Arab American University Graduates, the Palestine Human Rights Campaign, and the National Association of Arab Americans. The November 29 Coalition was a volunteer organization, as were several philanthropic organizations such as the United Holy Land Fund. It seemed unlikely any of them would be interested in me, a non-Arab with no experience, no academic training, and completely new to the issues. It appeared I had reached a dead end in my quest for a job related to the Middle East that didn't require me to leave the United States. Now that I was divorced and Jay was living near Cleveland, I had a responsibility to stay in close touch with him.

Prior to leaving for the New York conference, Professor Abu-Lughod called and asked if I could host a public lecture by Israel Shahak, a distinguished professor of chemistry at Hebrew University in Jerusalem, the chair of an Israeli human rights organization, and a survivor of the Holocaust. I ran it past our staff and was relieved there was no opposition. Fortunately, the hostile Christian zionist staff person was on vacation, but I had the rest of the staff on board. I booked a room in the church for the lecture.

When I returned from my New York trip and attended our Tuesday morning church staff meeting I was told the lecture was canceled. I was shocked because no one informed me or asked me to participate in the decision. Pastor Lewis said the local rabbi at Beth Emet synagogue called and urged him to cancel the lecture because the professor was deemed to be a radical leftist and a "self-hating Jew."

I countered, "Did you know this man is a distinguished Jewish professor at Hebrew University in Jerusalem and a Holocaust survivor? He is a citizen of Israel and happens to criticize Israel on its violations of human rights. I'm wondering why you didn't contact me to discuss this decision? Beyond these concerns, why can't we listen to the professor rather than canceling his presentation because the rabbi complained?" It was the same tactic used earlier to shut down our initial Middle East course, but this time it was a Jewish professor from Israel who was canceled. I lost the argument and had to call Professor Abu-Lughod and explain the cancellation. I was upset with how the senior pastor handled the situation and let him know my concerns with the process, or lack thereof.

Professor Shahak's lecture at Northwestern University was impressive, particularly his analysis of the deteriorating situation in Israel under the Likud government. Afterward, I picked up a flier promoting a new organization called the Palestine Human Rights Campaign, recently established by the Association of Arab-American University Graduates. The new director of PHRC, Jim Zogby, was visiting Chicago and Professor Abu-Lughod was hosting him. I asked Professor Abu-Lughod about the meeting, and he urged me to attend.

Jim Zogby gave an interesting presentation, and I was immediately attracted to the pragmatic focus on Palestinian human rights. He said Amnesty International, the preeminent human rights organization, would not take on Palestinian cases in the United States. The US Department of State was the same. PHRC's mandate was to raise Palestinian human rights as violations of international law and change the positions of the State Department and Amnesty International. There was some hope for change as the new Carter administration seemed open to adopting human rights cases.

I looked down the list of PHRC's sponsors and noticed several well-known clergy and academics like Edward Said, Noam Chomsky, Daniel Berrigan, Professor Abu-Lughod, and the folksinger Pete Seeger. After the meeting, I met Professor Ghada and Ayoub Talhami, who offered to host a follow-up meeting in their home in two weeks. I knew about the couple and had heard

Ayoub was one of the most respected Palestinians in the Greater Chicago community. By profession, Ayoub was an engineer in the City of Chicago's Department of Sanitation and Water Reclamation. Ghada had just completed her PhD in African studies at the University of Illinois – Chicago, and was looking for a full-time faculty position.

The Talhamis convened the meeting, and the first order of business was to vote on becoming the PHRC chapter in Chicago. It had unanimous support. Most of the dozen people present were well versed in Middle East issues, so I sat back and listened to the discussion. I was one of three non-Arabs at the meeting, which was fine with me. I thought Palestinians should take the lead and identify what projects to adopt.

The Talhamis were gracious hosts who went out of the way to make me feel welcomed. I was one of the last to leave that night, and Ghada and Ayoub thanked me for attending and asked if I would like to come back for dinner the following week. I responded in the affirmative. When I asked if I could bring anything for dinner, they responded, "Just bring yourself."

When I arrived at the Talhami home the following Saturday, I was greeted by the three Talhami children—Yousef (about twelve years old), Lamees (six or seven), and Ghassan (or Gus, about four). They ushered me into the living room as Ghada and Ayoub came out of the kitchen to greet me. The house was filled with delicious aromas from the homemade Palestinian food they were preparing. Lamees, a polite and efficient server, returned with a notebook and took my drink order. I interacted with the kids and was soon known as *Ammo* ("Uncle") Don, a title that continues to this day, even though all three are no longer children. We had a delightful evening as Ghada and Ayoub filled me in on the Palestinian community in Chicago and their stories growing up in Palestine.

The Palestine Human Rights Campaign gradually became a major part of my activism. I liked the focus of the organization on human rights cases and the opportunity to challenge the US government and organizations like Amnesty International. I raised the issue of addressing the theological issues around land and justice in relation to the Palestinians, and Ghada and Ayoub liked the idea. Ayoub reminded me that he heard Fr. Paul Tarazi lecture on these issues at the Presbyterian conference in LaGrange and said we could bring him back for a lecture. They suggested we propose the idea at the next PHRC chapter meeting.

A few weeks later at the PHRC chapter meeting, I submitted the idea of addressing the theological issues of land and covenant in Palestine. Most of the group was secular but they saw the increased relevance of the issue given the positions of the Likud Party and its growing alliance with Christian fundamentalists in the United States. We discussed a lecture or a weekend conference but were reminded that we were a small organization with no money, no mailing lists, and were unknown in the community. Ayoub said he would call Jim Zogby and propose the idea to him, perhaps the national office would be interested.

Jim was excited about the idea of incorporating theological issues into PHRC's justice mission. Ayoub, Jim, and I had a follow-up conversation on the telephone and began to explore the possibility of a conference. Jim thought we should hold the conference in Washington, DC, or New York City, as PHRC was fairly strong on the east coast. Ayoub and I were pleased with any location but did not want to give up on the idea of holding a conference in Chicago.

Ayoub and I traveled to Washington and attended a meeting at the PHRC office with Jim Zogby and Wes Granberg-Michaelson, editor of *Sojourners* magazine. Wes had grown up in the Chicago area in the evangelical community and was very aware of the Palestine issue and progressive on social justice causes. Wes convinced Jim that Chicago was an ideal location for the conference, given the strong tradition of evangelical organizations and progressive anti-war organizations in the region.

I proposed the Christian Life Center in LaGrange, Illinois, for the 1979 PHRC conference and when I met with representatives of the Sisters of St. Joseph, who ran Nazareth Academy on the same campus, they were pleased we were returning. When I told them about our lineup of speakers—including Fr. Elias Chacour, a Melkite Catholic priest from the Galilee—they were even more enthusiastic. Abuna Chacour had recently published the book *Blood Brothers* and I gave the people from Sisters of St. Joseph a copy. Another interesting speaker proposed by Jim Zogby was Zuhdi Terzi, a Palestinian Greek Orthodox layman from Jerusalem who was the PLO ambassador to the United Nations.

Once we mailed out the invitations to the conference announcing the list of speakers, I received a call from my friend and former colleague at First

Presbyterian Church in Evanston, Rev. Gary Skinner. Gary was the chief executive presbyter—essentially the bishop—of the Presbytery of Chicago. He had received a strong letter and phone call from the Chicago Board of Rabbis and staff at the Anti-Defamation League, Rabbi Yechiel Eckstein, who demanded the Presbytery cancel the conference.[28]

After Gary's call, I was eager to meet with him to address these concerns. The Middle East Task Force of the Chicago Presbytery was listed as a cosponsor of the conference, and the content of the conference had implications for the presbytery. Over lunch, Gary and I looked at the rabbi's concerns more closely. Gary noted the rabbi was furious that the conference included speakers such as Professor Abu-Lughod and Ambassador Terzi, thus "providing a platform for PLO terrorists." I pointed out that the invitation stated Terzi would attend the conference but not as a speaker. He would only be available to answer questions.

Recalling how the same arguments were used against Professor Abu-Lughod when he spoke at the Middle East series at First Presbyterian Church in Evanston, Gary was familiar with these tactics. He was a strong proponent of our First Amendment rights and believed the conference should go forward. He had already drafted his response to the rabbi's complaint and wanted me to review it prior to putting it in the mail.

His polite but direct response told the rabbi the presbytery had neither the power nor interest in canceling the conference. The Middle East Task Force, the Palestine Human Rights Campaign, and other cosponsors had a right to host the conference based on the First Amendment to the Constitution of the United States, which guarantees the right of free speech.

The conference took place on a beautiful May weekend in the Chicago area. Fr. Chacour was an instant hit with the audience, delivering his passionate call for justice and nonviolence while reminding them that he was a follower of his "compatriot in Galilee," Jesus of Nazareth. Emphasizing the Beatitudes of Jesus as a call to action, he joked about Rev. Robert Schuller's recent interpretation of the "Be Happy Attitudes." He considered this interpretation to be a foolish American distortion that missed the point of Jesus' message. Fr. Chacour said Jesus spoke in Aramaic, not English. The Aramaic word for "blessed" means "to be empowered," or "to rise up and get your hands dirty" in the difficult work of justice and peace on behalf of the poor and dispossessed.

Another conference highlight occurred when Wes Granberg-Michaelson rose to ask a question. Prior to the session, Wes told me what he was planning to do. He asked Ambassador Terzi, "What do you, a Palestinian Christian, think about Israel stealing Palestinian land and using the Bible to justify it?"

I was moderating the session and called upon the ambassador, who started to answer from his seat near the back of the chapel. Several people were unable to hear his response, so I invited Mr. Terzi forward to address the audience. The elderly gentleman was the only person at the conference wearing a suit and tie. I introduced him as the PLO's official representative to the United Nations, a Palestinian Christian from Jerusalem. I could see some people in the audience take a second look or whisper to their neighbor in amazement. I'm sure 99 percent of the audience had never seen an official of the PLO in person. Terzi was about as far from Yasser Arafat in appearance as anyone could imagine.

Terzi opened his Bible, another marked difference from what people expected, and read a portion of I Kings 21. In this passage, a poor Jezreelite (Canaanite) farmer named Naboth had his farm seized by King Ahab and Queen Jezebel. Terzi noted how the king coveted the land but Naboth protested, saying the land was all he had and it had been in his family for generations. It was his only source of income. The king told his wife, the notorious Queen Jezebel, that the farmer refused to give up his land. Jezebel concocted a plot whereby two "scoundrels" were paid to lie and accuse Naboth of blaspheming the king. As a result, Naboth was stoned to death and Ahab and Jezebel seized his land. Word of the evil deed reached the prophet Elijah who condemned the action and judged the king and queen harshly.

Terzi put down the Bible and said this is precisely what Israel is doing today, stealing land from Palestinian farmers and others with full support from the United States and many European nations. He noted that Naboth was not Jewish but a gentile, just like the Palestinians, making the parallels even sharper. "What is needed today, he said, are prophets like Elijah who will stand up and call Israel to account for its sins, stop the theft of land, and end the injustices inflicted on the Palestinians."

Terzi underscored his point, stating, "It's up to the Christians, Jews, and Muslims to correct the lies and false teachings now used to cover up the theft of Palestinian land. We need the people of faith to stand up for justice and be the prophets today like Elijah." The ambassador's message was well received.

He returned to his seat in the back of the chapel and the audience rose to give him a rousing ovation.

I caught Wes's eye and saw that he was smiling from ear to ear. The PLO ambassador's sermon was one of the highlights of the conference. It was time for the morning coffee break and our planning committee was scheduled to meet and evaluate the conference proceedings up to that point. As we walked past Terzi, we saw that he was surrounded by attendees waiting to speak with him. I couldn't help but smile at the irony. Neither the US government nor Israel wanted him to speak and relate to people, but he had simply answered a question and delivered a meaningful response.

Our planning committee was thrilled with how the conference was going and could not be happier with Ambassador Terzi's message. We decided to draft a statement to summarize our main points and see if we could get it published in a Christian journal. We outlined the key themes we had been hearing, and considered assigning a small group to draft the statement. Wes said it was difficult for a small group to draft a statement and volunteered to take our notes, isolate himself for a couple of hours, and work on a draft.

Wes was an outstanding writer. He presented his draft statement to the committee during the afternoon break, and we were in awe of its content, tone, and how it was framed in a Christian theological context. We made a couple of minor suggestions and asked Wes to read it at the end of the conference prior to the final benediction.

When Wes finished reading the statement, the audience responded with another round of applause. The powerful statement enabled us to end the conference on an inspirational note. I asked people to come forward and sign their names and affiliations to the statement. We decided to call it the LaGrange Declaration, and I suggested we aim for 2,000–2,500 signatures in the coming weeks and months.

Someone in the audience shouted, "Why not 5,000?"

"OK," I said, "we have a new goal."

Wes said, "*Sojourners* magazine will publish the declaration in their next issue." This was a fabulous offer that would boost our chances to reach the goal of 5,000 signatures. Moreover, I wasn't sure any other Christian journal would have the courage to publish a progressive statement on Palestinian rights and justice in the late 1970s. The religious and political climate was not conducive to support of the Palestinians.

Asserted within the declaration was the concept of a "two-state solution," a concept that was normal in 1979 but moribund today. (See chapter 20 for an analysis of the death of the two-state solution.) Otherwise, the declaration is remarkably relevant forty years later, as most of the key political and theological issues continue to be unresolved. Also unresolved are the religious distortions of issues such as the land, the covenant, and Israel's human rights violations against Palestinians.

One of the most important pronouncements in the declaration was "the Palestinians have a right to be represented by Palestinian leadership of their own choosing." Similarly, the declaration affirms "political self-determination" as critical to any just solution as is "the right of return for Palestinian refugees." Finally, the declaration challenged theologies supporting a "divine land grant to Israel" as "unbiblical," emphasizing "the Bible [does not] give the modern state of Israel a divine right to the lands inhabited by the Palestinian people."[29]

Framing the call for justice in the Israeli-Palestinian struggle within a biblical and theological framework was a relatively new perspective in the United States. We went to work promoting the LaGrange Declaration as we did not receive any press coverage other than a *Sojourners* article by Wes and the printing of the declaration. Almost immediately, the mainline Protestant and Roman Catholic journals attacked the declaration as "antisemitic."

An interesting example was the left-leaning *Christianity and Crisis* and the equally progressive *National Catholic Reporter.* The latter carried a column by leading feminist theologian, Rosemary Radford Ruether, who called the declaration "at its core an antisemitic document." I only knew of her by reputation, but I learned she was committed to other justice issues such as her opposition to the Reagan administration's Central America policy, civil rights for Black Americans, and her special interest in opposing antisemitism.

About six months after the LaGrange conference, a friend told me Rosemary's perspective on Israel-Palestine had changed. She was on a women's delegation to Israel/Palestine and while walking alone in the Old City of Jerusalem, she saw Israeli soldiers beating Palestinian youths for a minor infraction. When she questioned the military about their behavior, she was told, "These are just Palestinians, and you shouldn't question what we are doing." This was unacceptable. Rosemary had seen similar behavior in Central America and immediately asked for a tour of the illegal Israeli settlements. Having seen another side of Israel, she returned to the US and wrote an article in the National Catholic Reporter (NCR) about what she saw and how it had changed her thinking.

My friend Jim Wall, editor of *The Christian Century*, called and asked me to join him and Rosemary for lunch and discuss the change in her thinking about Palestine. Jim had been talking with Rosemary about a problem she had encountered since she wrote the NCR article. Rosemary showed me a letter stating that the "National Conference of Christians and Jews" was rescinding its invitation for her to deliver the keynote address at its annual convention. She was still upset about the letter. She had been a regular speaker and supporter of the organization for several years, but everything had changed once she wrote about how Israel was taking land and abusing young Palestinians.

I suggested she write more articles about the incident and see if *Christianity and Crisis* would publish them. Jim said he would consider publishing a "how my mind has changed" article by Rosemary. I asked if she would be censored by the *National Catholic Reporter* and she said it was not likely. I knew from my own experience that this kind of censorship and silencing were common in the secular and religious press and was grateful to have some company to challenge it. Palestine seemed to be one of a handful of issues where we were prevented from telling the truth about the reality on the ground. The censorship would become a constant issue for anyone advocating Palestinian rights and criticism of Israel.

The censorship reached the highest and most intense levels during the genocidal war on Gaza that began in 2023, but people on social media and several courageous journalists primarily in Gaza told the truth and paid for it with their lives. Other journalists, including progressive Jewish scholars, also stood up and told the truth. Increasingly social media networks were bought up by wealthy business organizations that were hostile to the Palestinian narrative but somehow the truth broke through and public opinion swung to gradually affirm the Palestinian reality.

Rosemary, her husband Herman, and I became close friends for the next forty years. We worked closely together as they both joined the Palestine Human Rights Campaign Board of Directors, led delegations to the region, and Rosemary's writing on the Palestine question accelerated. Rosemary and Herman wrote *The Wrath of Jonah,* a brilliant book on the conflict that included important theological analysis. When I took my sabbatical in 1987, PHRC hired Herman to serve as its interim director.

A surprising media opportunity came when I received a call from the syndicated columnist Georgie Ann Geyer, who wanted to discuss the LaGrange Conference. Having spent time in Chicago, she was pleased when I suggested we meet at my favorite restaurant, the historic Berghoff, a German eatery in the heart of the Loop. Once we placed our order, I handed a note to the waiter and asked him to deliver it to the head chef. A few minutes later, Muhammad, sporting his chef's toque, came out of the kitchen and sat down to talk with us. I introduced Georgie Ann to Muhammad from Beitunia, Palestine. I wanted her to meet a Palestinian refugee who was a highly skilled chef and a wonderful human being.

Geyer was a popular columnist who nevertheless had expressed some racist and Islamophobic tendencies, but in this case, she seemed to grasp the justice issues in the Israeli-Palestinian struggle, and her article was very constructive. The column, titled "Challenging the Biblical Claim to the West Bank," was published in newspapers across the US. In the article, the declaration received a positive review. Geyer quoted Wes Granberg-Michaelson, identified as the editor of the "thoughtful evangelical magazine *Sojourners*," (who) told her,

> If there is going to be a change, it will have to come from the US Christians who say Prime Minister Menachem Begin's claim to the Arab West Bank is a perversion of the Bible. Theologians and Biblical scholars alike say the idea of a divine claim to land or a divine blessing to a special, privileged people is totally without foundation. If we want to draw on the perspectives of the Bible, then we should draw on the perspective of justice for all.[30]

The year 1979 brought significant changes to my life. The LaGrange Conference and Declaration put our PHRC Chicago Chapter on the map and sent a strong signal to the churches about justice in the holy land. I decided to leave my full-time position at First Presbyterian Church in Evanston and work half-time at the church and the other half as the chair of our Palestine Human Rights Campaign in Chicago. I fell in love, and Drew McAllister and

I were married in June. I was living with two other families in Westminster House, the campus ministry at Northwestern University where Bud Ogle was a campus minister.

Westminster House served as our home with Bud and Donna Ogle and Martha and Paul Arntson, who became family. They helped me welcome Jay, who visited every three months for a weekend. Covenant Community, our house-church, became a centerpiece of our lives. The community consisted of approximately forty-five people including students, faculty, clergy, and others who met for worship on Sunday evenings and small mission and study groups. We discussed justice issues ranging from housing and youth work in a poor area of Chicago to gender inclusivity and liberation theology. The gender-inclusivity group challenged the community to adopt inclusive language in our hymns, welcoming and loving LGBTQ friends and developing theological positions that support them. They supported my interest in Palestine and were eager to learn more.

Drew and three women from Covenant Community left their teaching positions and opened a small elementary alternative school in the Good News neighborhood in Chicago. Bud and Joe and Nancy Gatlin led a mission group called Good News North of Howard in their multifaceted ministry with the poor in a nearby Chicago neighborhood. They were able to raise funds and purchase a hotel and renovate several apartment buildings while training men and women from the neighborhood with construction skills. The project provided housing for low-income families and in some cases the option of owning property through sweat equity in one of the buildings.

Drew and I were part of another mission group of twenty-two members called the Peace Tax Fund Group. Each person in the group withheld a portion of their income tax as an act of Christian resistance to war. We told the IRS our intentions in a cover letter with our tax returns. We were conscientious objectors to war and militarism. We did not keep the funds we resisted but deposited them in our war-peace tax account and made modest grants to local peace groups.

From time to time, we sponsored educational events for the community or the public. One of my all-time favorite public events occurred on April 15, 1980, when we rolled a ten-foot-tall "penny," made from a large wooden cable spool, twelve miles through Chicago neighborhoods to the downtown post office. The giant penny sported the logo "Not One Cent for War." We distributed fliers as we walked, we held interviews with Chicago radio stations, had one interview on the 10 PM television news, and talked with people as we walked. We held a brief rally at the post office and distributed brochures to people dropping off their tax returns.

~

I needed help with our follow-up efforts with our PHRC chapter and was able to hire a part-time field education student from McCormick Seminary. Jim Zazzara and I developed a modest Chicago- area mailing list, and the signatures from the LaGrange conference provided names from across the country. Within a year of the LaGrange Conference, the founder and first director of PHRC, Jim Zogby, announced he was leaving his position to become the national director of the American Arab Anti-Discrimination Committee (ADC).

With the national office of PHRC closing, our Chicago chapter was not convinced the new ADC organization would prioritize the work of Palestinian human rights. We called an emergency meeting of our Chicago group and decided our focus should continue to be on Palestine. The Chicago group asked if I could work more hours, in case we wanted to expand our efforts in Chicago. I said I was open to it, but we should decide on our goals. We had little funding and wondered if we could support a staff person. Then someone said, "Perhaps we should consider going national and rebuild the Palestine Human Rights Campaign." At that point everyone laughed, but the person who suggested it said, "Why not?"

I called Jim Zogby to tell him of our decision to continue as a Chicago chapter. He tried to talk me into becoming an ADC chapter, but I told him we were committed to keeping our focus on Palestinian rights. He offered to send us a partial mailing list, but he could not offer financial support. I said we would like to continue using the PHRC logo and Jim said he would send the artwork.

Two other chapters heard we were continuing as a PHRC chapter and asked if they could join us. I welcomed them and suggested they let Jim Zogby know of their decision. When our Chicago chapter met, I mentioned the two chapters people said we should not laugh about the idea of becoming a national organization. Gradually, we added other chapters and carried on the human rights action alerts and regular program of PHRC.

I contacted the Palestinian artist Kamal Boullatta at the advice of Professor Abu-Lughod. Kamal, a brilliant artist, designed the PHRC logo. He was pleased we were continuing our commitment to PHRC and offered to assist us any time we needed his work. I began to build a new board of directors with the help of Ayoub and Ghada Talhami, Husni Haddad, and Ibrahim Abu-Lughod. One of the active Chicago chapter members, Paul Mokhiber, agreed to serve as treasurer, and within a month we had a strong board of directors. Contributions continued to come in. By late June, we were able to cover my salary of $500 per month and start thinking about an office. Slowly but steadily, we started to rebuild the Palestine Human Rights Campaign.

Looking back on 1979 and the first half of 1980, I was facing more life changes than I could have imagined. My pilgrimage from the pastorate to Middle East work had suddenly become a reality, moving from half-time chapter director to national director of the Palestine Human Rights Campaign. I lost my full-time salary when I left the church but was able to work for $500 per month for the next year. I also remarried, despite having said "never again." Our communal living situation was a gift; the shared lifestyle allowed us to be engaged in meaningful work with minimal incomes.

Ultimately, I return to Wes Granberg-Michaelson's analogy of a pilgrimage, which has become so relevant for my own personal journey. Liberation was at the heart of the journey: theologically, personally, and practically. It involved a downward journey of dramatic changes in my vocation, a new marriage, support from a faith community, accepting a lower income, and starting the journey with justice in Palestine. The new directions involved risk, humility, steadfast faith in God, and openness to a new journey in life. Wes summarized my past eighteen months and future when he wrote:

> The pilgrim's loss of control is a liberating form of surrender. It is born from the countercultural conviction that we are not the masters of our destiny. Rather, in relinquishing ourselves to the messiness of lived experience, and to circumstances we know we are unable to control, we discover a Presence that has already unfolded us, sustained us, and gone ahead of us. It's grace."[31]

Chapter 14
A RINGSIDE SEAT TO THE ISRAELI INVASION OF LEBANON

"Tomorrow is yesterday. Violence naked and unbridled, has not been exhausted, old wrongs are still unattended, new ones wait the hour of revenge."

—Hussein Agha and Robert Malley, *Tomorrow is Yesterday* [32]

It was late January 1980, and we needed an office for the Palestine Human Rights Campaign in Chicago. For strategic reasons, I thought it would be important to find an office in downtown Chicago. Our financial resources were limited, and I needed to find free space for a few months while we tried to raise funds to cover rent and basic expenses. I started knocking on doors of churches and peace organizations in the Chicago loop but with little success. Most organizations wanted a hefty payment of two months' rent up front. I visited seventeen different churches and peace organizations but not one of them could offer free space.

My eighteenth visit was Christ the King Lutheran Church, located on the eighth floor at 202 South State Street, in the heart of Chicago's South Loop. I had an appointment with Pastor Erickson and when I entered the church office, he said, "Have we met before? You look very familiar." I did not recognize the elderly pastor but said, "I hope so, let me think." He offered me coffee and before I made my standard pitch, he exclaimed, "Now I remember. Last year during the Chicago blizzard, you and your friends at Westminster House took me in when my car was stranded on Sheridan Road in that horrible snowstorm. You rescued me from the cold, offered me dinner, and then you helped me start my car. I'll never forget your hospitality."

"Yes, yes, now I remember," I said. "Of course, that was it!"

He asked, "How can I help you?"

"Well, I have a favor to ask. I'm a Presbyterian clergyman and I have decided to embark on a new ministry related to the holy land, or as some say, the 'unholy land.' I've decided to leave the congregation I was serving in Evanston and start a small nonprofit ministry. I need an office, but we can't afford rent right now. We should be able to pay in three months. Would you have a small area where I could set up a table for half of each day, just to get started?"

He smiled. "Yes, we do have space. We could give you six months or so of free space and then you can contribute a couple hundred dollars a month… How about that?"

I exclaimed, "Thank you, thank you. I think God had a hand in this, given how we met and what I need to get started in this new venture."

Pastor Erickson's small congregation was subsidized by the Evangelical Lutheran Synod of Chicago. He showed me the space, which was more than adequate. I set up a table and telephone but needed to take it down and pack up our papers before supper as the church held evening meetings in the room. Pastor Erickson asked me to tell him more about the mission and type of work the Palestine Human Rights Campaign was doing. I told him about the origins of the group, gave him a copy of the LaGrange Declaration, the *Chicago Sun-Times* article by Georgie Ann Geyer, and the *Sojourners* magazine issue. They represented the only publicity we had, but Pastor Erickson was impressed, saying, "This sounds like important work. Let me draw up a small contract. When do you want to start?"

"How about tomorrow at this time?"

"Why not?" he laughed. "Tomorrow is our midweek worship and communion service at noon. Why don't you join us and then you can set up your office." I agreed and we shook hands. I said a little prayer of gratitude and we finally had an office.

About a month after we settled into our new office, Ayoub Talhami called and announced, "I have a great opportunity for you. The Democratic Party leadership is in Chicago and meeting at the Palmer House this week. They are holding hearings and we need to make a presentation to them on Palestinian human rights for the party platform. I think you are the one to make the presentation. The presentation is a three-minute statement and it will need to be tightly argued. I think you should do it. What do you think? It will be Friday morning, so that gives you a couple of days to prepare."

I thought about Ayoub's suggestion and said, "Either you, Ghada, Husni Haddad, or Professor Abu-Lughod would be much better. I'm still learning about the political issues."

"But you, as a Presbyterian clergyman, might have more credibility," he insisted. "They will react negatively to each person you named simply because we are Palestinians. I talked it over with the others and we think you should do it." I was already feeling over my head trying to rebuild a human rights organization from scratch, but this was an opportunity to contribute to the cause and learn something in the process.

Three days later I was at the Palmer House, just two blocks from our new office, waiting to deliver my statement. When my name was called, I took a seat before the committee and nervously made my presentation. When I finished, the chair led the attacks, stating, "Why in the world do you think the Democratic Party would adopt your antisemitic request? You did nothing but attack Israel, our strongest ally in the Middle East."

I blurted out something like, "Because Palestinians are a community suffering from well-documented human rights abuses at the hands of the Israeli army. The United States is supporting Israel to the tune of $15 million per day, and as tax payers we need to insist Israel abide by international law. The US Arms Export Control Act of 1977 is clear in stating US arms cannot be used against civilian populations. It's the law."

The chair did not answer my points. Instead, he allowed other committee members of the panel to continue their attack, making points taken right out of the AIPAC playbook, including, "Israel is a strategic ally of the United States and should not be singled out as you are doing. What about Egypt, Saudi Arabia, and the rest of the Arab world?" There were no positive comments. Feeling like a complete failure, I realized I should have known better and taken a different approach or stood by my original statement and not done it at all.

Afterward, Ayoub took me to lunch at the Berghoff. I was still reeling from the attacks, feeling like a complete idiot. Ayoub insisted, "You were great! You didn't back down and you made good points again and again."

"But it was a total disaster," I said. "There was not a single positive response to the points I made. Everything I stated opened me up for more attacks. We made no progress at all on the party platform."

Ayoub stressed, “Look, the Democratic Party is unabashedly pro-Israel and has been for decades. This is a small start. We need to make our case every four years and keep Palestinian rights in front of them, even if it takes years to wear them down. The truth will come out even if it takes twenty or thirty years.” When Ayoub said “wear them down,” I thought of the widow in Jesus’ parable of the unjust judge in the Bible (Luke 18:1–8). In the story, a poor widow takes her case before a judge who, the text says, “feared neither God nor man.” But the widow keeps coming before him to make her case. Finally, the judge says, “This woman is wearing me down. Give her justice.” The lesson is: “Stay the course. Wear them down. Be steadfast until you receive justice.”

—

Meanwhile, tension between Israel and the PLO was escalating in the spring of 1981. I was watching it closely. Israel and the PLO had been trading rocket attacks for weeks. Israel used its fleet of US-made F-16s while the PLO fired Katyusha rockets from South Lebanon. On July 17, 1981, Israel hit Palestinian sites in Lebanon with vengeance, killing 123 and wounding several hundred.[33] Arab and European analysts suggested the CIA had been notified and the United States was complicit in the attacks.

When these attacks began, I was suspicious of the CIA’s involvement and wondered how we could address this issue of “unconditional US support for Israel.” My time in front of the Democrats taught me we couldn’t make a dent in US support for Israel at the political level. In the case of the bombing of South Lebanon, Israel used US-made F-16s and bombs. There was speculation that Israel was field-testing US weapons on Palestinians as if they were guinea pigs. Justice seemed to be irrelevant in any case involving Israel, which seemed to be above the law, or at least that’s the way both the Democratic and Republican parties interpret a law on the books of the US Congress. As far as our elected representatives were concerned: who cares?

I did not have the documentation in my hands when I testified before the Democratic Party officials in July 1981, but gradually the truth came out that the US was coordinating the attacks on Lebanon with Israel. Ten years later, the Pulitzer Prize-winning journalist Seymour Hersh exposed the fact that US Secretary of State Alexander Haig met with the Israeli defense minister in May 1982 and gave him the green light to invade Lebanon. The Israeli air strikes in July 1981 were a prelude to the invasion of June 1982, and it was likely the 1981 attacks were authorized by the US. I was surprised to see the story reported in the typically pro-Israel *New York Times*.[34]

The Israeli air strikes of July 1981 hit PLO bases, a community center in the Rashidieh refugee camp, and a Shi'ite Muslim village in south Lebanon. US weapons were involved in the bombing raids. Now that the city of Sidon was struck, its large Shi'ite community was showing signs of fatigue and resentment toward the Palestinians, which was one of Israel's goals. The Israeli operation was viewed as a prelude to a far more extensive war in 1982. Sharon's strategy, as approved by the US secretary of state, was designed to eventually destroy the PLO's presence in Lebanon and change the current political regime.

The events of July 1981 through August 1982, foreshadowed the impunity Israel continued to have from Republican or Democratic legislators during its genocidal war on the Gaza Strip beginning in October 2023. For more than a year, the administration of Joe Biden, a Democrat, supplied Israel with the latest US aircraft, tanks, and bombs, including 2,000-pound blockbuster bombs. Israel dropped more tonnage of bombs on mostly Palestinian civilians in eight months than the US used during World War II. Street protests grew, as did major protests on university campuses in the spring of 2014. Polling showed nearly 70 percent of Democratic voters demanded a permanent ceasefire, but the Biden administration refused to demand one, nor did it demand a cut in US military aid to Israel as congressional laws require. Nothing seemed to sway the Biden administration from its support for what the International Court of Justice called "a probable genocide."

Within a few days of the July 1981 attacks, I received an invitation to travel to Beirut and see the evidence of the Israeli attacks and attend an international conference organized by a coalition of Lebanese and Palestinian organizations. These groups, part of the Lebanese National Movement, included Druze, Shi'ite, Sunni, the PLO, some Orthodox Christians, and several smaller secular Lebanese movements. I welcomed the opportunity for another learning experience and signed up to go.

Despite Air France losing my luggage for five days, the conference and side trips were important experiences for me. They provided clear evidence of Israeli aggression. The US media had either ignored the bombing raids in Lebanon or implied Israel was justified in responding to PLO rocket attacks on Israel under the guise of self-defense. Few asked whether Israel provoked the PLO rockets by bombing the Palestinian camps first. This same pattern of Israeli provocations followed by Hamas rockets has continued to the present day.

After arriving in Beirut, we were taken to several of the Palestinian and Lebanese Shi'ite areas bombed by Israel, including Rashidieh refugee camp (just five miles north of the Israeli border), Sidon, Beirut's refugee camps, and the poor Shi'ite neighborhoods, also known as the "Belt of Poverty" surrounding Beirut. We saw extensive destruction and displacement of families.

The conference provided film footage of the bombings at each of the above sites provided by Lebanese, Palestinian, European, and Japanese journalists. The documentation was thorough, the destruction and death indisputable. European relief and human rights organizations confirming the attacks included the International Committee of the Red Cross, Amnesty International (minus the US office), and Oxfam. Journalists and human rights advocates addressed the conference, raising such questions as: "Why does the US and European press continue to ignore Israel's aggression when they have documented evidence of the civilian victims?"

The conference had a clear bias toward its sponsors, the Lebanese National Movement, and the PLO. However, I could put that aside as they had independent eyewitnesses present the cases of the victims with clear evidence. No one had a credible answer to the question as to why the US and Europe ignored the facts. I came away from the conference more convinced than ever that the answer rested in the fact that the United States and several European governments were complicit in the attacks. They had either given Israel the green light or they helped fund the attacks and provided the aircraft and bombs.

I returned to Chicago after ten days in Lebanon with more insights into the political challenges surrounding the US-Israeli relationship. I was more aware that the Reagan administration was the most pro-Israel administration to date and that our advocacy faced more opposition at the highest levels of government.

As a result, the Camp David Accords under the Carter administration, signed on September 17, 1978, locked the United States, Israel, and Egypt into a treaty that excluded the Palestinians. Israel's Begin refused to reach an agreement on the Palestinian issue as President Carter had hoped, and by postponing it, Israel had free rein to pursue its military strategy with Egypt removed from the opposition. Israel was free to implement its anti-PLO strategy of regime change in Lebanon with minimal resistance from the Arab world, who went along with Israel's strategy of postponing any discussion of the Palestinian issue. Many analysts saw the July 1981 attacks on Lebanon as a dress rehearsal for a much larger war in Lebanon. No one knew when the war would begin, but by January–March, 1982, it was inevitable.

As the new version of our Palestine Human Rights Campaign grew, I was able to hire a second staff member, Karen Koch-Kreim. A year later we added Leila Diab, giving us two dedicated women: one an American married to a Palestinian and the other a Palestinian American from Chicago. We had grown to twelve chapters around the country and were issuing an average of two human rights action alerts per month, calling on people to put pressure on our State Department and Congress to intervene, and raising Israeli human rights violations wherever we could get media attention or educate the peace, religious, and human rights organizations.

The primary mission of PHRC was to raise cases of Palestinian human rights and gain more support from civil society in the United States. Our theme was "Palestinians have human rights too." In the early 1980s, Palestinians were not viewed as human beings and were expendable given the United States' and Europe's commitment to Israel.

We utilized case studies and everyday stories, bringing stories of real Palestinians to US audiences. We submitted our reports to the media, despite being met with minimal interest. We appealed to Amnesty International and other human rights organizations regarding their silence on Palestinian human rights cases. We increased our efforts to reach young people at universities and clergy in the churches. In 1981, Amnesty International USA still would not take Palestinian human rights cases. When I discussed this "Palestine exception" with a friend who was an active A-I member of a local committee, she said the organization did not want to offend its Jewish donors and members. She reminded me that the international office in London took on cases of Palestinians who were not involved in violence.

The fact that the leading human rights organization recognized Palestinians as equal human beings around the globe but not in the United

States seemed preposterous. I decided to join our local Amnesty International chapter, which was affiliated with Northwestern University. It was a convenient arrangement as the chapter met in our home, Westminster House. In my first meeting, I raised the case of a Palestinian prisoner who had been adopted by the international office in London. The prisoner had no history of violence and was arrested for a nonviolent protest at Birzeit University. I brought his case to our Evanston chapter and was told we could not adopt due to the current Amnesty International USA policy opposing Palestinian cases. I suggested we should challenge this policy as the rest of the world adopted this particular case. Why not us? Most of the chapter members were unaware of the disparity. The chapter leader was aware of the difference in the US but was unwilling to challenge the US office.

Realizing it would take time, I started to educate other members of the chapter about the human rights situation in the Palestinian territories. My first contact was Liz Stout, a friend from First Presbyterian Church in Evanston who I knew to be open-minded about justice issues. When she heard that most countries in the world took Palestinian cases and the US did not, she was totally on board. I supplied Liz with background information, and she was willing to talk with two friends who were also members of our chapter. I spoke to Shirley Taraki, another member, whose daughter taught at Birzeit University and was married to a Palestinian. Shirley was eager to challenge the policy and adopt Palestinian cases.

Gradually, I gained support from more than half the committee. In six months, I presented a new Palestinian case that the London office had adopted. This time the chair opposed the case, but we urged him to put it to a vote. The Evanston chapter voted to adopt the Palestinian case by a narrow 6–5 vote. Our Evanston chapter decided to write letters of support for the Palestinian case and inform the New York office of our rationale. The chairperson called the New York office and was told not to go public with the decision. We agreed not to go public yet and wrote the New York office asking for permission to make a public statement. Our request was declined.

Within a few months, Naseer Aruri, a Palestinian professor at the University of Massachusetts Dartmouth, ran for a seat on the Amnesty International USA board of directors. We were among the many organizations to mobilize people to join the group as dues-paying members and vote for Naseer. Despite a campaign by zionist organizations to smear Naseer with the "PLO terrorist" label, he won the election. It wasn't long before Amnesty International USA changed its policy and approved adoption of Palestinian cases. Finally, we were in compliance with the rest of the world, perhaps with the exception of Israel.

One of my major projects for 1981 involved organizing a post-Christmas trip to Lebanon, Syria, Jordan, Israel, and occupied Palestine. Our new board of directors decided we should organize a series of fact-finding delegations for Americans to see the Palestinian situation firsthand and then follow up with them when they returned to the United States. I started recruiting participants for the trip through our chapters, the new newsletter, and personal phone calls. By October, over forty people had enlisted. At least a quarter of the participants were from the Christian Laity of Chicago, a group led by my friends Rev. Hal and Betsy Edwards. We recruited educators, journalists and authors, clergy—both African American and Caucasian, and a variety of community leaders.

Meanwhile, as of early December 1981, Israel continued to attack PLO bases in Lebanon and intensified human rights abuses in the West Bank, East Jerusalem, and Gaza Strip. These actions continued despite a truce the United Nations had negotiated between the PLO and Israel, the first truce between the two parties since Israel was founded. The United Nations monitoring agency UNIFIL (United Nations Interim Force in Lebanon) reported several hundred Israeli violations by air, land, and sea between August 1981 and mid-May 1982. We protested the US silence on the matter to no avail. Tension was mounting amid consistent reports that Israel was preparing to invade Lebanon at any moment. Due to these alarming reports, roughly ten people dropped out of the trip.

By mid-December, we decided to go ahead with the trip. We had thirty-six people, including Hal and Betsy Edwards, my wife, Drew, Bud and Donna Ogle, author Grace Halsell (*Soul Sister*, *Journey to Jerusalem*), John Mahoney, director of Americans for Middle East Understanding, Janet Morrow, head of a Chicago city policy think tank and the wife of the president of Standard Oil. Rev. Darrell Myers recruited five clergy and activists from the Los Angeles area. We added Nick Wolterstorff, a philosopher at Calvin College, and his wife, Claire, joined us in Amsterdam where they were on a sabbatical. My good friend and mentor Husni Haddad, a historian and native of Syria, agreed to be a group leader and assist with translations and interpretation of the political situation.

We arrived in Beirut on December 28, 1982, and were welcomed by Gaby Habib, who had arranged a full program for us. After a day of orientation sessions on the history and politics of Lebanon, we left for a meeting with the Maronite leader and future president of Lebanon, Amine Gemayel. Gemayel was one of two sons of Pierre Gemayel, founder of the Phalangist Party and political patriarch of the Maronite community.

Back at our hotel in Beirut, my phone rang around midnight with an urgent call from Gaby, who had just spoken with Bachir Gemayel, the head of the Phalangist militia. Known for his cruelty, Bachir was furious after watching a report on Lebanese television about a "high-profile American delegation" that met with his brother Amine. We were far from a high-profile group, but there were no other American delegations visiting Beirut at the time. The report inflated our importance, and when Bachir learned MECC organized our itinerary, he threatened to kill Gaby unless we met with him.

Bachir was already responsible for two political assassinations and two massacres of Palestinians, so we took his death threat seriously. There was solid evidence that Israel and the CIA were financing the Lebanese forces, with an eye toward installing Bachir as president. The problem was that our delegation was scheduled to meet Lebanon's prime minister at 9 the next morning. Gaby proposed we divide the group in two, with me taking half of the people to meet Bachir Gemayel, and Hal Edwards and Husni Haddad taking the other half to meet with Prime Minister Salim al-Hoss. This satisfied Bachir and Gaby breathed easier.

Our extensive itinerary took us to Damascus for three days, Amman, Jordan for two days, then to Jerusalem, the West Bank, Gaza Strip, and Israel for ten days. In Jordan, we visited the remarkable archaeological site Petra and met with Greek Orthodox church leaders and Hanna Nassir, the exiled president of Birzeit University.

Our group had an unplanned, informal meeting with Senator Charles Percy of Illinois, who was attending a meeting at our hotel in Amman. Percy was one of the only members of Congress calling for dialogue with the PLO in 1982. (This mild support for meeting the PLO cost him his senate seat in the next election as the pro-Israel lobby supported his successor, Paul Simon, who was fully committed to Israel.) We crossed the Jordan River the following morning and visited the ancient site of Qumran where the Dead Sea Scrolls were discovered.

Our visit to the Gaza Strip—witnessing the extreme poverty while experiencing abundant hospitality from our hosts—made a lasting impression on everyone. Those who were not especially sympathetic to the Palestinian cause were usually won over by the hospitality. Our session with Haider Abdel-Shafi, president of the Gaza Red Crescent Society, also had a significant impact on our delegation. His graciousness and lucid analysis of zionism, including its goal of eliminating Palestinian nationalism, was clarifying and shocking. Dr. Haider ranked at the top of everyone's evaluations at the end of the trip.

Ten years later, Haider was the chief negotiator for the Palestinians at the Madrid Peace conference and eventually broke ranks with Yasser Arafat during the Oslo Accords. Abdel-Shafi believed Arafat was conceding too much to Israel with the Palestinians receiving nothing in return. Within a few months of the momentous signing of the Oslo Accords, in September 1993, Abdel-Shafi's warnings proved to be accurate. Israel had no intention of allowing a Palestinian state. The Oslo Accords merely set the stage for a more vicious military occupation.

In Jerusalem, we had an important session with the Israeli human rights attorney Felicia Langer and Israel Shahak, a Hebrew University professor of chemistry and the chair of the Israeli League for Human and Civil Rights. Throughout my decade as director of PHRC, they were my main sources for human rights cases and political analysis. We paid them a modest monthly stipend and I phoned them and transcribed their messages to be posted in our Action Alerts. Felicia was an aggressive and fearless attorney with a passionate commitment to justice for Palestinians. She did not win many cases, but the deck was stacked against her in the Israeli military courts where the army won 99.5 percent of the cases.

As Professor Shahak spoke to our group, I was grateful we had maintained a friendship through these many years. We encouraged our group to subscribe to the "Shahak Reports," a remarkable monthly collection of translations of news events from the *Hebrew Press*, compiled with comments by the professor. The Shahak Reports became a staple of my continuing education on Israel and Palestine. Professor Shahak told us the trained political eye can read between the lines and know what Israel was planning through a careful analysis of the Israeli press. He proceeded to predict a full-scale Israeli invasion of Lebanon in the spring of 1982, with the goal of destroying the PLO, undermining Palestinian nationalism in the West Bank and Gaza, and regime change in Lebanon. He was correct on all three predictions.

One of the most important reports we published from Professor Shahak's translations came in August 1982. It was a special report titled "The Zionist Plan for the Middle East" by Odet Yanon, which predicted Israel's goal of dividing the Middle East into cantons by pitting various ethnic and religious populations against each other. The project was well underway in Lebanon, where Israel was supporting the Maronite population and Phalangist Party. The author described a plan for Iraq, including regime change, and Iraq's division into three or four zones, thus weakening the country. Syria had a similar forecast to Iraq's. Israel's goal was to divide existing countries into competing units in order to give Israel military superiority across the region, a goal the US may have supported.[35] Israel's support of the US invasion of Iraq and the long US military presence demolished the central authority of the Saddam Hussein regime and led to Iraq becoming a failed state. The same pattern occurred in Syria, which is also a failed state. The only country in the region that may still pose a threat to Israel is Iran, where Israel has repeatedly assassinated its scientists and has attempted to bomb its nuclear reactor. The 1982 prophecy of Yanon's report has nearly been achieved by Israel and its powerful lobby in the United States.

Our Palestinian hosts in Jerusalem arranged an enlightening evening of dinners and conversations in homes with Birzeit faculty. We divided ourselves into five groups and had the opportunity to meet with leading personalities such as the acting Birzeit president, Gaby Baramki, and his wife, Hanan Ashrawi, Lisa Taraki and husband, George Giacomin, Suad Amiry and husband Salim Tamari, all of whom were Birzeit University faculty. The fifth group was hosted by Albert Aghazarian and his wife at their home in the Armenian quarter. Albert became a close friend and we worked together for the next decade primarily around academic freedom for Birzeit students and faculty.

We returned to the United States feeling grateful that the trip went well and that Israel decided to delay its invasion of Lebanon. The trip had a significant impact on each participant; some stayed in touch for several years. The PHRC board decided to increase the eyewitness trips, given the success of the one just taken. We set our goal to recruit people who could influence the media and US policy in Congress. Everyone told me I overloaded the itinerary and that people had become exhausted halfway through the trip as a result. It took me a few years to learn "less is more." There are so many sides to the Israeli-Palestinian struggle, and I wanted people to see it all.

We were unable to recruit members of Congress and their staff. Everyone was afraid of the pro-Israel lobby, which had a monopoly on trips to Israel and Palestine. Not a single member of Congress or staff member was willing to risk taking a trip with a Palestinian human rights organization. But we were able to recruit clergy, faculty, public school teachers, medical personnel, and journalists outside of the mainstream media, and put our emphasis on these constituencies.

We needed a new chair of our PHRC board and I was impressed by Nick Wolterstorff, a philosophy professor at Calvin College and later Yale University. Nick and his wife, Claire, were participants in the recent January 1982 PHRC trip and were deeply moved by the experience. Ayoub needed to step down as chair of the board, and Ghada said she would take the position at a later date. Her main priority was adjusting to her new teaching responsibilities as a professor at Lake Forest College on Chicago's North Shore.

I called Nick and floated the idea of him becoming chair. Nick was open to the idea but cautious as he was new to the Palestinian issue. I reassured him that we had several spokesmen for PHRC like Edward Said, Ibrahim Abu-Lughod, Husni Haddad, and many others, but we needed someone who could strengthen our board and provide legitimacy in academia and the churches. He covered both categories. Nick finally agreed and did a terrific job for at least three years before moving to Yale University.

In 1986, I was asked to testify before the House Foreign Affairs Committee on Palestinian Rights. I had developed a working relationship with the chief of staff of the House Foreign Affairs Committee, who told me several Christian fundamentalists were being lined up by AIPAC to testify. These included Jerry Falwell and Pat Robertson of TV's *700 Club*. I decided to ask Ray Bakke, a new PHRC board member and a professor with impeccable evangelical credentials. Ray agreed, as long as I wrote a draft of the presentation and allowed him to modify the text any way he wished.

Ray's presentation challenged the false biblical assumptions of Falwell and Robertson, who claimed, "God gave the holy land to the Jewish people." Ray's appeal with a Jesus-focused reading of the Bible and the demand for justice had a significant impact on the committee and angered AIPAC. He was able to cite numerous human rights violations, including the illegal settlements, and provide a political and theological rationale that essentially undermined the weak presentations by Falwell and Robertson.

Shortly after returning from the Middle East in January 1982, my thoughts turned to our next delegation. I decided to focus on Christian relief and development agencies, hoping to interest them in supporting Palestinian refugees in Lebanon. We extended invitations to several agencies including World Vision, World Relief, and Catholic Relief Services. None of them were interested, but Hal Edwards told me about a new Christian relief and development agency called Mercy Corps International. Hal thought they might be interested.

Mercy Corps had evangelical Christian roots and was linked to the singer Pat Boone, which raised a red flag for me. Pat Boone was one of the leading spokesmen for various pro-Israel causes and a passionate fundamentalist Christian zionist. I had my doubts when I called the son-in-law of Pat Boone, Dan O'Neill, president and chair of the board for Mercy Corps. Dan was married to one of the singing Boone sisters, Cherry, who chronicled her struggle with anorexia and performance anxiety in a best-selling autobiography.

When I reached Dan, he sounded a bit suspicious of me until I said I was a close friend of Hal Edwards. Once I began telling him about the trip Hal and I had led to Lebanon and Israel/Palestine, Dan was all ears. He exclaimed, "Wow, tell me more." I told him about our itinerary and gave a brief introduction to my background as an evangelical Christian. I added that I had recently discovered Middle Eastern Christians and Palestinian human rights. Dan jumped in and said, "I have made a similar journey. You should know that I volunteered in the Israeli Army in the 1973 war and worked with George Otis, a strong pro-Israel leader in the US. He recently set up a radio tower in South Lebanon and is broadcasting Christian programming in Lebanon on a station called the Voice of Hope." I was aware of the station as it was a pro-Israel, fundamentalist Christian zionist station broadcasting Western Christian and country music in English with fundamentalist pro-Israel Bible studies.

I proposed to Dan that we could organize a trip to Lebanon and recruit leaders from Christian relief and development agencies. He was in full agreement and asked for a few days to get his board's approval. I mentioned how useful it was to work with Gaby Habib and the Middle East Council of Churches as they know everyone in Lebanon and have a close working relationship with the PLO and the Red Crescent Society. "MECC will do all the logistics for us," I said. "We can make any suggestions so Mercy Corps can be fully involved with me in the itinerary." I faxed him a proposal with a suggested itinerary and we were in business.

Dan and the group's chair, Ells Culver, recruited nine people from three different relief and development groups, including a physician who served on its board and a cameraman who was to document the trip. As May drew closer, there were increased reports of the long-expected Israeli invasion but no definitive data. We decided to go ahead with the delegation.

Soon after the confirmation, I received a fax from Professor Abu-Lughod suggesting we consider postponing the trip for six months because the PLO was concerned the Israeli invasion could come any day. Dan, Ells, and I discussed a possible postponement but decided we should take the risk as no one had hard information on the invasion and our trip was only ten days in duration.

At the same time, PHRC worked with the United Holy Land Fund and the Red Crescent society to support a delegation of physicians and nurses. They planned to leave in early June, approximately ten days after our departure. A nurse from Northwestern Hospital in Chicago, Elizabeth Elliot, was the organizer of the medical group and worked closely with Mahmoud and Fadwa on arrangements.

The PHRC and Mercy Corps group arrived on May 27, and we began an ambitious itinerary including visits to four Palestinian refugee camps where we were introduced to several projects to be considered for funding and partnership with US agencies. We heard several lectures on the political situation in Lebanon and the history of the Palestinian refugees. On June 3, we drove to Jounieh for a meeting with Maronite and Phalangist party leaders. The medical group landed in Beirut on June 3 and were scheduled to begin volunteering in Red Crescent hospitals in Beirut that weekend.

Our group left the meetings in Jounieh shortly after lunch on Friday, June 4, for the hourlong drive to our next appointment. We were scheduled to meet the PLO spokesman Mahmoud Labadi at 3 PM at his office in the Fakhani district of Beirut. We were surprised by the heavy traffic traveling north from Beirut. The bus driver turned on BBC news and said an anti-PLO Palestinian group tried to assassinate the Israeli ambassador in London. We figured since it was an anti-PLO group there was nothing to worry about, but we were puzzled as to why so many people were leaving Beirut. It slowed us down considerably.

As we crossed the bridge into West Beirut just before 3 PM, two members of our group urgently requested that we stop so they could use the bathroom. I asked if they could wait just fifteen minutes so we wouldn't be late for our appointment. They said it was impossible and we had to stop. The driver said we could make a quick stop at our hotel, which was on the way to the PLO office and I could call Mahmoud Labadi's office from the hotel and apologize for our delay.

Our bus pulled into the Beau Rivage Hotel and the two men ran into the hotel. I stepped out of the bus, and at that precise moment, 3:05 PM, we heard massive explosions followed by the unmistakable sight of F-16 fighter jets flying overhead. The bombing was six or seven blocks from us, and we could feel the vibrations in our bodies. Israel continued bombing the Fakhani area, where we were supposed to be at that exact moment. This was one time I ever thanked God for my late arrival. I told everyone to get out of the bus and we ran to the hotel basement as the bombing intensified.

The bombing lasted twenty to thirty minutes, the entire hotel vibrating with each detonation. We could hear the F-16s sweeping in from the sea in waves, and we wondered if the targets were getting closer to us The Israelis hit several neighborhoods to the south of us, including the soccer stadium, the Cité Sportive. As the bombing intensified, I wondered if Israel was going to hit the large Syrian army base directly across the street from our hotel.

Standing in the basement hallway, I looked around and saw several members of our group weeping, their heads buried in their hands. I felt their anxiety and began to pray the Jesus prayer, synchronizing it with my breathing: "Lord Jesus, Son of God, have mercy on us." I used this simple prayer to elicit a sense of peace and center myself completely in God's presence. It restored a sense of peace within me and took away the anxiety. I thought of my family back home in the US and prayed our travel group would be spared. I prayed for the victims and the medical workers assisting them. I prayed for the protection of our group of doctors and nurses. I prayed for those most vulnerable in the refugee camps to be spared.

Looking across the room, I saw a beautiful young Palestinian mother wearing a hijab, gently rocking her baby, quietly singing in Arabic. She had a smile on her face and reminded me of Madonna and baby Jesus. If I were a painter, I would have captured this beautiful image of inspiration and hope in the midst of a deadly situation. I imagined she had been through this experience several times and knew how to manage it with grace and love. Showing each one of us how to cope, this young Muslim mother was a calming influence for those who watched her.

It was not lost on me that Israel was using US-made F-15s and F-16s and dropping bombs manufactured in the United States. My mood shifted immediately to a sense of outrage that our US tax dollars provided the weapons used to kill so many innocent people—usually civilians. I made a vow to raise this issue with my elected officials when I returned home. PHRC would need to enlist several organizations to challenge Congress on why the US Arms Export Control Act was not enforced with Israel.

As I write at the end of 2025, hundreds of us have been writing, visiting, and setting up remote meetings with our senators and representatives demanding they invoke the US Arms Export Control Act and stop funding Israel's genocidal war in Gaza. We also have the "Leahy law," which complements existing laws conditioning US military aid on human rights performance and international law. There is no question Israel has been violating US law—the International Commission of Jurists has already confirmed this fact. What political analysts call the "Israeli exception" is still in effect forty years later.

The bombing finally stopped, and I joined five members of our group and took the elevator up to the roof to see what had happened. We could see the Fakhani District around six blocks from us with smoke billowing up to the sky. Israel had hit several office and apartment buildings. Only time would tell how many died in this crowded neighborhood. I called Mahmoud Labadi later who said they were okay but the building next to them took a direct hit and at least a dozen civilians were killed and several wounded.

To the south, the Cité Sportive (now the Camille Chamoun Sports City Stadium) had smoke billowing out of several places where Israeli bombs had struck. We learned from BBC and Lebanese television broadcasts that evening that several thousand Palestinian refugees and poor Lebanese lived in the stadium. The broadcasts added that one part of the stadium might have been used as an arms depot by the PLO. Ambulances and fire trucks were rushing to the stadium and entering at one end. Suddenly, four F-16s flew in from the Mediterranean coast and bombed the stadium again, timing the raid to hit the ambulances, fire trucks, and medical personnel. Someone in our group screamed, "Bastards! How could they do this?" Good question. Bombing civilian targets was bad enough, but ambulances and medical personnel? This is beyond cruel. It could also be classified as a war crime. I knew it would never be investigated.

Our group was scheduled to have dinner with Fathi Arafat, Hedla Ayoubi, and the Red Crescent staff at the group's headquarters. It took a few attempts to reach Fathi by phone. When I finally reached him, I suggested that we postpone the dinner as they had endured a terrible tragedy and were coping with the dead and wounded. "Absolutely not," he insisted. "We are preparing now and it is important we meet with you. In fact, it is more important than ever as you have witnessed what we live with here."

I asked about our medical group. He told me they arrived in the late afternoon and were safe. He and Hedla would be meeting them tomorrow morning. Fathi said over 300 had been killed in the bombing raids and well over 1,000, perhaps as many as 1,300, were wounded or maimed. The overwhelming majority of the dead and wounded were civilians, while some medical personnel had been killed or wounded when the stadium was bombed. He did not have confirmed statistics at that time.

When our delegation arrived at the Red Crescent headquarters, Fathi and Hedla welcomed us with smiles and graciousness. I knew they were tired, and there was deep sorrow beneath their smiling faces, yet they prepared a giant plate of *makloubeh,* the Palestinian dish that translates to "upside down." It is a delicious blend of rice, vegetables, and in this case chicken, steamed in a huge pot. Once it is fully cooked, a large tray is placed on top of the pot and a strong person flips it over. Once the pot is removed, the successful *makloubeh* stands tall and proud like a perfectly prepared cake. The chef did the flipping honors when we arrived, and the presentation was picture perfect. It was served with a side salad, yogurt, pita bread, and other trimmings. *Makloubeh* has become my favorite Palestinian dish. Whenever I have it, I remember the memorable evening with Fathi and Hedla.

During our discussion after dinner, Hedla emphasized the sad fact that nearly all the deaths that day were civilians, including a large number of children, medical workers, and firefighters. We asked them about the Israeli justification for the war, which seemed to be an unprovoked assault. Fathi said Israel claimed its ambassador in London, Shlomo Argov, was wounded in an attempted assassination the previous day. He said the PLO had nothing to do with the London attack. In fact, it was carried out by the Abu-Nidal group, a tiny militia based in Iraq that was an anti-PLO organization. It had killed several PLO leaders and attempted to kill Yasser Arafat in seven separate incidents.

Fathi added, "Earlier today, Scotland Yard identified the Abu Nidal group as the party responsible for the attack and said the PLO had nothing to do with it. Israel's actions are completely offensive; this is in no way a defensive war. The PLO has sent no rockets into Israel so they started this war, but you can count on the fact that Israel and the Western media will say the PLO started it."

I added, "This also means Israel has intentionally violated US law by using US weapons and aircraft in an unjustified offensive capacity to kill innocent civilians." I mentioned the US Arms Export Control Act adopted by Congress in 1976. Fathi was unaware of the law and very interested in this fact. He said they would file a complaint with the United Nations and the US Congress. He asked me to write down these laws for him.

He added, "Israel has been trying for nearly a year to find an excuse to justify this war, but we haven't given them anything to justify an attack. Now they have invented an excuse and will try to sell it to the United States and the rest of the world." This was not the first time Israel had been involved in such an incident. Then he said, "I would not put it past Israel to have recruited the Abu-Nidal group to attack the ambassador in London."

The next morning, June 5, we visited the Gaza Red Crescent Hospital adjacent to Sabra and Shatila refugee camps. To this day, the hospital serves Palestinian refugees and poor Lebanese who are forced to live in the crowded camps and the poverty-stricken suburbs of south Beirut. We took a tour of the hospital and visited the wing hit by a bomb the previous afternoon. Several rooms were closed and under repair. Fortunately, patients had been evacuated during the bombing so there were no deaths or injuries at the hospital. Due to the large number of injuries during the Friday bombings, the hospital was filled to capacity.

Among the many parallels between the Israeli invasion of Lebanon in 1982 and the current genocidal war in the Gaza Strip, one is the Israeli claim of "precision bombing" that supposedly avoids places like hospitals and civilians including women and children. Despite Israel's use of artificial intelligence instruments in the Gaza genocide, IDF spokesmen have stated that when Hamas suspects are targeted, the deaths of 100 or more civilians in the building, including women and children, is an acceptable consequence. The cynical use of AI programs like the one named "Where's Daddy" allow for 2,000-pound US-made bombs to be dropped on apartment complexes, capable of killing over 300 people at a time and leaving a gaping hole where buildings once stood.

~

Following this visit to the rooms, we were on our way to a briefing by medical staff when there was furious activity and an alarm sounded. We were rushed to the basement and medical personnel began to evacuate patients and wheel them downstairs. Hospital officials told us Israeli aircraft had been sighted in the area and another bombing raid was possible. We remained in the basement for approximately an hour when we saw several ambulances arrive at the emergency entrance not far from where we were standing.

Nurses and medical personnel rushed to the ambulances and began to remove young girls, some screaming and others crying in pain as they were carried into the emergency ward on stretchers. We could see some were badly burned. We learned they had been on a United Nations-sponsored field trip, in clearly marked UN buses, when Israel dropped bombs on all three buses on the coastal road. Shortly after the ambulances arrived, a number of cars pulled up with families crying and wailing as they received news of their daughters' fate. Medical workers began to unload the first group of body bags with the bodies of girls who had been killed on the buses.

A second ambulance pulled up and more families arrived on the scene. Blood-curdling screams filled the air as they watched the body bags and wounded girls being removed from the ambulances. A nurse made her way to our group and informed us that nineteen girls had been killed and others had lost limbs and were in serious condition. One of the girls who had died, Saidi Sayed, was sixteen years old. Her mother and sister wailed, tears streaming from their eyes as the nurse translated the Arabic mantra her mother was wailing: "Saidi, Saidi, my baby Saidi, my baby is gone. Why O Allah, why? Is this our destiny?" The wailing haunted us, piercing our hearts and bringing us to tears.

The overwhelming collective grieving shook our travel group to the core. One of our men ran to the bathroom and vomited, overcome by the stress. We watched as one of the medical staff took the bag that contained the body of Saidi to a room beside the emergency exit. Saidi's sister tried to follow him, screaming, "Please, let me be with my sister. Please, please." She pushed her way to the door as medical people tried to calm her, but they could not hold her back. Two men we assumed were her father and brother came and embraced her as they all stood wailing by the door that closed in front of them. The poor inconsolable sister collapsed on the floor from exhaustion.

I had never seen such grief and agony in my life. An innocent school trip in well-marked United Nations buses brought such needless suffering to these poor people. It was another massacre in the long series of massacres Palestinians have suffered at the hands of Israel. The Palestinian nurse translating for us remarked, "I know these UN programs. I was a participant when I was in high school. Every bus is clearly marked with the large UN insignia on the roof and sides of each bus. The United Nations informs the Israeli military about their routes in advance. There is no question Israel knew what these buses were doing. They knew two days ago the times and the route the buses would be taking. Believe me, this was not an accident. You should investigate this incident with UNRWA and they will tell you the facts. A United Nations bus filled with high school girls should not be a military target."

This horrific event and the suffering it caused devastated everyone in our travel group. We were all mourning the senseless death of innocent teenagers paying the ultimate price simply because they were Palestinians. We were told the medical staff would not be available to meet us and the nurses apologized. Of course we understood and wished them God's peace and safety. We left the horrifying scene at Gaza Hospital and drove to a restaurant for lunch.

Most of the group could not eat, me included. I asked our bus driver if he knew where the US news offices for CNN, CBS, ABC, and NBC were located. He called his office and found the addresses. All were all within a few blocks of where we were having lunch. Ells stayed with the group while Dan and I drove to the offices. We rang the doorbells of CNN, CBS, and ABC but no one responded. Finally, we stopped at NBC and found Bureau Chief Mike Mallory, who answered the door. We told him what we experienced at Gaza Hospital, and he was very interested.

Mike called a cameraman and found a small park where he could interview Dan and me. We described who we were, why we were in Beirut, and what we had just witnessed. We went into detail about the scene at the hospital and the tragedy of the Palestinian schoolgirls. We noted the bombing of a wing of the hospital and the high number of civilian casualties, countering the myth of Israel's "surgical strikes hitting PLO terrorists." We made a strong case that the entire Israeli military operation was illegal and not provoked by the PLO. We also expressed anger at how our tax dollars were being used to finance the killing of innocent civilians, and the possible illegality of Israel's use of F-16s and US-made bombs against civilian targets.

Mike affirmed our message and warned us, "We know the news footage we sent yesterday was cut in the New York studio by Israeli censors, so very little, if anything, has been reported in the US on what has happened on the ground in Beirut the past twenty-four hours." This was depressing news and a new dimension of Israel's management of US media. Mike said, "There may be a chance your interview will escape censorship since you are Americans who witnessed this disaster. But I can't promise anything. I'll send the tape up to our station on the mountain immediately and they will transfer it to New York via satellite this afternoon."

We thanked Mike Mallory for caring about the issue and encouraged him to continue telling the truth. We alerted our families to start watching NBC, asking them to let us know if the report aired. By Monday morning we learned NBC did not air the interview. Mike Mallory was correct. The US and Israeli censors had successfully filtered the news and were broadcasting Israel's version of the events in Lebanon.

Studies were conducted on how the media covered the invasion of Lebanon during the June 4–July 15,1982, period. The first month of the news coverage was effectively monitored by the Israeli censors. Gradually, both print and television and radio news began to allow some, but not many, independent journalists to provide more accurate accounts. By the third week in July, the media coverage began to shift, offering accounts that were critical of Israel and the high numbers of civilian casualties for the first time.

When I returned to the United States the second week of June, I watched all the networks and listened to various radio broadcasts including National Public Radio. I was appalled by the uncritical pro-Israel reporting. Most of the TV footage carried a byline that declared, "The following report has been approved by the Israeli Defense Forces for broadcast." Our task was to challenge that narrative with what we had witnessed with our own eyes. If NBC News could not tell the truth, I wondered what chance we would have to challenge the Israeli narrative. I was about to find out.

Chapter 15

WHEN THEY CALL YOU AN EXTREMIST

"But though I was initially disappointed at being categorized as an extremist, as I continued to think about the matter, I gradually gained a measure of satisfaction from the label... Was not Jesus an extremist for love? 'Love your enemies, bless them that curse you, do good to them that hate you, and pray for them which despitefully use you, and persecute you.' Was not Amos an extremist for justice? 'Let justice roll down like waters and righteousness like an ever-flowing stream.' So the question is not whether we will be extremists, but what kind of extremists we will be. Will we be extremists for hate or for love? Will we be extremists for the preservation of injustice or for the extension of justice?"

—Martin Luther King Jr., "Letter From a Birmingham Jail"

Saturday evening I called for a meeting of our delegation in Beirut to process the tragic deaths we had witnessed that day and the impending Israeli war on Lebanon. Most of the people in the group had not experienced that kind of death and destruction. Everyone discussed their grief with openness and vulnerability. One man did not speak, but the rest of us welcomed the opportunity to process what was going on inside our hearts and minds.

Afterward, I asked the group if we should consider leaving Beirut in the next day or two because there were reports the Israelis might intensify the bombing and it was likely that the airport would be reduced to rubble. I reminded them of our upcoming meeting with the US ambassador to Lebanon at 9 the next morning, at which we might get an update on the situation. The group was split down the middle. Half wanted to leave as soon as possible, and the other half wanted to stay another week. I offered to call our travel agent after the meeting and ask him to begin rebooking flights back to the United States for those wanting to leave early.

Just as I was taking down the names for early departures, my friend Mahmoud Labadi, the PLO spokesman, walked into the room. We were glad to see him alive after the close call on Friday's bombing of the Fakhani neighborhood. With a note of cynical humor, he apologized for having to miss the meeting Friday, saying, "The Israelis have a way of disrupting our meetings with such rude actions as bombing our buildings."

Then Mahmoud turned to a serious matter. He said the main reason he wanted to see us, aside from thanking us for coming to Lebanon, was the latest intelligence he just received. "By all indications, it is now clear Israel will begin a full-scale invasion as early as tomorrow, or Monday at the latest. I urge you to rebook your flights now because it is likely they will destroy the airport after Western diplomats depart. The European and American diplomats are scheduling departures on Monday and Tuesday, according to our sources. You should probably leave no later than Tuesday at noon."

Then he explained, "We need you to return to the United States and tell people what you have witnessed here. You may know the Israeli censors are sanitizing the major US networks and the truth is not being told to the American people. The same is happening in parts of Europe. You are among the only people from the United States in Beirut now, other than your medical group, a few reporters whose dispatches are censored, and the diplomats. "We can't expect the diplomats to tell the truth because as in the case of the US, they are paid to support Israel."

He continued, "It's only people like you from civil society who can help us break this wall of silence. You will need to be courageous as you stand up to the lies the media will tell. There isn't much you can do here now so I'm sorry to say you should leave and your real mission is at home. I thank you again for being with us and I hope you will return so we can meet after the war is over—if we survive. You are very important to us and we are counting on you."

Mahmoud took a few questions from those who wanted to stay in Beirut, but I had made up my mind to return. Mahmoud was more emphatic about returning as he addressed those who wanted to stay. Then he excused himself. I gave him a hug before he left and told him he could count on us. I urged, "Please contact me at my Chicago number," and handed him a card with my contact information. "Just call or fax me with your updates and I'll send them to the rest of the group."

It was interesting to me that Palestinians like Labadi had never been in the United States, yet his political analysis was the only hope for Palestinians at the grassroots level. They knew the power of the pro-Israel lobby and that its influence on the media was so extensive in 1982 that the bottom-up grassroots approach was their best hope. Forty years later, the situation has only improved slightly; the small minority of members of Congress who support Palestinian rights and social media have opened up other forms of media that aren't under zionist control. Some churches have embraced Palestinian rights and justice, as have young Muslims and Jews under the age of forty, yet it has been the grassroots protests in the streets and on university campuses that offer the greatest hope. It may be decades before we can influence Congress and change the mainstream media.

He gave me another hug, his big smile beaming, and murmured, "Thank you so much for what you will do." I wondered if I would ever see him alive again. Mahmoud Labadi was a marked man.

Now we had clarity about our decision. We were needed in the United States, not in Beirut. As Mahmoud said, we would probably get in the way as their strong hospitality instincts would divert them from what they should be doing to survive. I told the group I had previously planned to stay another week, but Mahmoud's information was decisive. We needed to return to the US and start working to break the censorship and domination of the narrative the Israelis were spinning in the United States. I took a quick poll of the group, and now everyone was on board with an early departure. I called the travel agent and asked him to rebook us on the earliest flights possible starting the next afternoon. I also called Gaby Habib about the change, and he said it was a wise decision.

The next morning, we pulled up to the fortress-like American Embassy building in Beirut. A secretary told us we would meet the chief information officer, Ryan Crocker. After clearing security, we were taken to Crocker's office (he went on to have a long and distinguished career in the foreign service). Crocker, who was in his mid- to late-thirties, asked us why we were in Lebanon and wondered if we realized we were at risk. Finding this comment insulting, I simply responded, "Of course. We hadn't planned on a war. But now our primary concern is why our government is supporting this war. We've watched the US-made F-16s bomb mostly civilian targets including a hospital wing." I mentioned the bombing of UN school buses and what we witnessed at the hospital. "We've seen too much and are angry," I said. "Can you shed some light on why the US is subsidizing these attacks?"

I expected him to be defensive, but instead his response was diplomatic and measured. He said Israel needed to defend itself from PLO rocket attacks and the United States supported these efforts. I mentioned there had been no PLO rockets since the treaty the previous July, according to the United Nations, and that Friday's assassination attempt in London was not by the PLO but an anti-PLO group. Israel's use of US weapons was not defensive. They were the ones who started this war. The PLO did not fire the first rockets and bombs; it was Israel on Friday, June 4, and we had witnessed it.

Dan O'Neill followed up by detailing our experience the previous day at Gaza Hospital. He described the ambulances arriving with the bodies of nineteen teenage girls and several others who had been wounded and maimed by Israeli air strikes on United Nations buses. Dan also raised the Israeli bombing of the sports stadium. We learned later that several medics and civilians were killed in the raid. Dan asked, "Don't we have an ethical and legal responsibility as US citizens when our tax dollars are used to kill innocent civilians, including nurses and doctors?" Dan added that we had filmed the bombing and planned to show it in the US.

Crocker seemed caught off guard by our questions and was spared having to answer when a secretary burst into the room, announcing that Israeli tanks and soldiers just crossed the border into South Lebanon. The long-anticipated full-scale invasion of Lebanon had officially begun. Crocker muttered a curse and asked us to excuse him as an emergency meeting would have to be convened to deal with this new development. As he left the room, he advised us to leave Lebanon as soon as possible. It was clear: the war was on.

I called Gaby Habib from our hotel to check on the status of our flights. He said everyone was booked to leave on Tuesday morning, the earliest they could find seats. He said most westerners were leaving Beirut. I asked him about our nurses' group and he said they were doing well and were with Fathi and Hedla Ayoubi. I called Elizabeth Elliot, my friend in charge of the delegation, and told her we were advised to leave immediately and were flying out tomorrow. When I suggested she and the others might consider doing the same, she replied that they had only been there two days and were planning to stay, adding that as trained nurses and physicians, they might be needed to work in the hospitals. I wished them well and thanked them for being there.

On Monday morning we went to the MECC office and got our tickets from Gaby's travel agent. Gaby gave us some final words of appreciation and asked about the experiences that stood out for us. Nearly everyone mentioned the day at Gaza Hospital and the tragic experience of seeing the dead and wounded Palestinian schoolgirls arriving at the emergency ward. One person said the question of who the real terrorists were in this case, had struck him as important. He added, "And it's not the Palestinians as our media portrays the situation here." Someone else said our biggest challenge would be when we returned home and began to interpret our experience to the media, the churches, and our families.

As we were ending our session with Gaby, one member of our group told him, "Thanks for arranging the war—it made the time in Lebanon unforgettable." We laughed and closed with heartfelt prayers, primarily for Gaby and his staff, their families, and for all the people we were leaving behind. Their safety was foremost in our hearts. We were flying home tomorrow, but they could not leave. We knew the days and weeks ahead would be extremely difficult for them. We committed ourselves to pray and work on their behalf in the United States.

On Monday evening we held our final dinner and reviewed various ways we could work more effectively when we returned home. The next morning, after an early breakfast, we left for the airport. The group had grown to respect each other, and we were grateful for the experience, despite all the trauma we had witnessed. I was the only one booked on the Air France flight through Paris. Dan O'Neill told me later that he was on one of the last flights out of Beirut that morning, and he recognized several US Embassy staff who were on the same flight. We learned later that Israel bombed the airport early Tuesday afternoon, shortly after the US Embassy staff left. The timing of the airport bombing was no mere coincidence.

As I settled into my seat, I felt a sense of guilt for having abandoned our Lebanese and Palestinian friends. I thought about specific people, especially the vulnerable refugees and the poor crowded into apartment buildings that were now Israel's targets. What would the terror of the daily bombing do to children? Would they ever heal from the trauma? I couldn't help but feel I was abandoning them, but what could I do? The one saving grace was their plea that we all go home and tell their story. That was my mission for the coming months.

Once I landed in Paris, I had two hours before boarding my flight to Chicago. I called Drew with the new arrival time and asked her to contact my office and have them set up some interviews for me with radio and television stations. She offered to call my mom and dad to let them know I was on my way home and all was well. She was relieved I was safe and coming home early. I ordered a cup of coffee and a croissant, but my heart and mind were still in Beirut. The trip was so intense, I knew it would take a few days to adjust to being back in Chicago and begin taking up my responsibility to those I had left behind.

I was still haunted by the sound of F-16s bombing Beirut's neighborhoods. Every time I heard a plane taking off from the airport, I flashed back to the sound of the F-16s coming in from the Mediterranean. My anger was triggered immediately. How many people would they kill on this bombing mission? And one of the worst dimensions for me was how US taxpayers were footing the bill for this senseless killing. A delicious meal, a glass of wine, and I was asleep from sheer exhaustion.

Drew met me at O'Hare Airport, and it was good to be back in Chicago with Drew and our household. I called Mom, Dad, my sister, and Jay to let them know I had just returned and was safe. Just hearing their voices helped my transition to normalcy. My mind kept flashing back to Beirut, wondering what was happening as the war rolled out hour by hour. My office staff had booked three interviews, including one with a live interview opposite an Israeli general, on our Chicago NBC affiliate. They also set up a separate press conference, three radio interviews, and a meeting with reporters from the *Chicago Sun-Times* and the *Chicago Daily News*. I thanked them for a job well done and knew I had to hit the ground running the next day.

After a good night's sleep, I headed for the office the next morning and was greeted with warmth and hugs from the office staff, who were anxious to hear my analysis of the situation. Just then, a call came in from Tim Weigel, a sports reporter for NBC. He told me he was the anchor for the news program I was to be interviewed on later that day and that Israeli General Shromi would be in the studio but had insisted that I be somewhere else. I told Tim the guests should not be telling him how to do his show and that I would like to be in the same room with the general. I asked him to call the Israeli Consulate or whoever was arranging the interview and insist that we be interviewed together. Tim agreed and said he would call me back to let me know the outcome.

A few minutes later, Tim called back to say that unfortunately someone else at the station had already agreed to allow the Israeli general to be interviewed separately in the studio. I didn't believe him, but I bit my tongue, then I expressed my frustration and eventually agreed to do the interview. It meant I had to be interviewed in a park by Lake Michigan. I should not have been surprised by Israel's ability to control the news. At least I would have the opportunity to deliver my perspective, knowing full well that I had to be on high alert to analyze and repudiate the general's spin on the war.

I arrived in the park by Lake Michigan around 3:30 PM and found the NBC staff setting up their cameras and equipment. They hooked me up with a microphone and headset, and we were ready to go. They had a small monitor that enabled me to see the live news feed with General Shromi and host Tim Weigel.

The general spoke first, describing Israel's actions as a defensive necessity due to PLO rocket attacks on the Galilee. He insisted the Israeli air strikes were hitting PLO terrorists with "surgical precision" The general had already told three lies that I was ready to refute, but I knew I should take the offensive rather than simply refute his false claims.

Then General Shromi made a statement that was shocking and something I decided to focus on immediately. As the general concluded his opening remarks, he bellowed, "We believe Israel's 'Peace for Galilee' operation will be the final solution to the Palestinian problem."

Tim Weigel asked if I would like to respond to the general. Without hesitation, I replied, "Thank you for the opportunity. General Shromi, I can't believe what you just said. You stated, and I quote, 'the Peace for Galilee operation will be the final solution to the Palestinian problem.' Isn't that what Hitler and the Nazis said about Jews during the Holocaust? I have studied the Holocaust extensively and have always stood with Jews in their fight against antisemitism. I just returned from Beirut yesterday, and let me tell you what I observed firsthand. I have seen Israel's bombing raids hitting mostly civilian targets and can document everything I say with the reports of international medical and human rights organizations.

"My travel group watched from our hotel roof last Friday, June 4, as over 300 Palestinian and Lebanese civilians were killed that day. The first attacks were at 3:05 PM on the Fakhani neighborhood. We were huddled in our hotel some six blocks from the airstrikes and the hotel shook from the intensity of the bombing. A hospital wing was bombed that day and we visited it the next morning and saw the destruction.

"When the first bombing raid subsided, we went up to the hotel roof and saw US F-16s come in from the Mediterranean at 3:45 PM and bomb a stadium full of refugees. The bombs hit ambulances and medical staff who were summoned when the area was bombed shortly after 3 PM. On Saturday morning, June 5, our group had been touring that hospital and saw the damaged wing, when several ambulances arrived with teenage girls who were on a field trip in clearly marked United Nations buses. Their buses were bombed by Israeli jets on the coastal road south of Beirut. We cried as we saw nineteen body bags unloaded from the ambulances. Then came the stretchers carrying young teenage girls, shrieking and writhing in pain, some with their arms and legs blown off. By then their mothers and families arrived and were wailing in grief. It was a nightmare for these families. Your claim that the bombs are hitting terrorists 'with surgical precision' is simply false. What Israel is doing constitutes war crimes.

"Your army and air force are killing innocent children, women, and men, and as an American citizen, I am appalled that these are US-made weapons Israel is using illegally. This is a clear violation of the US Export Control Act that forbids US made weapons to be used in an offensive capacity against civilians. Israel started this war without provocation, and by hitting mainly civilian targets, it can be classified as a war crime, General. For you to use Hitler's language of a 'final solution' is immoral. How can you stoop this low and think you can get away with a few sound-bites? This carnage has to stop and your rhetoric about a 'final solution' is an absolute outrage."

The host asked the general to respond. Clearly flustered and on the defensive, he tried to walk back what he had said. "I meant the final solution in the sense of protecting our citizens in Israel." I did not let him off the hook. I circled back and repeated his assertion clearly borrowed from Hitler's plan to exterminate Jews. I asked, "Is this what the general is telling us? The Jewish state is planning to exterminate the Palestinian people?" At that point, Tim Weigel ended the interview.

I returned to my office and within fifteen minutes I had a call from Tim Weigel. He said their switchboard lit up during the interview, exploding with angry complaints about what I had said. Most people were saying I had delivered pro-PLO propaganda and should be censored. I later learned that Weigel's boss told him to never invite me back. I responded, "Look, I did not exaggerate one thing in that interview. Everything I said was accurate and I can confirm it with independent sources. The number of casualties I mentioned is less than what the Red Cross is reporting. I understated the situation and NBC needs to do their own investigation. Just talk to Mike Mallory, your bureau chief in

Beirut. The general offered you propaganda and was foolish enough to make the 'final solution' argument. I had to challenge him."

After I hung up, I wondered if I had been too aggressive. If I was coming across as too aggressive or angry, then perhaps I needed to tone down my statements so my case would be heard. My staff thought I had done a great job, but then they were biased. I could not have let the general get away with his racist remarks, including the reference to exterminating Palestinians or the fiction about Israel's "surgical precision."

Challenging a dominant narrative in the media when it involves the United States or a powerful nation like Israel will inevitably evoke strong responses. You'll be labeled an extremist or part of the lunatic fringe. I remembered the famous quote from "Letter from a Birmingham Jail," when Dr. King was accused by the white establishment of being an extremist. King wrote, "Will we be extremists for the preservation of injustice or for the extension of justice?" There is an uncomfortable price to be paid when you take a stand for an unpopular truth. I found it interesting that, two days later, General Shromi was recalled from his national media tour and replaced with a more moderate Israeli military spokesman.

I believe this was the first time I understood that the goals of zionism and the State of Israel were the erasure of the Palestinian people, whether slowly or in large massacres. The Nakba that began in 1948 was a continuous operation—as the early zionists stated, "inch by inch we will take the land." My awareness of settler colonial ideology and its goals of replacing the indigenous population was not developed at this time, but I began to grasp the goals of Zionism and the State of Israel with greater clarity after hearing the general invoke the "final solution."

The Palestinian organizations in Chicago and across the US and Canada were remarkably united that summer. In the past, some Palestinian political factions refused to cooperate with organizations espousing a different political line. These political divisions evaporated temporarily with the crisis in Lebanon. Our demonstrations in Chicago were large—500–750 strong—and spirited. We even had over 1,000 participants on two occasions that summer.

In mid-June 1982, PHRC was the lead organizer of one of the 1,000-plus demonstrations in front of the Israeli Consulate in Chicago. I called for a meeting of the seven or eight organizations that cosponsored the rally. We agreed in advance to rule out the most extreme slogans and chants, especially anything hinting of antisemitism and violence. The latter was a difficult point to negotiate, but I insisted on it or PHRC would withdraw. Despite the agreements, a group called the General Union of Palestinian Students (GUPS) showed up late and burned the US and Israeli flags during the demonstration. I knew there would be repercussions.

The next morning, I read my *Chicago Tribune* on the train as I headed for the office. I was eager to see if there was an article about the rally and if it had received fair coverage. About halfway through the first section I saw a picture of the students burning the US and Israeli flags. PHRC was mentioned in the caption as the chief sponsor of the rally. There was no article accompanying the photo despite the fact that I had given a long interview to a *Chicago Tribune* reporter, providing context and information about the high numbers of Palestinian and Lebanese civilian casualties.

The caption under the photo stated, "Palestinian protesters burn US and Israeli flags in front of the Israeli Consulate organized by the Palestine Human Rights Campaign." This was the only text. There was no mention of the Israeli invasion of Lebanon, the number of civilian casualties, documentation from the Red Cross, or anything I had said in the interview. We were made to look like the lunatic fringe burning the US and Israeli flags. The photo was a gift to the Israeli propaganda campaign.

With a sense of dread, I waited for the other shoe to drop. I prepared the staff to be peaceful as we would be receiving a series of threatening and ugly phone calls. There was no need to escalate the tension with what we said in response. I was especially concerned about threats to our female staff and told them to keep a careful record of all threats. I told them if there was an abusive call, to be sure to record it. (We had a recording device for phone calls.) I said if they were verbally attacked with threats of violence or sexual abuse, they should feel free to put me on the call, especially if it is a violent male on the other end of the line. We needed to report all threats to the Chicago police as they were responsible for our security. I hesitated but thought the FBI should be notified in select cases. At the same time, I did not trust the FBI as they were often working against us.

We did record several threatening calls, but the surprise came on the following day. The rental contract on our office space arrived in the mail, and I was eager to see it as it was about to expire the following week. I was shocked to read a certified letter stating that we would need to vacate the office space within two weeks. No reasons were given, but we knew the reason.

Our office building was owned by Arthur Rubloff & Co., a large Chicago-based reality company and a major donor to pro-Israel causes. We also learned the Pritzker family, owners of the Hyatt Hotels chain, was sponsoring Peace for Galilee bonds that went straight to the Israeli Defense Forces. These two agencies worked together in their support of pro-Israel causes and, in this case, financial support for the war in Lebanon. Rubloff & Co. was not pleased with an organization challenging Israel's invasion of Lebanon and burning flags at the Israeli Consulate.

We started packing, and I found a new office just two blocks away. After the flag burning, I told representatives of GUPS that they owed us a huge favor and could pay us back by helping us move to our new office. They were pleased to assist, and I made sure they got the message to check with me prior to taking such actions as flag burnings in the future. I understood their anger, but these actions have consequences and in this case we paid the price, not them. They were still gloating over having their picture in the newspaper, so I'm not sure they really heard me. The burning of the flag taught me to take more control of the demonstrations and alert our internal security people to intercept such actions before they happened.

When I returned from Beirut, I learned about the major anti-nuclear rally scheduled in New York City on June 12. Organizers were promising the largest anti-war demonstration since the anti-Vietnam War protests in the late sixties and early seventies. I knew some of the organizers from Chicago and New York and made a few last-minute appeals to see if they would include someone giving a two-minute statement on the war in Lebanon. I offered to come at no cost or to send my friend Rev. Tony Wolfe, my roommate on the recent trip to Lebanon who was director of the SANE/Freeze peace movement in Los Angeles.

Our request to offer a statement was turned down. One of the organizers told me the sponsoring organizations were scared to death their coalition would unravel if they raised the Palestinian issue and the war in Lebanon. He said they knew they would lose half of their major donors, who were sympathetic with Israel and unwilling to criticize the war. So much for truth-telling. Palestine was too controversial for the mainstream peace movement, even with a hot war in process as they met.

Unfortunately, this is still the case with many liberal organizations that adhere to the zionist narrative. We can review most of the mainstream Democratic senators and representatives or read the Democratic Party platform. At the same time, a new breed of progressive groups such as Black Lives Matter, many Hispanic progressive movements, young Jews, as well as organizations like Jewish Voice for Peace, If Not Now, and American Muslims for Palestine are growing into sophisticated and efficient movements, as are several other Muslim organizations. Nearly every mainline Protestant denomination today has a strong Palestine justice network and is taking strong positions on BDS (the Boycott, Divestment, and Sanctions movement), and using the apartheid analysis of Israel.

Dan O'Neill, Ells Culver, and I spoke regularly throughout the summer of 1982. They were working with the media and had some success in the Seattle and Portland areas with the Bullitt family, owners of a chain of television stations in the Pacific Northwest. Dan mused on one of our calls, "You know what? I think we need to return to Lebanon when the war is over." Each one of us had been thinking the same thing. We wanted to make a follow-up trip and bring proposals for specific projects we could support in Lebanon in partnership with the MECC and the Red Crescent.

Dan and Ells agreed to draft the relief and development proposals for medical projects. I offered to draft a proposal to educate Western evangelicals concerning the plight of Middle Eastern Christians and the Palestinian case. Most evangelical Christians in North America and Europe were unaware of the existence of 15 million Middle Eastern Christians. And they were often both ignorant and hostile to Palestinians due to their distorted interpretation of the Bible.

~

The summer of 1982 was a period of accelerated learning for me. I was struggling to adjust my political and theological analysis to incorporate the rising crisis caused by the Israeli invasion of Lebanon. One new insight was increasingly clear to me. The United States gave Israel the green light to invade Lebanon, and the Reagan administration was fully behind Israel and against the Palestinians. A related issue was that the CIA was working closely with Israel to destroy the Palestinian presence in Lebanon and push for regime change in Lebanon.

The most likely candidate for the presidency of Lebanon was none other than Bachir "The Butcher" Gemayel of the extremist Phalangist Party. I mentioned earlier how Bachir led at least two massacres of Palestinians and assassinated two of his Lebanese political opponents. He even threatened my friend Gabriel Habib, general secretary of the Middle East Council of Churches, because he did not meet with our American group. If Bachir became president of Lebanon, he would increase the role of Israel in Lebanon, which spelled doom for Palestinians.

I had no idea what to do about these political developments, but they provided important context for our thinking and how limited we were in resisting the cabal of Israel, the CIA, Mossad (Israel's international spy agency), and the Reagan administration. We did not have the base of support that could influence Congress, the State Department, or the people shaping Middle East policy in the administration. All that was left was to develop a stronger grassroots movement of opposition and try our best to influence the media and the handful of congressmen and women who would listen to us.

A colleague working at the United Nations told me to contact Don Betz, a professor from Oklahoma who was working part-time at the UN in New York. She said his project was something I should be aware of and get involved in if possible. I reached him by phone and Don explained his ambitious project. His dream was to organize an international movement of nongovernmental organizations focused on the question of Palestine and to develop a relationship between the NGOs and the United Nations. It was a plan to mobilize people at the grassroots level on every continent and connect them to each other and to the United Nations.

As I listened to his project I wondered if we could involve PHRC and other like-minded organizations in the emerging network. Don said this was his hope and that he would like to spend more time discussing it with me. He would be flying through Chicago the following week on his way home to Oklahoma and wondered if I could meet him at the airport for lunch. I said, "Absolutely yes, I'll be there."

We met at a restaurant at O'Hare Airport and the two of us found several interests in common. I liked Don immediately. He was intellectually sharp with a good grasp of the Middle East and Palestinian history in particular. He was an organizer whose vision for an NGO network was urgently needed. I was amazed by the scope of the NGO project, which was both global and local, and would build networks around the world focused on the question of Palestine.

The project was launched within a year with a meeting at the UN. Don returned to Northeastern Oklahoma University but served as the chair of the International Coordinating Committee on the Question of Palestine. The project was tied to the Division of Palestinian Rights, the main United Nations program assigned in 1975 to support the Palestinian issue.

~

The summer of 1982 brought more opportunities for speaking engagements than I could fulfill. Most were with various Arab American organizations, so most of my audiences were sympathetic. People were interested in my experiences in Beirut and my analysis of the situation. The second-most available venue was college campuses, particularly those with Arab student organizations. On a personal level, the opportunities were very rewarding, allowing me to build PHRC chapters in various parts of the United States.

One of the most memorable events of the summer of 1982 took place at the University of California, Santa Barbara. The local GUPS people invited me to address the student body. I urged them to reach out to churches, peace organizations, and faculty. When I arrived at their beautiful campus, I was pleased to see they had worked hard to build a large and diverse audience, despite it being summer.

I delivered my usual speech with slides covering the Israeli invasion, including scenes of the bombing of the UN school bus and the media cover-up. I concentrated on the high level of civilian casualties and how the war was entirely an offensive one started by Israel and, as such, illegal under US law. I urged the audience to raise these points with their senators and members of the House, calling for an end to the war and an investigation into its illegality. Most of the audience seemed receptive to my talk, with only a few hostile questions and statements, which was typical.

After the speech and the question-and-answer period ended, the student hosts suggested we go to a radio interview at a local station and then they would take me to dinner. As we were walking toward the parking lot, one of the students noticed a middle-aged man raising a gun, pointing it at me. The student rushed him from behind while the man was yelling about his intent to kill me for spreading PLO propaganda. The brave student grabbed his gun while another called campus security. The man was apprehended and later turned over to police.

Fortunately, he seemed to be a solitary actor. I'll forever be grateful to the student who acted quickly and risked his life to protect me. I thanked him profusely and gave him a few books on Palestine as a gift. He was a Palestinian from the West Bank and simply said, "This is our duty. We thank you for what you are doing for our people. This is the least we can do."

~

Another interesting opportunity arose at a speaking engagement I accepted in my hometown of Buffalo, New York. I had several invitations in the Buffalo area that weekend, starting with the church my parents attended in the suburb of East Aurora, where I attended high school. The talk at my parents' Presbyterian church was well attended. I was pleased to see a few of my high school classmates in the audience. The questions were a reminder that people had a very basic level of awareness. Few even knew where Lebanon was or why the Palestinians were in Lebanon. I recalled how little I knew just two years earlier and was reminded to assume nothing in terms of the knowledge base of the average American.

During the same trip, I was invited to address a large, primarily Palestinian group of Arab Americans in Buffalo. They were very appreciative of a local "white guy" bringing an eyewitness account of what was transpiring in Lebanon with the Israeli invasion. After the speech, a journalist from the *Buffalo Evening News* magazine approached me and asked if I would work with him on a major article on Buffalo's Arab community. This was a rare and wonderful opportunity as journalists rarely ask you to work with them.

The journalist was Anthony Cardinale, and we developed a good working relationship. He continued to call me after I returned to Chicago, and we worked closely on a cover story for the *Buffalo Evening News* weekend issue. Anthony was honest about having little to no background on the Palestinian issue and asked good questions about the history. I encouraged him to feature stories about local Arab citizens and explore their backgrounds and what the Arab community was bringing to Buffalo.

The article appeared, and it was a beautifully written overview on the Arab community in Buffalo with stories of four different community leaders, along with a historical section and a sidebar on the invasion of Lebanon. I called and congratulated Anthony and offered to assist him, if I could, whenever he needed. I asked if his editor supported the article, and he said he had the full backing of the editorial board; the minimal criticism they received did not pose a problem.

My other media event was an hourlong debate on a major Buffalo news station with fellow Buffalonian Wolf Blitzer. At that time, I was not familiar with Blitzer, who was a young staff member of the pro-Israel lobby AIPAC. Previously, he lived in Israel and was a reporter with the *Jerusalem Post.* The debate started with the host asking me to share my experiences in Beirut a few weeks earlier during the Israeli invasion. I described the attacks on civilians, including the girls killed in the United Nations delegation, and the disparity of the numbers of civilian deaths. Blitzer tried to debunk my eyewitness accounts of civilian casualties, claiming Israeli pilots were known for their accuracy and that they were killing PLO terrorists with "surgical precision."

This statement was all I needed to zero in on Blitzer's use of false propaganda. I noted there is no such thing as "surgical precision," as the independent Red Cross statistics show the unbelievably high number of civilian deaths. I highlighted it with the nineteen dead schoolgirls. Then I asked Blitzer if he had been in Lebanon and seen evidence to disprove my reports. I asked him specifically if he was in Beirut in June 1982 and if he had his own or eyewitness accounts that confirmed what I said. I suggested that he was using unreliable information from the Israeli military and the Israel Ministry of Information trying to whitewash the high death numbers. He changed tactics, calling me antisemitic, but when I called him out on the name-calling and pulled him back to my question, he avoided it. I asked it again and Blitzer had nothing concrete to offer in opposition.

During the call-in period, I was amazed by the large number of sympathetic voices and questions coming in, some with Arabic accents. A number of the callers were from nearby Hamilton and Toronto, Canada. The overwhelming number of callers either had facts about the situation or were themselves Palestinians or Lebanese who supported the information I was providing. A few years later I was shocked to hear that Blitzer had landed an influential post with CNN, given his pro-Israel bias and history with the leading zionist lobby.

The next evening, my dad and I relaxed in our living room with a beer. He told me that my trip to Lebanon and the fact that I was under bombardment by US fighter-jets had caused him to rethink several issues. After reading the material I was sending him, he had changed his thinking about US foreign policy. He cited President Eisenhower's famous warning about the military industrial complex taking over foreign and domestic policy. Dad said, "Tragically, Ike's warning has come true. I now see what has transpired under Reagan, and we are in deep trouble as a country. The Pentagon and military are now running policy and I see relationships with Israel and others as very dangerous."

I sat there open-mouthed in disbelief. This was my Republican dad, a veteran of World War II, staunch supporter of Richard Nixon and fan of Ronald Reagan. My heart leapt for joy. I tried to contain my enthusiasm so he would continue to share his insights. I remembered our years of struggle over issues like the Vietnam War, the militarization of our foreign and domestic policies, and the case of Israel. I was almost speechless.

In what seemed like a confessional moment, my dear father, who was a patriot among patriots, was having second thoughts. He said, close to tears, "If I had to do it again with what I know now, I never would have enlisted in World War II. I lost three years and missed seeing you grow up during those years. But at least I've seen the light." His willingness to be vulnerable with me was deeply moving, especially given our tension through the years about political and religious issues. After all, Dad was still the treasurer of the Republican Party of Western New York and was quite influential in his Republican circles.

I thanked him for his honesty and his willingness to share these thoughts with me. It was probably the most meaningful conversation we ever had. I got up out of my chair, walked over to him, and, on the verge of tears, gave him a huge hug. After years of arguments and political differences, we were fully reconciled, bound together in a profound moment of vulnerability, mutual compassion, and unconditional love.

Chapter 16
THEIR BLOOD CRIES OUT! THE SABRA/SHATILA MASSACRE

"Again I saw all the oppressions that are practiced under the sun. Look, the tears of the oppressed—with no one to comfort them... And I thought the dead, who have already died, more fortunate than the living... but better than both is the one who has not yet been, and has not seen the evil deeds that are done under the sun."

—Ecclesiastes 4:1–3.

"Anyone who can make you believe absurdities can make you commit atrocities."

—US Rep. Jamie Raskin, during the second impeachment trial of Donald J. Trump, 2021

The summer of 1982 was one of the most intense periods in my life. We were working twelve to fourteen hours a day at the PHRC office trying to mobilize pressure to end the brutal Israeli war on Palestinian and Lebanese civilians. We rarely achieved any significant victories, but we remained steadfast despite the odds against us. The Israeli narrative continued to dominate the US media and hold sway with the Reagan administration throughout the year.

Day after day, week after week, we tried to improve our strategies and learn from our mistakes in our attempt to disseminate the Palestinian narrative to the American people. Trying to change the mainstream US media and the Reagan administration's policy on Israel and the Middle East was like attempting to salvage a garden that had not been watered during a month-long drought. The problem was systemic and beyond our control due to the iron-clad commitment of the Reagan administration and the mainstream media to the Israeli narrative.

In July 1982, I traveled to Washington, DC, for a meeting with the House Foreign Relations staff and its chairman, Lee Hamilton. Hamilton was more honest about Middle East issues than most senators and representatives. He was well aware of the political game Israel and its lobby were playing and was sensitive yet cautious about the Palestinian issue. I asked him what it would take for his committee to end the war in Lebanon, and he said, "A stronger lobby from the Palestinians and mobilizing local support so we can stay in office once we take such a stand." He went on to say his office received daily briefings and regular visits from AIPAC and other pro-Israel lobby organizations and little to nothing on behalf of the Palestinian position.

Jim Zogby, cofounder of the American Arab Anti-Discrimination Committee, and I met with Undersecretary of State Elliott Abrams, who was responsible for the Israel portfolio. I brought my analysis of the invasion of Lebanon and photographs of Israel's attacks on civilians that I'd witnessed. Abrams stonewalled us and said US support for Israel was untouchable and the invasion of Lebanon was a defensive operation.

Jim stood up and challenged Abrams with a verbal undressing and pounded on his desk for added emphasis. It was a futile exercise. Later, it was revealed that Abrams had colluded with Israel in the Iran-Contra scandal, covering up Israel's training of the militias and death squads responsible for scores of murders of civilians in Nicaragua and El Salvador. Abrams was the human embodiment of high-level corruption which illustrated the impossible task we had in attempting to change US policy during the summer of 1982. He was later convicted of lying to Congress and removed from his post but pardoned by Reagan.

Decades later, President Joe Biden appointed Abrams to a significant administrative post related to the Middle East. Abrams still had influence with Republicans and Democrats, and was a major asset for the most extreme government in Israel's history under Netanyahu.

Despite the obstacles, we were determined to forge ahead trying to educate the public and build a movement of resistance to the criminal behavior of Israel and our own government. I often thought of the wisdom of Jesus' Parable of the Sower. The farmer in the parable continues to sow seeds, knowing some will fall on rocky and barren soil but others will find fertile soil and blossom. Regardless, the farmer never stops sowing seeds, undeterred by the possibility of failure. In the same way, our task to sow the seed of truth has to be pursued with *sumud* (steadfastness) as the Palestinians say, seeking fertile soil but never giving up on justice.

~

Our PHRC office organized a press conference for July 30, 1982 and invited three interfaith leaders and a secular human-rights attorney to speak. The purpose was to announce a new interfaith appeal directed at our two Illinois senators and representatives, calling for a permanent ceasefire and leading to a treaty that ended the war in Lebanon and lifted Israel's military blockade of Beirut. At the time, Israel was intensifying its carpet bombing of the city and the United Nations reported shortages of food and essential medicine in Beirut. The intensive Israeli bombing campaigns and high numbers of civilian deaths prevented Lebanese and Palestinians from burying the dead.

The day before our press conference, the United Nations Security Council adopted Resolution 515, demanding that Israel lift the blockade preventing humanitarian aid to Lebanon, by a vote of 14-0. The United States abstained rather than vetoing the resolution as Israel had requested, demonstrating a shift in US policy. We thought our strategy had a chance to receive modest media attention and hoped it would gain support from a number of Chicago area legislators.

When I entered the room designated for the press conference at the Chicago Methodist Temple, I was pleasantly surprised to see a large turnout of the mainstream Chicago media. The major television networks, newspapers, and several independent television and radio stations were present as were a handful of independent journalists. I made a brief statement introducing our appeal from interfaith leaders in Chicago and introduced the four speakers, each of whom delivered a three-minute statement. I felt confident we had made our points succinctly with a degree of urgency.

When it was time for the press to ask questions, the second person I recognized was a reporter from the *Chicago Tribune*. He stood and proceeded to blame the PLO for starting the war and threatening Israel's security. He grumbled, "Israel is fully justified in its efforts to remove this terrorist threat from the region."

My friend Gene Stoltzfus, founder of Christian Peacemaker Teams, leaned over and whispered, "I know this guy. He does not believe what he's saying.

There's something weird going on and we need to talk to him privately."

After the press conference, Gene and I approached the *Tribune* reporter and asked him about his hostile statement. He asked us to go to a side room away from the crowd and confided, "Please don't use my name or make public what I'm about to tell you. It must remain confidential. Do you promise?" We agreed. He continued, "Before I came here this morning, my editor called a number of reporters into his office and urged us to avoid the Palestinian perspective in our reporting. He said if you happen to encounter it, confront it aggressively with Israeli talking points." Then he showed us the guidelines distributed by the Anti-Defamation League with talking points on how to defend the Israeli Defense Forces Peace for Galilee campaign, aka Israel's war in Lebanon.

He said, "The only way I can introduce your perspective in my reporting is to frame it from the perspective of the Israeli talking points. If I fail to do that, my report will be cut immediately."

Gene and I looked at each other. We were not surprised. I asked the reporter if we could jot down the Israeli guidelines, and he gave us a few minutes to make notes. I said, "I understand the pressure on you, but please, just try to tell the truth without taking sides. That's all we ask. This particular appeal is a humanitarian issue and it should not be politicized as Israel is doing. Reporting the Israeli military's talking points day after day just plays into their censorship of the reality on the ground." He assured us he was aware of the problem but added, "Look, I can't afford to lose my job over this issue. I hope you understand."

We understood but urged, "Please do what you can to stop the disinformation campaign."

The next morning, I picked up the *Chicago Tribune* and found the article buried in the back of section one. Sure enough, the first half of the article was straight out of the Israeli playbook. But the final two paragraphs were different. They reported the facts as we had stated them at the press conference. The reporter included the faith leaders' appeal to Illinois legislators to support a ceasefire and attend to the humanitarian needs in Beirut. We had achieved a modest victory.

This incident prompts me to wonder how far we have come in forty years of advocacy for Palestinians. In many ways the mainstream media is still effectively managed by the Trump administration in collaboration with the pro-zionist organizations that are advocating for Israeli policies. The censorship is still a major factor with the *New York Times*, NBC, CNN, and other major news outlets. But Israel does not have the same control over social media. Yes, the majority of our legislators in the US, Canada, and Europe are towing the line with Israel and their monitors, but not all. Forty years ago, we did not have strong Muslim and Jewish organizations advocating for Palestine, and we did not have Palestinian justice networks in our churches. Perhaps the most important matter is that young people under forty are not buying the zionist rhetoric and are extremely critical of colonial powers, including Israel. The marches, campus protests, and social media messaging in opposition to the Israeli-US genocide in Gaza represent the most important shift yet, while the Trump administration in coordination with the pro-Israel lobby has shut down campus protests and threatened free speech at most US universities. It may be a temporary victory for Israel until the courts resolve the matter.

—

Shortly after returning from Lebanon in early June 1982, I began to have nightmares for the first time in my life. I knew from three years of Jungian therapy that my anger and frustration were buried in my subconscious memory, and it was showing up in a series of recurring dreams centered around an incident that occurred the summer after my junior year in college. I was working in a steel mill in Buffalo and was assigned to the night shift. Every night I started my work by climbing a twelve-foot-high platform surrounded by a dozen ingot molds, which had been poured in the morning. I worked with my friend John, a gentle giant who was the starting center on the University of Pittsburgh football team. Our job was to knock out the pins at the top of the molds as we worked from the bench, then go back to the ground and remove the other pins.

One hot July evening, John and I climbed the stairs with our sledgehammers and started knocking out the top pins. Suddenly, John yelled, "Hey Don! Look out! There's a crane dumping hot iron behind us. Let's get out of here!" We ran to the opposite end of the bench and the crane followed us, continuing to pour hot iron. I could hear it sizzling on the bench behind us. Our only option was to jump off the bench and run to an area where the crane could not reach us. Thankfully, we were fit enough to make the twelve-foot jump and ran to an area beyond the range of the crane.

A group of workers who saw the crane dumping hot iron as it pursued us started yelling at the operator. A few veterans said they had never seen anything like it in two decades at the plant. Meanwhile, John and I were gasping for breath, wondering what had just happened. The plant supervisor finally arrived and demanded the crane operator come down to where we were standing. When the man arrived on the scene, we could see he was drunk. He mumbled, "I was just having some fun trying to scare the college guys with a little hot iron." He was fired on the spot.

My recurring nightmare drew from that experience at the steel mill with an added twist. Since I slept on my stomach, from time to time my arm would fall asleep. That sensation triggered a nightmare that transported me to the midst of the bombing of Beirut. The tingling nerves morphed into my arm burning from Israeli cluster bombs or something like napalm dropping all around me.

I would wake up from these nightmares in a cold sweat, yelling, "My arm, my arm has been hit!" and shocking everyone in the house, especially Drew. My right arm was my pitching arm. I had been careful to protect it since high school, holding on to my fantasy of pitching in the Major Leagues. Losing my right arm would be a devastating personal loss. This nightly terror was evidence that the stress and frustration of our political efforts that summer and the bombing I had experienced in Beirut were combining to wear me down.

After one session with the therapist, the nightmares stopped. Once I named and identified the source, they ended. As I reflected on this experience, I was embarrassed with the focus on my suffering. My focus should be on the Palestinian and Lebanese children and civilians coping with two months of daily bombing raids. I was exposed to the bombing for a mere five days. I could not imagine the long-term effects of living with this daily pain and fear, especially among children. I often think of the children and elderly in similar bombings, whether in Syria, the Ukraine, Gaza Strip, Israel, Lebanon, Yemen, Iraq, Iran—wherever. I can't begin to imagine the trauma both children and adults in the Gaza Strip and now the West Bank have experienced as they have witnessed parents, partners, and friends murdered in front of them. Most have no one to help them process the severe damage done to their hearts and minds in the trauma will remain unresolved..

~

I turned forty on September 3, 1982, and while I did not make a big deal of the birthday, I knew it was a threshold of sorts. I thought about the gift of forty years of life and wondered what was next for me. Working on interpersonal issues was one significant project to which I was committed for the future. I had married Drew McAllister two years earlier, eager to be a good husband and father, but the marriage was not going well. What began as love between us quickly evaporated into constant tension, and we grew apart. I thought I was ready to try marriage again, but I may have fooled myself. Or was the problem more basic? Maybe we just weren't a good match.

Trying to be a good father to Jay was another commitment I vowed to make a high priority, but it was a challenge. He lived many miles away in the Cleveland area. My work with PHRC was fulfilling but I needed to work on the issues at home. My personal faith was in a transitional phase as I continued to embrace liberation theology and move away from my evangelical roots. My hunger for justice was challenged by the injustice I saw daily—not only in the Palestinian case but also in the scourge of racism we faced at home in Chicago.

I found meaningful support and fellowship in our household and in the Covenant Community, with its radical commitment to God's love and search for justice. Jesus continued to be the center of my faith in new and inspiring ways that drew from liberation theology and the call to prophetic ministry. Now that my time in the institutional church was officially behind me, I felt liberated as new horizons for ministry and service were born through my work with PHRC and Covenant Community. Perhaps I needed to stay the course. My life was, for the most part, loving, deeply meaningful, and filled with compassionate friends who were engaged in peace and justice and were supportive of Drew and me, come what may with our relationship.

~

I stayed in touch with Dan O'Neill and Ells Culver of Mercy Corps throughout the summer as we tried to encourage each other to maintain our resistance to the war in Lebanon. One morning Dan called and cautioned, "I hope you're sitting down. We have some shocking news. Let me get Ells on the line." Apparently, Mercy Corps had just learned that one member of our recent delegation to Lebanon was an undercover CIA agent. They said the person in question was the one guy who was not crying that Saturday morning in Beirut when the teenage girls were brought into the hospital in body bags. I knew immediately who they were referring to.

Ells said he was the brother of an influential member of Mercy Corps Board of Directors who held a prominent position in the Reagan administration. Dan and Ells said they felt terrible about the development, but I said, "Yes, but it's not surprising. Why wouldn't we be used by the CIA in this way? We were the perfect cover as a human rights group with Christian relief and development agencies. There is no need to apologize. This summer I've had to deal with two attempts by the FBI to infiltrate our PHRC Board of Directors. In both cases we figured it out and kept them off the board but I'm sure they will continue to infiltrate us. We may have one on the board now and I don't know it."

Most of my calls with Dan and Ells ended with a discussion about when we would return to Beirut. By mid-August the war began to wind down and a treaty was negotiated by Saudi Arabia, France, and the United States. They mediated the agreement for the PLO to withdraw from Lebanon in exchange for protection of the large number of Palestinian civilians left behind, primarily refugees in the camps scattered throughout Lebanon. The PLO leadership and military did leave Lebanon and were distributed in various Arab countries, primarily Tunisia, Algeria, and Yemen.

In the only concession to the PLO, the United States made a commitment to provide protection for the 350,000–400,000 Palestinian civilians who lived in Lebanon. These populations were suddenly vulnerable to attacks from Israel or the Phalangist militias. The PLO knew this and demanded security for the Palestinians left behind and the United States guaranteed it. France was to have a minor role in providing protection.

Palestinian concerns were elevated when Bachir Gemayel, head of the Phalangist militia, was elected president of Lebanon on August 23, 1982. Bachir had a history of hatred toward Palestinians and as noted earlier, he was involved in at least two massacres, including Tel al-Zaatar. Despite these factors, the treaty seemed to be holding in the early days after the PLO's withdrawal, but it was an uneasy period for Lebanon. Israel was still occupying half of the country from the southern border to the whole of West Beirut.

Dan, Ells, and I decided to fly to Lebanon in mid-September 1982. We agreed to rework our three proposals, two of which we planned to submit to Gaby Habib and the Middle East Council of Churches and one to the Palestinian Red Crescent Society. We booked our flights with a departure on September 16, with a rendezvous in Cyprus. The Beirut airport was still closed, so we planned to take a boat from Cyprus to Beirut. I contacted Gaby at MECC and Hedla Ayoubi of the Red Crescent. They agreed to host us but cautioned that we should stay in touch and monitor political developments closely because anything could happen. They were very worried about what Israel and Bachir Gemayel might do to the Palestinian refugees.

On September 14, 1982, President Bachir Gemayel of Lebanon was assassinated after just three weeks in office. Dan, Ells, and I checked in with each other and concluded that we should still go. Little did we know what was transpiring behind the scenes. No one knew who was responsible for the assassination, but speculation pointed to the Syrians or Palestinians, and some even suspected Israel. The Palestinians were unlikely candidates—they were leaderless and had no military presence since the PLO had evacuated. Syria or a Syrian militia aligned with the Lebanese opposition was the more likely culprit. Some of these groups had the capability for a sophisticated explosion of this magnitude.

When I picked up my airline tickets from Mahmoud and Fadwa Naji at Salaam Travel, they asked me to carry a check in the amount of $50,000 to the Red Crescent Society from the United Holy Land Fund. We knew how difficult life had become for Palestinians, and we worried about the Red Crescent Hospitals as possible targets of Israelis and the Phalangists. Feeling honored to take the check, I folded it carefully and placed it in a secret compartment in my wallet.

As Drew drove me to the airport the next afternoon, she seemed relieved that I was finally leaving after spending a summer preoccupied with the war in Lebanon. I left Chicago on September 16, and after two connecting flights, I landed two days later in Cyprus. Dan and Ells were waiting for me, and we rushed to catch a taxi to the Port of Larnaca and the boat to Lebanon. We were on the road no more than ten minutes when the driver turned on BBC World News. The lead story was about a massacre underway in the Palestinian refugee camps Sabra and Shatila in south Beirut. The BBC account—the first international media report of the massacre—painted a savage picture of what was taking place. All transportation in and out of Lebanon had been canceled and Beirut was in a state of complete chaos. The driver said there would be no boats to Beirut for the immediate future. We asked him to take us to a hotel near the port in Larnaca.

We monitored the BBC accounts at the hotel on our shortwave radios every hour. The BBC reports speculated the Phalangist militia attacked the camps in revenge for the killing of their leader, Bachir Gemayel. Since no evidence had been presented to confirm who was behind the assassination, the Lebanese government called for new elections. Amine Gemayel, Bachir's brother, was the presumptive front-runner in the next presidential election.[36]

By Sunday evening, the boat to Beirut was back on schedule with a 6 PM departure and an arrival time of 7 AM in the port of Jounieh. When we arrived, we saw two US friends, Dick Butler from Church World Service and Dale Bishop of the United Church of Christ Middle East Desk, preparing to board the boat back to Cyprus. Dick urged us to hurry to the MECC office as events were developing quickly. This was precisely our plan. We took a taxi to the office and greeted Gaby Habib, who was about to convene a meeting with twenty-five nurses and physicians who were volunteering with MECC in the refugee camps.

Gaby pulled us aside and said the situation was extremely tense in Beirut. He wanted us to go immediately to Sabra and Shatila so we could see the situation for ourselves. He told us that several physicians and nurses from their group had been stationed in the camps and some were eyewitnesses to the atrocities. Most of them were traumatized. Meanwhile, Israeli troops were coming up the street searching buildings. Gaby needed to hold the meeting immediately and move the nurses and physicians to a more secure location before the Israelis arrived and interrogated everyone.

As we were leaving, I ran into Swee Ang, a dynamic British-Chinese surgeon who was volunteering with MECC. She had been in Gaza Hospital adjacent to Sabra and Shatila refugee camps during the massacres. Swee was a youthful four feet eleven inches tall, but her stature belied her enormous courage. After introducing herself, she asked if we could meet her after we returned from the camps. She handed us a phone number and we promised to call her.

After Dr. Swee went to her meeting, a nurse from the US, Ellen Siegel, told us Dr. Swee could be in some trouble with the Israelis as she had sent the telex to the BBC about the Sabra and Shatila massacre. It was the source of the first international news broadcast that we heard in Cyprus. Ellen admitted she was glad Swee had filed the report but feared that it could put the MECC in jeopardy if the Israelis traced it to the group's telex machine.

From that moment on, Dr. Swee became a lifelong friend. We have stayed in touch over the years through our common commitment to the Palestinian people. I later learned that she had also grown up as a Bible-believing fundamentalist Christian zionist, in Malaysia. In her book *From Beirut to Jerusalem*, she recounts her story. Thomas Friedman of the *New York Times* published his own very successful book with the same title, although Swee's volume had been in print for a year before Friedman's account appeared.

~

We quickly left the MECC office and Gaby arranged for a driver to take us to the southern edge of Sabra and Shatila refugee camps. We walked past a tall office building that had been commandeered by the Israeli Defense Forces as a staging point for their operations. With their powerful military binoculars, the Israelis could easily observe what was happening in the camps. They watched us walk past them as they continued to monitor the Red Cross and Red Crescent efforts to recover bodies. We walked down the dusty road to the camp when medical workers approached us and handed each of us a handkerchief doused in generous amounts of cologne. The worker instructed us, "Hold the cloth over your nose as the smell is very bad. It will make you sick if you don't use this." It was a hot day, well over ninety degrees Fahrenheit and very humid. The bodies of the dead had been decaying in the heat for at least two days and the smell of death permeated the air.

As we drew closer to the workers, we witnessed chilling scenes of families arriving for the first time to see if there were any bodies or even parts of bodies of loved ones under the rubble. What I witnessed then was a glimpse of what Palestinians have been going through on a daily basis in the Gaza Strip since October 7, 2023, trying to rescue the bodies or body parts of loved ones trapped under the rubble. Nearly all of their tiny houses and shops had been bulldozed by the Phalangists to make sure everyone was dead and the Palestinians would leave Beirut. We went over to one of the remaining shops, a shell of a building, and overheard the owner being interviewed. A journalist translated the owner's story and I recorded the translation:

> I was working in my shop around 4 PM on Thursday (September 16) when commandos entered from the south. They began shooting left and right. I could see the Israelis posted behind them at the tall apartment building. Just prior to their entry, Israeli tanks had shelled us from the southeast, then the commandos arrived within an hour. Once darkness fell, the Israelis put up flares so the killing could go on all night. I ran from my shop once the shooting started and was lucky to hide in a small

mosque on the edge of the camp. So many others were not so lucky.[37]

We crossed the dusty street and caught a glimpse of a team of Red Crescent personnel pulling a decayed corpse from the rubble. I had to turn away and hold back tears when I saw the decayed corpse of a small child. I walked to the next group and a Red Crescent worker held up the arm of a child. A woman, who I assumed was the girl's mother, screamed in agony when she saw it. She wailed as she cried out to Allah and cursed Israel, Lebanon, and the United States for abandoning the Palestinians. Death and grief were surrounding us at every turn.

Dan, Ells, and I agreed to split up and do our best to record and photograph what was appropriate. I had a small tape recorder and notepad but rarely took photos. I thought it best to respect peoples' privacy and took only a few photographs. Walking down the road, I met an elderly man, Ahmad, perhaps in his sixties, who was willing to discuss how the massacres took place. He spoke excellent English and was eager to talk. Ahmad said he left his home on Wednesday to purchase supplies for his store. He tried to return home early on Thursday evening, but Israel had sealed off all entrances to the camps.

He had just arrived to see what was left of his shop and his home. It was then that he learned that most of his family has been killed. I could not begin to imagine the pain he felt. "This is our fate as Palestinians," he said. "My son escaped from the massacre, but my wife and two daughters were murdered. What can I do? This is our destiny."

Ahmad said most of his information came from his neighbors in the camp, a couple who had survived the massacre by playing dead beneath family members who were murdered by the militias. He told me the killers were from various Lebanese militias, many of whom seemed to be on drugs because they slurred their words and their minds were crazed with violence. He identified a southern Lebanese accent in the group and surmised they could have been part of the Israeli-controlled Southern Lebanese Army. The neighbor survived but witnessed his sister being shot to death and raped. Then one of the militiamen sliced off her hand so he could take her bracelets and rings.

Since Ahmad was unable to return to his home in Shatila camp on Thursday evening, he stayed with a friend in an apartment building a few blocks from the camps. They saw the flares put up by the Israelis on Friday evening so the killing could go on into the night. He heard the United States was supposed to assume responsibility for protecting the Palestinian and said all Palestinians knew the United States would be in charge of their security. And as we could see, the United States did nothing.

Eventually, the story of how the US fumbled—or intentionally reneged on—its commitment to provide security for Palestinians emerged. As it was not a priority, and at the request of Israeli Defense Minister Ariel Sharon, the US pulled back its Marines, who were supposed to supervise the PLO's withdrawal. Had the Marines been redeployed to monitor the Palestinian refugee camps, the massacres would have not have occurred. Instead, the Marines returned to their ships and had an extended break. I'm certain that if the Palestinians were Jews or white people, the United States would have left the Marines in Beirut to provide protection. Since they were Palestinians, they were expendable.

I was overwhelmed with grief after interviewing the two shopkeepers. Everywhere I looked there was another family returning to discover the inestimable loss of loved ones, their homes destroyed, their modest businesses gone. I heard another mother crying out to God in Arabic, "Why O Allah? Why, why, why?" Who knows what she had seen—a decomposed body, a body part of a son or daughter, or the enormity of the incalculable loss of her family and home. I looked for somewhere to sit and pray for a moment so I could gain control of my emotions.

Ahead of me was a mound of dirt where a few others were sitting. I took a seat and tried to center myself in silence. But there was no escaping the horror, whether from the smell of death, the piercing screams of loved ones, or the destruction around us. Trying to find peace within myself, I reached out to God in prayer. I prayed for those who were crying and grieving after losing a loved one. I prayed for the rescue workers who had an unfathomably difficult job.

My prayers became wordless as the appropriate language escaped me. All I could do was sit in silence and try to meditate on the thought that God was somehow here, even though our eyes saw little evidence. I reflected on the fact that God was present when his own son, an innocent young man of thirty-three, was crucified after a corrupt justice system condemned him to death on a cross. His body was savagely sliced open by a sword and nails driven through his hands as he hung on a cross.

I turned to a journalist who was sitting beside me, weeping, on the dirt pile from the mass grave. I asked if she was OK, then apologized for addressing her in English. "Please forgive me," she said through her tears. "I can't help myself. Watching this is so difficult."

"You are doing the right thing by attending to your emotions," I told her, and asked where she was from. She said Paris, and that she was part of two French news teams that had been in Lebanon for two weeks. As Red Crescent workers carried body bags to the bottom for burial, I asked her how many were buried here. She said she had lost count, but then she directed me to look to my left. "They are digging another mass grave because this one won't be big enough."

"Oh my God," I gasped. "This is beyond belief."

"Yes," she said. "This is a war crime."

"Do you think anyone will be tried and convicted?"

"Absolutely not," she scoffed. "They will all get away with it. History seems to say so, don't you think? No one ever pays for crimes committed against Palestinians."

"I'm afraid you're right," I said. "My country will always run interference for Israel and protect them. I'm sure the US is complicit in all of this."

Indeed, we had no reason to think that the United Nations or international courts would ever bring Israel and the Lebanese forces to trial, and we were correct. More recently, nations like South Africa, Ireland, and Norway, have shown a willingness to abide by international law and challenge the colonial powers in their attempt to white wash Israel's crimes and their own.

With emphasis, she responded, "I'm glad to see an American is here who thinks like this."

As we spoke, a Muslim cleric walked by and I excused myself as I ran to catch up with him. The sheik was deep in thought, reciting verses from the Qur'an as he walked. I expressed my condolences and asked if I could speak with him. I asked if he was from the mosque at the edge of Shatila camp, and he said he was. Then I asked if he had been able to estimate the number of dead from the massacre. He responded, "It is still too early to know but it has to be between 2,000–3,000,[38] but added, "We will never know. The Israelis and the Lebanese militias removed a large number of bodies in several truckloads. I saw this with my own eyes on Friday evening. No one knows where the bodies were buried and we may never know. Only Allah knows." I thanked him and wished him *As-salaam Alaikum* ("God's peace").

"Please, when you return home, tell the world what has happened here."

"I will," I promised. "I absolutely will."

~

What happened in Sabra and Shatila matches the textbook definition of genocide. The Rome Statute has become the international standard for defining the crime of genocide stating it includes "any of the following acts: murder, extermination, enslavement, deportation or forcible transfer of a population, imprisonment, torture, grave forms of sexual violence, persecution, enforced disappearance of persons, the crime of apartheid, and other inhumane acts when committed as part of a widespread systematic attack directed against any civilian population."[39]

By denying certain facts in the case of the Sabra and Shatila massacre, the Israeli trial of Ariel Sharon and several generals involved in the crime (the Kahan Commission of 1983), established that they were "indirectly responsible" for the atrocities committed in Sabra and Shatila, while the Lebanese militias were guilty of "primary responsibility" for the massacres. General Sharon was removed from his office as defense minister but was allowed to remain in government as a minister without portfolio. In 2001 he became the prime minister of Israel. He was never brought to justice although he played the primary role in this and two other massacres of Palestinians. In 2014, the *New Yorker* asked Bernard Ashravi, a professor of political economy at Dartmouth, to write an article assessing Ariel Sharon's career. His article opened with a remarkable paragraph that set the tone for his assessment:

> In 1930, George Bernard Shaw rose to toast Albert Einstein, and said, "If you take the typical great man of our historic epoch—and suppose I had to rise here tonight to propose a toast to Napoleon. Well, undoubtedly, I could say many, many flattering things about Napoleon. But about that greatness, Shaw deadpanned, something else would have to be considered, "perhaps the most important thing"... which is that it would perhaps have been better for the human race if he had never been born.[40]

The British journalist Robert Fisk once reflected on those who are silent in the face of massacres and genocide. He called upon journalists and all eyewitnesses to atrocities to "tell the truth or you could be enabling the next massacre. Those silenced by the Turks over the Armenian genocide are complicit, as were Germans who were silent during the Holocaust, and now the Sabra/Shatila massacre demands of Israelis, Lebanese, US citizens, and others to stand up and condemn the atrocity." In one of his last interviews, Fisk said:

> Journalists, I have always thought, must also be historians—not just fulfilling the old cliché about being "the first witnesses to history"—but by retelling, with ever more detail, the stories of the past, even when no survivors are left alive, and when powerful nations deny the truth of Armenia's suffering, just as Holocaust-deniers continue to taunt the Jews over the most tragic years of their history... Name the bad guys, I always say—and that applies to long-dead Turkish army officers who slew the Armenians just as it does to German SS officers who gassed the Jews. And, yes, the same applies to all the massacres of the Middle East. Name the still-living bad guys. And don't be afraid of those who claim that this is not objective. Mass murder is a war crime and we journalists surely oppose such iniquities. Looking back on it, that's why I was padding across those mass graves in the Sabra and Shatila camps 37 years ago.[41]

As I write in October, 2025, the Trump-Netanyahu peace plan has failed as Israel violated the ceasefire daily for three consecutive weeks and blamed Hamas for not delivering the bodies of Israeli hostages. Meanwhile, Hamas does not have the machinery to unearth the bodies that remain under the buildings Israel destroyed. Israel has also limited the humanitarian aid and medicine the so-called "peace plan" proposed and Palestinians are dying of hunger, disease, and the continued bombing. The US-Israel imposed peace plan has been exposed as an attempt to normalize a resumption of the Israeli-US genocide with Israel occupying over 50 percent of the Gaza Strip. Some analysts have stated the US-Israeli goals include Trump's plan to turn Gaza into a "Riviera" and expelling the Palestinians to third countries. If Israel and the US are successful in this "normalization strategy," they will also undermine the International Court of Justice and the International Criminal Court litigation on genocide and war crimes of the last two years, repeating the same pattern that followed the Sabra-Shatila massacre, and avoiding consequences for the US, Israel, and other countries that financed the genocide. Now it is the responsibility of every citizen and organization in the global community to demand that justice is done and that a political solution to the Palestine question be instituted immediately.

Section V:
Ch. 17–19

Palestine is Still the Issue

Every moment and every event of our life on earth
plants something in our soul.
For just as the wind carries thousands of winged seeds,
so each moment brings its germs of spiritual vitality that come to rest
imperceptibly in our minds and wills....
If I were looking for God, every event and every moment would sow,
in my will, grains of God's life that would spring up one day
in a tremendous harvest.

—Thomas Merton

Chapter 17
MY JOURNEY WITH EVANGELICALS AND JUSTICE IN THE UNHOLY LAND

"What are the things that you can't see that are important? I would say justice, truth, humility, service, compassion, love. You can't see any of those, but they're the guiding lights of life."

—Jimmy Carter, US president, 1977–1981

Friends told me to stay home and not visit the Middle East. They said I was bad luck for the region. After all, three of my last four visits to the Middle East coincided with catastrophe: Israel's bombing of South Lebanon in July 1981; the Israeli invasion of Lebanon in June 1982; and the Sabra and Shatila massacre in September 1982. Regardless, I wasn't taking these events personally and continued preparing for my next trip—a five-country listening tour with my evangelical friend Ray Bakke—in the fall of 1986.

After he read my doctoral dissertation, particularly the last chapter proposing a new evangelical organization, Ray suggested that we embark on the listening tour of the region, stopping in Cyprus, Syria, Jordan, Israel, Egypt, and the occupied Palestinian territories (West Bank, Gaza Strip, and East Jerusalem). Due to the civil war, we decided to skip Lebanon and also Iraq. We planned to depart on October 10, for a three week tour.

Our main objective was to ask Middle East religious and political leaders about the most critical issues facing the Middle East for the immediate future. We were also eager to learn if there was a need for a new evangelical Christian organization that was sensitive to the key issues in the region—one that might challenge the growing influence of the religious right and zionist religious themes in Western churches.

Ray had impeccable evangelical credentials as a former Baptist pastor. He served as a consultant to World Vision International—the world's largest evangelical relief and developmental organization—and was a leader of the Lausanne Committee on World Evangelization (established by Billy Graham and other evangelical leaders). A professor at Northern Baptist Seminary near Chicago, he was a member of our Palestine Human Rights Campaign board of directors and had recently testified on our behalf before the House Foreign Affairs Committee on Palestinian rights in Israel and the occupied Palestinian territories.[42]

Our stopover in Cyprus was limited to one day for meetings with our colleagues at the Middle East Council of Churches. Gaby Habib arranged most of our itinerary with help from his assistant Larry Ekin, with whom we met as Gaby was still in Beirut due to urgent business. We spoke to Gaby on the phone to express our gratitude and he gave Larry a few last-minute changes. We left the next morning for Damascus.

Damascus is the oldest continuously occupied city in the world. It was a center of the early Christian church until the seventh century CE when it was established as the capital of the Omayyad dynasty of Sunni Islam. Our first stop in Damascus was the Church of Ananias, where Saul was mentored after his conversion to Christianity, when his name was changed to Paul.

Our host in Damascus was Rev. Adeeb Awad, a Presbyterian pastor and campus minister at Damascus University. At the Church of Ananias, he pointed out the house where Paul escaped his opposition when he was let down in a basket (Acts 9:11). We walked down Straight Street, in the heart of the Christian district, with several upscale shops and restaurants. We stopped for dinner and reviewed our schedule for the next three days with Pastor Awad.

After dinner, the pastor suggested we drive up to the mountain that overlooks the massive urban area encompassing Damascus and its suburbs. The lights of greater Damascus stretched as far as we could see as we looked north, east, and south. In 1985, about 1.5 million people lived in Damascus, and its suburbs added another half million. Rev. Adeeb pointed out several key sights such as the old city and Umayyad Mosque, where he said we could view the head of John the Baptist. (The Coptic Orthodox Church also claims to have John's head in a monastery.) He pointed to other sites, including government buildings and the University of Damascus with over 100,000 students.

In addition to showing us the beautiful panorama of Damascus, Pastor Adeeb said there was another reason to bring us there. It was the safest place in greater Damascus where he could talk freely without fear of someone listening to his conversation. Syria was a police state with an efficient *Mukhabarat* (military intelligence). He estimated one of every six people in Syria worked as an underground agent, so you never knew when you were being monitored, even in your own family.

Nevertheless, he said the Christians were experiencing more freedom than they had seen in decades. They had only two restrictions to abide by—they could not evangelize Muslims and they could not criticize the Ba'ath regime led by President Hafez al-Assad. Rev. Adeeb said Assad and most Syrian leaders were from the minority Alawite sect, an offshoot of Islam. A handful of Christians were also in government, but Syria was essentially a military dictatorship ruled by the secular Ba'ath. He recalled the uprising in February 1982, when the mostly Sunni Muslim Brotherhood challenged the Ba'ath regime and was massacred in the city of Hama (about 120 miles north of Damascus). No one knows how many died, but estimates ranged from ten- to twenty-thousand. It seems ironic that in November 2024, a coalition of fundamentalist Sunni Muslims forces led by Hay′at Thrir al-Sham (HTS) overthrew the six decade rule of the Assad family in Syria. The coup was guided by Turkey with possible support from the CIA and Mossad. Israel expanded its border around the Golan Heights and now occupies an expanded section in south Syria.

Our first appointment the next day was with Mahat Khouri, director of the Family Bookstore and a prominent Christian member of the Ba'ath Party. She was also a member of parliament and was well connected in the government. Like Gaby Habib, Mahat was an Antiochian Orthodox Christian and active with the Middle East Council of Churches.

Ray and I arrived at the Family Bookstore. Mahat was waiting for us with coffee and pastries. We had met previously in Beirut, at a MECC meeting, but this was my first visit to the Family Bookstore, which was one of the finest of its kind in the Middle East, frequented by Syrian Muslims and Christians alike. Damascus intellectuals gathered there monthly for Mahat's lecture series. She showed us the impressive schedule of speakers and gave us a tour of the bookstore, noting the extensive collection of books, magazines, and journals in Arabic, French, and English.

We asked her about the three major issues the Middle East was facing and she emphasized the problematic role of Israel and the United States in the region, the rise of extremism in Islam, Judaism, and Christianity, and the Palestine issue. She said, "Let me add a fourth. I'm worried about the future of Christians in the Middle East. Right now, we are protected in Syria, but this could change overnight. Make sure you mention this and you will hear more from my patriarch Ignatius IV. He keeps emphasizing this issue." Tragically, her fears were confirmed during the bloody Syrian civil war that began in February 2011, leaving the country a fragmented, failed state, with Christians reduced to approximately 1 percent of the population.

Mahat told us about some of the speakers she recently hosted in the lecture series. Most of the names were unfamiliar, but I did know Sadiq al-Azm, a professor of philosophy at the University of Damascus and one of the early critics of orientalism. I heard Sadiq deliver a lecture two years earlier at an AAUG conference and was impressed by his scholarly analysis of orientalism. Mahat said we were in for a treat in an hour as Kamal Salibi of the American University of Beirut would discuss his controversial new book, *The Bible Came from Arabia*.

Salibi was a brilliant historian, with a PhD from the University of London where he studied under Bernard Lewis, the famous orientalist. His controversial thesis claimed the events mentioned in the Bible did not take place in Palestine but in the western region of the Arabian Peninsula, the Hijaz. Salibi argued that the original texts of the events were changed by rabbinic scholars during and after the Babylonian Captivity. The Jewish scholars changed the location of the ancient events and relocated them in Palestine.

As strange as these ideas sound to the Western ear, Salibi provided compelling archaeological evidence and historical data to support his thesis. We listened intently and we each asked clarifying questions during the discussion. It was a fascinating exchange, and the assembled audience was sympathetic with Salibi's thesis. Ray and I were not persuaded as he did not seem to account for the overwhelming amount of archaeological evidence confirming the authenticity of the sites in ancient Palestine. Salibi did cause me to wonder if my Western education gave me a bias against his analysis.

Before we left the bookstore, we thanked Mahat for the fascinating morning. Earlier she mentioned that the Palestinian leader Bassam Abu-Sharif was one of the lecturers. He was the chief spokesman for the Popular Front for the Liberation of Palestine, an important wing of the PLO. I thought it would be good for us to meet him. I asked if she had a number for him, and she offered to introduce us. She handed me the phone, and I shared with Bassam the purpose of our trip and wondered if he was available that afternoon or evening. He suggested dinner and named a restaurant.

We met Bassam at a beautiful outdoor restaurant in an upscale Damascus neighborhood. A dedicated Marxist, he worked closely with George Habash, founder and general secretary of the Popular Front for the Liberation of Palestine. Bassam was rumored to have been one of the masterminds of the PFLP hijackings of the Pan Am, TWA, and Swiss Air flights, eventually blown up in Jordan. In the early 1970s, the PFLP led the Black September attempt to overthrow King Hussein's government. After Jordan expelled them in 1970, the PFLP settled in Damascus while Arafat and the Fatah Party settled in Beirut.

Bassam was initially stationed in Beirut after leaving Jordan and was working in the PLO office when he was the victim of a mail bomb assassination attempt by the Mossad. He had serious burns on his face and one hand was crippled. When we met him, he was the chief spokesman for the PFLP, but not long after our meeting he renounced armed struggle and returned to Beirut as Arafat's chief spokesman of the Fatah wing of the PLO.

Bassam was a student of US politics and was interested in how our approach to evangelical Christians could challenge the growing Israeli alliance with conservative Christians. Ray discussed his experience testifying before the House Foreign Affairs Committee and challenging Jerry Falwell and Pat Robertson. As expected, Bassam said the Palestine question was at the heart of the Middle East conflict. He encouraged us to keep the Palestinian issue in the top three of the many issues we were about to hear from Middle East leaders.

The following day we met with Patriarch Ignatius IV, head of the Antiochian Orthodox Church, which remains one of the strongest Arab Christian denominations in Syria, Lebanon, North America, and Australia. The most striking point in our session with the patriarch was his perspective on the future of Middle Eastern Christians. He pointed to several recent cases, including the civil war in Lebanon, attacks on the Coptic Christian churches in Egypt, and Israel's crackdowns on Palestinian Christians and Muslims, as evidence.

The patriarch said he was concerned about the future of Christians in Iraq as Israel and the United States were rumored to want regime change there. He said if Saddam Hussein was toppled, Iraq would fall into civil war immediately and the Christians would be at risk as would some Muslim minorities. He made the shocking statement: "If these trends continue, Christianity will soon disappear in the Middle East. The current generation of Middle Eastern Christians could be the last." He cautioned us to be careful not to demonize all Muslims. We needed to build bridges with the Muslim world while we supported Middle Eastern Christians and the Palestinian cause. After the devastating Syrian civil war and the mass exodus of Christians, the patriarch's grim predictions do not seem that outrageous.

On our final day in Syria, we visited a friend from Chicago, Claire Brandabur, a Fulbright scholar in her third year of teaching at Al-Ba'ath University in Homs (100 miles due north of Damascus). She requested that we meet in a remote park so she could be "completely frank" with us.

Claire emphasized how careful she had to be with every conversation, every written document, lecture, correspondence, and even casual conversations at dinner with friends. "You never know who is in the secret police," she said softly. "I'm not being paranoid because I love living here, but I have learned the hard way."

Claire shared that while teaching an English literature course at the university, two students took offense to one of her lectures on American revolutionary literature. They reported her to authorities as a possible "subversive" promoting the overthrow of the Ba'ath regime. Fortunately, the president of the university, a high-ranking Ba'ath Party member, was able to have her case dismissed. If it weren't for him, Claire would have been imprisoned as a spy or deported. Claire urged us to do whatever we could to keep the Palestinian case at the top of our agenda and to work on educating US evangelicals.

~

We flew to Amman early the next day and were met by Salim Musallam, director of MECC's Jordan office. MECC's work was primarily with Palestinian refugees and maintaining good relations with the local churches. Christians comprised approximately 7 percent of Jordan's population. They were not subjected to the strict monitoring we heard about in Syria, but they had to be careful. Evangelizing of Muslims and criticism of King Hussein and the regime was strictly forbidden. Salim had recently retired from a high-ranking position in the Jordanian military intelligence and was well connected to Jordanian politicians.

He took us to the Jordan Radio and Television studios for a live interview. We spoke openly and critically about US policy toward Israel under the Reagan administration and the growing influence of Christian zionists in US politics. We emphasized the need for closer ties between evangelicals in the

United States and Christians and Muslims in the Middle East. We added that the plight of the Palestinians was high on our agenda.

As we were driving to our hotel, Salim expressed how impressed he was by what we had said. He thought King Hussein should meet us, if possible, and asked if we would be willing to meet the king. Wide-eyed with delight, we quickly responded, "Yes, of course." We assumed a meeting was unlikely, and at best it might be the next day. We planned to clean up and have a relaxing dinner at a restaurant Salim recommended. Within fifteen minutes, Ray was in the shower and Salim was phoning. He asked, "Could you be ready in fifteen minutes? We have an interview with the king at 4:30 PM."

"Absolutely! We'll be downstairs waiting for you." Salim drove us to one of King Hussein's five places where we were received by the Head of Palace Affairs, Adnan Abu-Odeh. Within twenty minutes we were ushered into the king's office, where he welcomed us. Initially I was struck by how short the king was as we towered over him. He was warm and gracious, treating us with respect as if we were important envoys. He said, "I just watched your interview on television and am most interested in your perspectives as evangelical Christians. I was not aware there were evangelicals in the US who held your views. This is most encouraging."

The king showed us the morning edition of the *Jerusalem Post,* featuring a lead story on the International Christian Embassy in Jerusalem titled "Feast of Tabernacles." According to the article, three thousand "evangelicals" from all over the world were in Jerusalem to praise Israel and its settlement program. Then he turned to an editorial by the director of the ICEJ, Jan Willem van der Hoeven, a Dutchman, who proclaimed, "God has given this land to Israel, not the Palestinians. We have come to celebrate Israeli sovereignty over all of this land."

We shook our heads and said there is a need to consolidate evangelicals who oppose this extremist position. I said, "This is why we are here. We are meeting with religious and political leaders to give us their top priorities for the immediate future of the issues that will shape the Middle East."

The king responded, "Your efforts are more urgently needed now than ever. We are very worried about the rise of Islamic extremism here, even in Jordan. The Christian zionists stir up people, including the Muslims, and we worry about attacks on churches. Thankfully it has not come to that. More than 90 percent of the Muslims in Jordan welcome Christians and there are no problems."

Then the king brought his chair forward for emphasis. "In all seriousness," he said, "we are very concerned about a few sheiks here who are preaching a form of Islamic extremism. We value our Christian communities here and we are committed to protect them." Then the king made a remarkable statement: "If the extremist Muslims take over and drive out the Christians, we moderate Muslims will be driven out right behind them. In many ways the Christians are the glue that holds this delicate religious balance together. We need to protect them to ensure our future as Muslims."

Today the ICEJ and other fundamentalist Christian zionist organizations are aligned with the militant Temple Mount Faithful and other Israeli extremist organizations calling for the Third Temple to be built in place of Al-Aqsa Mosque and the Dome of the Rock. This is an extremely sensitive matter for Muslims as Al-Aqsa is the third-holiest mosque in Islam, and the Dome of the Rock represents an important landmark as the place where the prophet Abraham almost sacrificed his son. It is also where Muhammad made his night visit to Jerusalem and mystically had the vision or rising to the seventh heaven. Any attempt to attack or remove the famous mosque or Dome of the Rock will ignite tension and possibly lead to war, yet both Jewish and Christian extremist groups continue to call for the removal of the Muslim holy sites "by any means available to them."

We were amazed and grateful for this strong affirmation of respect and support for the Christian minority from the Jordanian monarch. We could sense the urgency in the king's voice and his concern over the threat posed by Islamists and the Christian zionists who were stirring the threat. This final statement from the king was similar to what we had heard in Damascus from Patriarch Ignatius IV. What was planned as a fifteen-minute conversation with King Hussein had turned into more than an hourlong dialogue. He wished us well and added, "If there is anything we can do to support your efforts, please contact us."

We left for the Allenby Bridge early the next morning. Despite a delay at Israeli customs where I was questioned about four Arabic books that I was carrying for Birzeit faculty, the crossing was uneventful. Our dear friend, the Birzeit president in exile, Hanna Nasir, had asked me to carry four physics and biology textbooks in Arabic to the West Bank campus and assumed that it would not be a problem. The delay over the textbooks was minimal, and fortunately the authorities did not search my wallet, which still contained the check from Hanna to cover Birzeit salaries for the month.

We took a *serveese* to our hotel in Jerusalem and heard the breaking news that Israel had kidnapped Mordechai Vanunu, the Israeli technician who exposed Israel's nuclear secrets to the media. An Anglican priest from Australia who claimed to be Vanunu's pastor was in Jerusalem appealing Vanunu's case to the Israeli government. As we were checking into our hotel, we learned Vanunu's pastor was staying in a hotel just two blocks from ours. We put our luggage in our rooms and walked to his hotel.

Coincidentally, Ray knew Vanunu's pastor, the Rev. John McKnight, who had attended one of his urban ministry seminars in Sydney. John was trying to organize a press conference to draw attention to the Vanunu case and request that he be granted asylum in Australia. We offered to assist him as I had some experience arranging press conferences in Chicago and had friends in Jerusalem who could help us with current press lists.

I wondered if the Israeli government would prevent us from holding a press conference, but we had to go ahead and take that chance. I suggested we rent a room in the American Colony Hotel for the press conference, as many international journalists were staying there. We started telephoning and faxing the local media to inform them of our press conference, scheduled for 9 the next morning. Taking a stack of press releases to the American Colony, I booked a room and stuffed the hotel mailboxes with press releases. We had no idea how well attended the press conference would be, given Israel's ban on media coverage of Vanunu.

The backstory on Mordechai Vanunu is important and it reads like a spy thriller. He is a Moroccan Jew whose family settled in Be'er Sheva in the 1960s. He was working as a technician at Israel's secret nuclear facility at Dimona in the Negev Desert when he became increasingly troubled by Israel's secret nuclear program. One day he decided to photograph every room in the facility and promptly quit his job. He left Israel for an extended vacation in India, taking the photos with him. At this point, he had no idea what he would do with them.

After a month in India he traveled to Australia and ended up in Sydney. One day as he was walking to his hotel, he noticed an announcement on an outdoor church bulletin board promoting a Wednesday evening discussion series titled "Following Jesus into Places of Conflict." Intrigued by the topic, he decided to attend. After several weeks of stimulating discussions, Mordechai told the pastor leading the series, the Rev. John McKnight, about the photographs of Israel's nuclear arsenal in his possession. He still had no idea what he should do with them.

Rev. McKnight began to meet with Mordechai on a regular basis, seeking guidance in this monumental decision. Their meetings increased and by late June 1986, after a long theological and philosophical struggle, Vanunu converted to the Christian faith. He was baptized in August and continued to meet with his pastor. After John led a session on "Christian Responsibility and Nuclear War," Mordechai was convinced the photos needed to be published. He was fully aware of the risks involved in such a decision.

Rev. McKnight challenged Mordechai to be certain this was the best decision possible and that he was ready to face the consequences. Together they carefully explored several publishers and Vanunu settled on the London *Sunday Times*. After weeks of careful vetting of the photos for authenticity, the *Times* flew Vanunu to London and the story broke on October 5, 1986. Prior to that date, Israel had been coy about its nuclear arsenal, claiming "it would neither introduce nuclear weapons to the Middle East nor be the first to use them." Now the mask was off, and the photos published in the *Times* exposed Israel's advanced nuclear program.

Pastor McKnight stayed in daily contact with Mordechai during his trip to London, but suddenly Mordechai went silent. McKnight learned Mordechai had been drugged and kidnapped by Mossad and was taken to Israel. The pastor purchased a ticket and flew to Tel Aviv. In his last phone call with Vanunu, Rev. McKnight remembered Vanunu saying, "My life is in danger."

The press room at the American Colony was filled to capacity the next morning as Rev. McKnight addressed the media. He appealed to Israel to live up to its claim as a thriving democracy and either put Mordechai on trial with attorneys of his choice or grant him amnesty in Australia or Norway. The questions for Rev. McKnight that morning were generally sympathetic, but some were hostile, accusing Vanunu of being a traitor.

Israel ignored Rev. McKnight's appeals and sentenced Mordechai Vanunu to prison for treason. During his eighteen years in prison, much of it in isolation, a family in Minnesota attempted to adopt him as a family member and provide him with a home in the United States. Israel rejected any and all overtures. When Vanunu was finally released, he was restricted to staying in Jerusalem, unable to leave the country and closely watched around the clock by Israel's secret police. The Anglican Church in East Jerusalem provided housing and support. Mordechai said his faith was the only thing that kept him sane and brought him through this ordeal.

I saw Mordechai regularly at St. Georges over the succeeding years. The last time I spoke to him was after worship at the Lutheran Church of the Redeemer in mid-December 2019. My wife, Linda, and I offered to take him to lunch, but unfortunately, he was unable to accept our invitation due to tightening restrictions and monitoring. As I write in 2025, we understand that he has been able to move to Jaffa but is still closely monitored and restricted from leaving Israel.[43]

While the bulk of our time in Jerusalem was consumed with the dramatic events surrounding Mordechai Vanunu, Ray and I had several very productive meetings with other leaders. We met with Samir Kafity, the Anglican bishop of Jerusalem and the Middle East, who was very enthusiastic about our project and encouraged us to move forward with haste. As a Palestinian Christian, the bishop was very aware of the influence of Christian zionism, which he viewed as "a heretical theology." He encouraged our plan to establish an evangelical organization and put the Israeli-Palestinian struggle and the challenge of Christian zionism at the top of our priorities.

We left Jerusalem and traveled north to the village of I'billin in the Galilee to meet Fr. Elias Chacour, who by 1986 was very popular in Europe, the United States, Australia, and Canada. Abuna, as he was known around the world, pledged to be available to assist us in any way possible as he saw our outreach to evangelicals as a high priority. We asked him if he was willing to come to London or Washington, DC, for our "founding meeting," and he agreed, with his familiar caveat: "*Inshallah*, pending my schedule."

The next day, we left Tel Aviv for the short forty-five-minute flight to Cairo, our last stop on the journey. Our first meeting in Cairo was with our mutual friend and host, Bishop Samuel, the bishop of Social Development and Ecumenical Relations for the Coptic Orthodox Church. During our discussion, Bishop Samuel urged us to emphasize the delicate situation facing the Coptic Christians but to be careful as to how we represented the church's position concerning the government of Egypt and Islam. He asked us to be respectful of Islam and avoid any Islamophobic statements. Tension was high in Egypt as there had been a series of violent attacks on Coptic churches by an extremist branch of the Muslim Brotherhood.

The bishop informed us that Pope Shenouda preferred to negotiate quietly and directly with the Egyptian government and Muslim leaders on these matters. The bishop added his concern about the rise of Christian extremists not only in the United States but also in Egypt, saying, "this is an issue where we need your help in the West. These people are coming to Egypt and their hostile message about Islam makes the Muslims angry and understandably so." Bishop Samuel added the need to affirm the Christians of Egypt but to never demonize Islam. He noted how this is a problem with many Western Christians, particularly some evangelicals.

The next day, Ray and I left to visit Pope Shenouda at his monastery, St. Bishoy, about an hour and a half west of Cairo. Arriving at his monastery, Ray and I marveled at the lush trees, flowers, vegetables, and fruit growing around the walls and inside the monastery grounds. We were told the monks who work the grounds were experts on gardening and irrigation methods in the arid desert climate. The Egyptian government recently hired them as consultants to the Department of Agriculture. The monk who welcomed us joked, "We have the advantage of prayer that helps our trees and fruits grow better than those of the government."

We were taken to His Holiness' simple study, where we renewed our prior acquaintances with him. We brought greetings from Gaby Habib and mentioned some of the meetings we had during our journey. We mentioned the goals of our trip and he smiled and was pleased to hear about the focus on western evangelicals. When we asked about the Palestinians, he added, "The Copts of Egypt always stand with the Palestinians."

The pope surprised us by declaring that he had banned Christian pilgrimage to Palestine and Israel until the "illegal Israeli occupation ends." He mentioned his long friendship with Yasser Arafat, noting they were at Cairo University together and had supported each other since that time. We were grateful for the visit and knew we had an important advocate for our work with evangelicals. The Coptic Orthodox Church was growing across the United States and Canada, and we needed to make connections with them. His endorsement of our work was of great importance.

Then he changed topics and mentioned the rise of Christian extremism and Christian zionism, which brought serious problems to the majority of Christians in the Middle East. He emphasized how the rise in Christian extremism, and especially Christian zionism, made Christianity look like a Western export. "Christianity was born and flourished here in the Middle East," he said. "We need to correct these Western aberrations as they portray Christianity as a kind of pro-Israel movement and turns God into a real estate agent for Israel." Pope Shenouda thought a new evangelical organization that worked closely with Middle Eastern Christians would be welcomed by the Christians and most Muslims in Egypt and across the region.

The next day we boarded our flight home, more than grateful for the meetings, both high-level and at the grassroots. We filled several legal pads with notes from our visits and had tapes and plenty of photos for presentations. Our next task would be to look for a coherent pattern of ideas so we could prioritize the issues. We discussed possible goals and a mission statement on the flight, and it seemed Ray and I agreed on the key findings. We were convinced after the three-week journey that we had clear evidence and support from Middle East leaders for a new evangelical organization.

After returning to Chicago, Ray and I worked separately for a few days and then met for lunch. We quickly found that we agreed on our three top priorities. Priority one was the establishment of a new organization to educate Western evangelical Christians about the historic witness and presence of the 15 million Christians in the Middle East. The second priority was to challenge the emergence of the Christian right and particularly Christian zionist doctrines and their influence on all Christians and Muslims in the Middle East. In this context we noted the dangerous growth of Islamophobia among the Christian zionists and others that needed our attention.

Our third priority was to call for evangelicals to support a just resolution of the Israeli-Palestinian political struggle based on international law and a negotiated political settlement. Above all, we needed to challenge the false teachings and influence of Christian zionism as it relates to the Palestinian people and claims that God gave the entirety of historic Palestine to the Jewish people. This and other false teachings of the Bible must be addressed by Western evangelicals. We added a fourth priority, which became important in our mission: establish closer relationships between Middle Eastern churches and churches in the United States.

We sent these goals to Gaby Habib for feedback along with our thanks for his arrangements, which made our trip possible. We had overwhelming support for a new evangelical organization to implement these goals and wondered what Gaby thought about convening a small group of Western evangelicals and a few Middle Eastern Christian leaders to launch the group.

A few days later we had an extensive telephone conversation with Gaby. We agreed on the goals and a meeting to launch the project. We considered various options and Gaby suggested London, England, as it would be easy for Middle Easterners and North Americans to meet there. Surprisingly, Ray divulged that he had already discussed the proposed organization with approximately fifteen evangelicals from large organizations who wanted to attend the inaugural meeting. Most could pay their own way. Gaby was pleased with a core group of fifteen and said he would recruit five Middle Eastern Christians to join us.

Ray suggested that we launch the meeting at Rev. John Stott's Center for Contemporary Christianity near Trafalgar Square in London. Rev. Stott was one of the leading evangelicals in the world, and his name would provide significant legitimacy to our efforts. He was close to Billy Graham and chaired the Lausanne Committee for World Evangelization, the largest evangelical organization in the world. Ray had worked with Rev. Stott, and we agreed to have our founding meeting at his center with approximately twenty leaders from Western evangelical organizations and Middle Eastern Christians.

The founding meeting at London's Center for Contemporary Christianity convened on September 18–19, 1987, hosted by Rev. Stott. Ray and I led the meeting with twenty-two in attendance: five from the Middle East, fourteen from North America, and three from England. Organizations in attendance included the Southern Baptist Convention, World Vision International, Young Life, the National Association of Evangelicals, InterVarsity Fellowship, and the Lausanne Committee for World Evangelization. Gaby brought Fr. Chacour, Rev. Adeeb Awad from Syria, Rev. Munir Adeeb from the Anglican Church, and Bishop Samuel from Egypt. We reached consensus to call the new organization Evangelicals for Middle East Understanding (EMEU).

We decided to issue a press release announcing the new organization. Then we asked Gaby Habib to draft a letter on behalf of Christians of the

Middle East to 150–200 US and British evangelicals, inviting Western evangelicals into a relationship with Middle Eastern Christians. The Middle East Council of Churches was the main partner for EMEU in this new initiative. We eventually received a positive response from over 100 evangelical leaders. We invited them to a meeting in Washington, DC, chaired by the chaplain of the US Senate, Rev. Richard Halverson, a well-known evangelical. Gaby attended the meeting and followed it with a two-week tour of the United States and met personally with several leading evangelicals.

Ray asked me how I did in fundraising to cover expenses for the London meeting. I told him we covered all the expenses and reimbursement checks to the participants were in the mail. He then said, "May I ask who donated the funds?" I told him to keep it in confidence that the donor was a wealthy Palestinian from London. The beautiful part of this was he was very enthusiastic about the project because it was designed to educate Western evangelicals. I added, "Isn't that a nice touch and how God works? A Palestinian Muslim has made it possible for us to launch an organization designed to educate Western evangelicals."

Chapter 18

A REVIVAL OF RESISTANCE IN THE UNHOLY LAND: THE FIRST PALESTINIAN INTIFADA

"There is no getting away from the fact that as an idea, a memory, and as an often buried or invisible reality, Palestine and the people have simply not disappeared. No matter the sustained and unbroken hostility of the Israeli establishment to anything that Palestine represents, the sheer fact of our existence has foiled, where it has not defeated, the Israeli efforts to be rid of us completely."

—Edward Said

Everything changed in the Middle East on December 9, 1987, at least for a few years. The previous thirty years saw Israel in complete control of the Palestinians in both the occupied territories and within Israel proper. On the surface, the Palestinians were in serious political decline by the fall of 1987. The PLO was isolated in far-off Tunisia, Algeria, and Yemen. The United States seemed to be closer to Israel than at any previous time and consistently ran interference for it in the United Nations and other international venues. Israel seemed to have no international accountability and could do whatever it desired with the Palestinians.

Even the Arab world was showing less interest in the Palestinian case, with some governments reducing their foreign aid to the PLO. The decline of the celebrity status once held by the Palestinians in the Middle East was clear when the Arab summit convened in Amman, Jordan on November 8, 1987. When Yasser Arafat and the PLO delegation arrived at the Amman International Airport, nobody was there to meet them. This was an insult of the highest magnitude in the Arab world and was televised for everyone to see.

I watched the reports from our temporary new home in Cyprus, amazed that in this pre-cable period we could pull in distant stations from Jordan,

Israel, Lebanon, Turkey, and Egypt. Jordan television covered the snub in detail since the kingdom was hosting the summit. The reports indicated the glory days were over for Arafat and the Palestinians.

One month later, on December 9, 1987, Gaza's desperately poor and densely populated Jabalia refugee camp lit a fuse that transformed the region overnight. An Israeli military truck plowed into a station wagon filled with Palestinian day laborers hoping to work in Israel. Four Palestinians were killed and eight were seriously injured in the incident. Every Palestinian believed it was deliberate; they had seen this kind of military action countless times.

Word of the incident spread quickly, and Jabalia's residents took to the streets. Suddenly the Israeli military patrols were confronted by hundreds and later thousands of angry protesters. A spirit of defiance and fearless aggression was evident as protesters burned tires, blocked the streets, and pelted the Israeli army with stones. The Palestinians were showing a new spirit of defiance and fearlessness as the youth, in particular, rose up and resisted the Israeli army.

To say the Palestinian Intifada began on December 9 would be to ignore the months and years of Palestinian resistance and suffering that preceded it. Palestinians had been resisting the brutal Israeli occupation daily since it began in June 1967. In fact, Palestinians had been resisting zionist colonization since the 1920s under the British Mandate and a major revolt occurred between 1936–39. The revolt was violently crushed by the British and zionist militias armed and trained by the British, leaving over 20,000 Palestinians dead and most of the leadership exiled from Palestine.

By the fall of 1987, the Palestinians had seen enough of Israeli's repressive occupation and colonization of their land and an explosion was inevitable. Localized incidents were one thing, but mass resistance across the Palestinian territories was considered impossible. The Israeli military system of control was thought to be too efficient, and its occupation had been on cruise control for several years. The military efficiency was the primary reason for Israel's effectiveness, and a system of paid collaborators increased its effectiveness. However, what happened in the Gaza Strip on December 9, 1987, seemed to come out of nowhere. This event echoed from Gaza's slums to the West Bank within twenty-four hours.

It is beyond ironic that the Gaza Strip was the location of a massive nonviolent protest movement called the Great March of Return that began on March 30, 2018, and continued every Friday for a year and a half. Gazans of all ages went to the Israeli military fence surrounding the Strip and flew kites, burned tires, and chanted about their right to return. They were completely unarmed, and nonviolent discipline was maintained. Israel's response was to deploy tanks, armed soldiers, and snipers, who killed over 200 and maimed others, shooting in the kneecap or head.

On October 7, 2023, Gazans broke out of their prison, led by Hamas, and sadly killed nearly 1,100 Israelis and took over 200 hostages, marking the most serious threat to Israel's security since the October war of 1973. The tragic genocidal war of 2023–25 ensued, killing approximately 70,000 Palestinians, with an untold number still under the rubble[44]. The resistance action by Hamas did put Palestine back near the top of the unresolved issues of Middle East peace and justice after the US and Israel had successfully marginalized their case. But at a terrible cost in Palestinian life, and Hamas remains guilty of war crimes by killing innocent civilians and taking hostages from Israel.

Following the December 1987 protests in Gaza, resistance events swept through the West Bank and East Jerusalem the next day. The crowded and bustling cities of Ramallah, Hebron, Nablus, East Jerusalem, Tulkarm, and Bethlehem all saw protests. Soon they spread to the small villages and refugee camps across Palestine and inside the Green Line, where the Palestinian Israelis rose up in an uncharacteristic rebellion. The Intifada (literally "the shaking off," generally understood to mean "uprising") was underway, a predominantly nonviolent mobilization of resistance in every sector of Palestinian society.

Watching the daily news of the Intifada from Cyprus inspired me to take one of the short forty-five-minute flights to Tel Aviv and experience the Intifada firsthand. I talked it over with Drew and the kids, and as long as I was back by Christmas Eve (with extra presents) they supported me making the trip. That gave me ten days in the Palestinian territories. I spoke to Gaby Habib, my boss for the sabbatical, and he had already been thinking about sending me to the West Bank and Gaza Strip. He said my background in human rights and connections with Palestinian and Israeli organizations would be useful for MECC. Gaby said the churches need to respond to these developments in Palestine.

Gaby asked, "How soon can you leave?" I said in about two hours. He laughed and ordered a taxi to the airport. "I trust you have cleared this with your family," he said. I assured him they were supportive as long as I brought back a few extra gifts for Christmas Day. I called my friends in Jerusalem to tell them I was arriving that evening, and they agreed to meet me at the airport.

My first stop was a briefing on the latest developments with Kathy Bergen and Jan and Samir Abu-Shakra in East Jerusalem. They were working at the Palestine Human Rights Information Center (PHRIC) in East Jerusalem and had between eight and ten field workers deployed from Gaza and Hebron in the south to Jenin and Nablus in the north. Our Palestine Human Rights Campaign in the United States was a sister organization. About a year earlier, I signed a working agreement with the respected Palestinian leader Faisal Husseini, who was the host and local sponsor of PHRIC. Jan had a PhD in sociology and was married to a Palestinian attorney, Samir Abu-Shakrah.

The North American coordinator was Louise Cainkar, a brilliant young sociologist working out of our Chicago office, having just received her PhD from Northwestern University. Louise and Jan turned this joint project into a major source of timely data on the Intifada, providing the latest human rights information to human rights and legal organizations, the media, and several governmental and nongovernmental agencies around the world.

When I arrived in Jerusalem on December 13, 1987, I was amazed by the degree of creative energy in the Palestinian streets. The atmosphere had dramatically shifted as young Palestinians competed with the Israeli army to see who owned the streets. The first two nights, I stayed with Jan and Samir, who continued to update me on the latest developments. Their field workers submitted daily reports from different regions of occupied Palestine. They were meticulous in checking and cross-checking each incident multiple times. The PHRIC/PHRC database operation was remarkably efficient and accurate, and was the leader in tracking the Intifada.

Jan and Samir emphasized the heavy price Palestinians were paying, yet their resistance was increasing. PHRIC confirmed and catalogued each Palestinian who died according to their name, age, location, and in some cases the type of fatal injury. The field workers were highly trained in detailed research and reporting methods and were careful to leave nothing to chance. Jan and Samir suggested I spend a couple of days in the Gaza Strip with one of the field workers so I could experience the resistance that was overwhelmingly nonviolent.

After a couple of days in Jerusalem and the West Bank, it was clear this level of coordination, and sacrificial suffering among Palestinians was unlike anything we had seen. When we got up in the morning, there was a *bayan* ("briefing") with the day's goals and actions slid under the apartment door or placed on the car windshields. Samir said the *shabab* ("Intifada youth") distributed these briefings in the middle of the night and the *bayans* came from the underground leadership. No one knew the identity of the underground leadership or where they were located, which left the Israelis clueless and frustrated.

Each bayan was dated and mentioned the most recent martyrs with their ages, hometowns, and means of death. It also included times and locations of demonstrations in each city. There were instructions for shopkeepers with a rotating schedule of times they were to close their shops (e.g., East Jerusalem at 2 PM, Bethlehem at 1 PM, Hebron at noon, etc.). People were reminded to boycott all Israeli products and to maintain nonviolence in their demonstrations. Significant events in Palestinian history were briefly mentioned and honored at demonstrations.

Jan said the shabab played significant leadership roles at the demonstrations by rallying people of all ages to come out to the streets. They were also active in disciplining the shopkeepers who did not honor the closure of businesses at the precise time designated by the *bayans*. A shopkeeper who ignored the closing time might find a broken window or graffiti written on their front door as a reminder.

Women played a major role in the Intifada. Several popular women's committees mobilized women and children in various solidarity actions ranging from demonstrations to medical relief. Zahira Kamal, Rita Giacomin, Um-Khalil, and Rima Tarazi of In-Ash Al-Usra were among the many women I met who were leading popular committees in health, education, and local organizing. Women were involved at every level, and some analysts said they were the backbone of the resistance.

One of the largest organizations I met was the Medical Relief Committee led by Drs. Mustafa Barghouti and Rita Giacomin of Birzeit University. Their mobile clinics and training in emergency medicine was highly effective throughout the West Bank. In the Gaza Strip, similar training and relief was coordinated by the Red Crescent Society and the main hospitals. The YWCA and YMCAs also deserve mention in the discussion of mobilizing and training women in health and medical services.[45]

I was eager to spend a few days in the Gaza Strip, where I was met by Walid, a PHRIC field worker. Walid had recently finished college at the Islamic University and was one of two field workers for PHRIC covering human rights cases in the most densely populated area on earth. We drove to the edge of the massive Jabalia refugee camp in the north of Gaza, where we saw the shabab, some as young as eight or nine years old, hurling stones at Israeli jeeps and burning tires in the street. The energy and courage of the *shabab* was remarkable, considering the heavily armed Israeli military.

We watched one incident unfold as a military jeep stopped abruptly after it was hit by a barrage of stones. The shabab scurried through the narrow alleys, easily losing the IDF soldiers in the maze of the densely populated Jabalia camp with nearly 100,000 refugees packed into one square mile. We noticed other *shabab* flying kites with the colors of the Palestinian flag, outlawed by Israel and punishable by serving time in prison. The kites became a sport and a form of resistance that annoyed the Israeli military, because the *shabab* never gave up.

Walid drove by another large demonstration near Beach Camp and pointed to two young Palestinians on bicycles. He told me to watch them, observing how the leaders were directing the demonstration from their bicycles. The two leaders cycled in and out of the crowd shouting directions to the protesters. He estimated the two boys were no more than fourteen years old, yet they had complete command of the demonstration numbering around 300 people. Walid said this pattern was common throughout the Gaza Strip. There was no need for adults to tell them what to do.

Walid drove to another street where we saw a small demonstration in front of a mosque. He said, "Watch this one closely. It has us puzzled. Do you notice anything unusual about this event?" I paused and then noted that it was similar to other demonstrations, but smaller. Walid said, "We could wait here for two hours, and you will find the Israelis never bother them."

"Why?" I asked.

Walid explained that they were a new Islamic organization named Hamas, and the Israelis seemed to be encouraging them for some reason.

"We believe the Israelis are trying to divide the Palestinians by pitting one Muslim group against the popular resistance and its leadership." It was the old divide-and-conquer tactic. "We will be watching this development closely," he added.

Walid and his family graciously hosted me at their small cinder block home for three evenings. They were a family of seven children and three adults (including a grandmother) living in four tiny rooms. Walid was the only one who spoke English, so he did all the translating. We sat in a circle on the floor for dinner around a beautiful platter of *musaqa'a* with chicken. We had simple conversations, but after we got to know each other they had several questions. They wanted to know about my family and especially the children. I passed around pictures, and they liked a picture of my second son, Matthew, as a baby in a kaffiyeh—a Palestinian scarf worn by peasants and a symbol of resistance.

Walid's mother asked me, "Why are you, an American and a Christian, supporting the Palestinians?"

I told them there was a growing movement of supporters of Palestine in the United States and Europe who are Christians, Jews, and Muslims, as well as many secular people. "We understand the Palestinian struggle and support it, but we have little power with our government," I explained. "We believe the Palestinians deserve justice and the big powers like England and the United States have supported the zionists and Israel as they have taken your land. We hope our movement will grow so we can stop the weapons and funding the US gives Israel."

When it was time to sleep, Walid asked if I would take his bed in the room he shared with his three brothers. He explained that he was worried the IDF was following him and might break into the home in the middle of the night, which was their pattern. He was moving from house to house every evening as he suspected the IDF wanted to silence his reports about Israel's human rights violations. I was happy to oblige. The first night I slept rather restlessly, but the second and third nights were easy. The experience made me more aware of the risks taken by our field workers and anyone involved in the resistance.

When I returned to Jerusalem days later, I arranged a series of meetings with church leaders. I was able to visit representatives from most of the Christian denominations that had a presence in Jerusalem. The bishops and priests were reluctant to have their churches engage in solidarity actions during the Intifada. They were very supportive of the Intifada but hesitated to get involved personally, with a few exceptions. This dynamic was about to change.

On my last Sunday before Christmas, since I was in Jerusalem, I wanted to attend worship at St. George's Anglican Cathedral. Several friends told me about the Rev. Naim Ateek who was different from the rest of the priests and bishops. They were right. Rev. Ateek preached an Advent sermon on Jesus' birth into poverty and oppression under the Roman Empire. His message was a call for justice and solidarity with the poor and marginalized. I was determined to introduce myself and have a conversation with him after the service.

Before the benediction, Rev. Ateek invited the congregation to stay and join him for coffee and a discussion of the sermon in light of events of the Intifada. Joining Rev. Ateek in the discussion was Palestinian attorney Jonathan Kuttab, whom I had met a few years earlier at a conference in the United States. They discussed the sermon and the biblical texts for the day and applied the Christian faith to justice and the need for involvement in the Intifada.

The group in the talk-back session numbered around thirty-five people, and after Naim and Jonathan spoke, people began to share concerns. A man said his son was arrested and had been in prison for a week and asked us to pray for him. Jonathan offered his legal services if they were needed. A mother from another family said she was worried about her three boys who were all active in the demonstrations. She asked them to stay home but they would not listen as all their friends were involved. She said they were not afraid, but she was worried about what the Israelis would do to them.

The discussion continued with an appearance by four human rights workers from Christian Peacemaker Teams who had driven up from Hebron reported on the intense confrontations between the military and the people. They mentioned their concern over the excessive violence the military was using against nonviolent demonstrations. One CPT member spoke up, saying, "We are all committed to nonviolence but the Israelis have no respect for it and only know brute force. There is little hope in trying to appeal to their consciences."

I would soon learn that these post-worship talk-back sessions had become popular and word began to spread about their value. For most of the sessions, either Jonathan Kuttab or Ken Bailey, a New Testament scholar, provided commentary and application. The sessions were pastoral and prophetic at the same time and provided mutual support and inspiration for members and local activists. The prophetic dimension was a major emphasis as the sermons and responders called the congregation to be guided by the liberating message of Jesus and the Hebrew prophets.

I was pleased to meet Gerald Butt, a familiar name to avid listeners of the BBC World Service. Gerald was the Jerusalem correspondent, a faithful Anglican, and a regular worshipper at St. Georges. Gerald offered thoughtful insights during the feedback sessions based on his faith and experiences as a journalist covering the Intifada. He was a refreshing contrast to the US journalists, who appeared fearful of getting too close to the Palestinians.

I met with Jonathan and Naim separately and mentioned the MECC's hope for a statement from the heads of Churches in Jerusalem concerning the Intifada. I told them the MECC was willing and able to distribute it around the world if they could secure a statement. Naim said he had been thinking about the same thing and was ready to work on it. He said it would take a few weeks as many of the church leaders were cautious. He reminded me the Israelis were sure to punish church leaders through various forms of intimidation like fines, house arrest, and revoking their travel privileges.

I said, "Whoever you can get to sign a strong statement will be fine and I know you need to be careful about how you send it to us. If you can find a separate and secure fax machine, we will disseminate it around the world on your behalf. Do what's necessary to protect yourselves." Jonathan said finding a secure fax machine would not be problem and he knew of one we could use. Both Naim and Jonathan affirmed the plan.

By the end of January, Naim was able to convince a majority of the heads of churches in Jerusalem to issue their first global appeal regarding the Intifada. The open letter was the first of its kind in history from the heads of churches in Jerusalem in support of a social justice movement like the Intifada. Prior to this, individual church leaders had issued statements, but this was nearly all the bishops, archbishops, and patriarchs speaking in unison.

We had been working as an MECC staff in Cyprus to be ready for transmitting the letter. We updated our contacts on every continent, including councils of churches, news outlets, and key political leaders, church associations, interfaith organizations, humanitarian organizations, and both religious and secular media. We made several follow-up calls to make sure key people received it and urged them to give it priority attention as it was an unprecedented statement.

Within days we began to see results. Framing the statement as an appeal from the Christian churches of the holy land gave it a sense of legitimacy. Several church leaders around the world issued solidarity statements in support of the Intifada and called for a peaceful and just resolution to the Israeli-Palestinian struggle.

In May 1988, with considerable fanfare, Israel claimed that it had arrested Mubarak Awad, my good friend and the cousin of Jonathan Kuttab. Mubarak was the president of Nonviolence International and a disciple of Dr. King and Gandhi. He and his wife, Nancy, principal of the American Friends School in Ramallah, were temporarily living in Ramallah. Israel placed Mubarak in solitary confinement and made a media sensation out of his arrest, calling him "the leader of the Intifada." This maneuver only fueled global interest in the Intifada, and since the underground leadership remained a secret, the deportation of Awad backfired on Israel.

The First Intifada was a homegrown, grassroots mobilization of the Palestinian people—not a new phenomenon. It was a movement of, by, and for the Palestinians living under Israel's military occupation. The PLO had nothing to do with it and in fact had to catch up with the phenomenon. Mazin Qumsiyeh's *Popular Resistance in Palestine* offers an extensive survey of 100 years of mostly nonviolent resistance. His volume begins with expressions of Palestinian resistance under the Ottoman Turks in the 1890s and underscores the concept of popular or grassroots resistance.[46]

I made four trips to Palestine in 1988, most on behalf of the Middle East Council of Churches. In April 1988, our family took the overnight boat from Cyprus to Haifa. My two younger children, Matt and Anna, got to experience the Intifada at the ages of four and three respectively. They played with Jan and Samir Abu-Shakrah's boys and attended their preschool, learning a few Arabic words. The main reason for the April visit was to attend and monitor the convention organized by the International Christian Embassy–Jerusalem. The ICEJ originally planned to have a massive Christian zionist convention commemorating the centennial of the founding of zionism in Basel, Switzerland. They were planning to host 5,000–10,000 zionist Christians to flood Jerusalem and declare their love of Israel.

My previous trip, in March 1988, involved local organizing for groups to challenge the ICEJ conference. Kathy Bergen and I convened a group of international volunteers and office workers who drafted a statement that local Christians could adapt for the Arabic and Hebrew press. We also planned a small protest for the opening night of the conference when Prime Minister Shamir of Israel was scheduled to speak.

Kathy and I visited the ICEJ headquarters in March to register for the conference and obtain the final schedule. We asked about the anticipated number of attendees, and they said they originally hoped for 5,000–10,000 but due to the Intifada they were expecting 2,500–3,000 from around the world. I was surprised when the receptionist asked if we would like to meet with Johann Luckhoff, the director of ICEJ. I worried he might recognize my name as I had published articles in *Middle East International*, a widely read London news magazine, criticizing the ICEJ and Christian zionism. Fortunately, he did not seem to know me.

In the course of our conversation, he asked what I knew about Christian zionism. I discussed some of my research at the British Museum including the early movement of British Restorationists, such as Rev. Thomas Brightman (1685) and Sir Henry Finch (1743). This seemed to be new information for him, and he was fascinated. He asked if I would be willing to deliver a paper at the upcoming convention, and I had to make a quick decision. I thanked him profusely but declined. I realized it would compromise my role with MECC and the Palestinians, and worse, my lecture could be manipulated if the group were to publish it without my critique.

When I returned to Cyprus in March, I worked with MECC to call upon church leaders across the Middle East to make strong statements at their churches and in the media rejecting the false message of the Christian zionists and denouncing how they were distorting the Bible and Jesus' message of love, justice, and inclusivity.

I wrote a monograph titled "What Is Western Fundamentalist Christian Zionism?" The monograph was translated into Arabic and we sent thousands of copies of both the Arabic and English versions to Lebanon, Syria, Jordan, Jerusalem, and Egypt. We were able to publish excerpts in several Christian journals around the Middle East.

When the ICEJ conference opened in Jerusalem, Patriarch Ignatius IV in Damascus and Pope Shenouda of the Coptic Church appeared on Syrian and Egyptian television denouncing the ICEJ conference as a false version of Christianity. Pope Shenouda called Christian zionism a Western heresy. The Palestinian press reported on the statements from the patriarchs.

On April 10, 1988, Kathy, Drew, and I were joined by our young volunteers and were curious about what we were about to experience. We were shocked by the low attendance. The original projection was 5,000–6,000 participants, which was reduced to 4,000 five months prior, then again lowered to 2,000 in March. We counted the attendees, who numbered a mere 700 participants, many of whom were presenters, staff, and ICEJ volunteers. The ICEJ gala convention was another casualty of the Intifada as most ICEJ supporters around the world decided to stay home.

I remembered seeing a television ad in Chicago before we left for Cyprus promoting Israeli tourism with the theme "Israel: Just a Stone's Throw Away." The ads were pulled in mid-December when the Intifada broke out as the Palestinian *shabab* used stones like the Old Testament's David as their means of resistance to Goliath—the Israeli tanks and military forces.

Not only did Israel's tourism collapse, but Israel lost control of the news media. Within six months, the news coverage started to shift from the usual pro-Israel narrative to showing a violent Israeli army fighting Palestinian children armed only with stones and slingshots. The nonviolent strategies of the Palestinians slowly began to gain more sympathy in Europe and North and South America.

The one audience celebrating the violent rhetoric of the Israeli military and political leadership were the Christian zionists. As we watched and listened to the ICEJ convention—featuring contemporary Christian music and dancers singing praises to Israel—we felt a cult-like atmosphere as they seemed to be literally bowing down to worship at the altar of the Israel Defense Forces and the nation of Israel. What we witnessed was pure idolatry. The ICEJ was nothing short of a cult in love with the nation of Israel that twisted the Bible to fit its false political ideology of praising Israel, not God.

After the dancers and praise songs for Israel concluded, it was time for Prime Minister Shamir's speech. Despite the secular Shamir's failure to mention the Bible in his violent rhetoric against the PLO and Palestinian terrorists, the audience hung onto his every word. There were several standing ovations as the prime minister railed against the Intifada as a "vile force of antisemitism calling for the destruction of Israel." Shamir denounced the Intifada as "an evil plot orchestrated by the terrorist PLO in their futile attempt to undermine the security of the country." Of course, Shamir ignored the fact that the Intifada was a homegrown and directed resistance, primarily nonviolent, against decades of Israeli oppression.

Shamir concluded, "What is happening in Judea and Samaria and Gaza is a continuation of the Arabs' war against the Jewish people. We have not returned to *Eretz Israel* ("Greater Israel") to be frightened by rocks and stones and firebombs. Here we are and here we will stay forever." The audience stood and screamed its praises for Israel. We left immediately as we had a project to launch.[47]

Our experience at the ICEJ conference was a reminder of how dangerous Christian zionism was for Palestinians. Palestinians had no place in this theology aside from being "in the way" while zionists stole their land. The Christian zionists were forming partnerships with militant zionist settlers who viewed Palestinians as Philistines and Canaanites who were to be exterminated or driven out of the country. What we were witnessing was settler colonialism with a false Christian veneer. We had our work cut out for us as they were gaining prominence and power in the right wing of the Republican Party alongside Ronald Reagan. We had to wonder where this type of extremism in Israel and the Republican Party would take Israel and the United States. We would soon find out.

Chapter 19

IN AND OUT OF ACADEMIA

"Ye shall know the truth and the truth shall make you mad."

—Aldous Huxley

I left my position at the Palestine Human Rights Campaign in the fall of 1989 after ten years as national director. My new position was with my friends Dan O'Neill and Ells Culver—the three of us were leaders of Evangelicals for Middle East Understanding (EMEU) and we organized clergy and led academic delegations to Palestine and Israel. The work was fulfilling, and it allowed me in my new position to expand our work with evangelicals by introducing more people to the justice issues in Palestine through the Middle East Programs at Mercy Corps International.

After celebrating my third year in the position, I received a disturbing phone call from my colleague Lowell Ewert at Mercy Corps headquarters in Portland, Oregon. Lowell had just overheard a conversation among staff about the changes they anticipated under the new Mercy Corps director, who would be assuming his position within a month. Lowell said it was clear the new director planned to terminate the Mercy Corps programs with Palestinians and put more emphasis on contracts with the US government through US foreign-assistance grants. The new director's views were not sympathetic with the Palestinian issue, and he wanted to distance the organization from it.

Suddenly my job at Mercy Corps was in jeopardy. I was grateful Lowell was looking out for me, but the writing was on the wall. Lowell advised me, "To be absolutely candid, Don, you should activate your résumé now and start looking for another position immediately." Once again, justice in Palestine created a problem for me, but I believed another door would open so I could remain focused on that very issue.

Within a week of my conversation with Lowell, a friend from my church called and invited me to lunch with her and another professor at North Park

University in Chicago. She said they would like to explore the possibility of having me teach a course on comparative religions at the university. I was intrigued by the idea, and the thought of teaching again was something I welcomed.

She told me the course would be in the fall semester, which was two months away. It seemed like a quick turnaround, but it gave me time to prepare. I knew very little about North Park University aside from its outstanding basketball team, which won the small college national championship two of the previous three years. As for comparative religions, I did have a good working knowledge of Buddhism, Islam, Judaism, and Christianity.

During our lunch meeting, it became clear they were more interested in my theology than my academic background. I was prepared to make a strong case for my teaching experience at two seminaries and my familiarity with four major world religions, but they wanted to know if I was an evangelical Christian. I was honest and mentioned my hybrid theology was a blend of *Sojourners* theology of social justice plus the insights I have gained from liberation theology, Eastern Orthodox spirituality, and Calvin's reformed theology. They pressed me on my Christology, and I responded that Jesus' life and teachings were at the heart of my theology. They said, "That's good enough for us."

They offered me the job on the spot, and I signed a contract over coffee and dessert. I was excited to get back in the classroom. By the end of August 1994, I was an adjunct professor and enjoyed my interaction with the students. I was on a tight schedule with my EMEU responsibilities as we were planning a major conference in the Middle East, but I was fulfilled and grateful for the dual assignment.

One day as I walked through the halls of the university, I saw a billboard promoting North Park's four academic and cultural centers: Scandinavian (the tradition of the Evangelical Covenant denomination), Africana, Latin American, and Korean. I began to wonder if North Park might be interested in a Middle Eastern Center. There were a few Muslims and Arab Christians on campus and a small Palestinian and Muslim community in their Albany Park neighborhood.

I discussed the idea with my colleague Ray Bakke, chair of the EMEU board of directors, and he thought we should pursue it. He asked me to draft a proposal for a Middle East Center at North Park that would include EMEU.

Ray knew David Horner, the president of North Park, and offered to give him a call to see if there was interest in our proposal.

David offered to meet us for lunch at Tre Kroner ("Three Crowns"), a delightful Swedish restaurant located across the street from North Park University. We discussed the proposal including the possibility of bringing EMEU to North Park as part of a Middle East cultural and academic center. David was a shrewd poker player, so we could not read him, but he expressed interest in our proposal. He asked for a couple of weeks to discuss it with a few faculty and the university's board of directors. I offered to pay for lunch and pulled out my credit card only to be told by the waiter, "Sorry, we don't take credit cards."

I had $5 in my wallet and Ray had $3. David had to pay for lunch, which was very embarrassing. I made a nervous joke about our lack of financial resources, which may not have been the best move when you are trying to land a job and impress the university's president. David took it in stride and said he recently had a similar problem with a donor he was trying to recruit.

Within a week, I received a call from David Horner. He was very positive about the proposal and suggested we meet again the following week. He proposed another lunch at Tre Kroner, and I promised to pick up the check this time. He said he was especially interested in bringing EMEU into the university and wanted to hear more about the organization.

David said the North Park Board of Directors and key faculty liked the proposal and thought it was a natural fit with the Evangelical Covenant denomination, the affiliation of North Park. Then he said there was one more hurdle for us to clear, namely Paul Larson, the president of the denomination. If Larson approved, we could proceed to a contract.

I did some research on Paul Larson and discovered he was involved in Christian-Jewish dialogue with mainline zionist organizations in Chicago. David said Larson had questions about my involvement in Palestinian issues and was concerned I might be antisemitic. I was familiar with how zionist organizations opposed advocacy for Palestinian human rights by arguing it is antisemitic and threatened the security of Israel. I was concerned about Paul's orientation but thought it best to be completely transparent on the Palestine question.

Larson needed two lunch meetings as he zeroed in on my support for the Palestinian cause. He questioned my critique of Christian zionism and had read my recent articles in the *Christian Century* and *Sojourners* magazine. Our initial lunch discussion left him with more questions. Clearly my advocacy for Palestinian human rights and my strong critique of Christian zionism were major obstacles for him.

During our second meeting, I explained how the zionist narrative denies arguments from theology concerning justice and international law in relation to Israel's treatment of Palestinians. I said Israel should be evaluated like any other nation on these matters and to criticize its human rights performance is completely legitimate. Israel is not above the law, and to claim it is an exceptional case places it above the law, including the Ten Commandments. The same can be said about Christian zionism. I said these issues are protected free speech under the US Constitution but are also issues Christians should be able to debate in a reasonable manner without being bullied and called antisemitic for taking these positions. I referenced my long history of supporting the right of Jews to have security and equal rights. I added that I would always stand in opposition to antisemitism, but criticizing Israel's violations of international law and Christian and Jewish ethical positions are not forms of antisemitism.

Larson said he had not considered these arguments, and it seemed to be a turning point in our discussion. He said I had passed the test. The next day, I signed a contract. I had a new position as the director of the Center for Middle Eastern Studies and a professor of Middle Eastern Studies. It was another example of how God works in remarkable ways. I realized there were sensitive issues surrounding the Palestine question and my critique of Israel and Christian zionism. I needed to be aware but was not about to remain silent about the Palestinian case for justice. For the moment, I was thankful a door opened at the university when the door closed at Mercy Corps.

I was welcomed by several new faculty members and students, including two Palestinian students who were brought to North Park on a Palestinian scholarship program. Suhail Qumri and Nakhleh Hussary, both from the West Bank, became good friends and worked closely with me in organizing the new Middle Eastern Center. Gary Burge started the student scholarship program before he moved to Wheaton College. Gary and I worked together at EMEU, and I valued his work as a respected New Testament scholar.

I started teaching a full course load at North Park in the fall of 1995 and we launched the Center for Middle Eastern Studies in early November of that year. I invited Elias Chacour to be the keynote speaker for the launch of the new center. Anderson Chapel was filled that evening, and Paul Larson and David Horner each had brief roles in the program. Abuna Chacour gave an inspiring address and received a standing ovation from the full house.

North Park University was the first evangelical college or university in the United States with a Middle Eastern studies center. The Palestinian students became the core leadership for our new Middle East Student Association (MESA). We added Mai Khader from Al-Ram (between Jerusalem and Ramallah) the next year followed by Rana Kasis of Birzeit village. With Suhail's brilliant knowledge of technology (to offset my incompetence). they brought an energetic willingness to assist me with office work related to the Middle East Center and were the core leadership of MESA.

I set up a relationship between North Park and the Sabeel Ecumenical Liberation Theology Center in Jerusalem to help guide the Palestinian Scholarship Program. Naim Ateek and his staff helped recruit students. Once they narrowed it to the three strongest candidates, I joined them for the interviews in Jerusalem. Naim, Cedar Duaibis, and Samia Khouri and I made the final selection each year. It was important for us to have Palestinian input and legitimacy as they knew how to recruit and involve the parents in the process.

MESA became a strong campus organization, thanks to the dedication and hard work of our Palestinian students. They usually had more influence than I did in winning faculty and student support for the Palestinian issue. The MESA group won the campus award as the most effective student organization for three consecutive years. MESA included several international students, particularly Swedish students, in its programs, and some of them were MESA officers. One of the Swedish students was Targol Hassankhani, an Iranian who emigrated to Sweden with her mother. Targol served as president of MESA and was a strong leader. Most Palestinian students made the dean's list for three of their four years at the university. Roughly half of the Palestinian students went on to pursue PhDs or master's degrees.

One of the Chicago Palestinian students was Fouad Saba, who was a member of St. George Antiochian Orthodox Church in the Chicago suburb Cicero. The church was a strong supporter of our program at North Park under Fr. Nicholas Dahdal. When Dahdal retired, Rev. Fouad Saba became the head priest of St. George's and Suhail Qumri and his wife were active members, as were Muna Kuttab and her husband Wanees Zarour. I am still in touch with most of the students and all have successful careers and wonderful families.

I encountered an interesting problem with the faculty shortly after I started my work at North Park. When it was time for the first Palestinian student to graduate, a conflict arose over the graduation ceremony. North Park usually had twenty-five to thirty international students graduating each year and the students marched into the ceremony carrying the flag of their country. I had not participated in the commencement ceremony at that point, and a Palestinian senior came to my office and said he had a problem. The school was insisting that he carry the Israeli flag. He grew up in Ramallah under military occupation, so I understood his refusal to participate. Our problem was the faculty member in charge of the ceremony did not share our understanding.

I agreed to meet with the faculty member. When we sat down to discuss it, I asked what she knew about the situation these Palestinian students faced growing up under a severe military occupation. She had no idea about it, so I began to explain what I had experienced during my visits and what their daily reality was like. She began to open up about the problem, and I offered to write a proposal about why the student should carry the Palestinian flag.

I wrote a five-page analysis of the history and occupation. Her committee read it and agreed the student could carry the Palestinian flag. When he marched into the auditorium proudly displaying the Palestinian flag, a huge cheer went up from his parents, the MESA students, and several international students sitting in the audience.

The EMEU partnership with North Park University's Center for Middle Eastern Studies (CMES) worked well, and our MESA group and lectures at CMES were gaining popularity in the community as well as on campus. The first five years were busy, and eventually the workload became overwhelming. I was teaching a full load of classes, raising funds and organizing the programs for the Middle East Center and for EMEU, and served on faculty committees and as faculty advisor to MESA. I was concerned I would burn out, and my secretary, Sylvia Klavins-Barshney, would as well. We were exhausted but loved the challenges.

I spoke to the chair of the CMES board, the wise and efficient Dr. Pauline Coffman, and we agreed to let go of the EMEU relationship. I was unable to give it the time it deserved and knew my friend Marilyn Borst would be a better director. EMEU was agreeable to the change, and I appreciated the freedom to concentrate on the growing responsibilities at North Park.

Before we made the change, I had one final initiative that needed EMEU's and North Park's support. I was receiving reports from Christian zionist sources claiming the Palestinian Authority (PA) had been persecuting Palestinian Christians. When the reports became an official bill on the floor of the US House of Representatives by Rep. J.T. Watts of Oklahoma, I knew we had to investigate the situation.

I was well aware that Israel had used this accusation on several occasions in an attempt to divide Palestinian Muslims from Christians. It was never successful, but they were doing it again. I decided to organize an evangelical fact-finding mission to Israel and occupied Palestine. The EMEU board and the CMES board both adopted the plan, and I raised funds to cover airfare for six participants.

I called my friend Brother Andrew, an internationally known evangelical leader from Holland who gained fame as "God's smuggler" in the 1960s when he made a career out of smuggling Bibles to churches behind the Iron Curtain. Now he had taken great interest in Islam and was very sympathetic with the Palestinian struggle through his new organization, Open Doors.

Steve Haas, former staff member at the Willowcreek megachurch near Chicago, was a vice president at World Vision International and was keen to participate. I recruited three pastors and a physician for the trip. We still needed a journalist, and I called the leading evangelical magazine, *Christianity Today,* but was declined. I suggested they consider one of my top students at North Park, a gifted writer who had published articles with other Christian journals. I sent them a few samples of her writing and they agreed. Peri Stone became our journalist, and she was an important part of our delegation.

We had an ambitious agenda with over forty meetings in our ten days, including leaders of Christian and Muslim organizations in the Gaza Strip, West Bank, East Jerusalem, and Israel. We met with three of the top leaders of Hamas, who loved Brother Andrew because he visited them five years earlier when Israel expelled them to a mountain in South Lebanon in the middle of February. Brother Andrew's visit with blankets, food, and Bibles was warmly received, and was now famous among the leadership of Hamas—quite an accomplishment for an evangelical leader.

Thanks to Brother Andrew's contacts we were able to meet with leading clergy, politicians, professors, students, and Christian leaders. Brother Andrew was invited to deliver a talk at the Islamic University in Gaza and was received like a celebrity. The love and respect the students and faculty had was truly inspiring. The President of the University shared the story of Andrew visiting more than 400 leaders from Gaza expelled by Israel to south Lebanon in the middle of winter, and how Andrew brought food, blankets, and Bibles to them. Andrew received an extended standing ovation and was mobbed by students and faculty who simply wanted to shake his hand.

We also met with two human rights organizations and three Christian zionist groups in Israel and West Jerusalem. The Christian zionist organizations were the primary source of the claims against the PA, but we suspected the government of Israel was working with them. In Jerusalem we met with Jessica Montell, director of B'Tselem, the prominent Israeli human rights organization, who had thoroughly researched the case. She confirmed the accusations were completely false. Jessica added they had irrefutable evidence that the PA was innocent. B'Tselem had a paper trail of evidence, as did Al-Haq, the Palestinian human rights organization in Ramallah. She said the case involved two Palestinian collaborators who sold Palestinian land to an illegal Israeli settlement company. They were caught by the PA, imprisoned but never tortured, and were released after three months. At that time, they were living in the large Israeli settlement Ariel.

Then we met with Clarence Wagner (no relation), director of the Christian zionist organization Bridges for Peace. He told us reports of PLO persecution of Christians were accurate. When we told him B'Tselem said these reports were fabricated, he became angry and claimed he had accurate sources to refute B'Tselem's claims. When we asked to see it, he said it was highly confidential and he could not give it to us.

We interviewed about a dozen Christian and Muslim clergy and heads of leading organizations in the West Bank and Israel, and nobody knew of a single incident of Palestinian Authority torturing or abusing Palestinian Christians. The only case anyone knew of involved a domestic incident where a Christian girl in Beit Sahour eloped with a Muslim boy. Both families were opposed to the relationship, and it stirred some tension in the community. However, the case was finally resolved by our friend Zoughbi Zoughbi of the Wi'am organization, who used the traditional Palestinian mediation process called *sulha* ("mediation or reconciliation").

Toward the end of our tour we met with Uri Mor, director of Israel's Ministry of Religious Affairs. At the outset of our meeting, Mor spoke as if the reports of PA torture were true, citing the International Christian Embassy and Bridges for Peace reports. We informed him that we had met with both organizations, which would not verify their sources. To the contrary, the human rights organizations al-Haq and the Israeli group B'Tselem had evidence the allegations were false.

A smile came over Mor's face. He sat back and admitted the case was fabricated by the prime minister's information office. He admitted that he was impressed by our research and added, "Honestly, from time to time, Prime Minister Netanyahu's people like to do this to keep the PA on the defensive." We asked him to confirm that it was propaganda and make a public statement to clarify the fabrication, but he refused. We issued a press release that received significant coverage, including in the BBC World Service and *Christianity Today*.[48] I submitted our documentation to the Oklahoma congressman and the committee reviewing the case, and it was eventually dropped.

Our Center for Middle Eastern Studies board of directors helped oversee our lecture series, fundraising, student scholarships, MESA, and the academic program. Our board chair, Pauline Coffman of the North Park faculty, was an amazing administrator who helped me negotiate issues throughout our fifteen years of growth and success. We were able to cover all of our program expenses thanks to a generous group of board members, led by Norm and Alice Rubash. Norm had recently retired as director of Standard Oil operations in the Middle East, and with his wife, Alice, were very generous donors and strong supporters of the Palestinian issue.

Our lecture series brought a variety of leading voices to campus, and we were able to design the topics to cover a range of Middle Eastern countries and issues. The Islamic scholar Mahmoud Ayoub of Temple University was a frequent lecturer as was Rami Khouri, the Beirut journalist who was a lecturer at Harvard University's Kennedy School. Another speaker was Harvard scholar Sara Roy, daughter of Holocaust survivors and the world's leading authority on the Gaza Strip. Ali Abunimah, co-founder of Electronic Intifada spoke with his father, former Jordanian ambassador to England and later the United Nations. We also hosted Pope Shenouda, patriarch of the Coptic Orthodox Church, and

North Park University bestowed on him an honorary Doctor of Divinity. The North Park Chapel was filled with Coptic Orthodox friends, and the priests added ceremonial incense to provide an Eastern Orthodox atmosphere for the evening.

In early April 2002, I received a call from Marda Dunsky, who was teaching at Northwestern University's Medill School of Journalism. Marda asked, "How would you like to host the British journalist Robert Fisk of *The Independent*?"

Without hesitation, I responded, "Absolutely!" I was an avid reader of Fisk's reports in the British daily and read his book *Pity the Nation* on the tragedy of Lebanon. I asked Marda, "How much will it cost for us to host Robert Fisk?"

She said, "Nothing! Northwestern University has already paid for his hotel and airfare plus an honorarium. The university president came under pressure from the usual suspects and just canceled the event. Robert Fisk is all yours. What do you think?"

Eager to accept, I told her I would have to run it by the North Park dean and president. "I'll get right back to you within twenty-four hours," I promised.

I briefed the dean and president about Fisk's writings and that he had interviewed Osama bin-Laden on three separate occasions in the 1990s and Fisk was critical of U.S. policy in the Middle East.[49] I said we may receive some criticism for this but Fisk does not endorse bin-Laden's views and this is a great opportunity for North Park University. Both the dean and the president approved the lecture. I called Marda to confirm it and started promoting the event.

We had only ten days before the lecture but were able to publicize it fairly well. I knew we were about to incur the wrath of various pro-Israel organizations in Chicago and conservative faculty at North Park. As interest grew, I moved the lecture to our largest auditorium on campus, which had a maximum capacity of 500 people. I alerted security on campus and the Chicago police to be on alert before and during the lecture. Other than the usual protest by three to four members of the Jewish Defense League, who I told to protest across the street but not on campus, there were no protests inside the auditorium or on campus. We counted 521 people in the standing-room audience in the auditorium. The North Park security informed me the fire code stated we could not go over 500 participants.

Fisk's hourlong lecture was titled "September 11: Ask Who Did It, But for Heaven's Sake, Don't Ask Why." Early in his lecture Fisk said he hated journalists and politicians who focused on the "who and where" questions but always ignored the "why." He explained the "why" question of September 11 in no uncertain terms, pointing directly to the misguided policies and actions of the United States, Israel, Saudi Arabia, and the Islamists who were empowered by those misguided policies. He was highly critical of the Western governments and Israel. Fisk singled out British, US, and Israeli interventions in the Middle East dating back to the Balfour Declaration, the CIA overthrow of the democratically elected government in Iran in 1953, and what he called the "bogus" case for the US war with Iraq. I noted the strategic role of Israel and the pro-Israel lobby in the United States, which worked closely with the new conservative movement to press the case for the US to attack Iran.

Fisk drew several standing ovations from at least two-thirds of the audience. He predicted, "If Saddam's regime is removed and the United States attempts a 'regime change,' the balkanization of Iraq will cost the United States dearly in an unnecessary and unwinnable war. The US will be in for decades of war and achieve nothing but further destabilization of the Middle East." In hindsight, most of Fisk's predictions during his 2002 speech were confirmed within ten years.

We sent out a press release two days before Fisk's lecture and another on the morning of the event. Our friends at National Public Radio in Chicago said they were already scheduled for the day but wondered if I could send them a high-quality tape that they would later air. I sent the tape by courier after the lecture, and the host of the popular Worldview program, Jerome McDonnell and his assistant Steve Bynum aired the entire fifty-five-minute lecture two days later. When I checked in with Jerome and Steve a week later, they said the interview set a record at Chicago Public Radio for the most hate mail, emails, phone calls, and opposition in the station's history.

The fallout from the speech at North Park was minimal, at least on the surface, but from that point forward, whenever I gave lectures at local universities, our programs at the Middle East Center were scrutinized by the pro-Israel organizations. One evening I was cleaning up the chapel after a lecture and overheard a conversation on the payphone in the back of the chapel that caught my attention. I knew immediately who the caller was. It was Chaya, who always sat at the front and took copious notes and asked leading questions of our CMES speakers. I confronted her and said, "Chaya, perhaps you were not aware I was standing around the corner and heard your full report to your 'handlers.' Next time could you at least be accurate about what I said and what the speaker addressed? Your report was completely dishonest."

Another important event at our center occurred in April 2005, when I organized a Center for Middle Eastern Studies-sponsored seminar on Christian zionism titled "Israel, the Bible, and the Future: Premillennialism and Christian Zionism in America." I invited leading authorities on the topic of Christian zionism including Barbara Rossing of the Lutheran School of Theology (*The Rapture Exposed*), Timothy Weber (*Living in the Shadow of the Second Coming*), Stephen Sizer (*Christian Zionism: Roadmap for Armageddon*), Gary Burge (*Whose Land? Whose Promise?*), and Yaakov Ariel (*Evangelizing the Chosen People*). I also invited Rev. John Hubers of the Middle East Staff, Reformed Church in America and Jay Phelan, president of North Park Theological Seminary. I decided to serve as moderator and not deliver a speech.

Gary Burge called and said we should invite Yehiel Poupko, a rabbinic scholar of the Jewish Federation of Greater Chicago. My first thought was, "No, inviting him would be a mistake as he is a very hostile force and would be disruptive." Gary insisted we invite him, and perhaps in a weak moment, I agreed. The rabbi accepted the invitation and agreed to deliver a lecture called "Christian Zionism in Theological Discourse: A Jewish Perspective."

On the day of the conference, Anderson Chapel was filled with approximately 350 in attendance from the university, various churches, and interested parties in the region. On Thursday evening, Dr. Weber gave an excellent keynote address on the history of Christian zionism in the context of premillennial theology. Rabbi Poupko spoke on Friday morning and proceeded to deliver one of the most hostile, unacademic rants imaginable.

The rabbi's presentation was essentially an attack on Stephen Sizer, Naim Ateek, and me as antisemites who hate Israel. He went twenty-five minutes over his allotted time and finally walked off the stage to the cheers of his six friends from the Jewish Federation. The remaining 345 people were stunned and silent. I responded by joking, "Well you can't accuse us of being one-sided after that performance." I added an apology noting, "Not only did the speaker fail to address his assigned topic, but he went twenty-five minutes over the agreed time, forcing us to cut the lunch period by fifteen minutes so we can get back on schedule."

After my class that afternoon, I convened a meeting with the speakers and our board of directors. I suggested we consider a project that would enable us to continue educating people about the dangers of Christian zionism. We decided to organize a website as an educational resource for students, clergy, and other interested parties. We discussed posting timely articles and videos and creating resources critical of Christian zionism.

Someone suggested we check on the availability of the domain www.christianzionism.org. I knew Stephen Sizer was technologically savvy so I gave him my credit card suggesting he purchase the domain if it was available. Within ten minutes Stephen returned and announced, "Done! We have www.christianzionism.org for $50 on your card." The website continues to operate, with an anonymous editorial committee of evangelicals working to reach evangelical constituencies with critical articles, interpretative tools, and personal stories in the section Why I Am Not a Christian Zionist. Rabbi Poupko and others at the Jewish Federation forced the North Park administration to drop the website from the Center for Middle Eastern Studies web page, but John Hubers took it over and did a superb job managing it for twelve years.

~

Looking back to the global awareness of Christian zionism in the year 2005, we could not have imagined how quickly it would rise to significant political power in the United States, South and Central America, Africa, and Southeast Asia. Who could have imagined that a future vice president of the United States and the secretary of state would have encouraged the mobilization of Christian zionist voters to lobby for moving the US Embassy from Tel Aviv to Jerusalem and encourage Israel to annex the West Bank and East Jerusalem? Who could have imagined the prime minister of Israel joining the US president at a ceremony marking the opening of the US Embassy in East Jerusalem with militant pro-zionist prayers and remarks from the leaders of Christians United for Israel? Who could have envisioned the presidents of Brazil and Nigeria promoting Christian zionist support from their countries for Israeli leaders to declare zionist sovereignty over all of historic Palestine as a fulfillment of biblical prophecy? And who could have anticipated Christian Zionist ranchers engineering pure red heifers to be used as sacrifices by Levitical priests in anticipation of the erasure of the Dome of the Rock and Al-Aqsa Mosque and the building of the third Temple? Or the Republican Speaker of the House hosting a rabbi from the Temple Mount Faithful at a Washington, DC fundraising event for the Temple Mount project with several members of Congress in attendance?

—

In 2007 I was preparing for my tenure review at North Park University. After a year of review, the faculty tenure committee unanimously recommended me for tenure. Our faculty was being reorganized and all the center directors were placed in the new humanities division, with the exception of me. I appealed the decision, and the provost denied my request, insisting I had to remain in the conservative Biblical and Theological Studies Department. I was suspicious the provost and a few faculty were playing a political game with my tenure issue. I was not surprised when the department denied my tenure, meaning I had no department to host me. I appealed the ruling, but the president denied the appeal. This was academic checkmate for me. Several faculty protested the decisions to no avail. The writing was on the wall for my academic career.

A few years earlier, June 2004 to be exact, the Presbyterian Church (USA) adopted a resolution at its national assembly to begin a process of ethical investment regarding companies involved with the Israeli occupation. This is church language for the BDS movement. Our Middle East Task Force in Chicago was promoting the resolution throughout Chicago with meetings, presentations in churches, and disseminating written support. I was active speaking every weekend in churches and universities—at one point realized I had an engagement every weekend for three months.

For me it was a matter of Christian ethics. I did not wish to profit from other people's suffering. Since my pension was with the Presbyterian Church USA, I did not think it was ethical to have our pension funds tied up with the Israeli military or companies operating illegally on land stolen from Palestinians. It took our Presbyterian Israel Palestine Mission Network (today the organization's name is the Palestine Justice Network) a full ten years before the resolution was finally adopted in June 2014. I was a minor player but thankful for the hard work of so many Presbyterian colleagues. The Presbyterian General Assembly was the first Christian denomination to adopt a BDS resolution in the United States.

The zionist organizations in Chicago were monitoring me closely and issued regular protests with the president or provost. I claimed I had a right to support BDS as a nonviolent instrument of social change, used effectively at the Boston Tea Party, the civil rights movement, the anti-apartheid movement in South Africa, and by Israel and leading zionist organizations. I had a right under the First Amendment to the Constitution to participate in BDS strategies and legitimate political criticism of Israel. Who was the Jewish Federation, the Anti-Defamation League (ADL), or anyone else to dictate the terms of my thought process and legitimate criticism of Israel's political strategies? Besides, they all used BDS strategies on numerous occasions, and their attempts to silence me or anyone else were duplicitous.

The tenure process came to a head during the fall semester of 2009. In mid-October, I received a call to meet with one of the administrators of the university. He seemed nervous when he announced, "Don, we have decided to close the Center for Middle Eastern Studies due to financial concerns." I challenged him immediately, noting our board raised every dollar of its program and operating budget, and it did not cost the university a cent. I asked to see a budget. "I do not believe for a minute you are proposing to close the Middle East Center as a financial problem," I said. "This is purely political and it involves outside pressure." I handed him the accounting with the CMES budgets and sources of income and expenses for the previous ten years. I asked for the university's financial records to prove we were a financial drain on the institution. To this day I have not received an answer to my questions about the budget from any university administrator.

I could see that my time at North Park was evaporating faster than I had anticipated. The political maneuvers blocking my tenure despite the unanimous faculty recommendation, terminating the Christian zionism website, closing the successful Center for Middle Eastern Studies with a fake rationale, all pointed to my termination.

I decided to meet with the university president. I assumed the proverbial buck stopped with him. When I arrived at the his office, his secretary said he was delayed and would arrive in about thirty minutes. I told her I would wait. She was a kind and thoughtful person and we had developed a good relationship through the years. She mentioned she had an errand to run.

Once she left, I went to her desk and began thumbing through the president's appointment book, which listed monthly meetings with Rabbi Poupko and the Jewish Federation dating back at least nine months. I photographed the meeting appointments with the federation, figuring they could prove to be helpful if and when I pursued litigation.

The president returned. I made my case, stating I had documented evidence proving the closing of CMES was not based on economics but rather was from outside pressure.

"No, he insisted, "it is purely a financial matter."

I leaned over the desk and clarified, "Let me repeat. From its inception fourteen years ago, the CMES board has raised every cent of its program without taking a dime from the university. I believe the closing of the center is due to outside pressure. If this is the case, the university's decision becomes a First Amendment issue, leaving you in a vulnerable legal position."

I could see by his body language that he had a visceral reaction to this statement. He repeated, "No, it is a decision based entirely on financial issues." I told him I needed to see the proof on paper and that I had already requested the same from the provost. I informed him I would be meeting with an attorney next week who was a specialist in these matters. Our meeting ended abruptly.

The next day, I contacted the Illinois chair of the American Association of University Professors and asked for its top three lawyers in the Chicago area who specialized in tenure and First Amendment cases for faculty. He gave me three names. I asked who was the most successful of the three and he gave me the name and phone number. I called and set up an appointment for the end of the week.

I met with the attorney for forty-five minutes, trying to maximize my time as he charged $650 per hour, so I kept my bill at $500. After hearing the details of my case, the lawyer assured me, "You have a very strong case, and you seem to have strong supportive evidence to challenge the administration on two levels: the closing of the center and your case for tenure. I expect the next shoe will drop soon concerning your contract."

"Yes, I'm anticipating this scenario," I sighed. The attorney responded, "You may be able to win this case, but the university could string this out for two to three years and you will be looking at legal fees and court expenses that could approach $50,000 or more. Do you have the resources for this kind of a legal battle?"

I replied immediately, "No way, absolutely not."

This was not the news I was hoping to hear, but it was the grim reality. My resources were tight. My daughter Anna still had two years of college at over $30,000 per year, and I was barely able to pay my mortgage as I refinanced it to cover her tuition. Now I was approaching the underwater mark. At best I had $1,200 in savings and no stocks or investments. I had no alternative. I could not fight this case in the courts, and I wasn't about to go to wealthy friends and beg for a loan. I had to prepare myself for the end of my teaching career at North Park University.

I began to intensify my meditation and prayer time because I was angry as hell at the university for its lies and the injustice of my case. I spent an hour in meditation and prayer every morning, trying to let go of the anger and center myself in God's love. It took at least two months of daily, disciplined meditation exercises and prayer before I began to sense the anger was finally lifting. For the first time in my life I had trouble sleeping, but finally the negative feelings shifted. I was still vulnerable, but I started sleeping through the night again. I was slowly coming to accept the injustice of losing my job. However, I was not about to tell the president or administration. I decided to drop the legal challenge as I still needed to negotiate a severance package.

When I received the notice of my termination at North Park, I almost took it in stride. It still irritated the hell out of me, but I knew there was no alternative. One of the tasks before me was to accept the gratitude people were showing and accept their support as a gift that was more important than the unfair termination. There were multiple cases of gratitude and support I received from students, faculty, and even parents of students.

Among the many faculty who expressed support was the remarkable Cherie Meacham, chair of the humanities division. Cherie went so far as to threaten to resign if I was not reinstated. When the administration failed to comply, she resigned from the largest and most powerful division in the faculty. Another stalwart friend who went to the mat for me was Leona Mirza, a math professor who challenged the president and provost with data on the revenue I brought to North Park, whether from the Middle East Center or the number of tuition-paying students in my classes. I'll always be grateful for her support.

My closest colleague, Bob Hostetter, chair of the communications studies department and a close ally on Middle East peace and conflict transformation, was always there to listen and provide feedback. He told me a significant number of our students met with the president and provost, requesting that I be reinstated. When the administration refused, the students demanded a "town meeting" so students and faculty could engage directly with the administration.

When the administration rejected their request, the students leading the protest began to implement the methods Dr. King used during the civil rights movement to leverage social change. Bob Hostetter and I taught these methods in our Introduction to Conflict Transformation class and used "Letter from a Birmingham Jail" as our source. And now the students were applying them step by step: (1) Gather all the relevant information; (2) Meet with those in authority and make your case for a change; (3) Mobilize support and make your case; (4) Use nonviolent strategies to mobilize mass support. We celebrated the fact that our students were putting our classwork to immediate use in direct action strategies including sit-ins, boycotts, and marches.

The administration relented under pressure and held the town meeting. I decided not to attend as I knew the students had the situation under control and my presence could be a deterrent. It was a valiant stand but the students ran out of time when graduation came and they had to leave for summer jobs.

The letter confirming my termination arrived on April 15, 2010. Shortly thereafter, a surprise occurred. I was at home preparing for one of my last classes when Bob Hostetter called, urging me to join him for one of the last chapel services where the administration was presenting academic awards to students. He said it would be rewarding to see some of our best students honored.

About halfway through the service, I heard my name called, announcing that I was receiving the coveted Zenos Hawkinson Award, the highest faculty honor for teaching excellence at the university. This acknowledgment was totally unexpected and a beautiful expression of affirmation. It was the faculty's decision to give me the award, which made it especially meaningful. The administration was unable to veto the decision. This award is an honor I will always cherish.

An equally surprising event came a week later at the final chapel, when I received the award as the "faculty of the year," by vote of the students. I felt doubly blessed that my teaching career at the university was affirmed by the two most important constituencies, the faculty and students. I was glad the president and administration were there to see both awards.

Meanwhile, I had been sitting on a letter from the president and board of directors offering me a year of full salary and pension with a long list of legal conditions. It was a simple case of procrastinating the penultimate step in severing my relationship with the university. I learned that the university usually offers a six-month salary severance with departing faculty. Offering me a full year of salary and pension was generous. By signing the agreement, I waived any form of litigation or grievance procedures against the university. I had already crossed that bridge in practical terms, and I signed the agreement.

I dropped off the letter at the president's office, and his secretary told me she was sad I was leaving. I know she meant it—she had become a thoughtful friend. I couldn't say the same for the president, who consistently avoided me before and after our final conversation. I was not surprised when he failed to come out and say goodbye although he was in the office. Both the president and administration played a cowardly role throughout the process, and I never heard a word from them again.

A few days later there was a wonderful surprise party for me at a local restaurant, organized by faculty and activists throughout Chicago with whom I had worked for over thirty-five years. Over 100 people attended. Days after this celebratory farewell, my last task was to unpack and move out of my university office. The university did not allow the custodians to assist me, and the only students available were two of the Middle Eastern students, who were glad to help.

My office had floor-to-ceiling, built-in bookcases on three walls. We loaded over fifty-five boxes of books into a rented U-Haul, and I left campus for the last time. I drove home up McCormick Blvd. and reminisced about the fifteen years of making that drive every workday. I was actually amazed I had lasted that long. I breathed easy, and despite my exhaustion, I had a smile on my face and peace in my spirit. The harassment of the final six months at the university was behind me.

I crossed Howard Street in the U-Haul and noticed a light mist of rain was beginning to cover the windshield. I hoped against hope that the rain forecast for the afternoon would hold off until I unloaded the truck. By the time I parked in front of my house, the sky opened, and a heavy downpour pounded the pavement. I ran up the steps of the house and let my dear dog Miles Davis Wagner out to relieve himself. After he was back in the house, I started to unload the truck—alone. My neighbor had promised to help, but when I called him, his plans had changed. Sweating like crazy, I worked for at least two hours and moved all fifty-five boxes into my small study, stacking them floor to ceiling.

I had twenty minutes to return the truck without a late fee, so I loaded Miles in the front seat and returned it to U-Haul. Miles and I got in my car, which I had parked there in the morning, and I decided to pick up my favorite Chicago-style stuffed pizza and beer for dinner. I returned home, fed Miles, said a prayer of gratitude, and spent the evening eating the best pizza on the planet while flipping between the Cubs and White Sox games.

The feeling of liberation brought a sense of gratitude and peace. I wasn't concerned at that point about what I would do next. That could wait. On that evening I knew the worst was behind me, and for a few days I postponed thinking about what was next. I knew I was surrounded by a large company of friends and family who shared my commitment to justice in Palestine. I also knew God would open another door. For the moment, it was time to completely relax with my faithful dog at my side. I planned to spend a month caring for the garden, praying, reading, and enjoying a brief phase of life with no major responsibilities.

About a year later, my good friend Tom Getman called from Washington, DC, during a break in a Christian and Jewish dialogue meeting he was attending. Tom told me that another participant pulled him aside during a coffee break and forcefully stated, "If you do not forswear your friendships with Don Wagner, Naim Ateek, and Gary Burge, you will be excluded from this conference." Tom was not about to be bullied and responded that he had no right to tell him who his friends and associates should be—and he was talking about three of Tom's most treasured friends. Tom later learned the man was Rabbi Yehiel Poupko of the Jewish Federation in Chicago.

Tom and I laughed as we recalled how both of us had been through the bullying wars with the pro-Israel lobby. If it wasn't Rabbi Poupko, it would be someone else. The bullying and intimidation just made us more committed to work for justice in Palestine. It confirmed we were doing something right, and we knew the Palestinians and progressive Jewish friends paid a heavier price than we ever would. Indeed, we were honored to be part of the great company of witnesses who will never surrender until Palestine is free.

Perhaps the most intense censorship and bullying by pro-Israel zionist organizations I have seen in the past thirty years has occurred since October 7, 2023. Whistleblowers have exposed the State Department, Congress, the *New York Times*, MSNBC, ABC, CNN, and most of the major networks. Congress and Presidents Biden and Trump have been on the wrong side of history in their bipartisan support of weapons to Israel and their pathetic defenses of financing Netanyahu's genocide. The student protests were effectively silenced in the spring of 2024; many students and faculty lost their jobs, some were imprisoned, others dismissed from school. In Palestine, upwards of 70,000 have paid with their lives. By comparison, I am privileged as a white male who has several options, and my life and liberty are not at risk. But the cause of Palestine lies deep in my spirit and like these students, I will not compromise the truth as I see it and I will continue to be faithful to this cause as long as I live. I believe Palestine is the test case for preserving the global justice system based on international law. Challenging zionism and Christian zionism are also essential if we are to preserve the Prophetic witness of the Hebrew prophets and the power of the liberating Gospel of Jesus. Whatever our belief system or ethical and moral value system, we can join the great cloud of witnesses who have the responsibility as human beings created equal in the eyes of God to resist the evils of settler colonial domination and the heretical claims of zionism and Christian zionism. This may be the Kairos moment for Palestine to move to center stage and for justice and peace to triumph at last for every resident of Palestine and Israel.

That moment of reflection was the turning point for me. The spiritual disciplines of prayer and meditation provided solace. I started each day sitting by my garden with Miles at my side. The meditation and prayer time were my lifeline and anchor. I was not worried about what the future held. Throughout my life, God had opened a door when another one closed. This was part of the "downward journey to justice, liberation, and hope." My challenge was to maintain that consciousness of hope, trust, and steadfastness. I needed the next door to open, but it took much longer than I anticipated.

Section VI:

Ch. 20

Liberating Your Mind: Zionism, Christian Zionism, and Resistance

"Our challenge is to liberate our minds from notions of powerlessness and subservience to political leaders. It is nothing short of revolutionary liberation from old ways that shackle brains and developing new paradigms for sustainability and coexistence with each other and with nature."

—Mazin Qumsiyeh, November 3, 2021

Chapter 20
FALSE GODS IN THE UNHOLY LAND: LIBERATING ISRAEL AND PALESTINE FROM ZIONISM AND CHRISTIAN ZIONISM

"The land of Palestine is colonized by the military and the Bible."

—Rev. Dr. Mitri Raheb

I am the product of two types of Christian zionism and was unapologetically committed to political zionism until my mid-thirties. As mentioned in chapter one, I was influenced by the premillennial dispensationalist beliefs including the Rapture, the Battle of Armageddon, the second coming of Jesus, and why a revived state of Israel was necessary for this scenario to unfold. These beliefs were reinforced as I read my parents' Scofield Reference Bible and by the preaching and Sunday school lessons I encountered during my preteen years in church every week.

But was I a Christian zionist? I was not active in a political sense for zionist causes, yet I did hold these beliefs about the new state of Israel's central role in the latter-day events. I believed the Antichrist was alive and would eventually attack Israel from the north and the final battle of Armageddon would commence. I would be "raptured" or removed from history before the global tribulation would encompass the planet. But was I a true Christian zionist? It depends on how one defines Christian zionism, which will be a central feature of this chapter.

My first goal is to define and summarize two types of evangelical or fundamentalist Christian zionism and Jewish political zionism. I will examine their history, relationship, and why the historical context of their emergence is important in understanding present day events. I will also introduce a third type of Christian zionism: the mainline Protestant and Roman Catholic version that is often forgotten. My second goal is to interpret the historical context, including when they emerged and how they developed politically and theologically, and the type of nationalism they follow. Third, I will analyze and critique them with settler colonial analysis and liberation theology, providing the reader with a brief introduction to these essential tools and a framework for further analysis. In the background of all three goals is the use and misuse of the Bible and, as Rev. Mitri Raheb noted, "The land of Palestine is colonized by (the Israeli) military and the Bible."

I. Defining Christian Zionism and Its Early History

I have been researching and writing about Christian zionism for over forty years, having researched the topic for my doctoral dissertation. In my research I became aware that Christian zionism was the product of various theological movements since the Protestant Reformation and was surprised to learn Christian zionism predated Jewish political zionism.

While the Protestant Reformation in sixteenth-century Europe was the source of the theologies that became Christian zionism, its influence was indirect through various millennial movements that emerged on the continent and in England in the seventeenth and eighteenth centuries. During my doctoral research I discovered the writings of Rev. Thomas Brightman, a British clergyman, whose pamphlet "Apocalypsis Apocalypseos," written in 1585, led me to believe he was the first Christian zionist. When I read the original text in the British Museum I was elated with the discovery. But was he a Christian zionist?

Theologically, Brightman was a "restorationist," believing the Jewish people must return to Palestine and be converted to Christianity in order to ensure Jesus' second coming. While "restorationism" was one of the evangelical movements that prepared the way for Christian zionism, it did not include a political program, nor was it affiliated with Jewish political zionism, which was not established until 1897. There were several other "restorationists" such as Sir Henry Finch, a member of the British Parliament, whose pamphlet "The World's Great Restauration" stated the following in 1621:

> Where Israel, Judah, Zion, and Jerusalem are named, the Holy Ghost meant' not the spiritual Israel, or the Church of God collected of the Gentiles, or\of Jews and Gentiles both—but Israel properly descended out of Jacob's loynes...there and such like are not allegories, setting forth

> on terrene similitudes or deliverance through Christ but meant literally and really the Jews.[50]

Again, Finch was a "restorationist" as the title of his monograph suggests, and while a member of the British Parliament, he did not have a political program. At this point, it is important to offer a definition of Christian zionism and I have opted for a more precise version offered by Robert O. Smith: "Christian Zionism is a politically mobilized strand of Christian fundamentalism committed to preserving Jewish control over all of historic Palestine to ensure the realization of the movement's own end-times hope."[51]

I have changed the definition I originally published in *Anxious for Armageddon* nearly thirty years ago. It was far too broad and focused more on the restorationist theology and premillennial dispensationalist theology rather than the political dimension. I included Rev. Brightman, Sir Henry Finch, and John Nelson Darby without citing the need for a political system and affiliation with Jewish political zionism. Brightman, Finch, Darby, and many others should be called forerunners, or precursors, who prepared the way for political Christian zionism but cannot be properly called Christian zionists.

A second type of Christian evangelical belief that I and most analysts include with political Christian zionism is called premillennial dispensationalism, which is the popular end-time theology I embraced as a child. The Irish Anglican John Nelson Darby (1800–1891) is often credited with systematizing these beliefs and inventing the doctrine called the Rapture. Darby did not invent this doctrine, but he was the first to synthesize and popularize these doctrines in the system he called premillennial dispensationalism. This fancy theological term simply means the return of Jesus will occur before he establishes his millennial kingdom following the defeat of the Antichrist in the final battle of Armageddon. A revived state of Israel plays a central role as it will be the theater where that final battle will take place in the Valley of Megiddo. Prior to the battle, "born-again Christians" will be drawn up to heaven in a dramatic event based on a misreading of I Thessalonians 4.

Following the Civil War, Darby brought these teachings to the United States in six speaking tours. In the process, they were popularized and eventually blended with "restorationism" and political Christian zionism. The theologian Donald M. Lewis provides an excellent overview of this process in his *Short History of Christian Zionism*.[52]

II. The Importance of Historical Context

Let me turn to my second goal and discuss the historical context for the rise of Christian and Jewish political zionism. When I taught a course on the history of the Palestinian-Israeli political struggle, on the first day of class I asked students to jot down their answers to three questions: Where (what continent); when (approximate decade), and why (precipitating events) did this modern political struggle begin? I was not asking about ancient biblical history but the modern era.

Some students answered that the year was 1967 when Israel defeated three Arab armies in the Six-Day War and occupied East Jerusalem, the West Bank, Gaza Strip, Sinai Peninsula, and Golan Heights. While these events are very important, the struggle originated much earlier. Other students suggested 1948, when Israel became a state and expelled half the Palestinian population in the Nakba. I noted that some history books say the struggle began in 1948, but they miss important events in doing so. Again, the origin is much earlier.

Others pointed to the Balfour Declaration of November 1917, which I affirmed as extremely important and much closer in time and location to the answer. I added that important developments would still be missed unless they looked to an earlier date and a slightly different location. I suggested the precipitating events did not occur in Israel or historic Palestine because Jews, Muslims, and Christians were living in peace and respecting each other's holidays and beliefs. At the turn of the 19th century, the population in Palestine was 93–94 percent Palestinian with the majority being Muslim and around 15 percent of them Christians, and 5 percent Palestinian Jews, and perhaps 1–2 percent from elsewhere. As the historian Ussama Makdisi details in his important volume *The Age of Coexistence*, Palestinian Jews, Muslims, and Christians lived together with respect for each other before Zionism and the British occupation unravelled their peace beginning in the 1920s.[53]

In fact, the modern Palestinian-Israeli struggle began in Eastern Europe, particularly with the brutal antisemitic pogroms in Russia and other regions from the 1860s through the 1890s. Political zionism was the response to antisemitism by a small minority of European Jews. Political zionism did not exist in Palestine. Again, this is primarily a European and Christian phenomenon with a long history dating back to the early church, including the Crusades and the Reconquista of the Iberian Peninsula, and later Germany, Austria, France, and the Russian Empire.

In the modern era, Eastern European Jews realized they would never be safe in Europe given the depth of antisemitism. An example was Dr. Leon Pinsker, the beloved physician of Odessa (in today's Ukraine) who had always practiced assimilation, believing Jews must remain loyal to the dominant culture and ruling nation. When pogroms broke out in Odessa in 1871, the Pinsker home was torched and his family threatened. In response, Dr. Pinsker wrote a pamphlet titled "Auto-Emancipation," where he applied medical analysis to demonstrate why antisemitism was an incurable European disease, called "Judeophobia," that put Jews at risk throughout the European continent.

Pinsker's prescription was for Jews to develop a national consciousness and seek a homeland either in Palestine or elsewhere. He became the chairman of Hovevei Zion ("Lovers of Zion") and established the first Jewish settlement in Palestine. The movement grew slowly, and in 1897 it joined Herzl's World Zionist Congress. Pinsker is an example of a precursor of zionism as he was writing and organizing in the 1880s before political zionism was official.

As various types of nationalism were emerging in Europe during the nineteenth century, zionism followed what is called "romantic" or "blood zionism," whereby the organizing principle of the proposed state was ethnic, or Jewish, such as "Germany for the German people." Various authoritarian movements have adopted this principle, such as under Mussolini ("Italy for the Italians") and later a more rigid form of authoritarianism under Hitler's National Socialist (Nazi) Party, which excluded Jews, Romani, and any other ethnic, racial, or religious group as "foreign."

III. Early Christian Zionism

Rev. William Hechler, an Anglican clergyman and chaplain to British troops in Vienna is one of the early examples of political Christian zionism. Hechler befriended Theodor Herzl and offered to assist him in contacting the German kaiser and Ottoman caliph to request land for a Jewish state. Herzl thought the elderly cleric was a Christian fanatic and not to be taken seriously. Herzl recorded his suspicions in his diary after Hechler knocked on his door and announced "I am here to help you as you are the answer to my prayers for the Jewish people."

During their initial meeting, Hechler mentioned his high-level contacts with the kaiser's family and the Ottoman caliph. From that moment they became a team, and Hechler did deliver high-level contacts with colonial powers. Herzl was seeking land to be donated for a Jewish homeland, but both the German and Ottoman empires rejected him. Herzl and Hechler formed a partnership that lasted several years, searching for sponsorship of the zionist program. Hechler was one of the few non-Jews invited to the First World Zionist Congress in Basel. Hechler was also the only person besides Herzl's family at his bedside when Herzl was dying. The zionist leader told Hechler, "You are the father of Christian zionism."

Hechler was not the first Christian activist to support the Jewish zionist idea before zionism was officially launched. One important transitional figure who was both a precursor to the zionism idea and, in the minds of some, a true Christian zionist was Lord Shaftesbury. A prominent member of the evangelical lobby the Clapham Sect, known for the work of William Wilberforce who campaigned to end slavery in England, Shaftesbury led the campaign to end child labor abuse. He is also known for advocacy for a Jewish homeland in Palestine. Shaftesbury's theology was a blend of "restorationism" and premillennialism, with a clear understanding of the need for a Jewish homeland in Palestine.

Shaftesbury's mission was to encourage Jews to settle in Palestine where they would be evangelized and converted to Christianity in order to hasten the second coming of Jesus. There is some dispute over who was first but many scholars say Shaftesbury is credited with coining the phrase "There is a country without a nation; and God now in his wisdom and mercy, directs us to a nation without a country." It is likely that the zionist movement adapted the phrase to become its motto, "A land of no people for a people with no land." Shaftesbury first used the phrase in the publication "The Quarterly Review" in 1839, nearly sixty years before the zionist movement was born.[54] Shaftesbury and his colleagues were successful in convincing the British Parliament to erect an Anglican cathedral in Jerusalem, whose purpose was to convert Jews to Christianity.

It is important to note how the "land of no people" label was used by both Jewish and Christian zionists to advance the myth that Palestine was an empty land waiting to be settled. "A land of no people" was actually home to a thriving Palestinian Muslim and Christian community with a small (5 percent) Sabra, or Palestinian Jewish, community, all of whom were indigenous to this province of the Ottoman Empire called Palestine. Their roots go back to the ancient Canaanites, who were Semites, so the descendants of these Palestinians have more Semitic DNA than the European or Ashkenazi Jews who were the majority of the wave of European Jewish settlers after 1920.

The tragedy of "the land of no people" myth is how Herzl and the early zionist fathers, with support from the Christian zionists, advanced the myth. They used it to justify the removal or expulsion of the Palestinians, and eventually provided a false justification using biblical references such as the Book of Joshua and the conquest of Canaan. It is these myths that paved the way for the unending Nakba that has now accelerated in the Gaza Strip since October 7, 2023.

There are indicators that if Israel's genocidal war does not end, it will continue in the West Bank and East Jerusalem and possibly with the 20 percent Palestinian population of Israel inside the Green Line, which seems to be the goal of the present Netanyahu government. It is shocking to see how the churches and both Christian and Jewish zionist are silent about demanding a ceasefire and cutting military aid to Israel and thus are supporting the genocide of Palestinians.

The third early example of Christian zionism was William E. Blackstone, a Chicago area layman who was influenced by John Nelson Darby and the evangelist Dwight L. Moody. Robert Smith calls Blackstone "America's first quintessential Christian zionist."[55] When Blackstone's *Jesus Is Coming* was published in 1978, it became a runaway bestseller, popularizing Darby's end-times beliefs and blending them with "restorationist" theology. Translated into more than twenty languages, the book popularized Christian support for the zionist ideas before Jewish zionism was official.

Blackstone is credited with organizing the first zionist lobby in the United States in support of a Jewish state in Palestine. In 1891, he convened a conference in Chicago and launched a petition drive requesting that President Harrison support a Jewish state in Palestine due to the pogroms in Eastern Europe. Blackstone was able to enlist financial support from John D. Rockefeller, J.P. Morgan, and the publisher Charles B. Scribner. The petition was published in newspapers from Boston to St. Louis. Signatories included several US senators, representatives, and the chief justice of the Supreme Court. President Harrison turned down the petition, but Blackstone's project remains the first example of a pro-Israel lobbying in the United States. In 1915, Justice Brandeis of the Supreme Court, a leading Jewish zionist, honored Blackstone as a true zionist and a "Righteous Friend of the Jewish people."

These three examples demonstrate how Christian zionists were involved in political strategies to support zionism and its goal of establishing a Jewish state before Herzl's official launch of the zionist movement in 1897. They also provided a false Christian justification of what is called settler colonialism and the goal of replacing indigenous Palestinians with Jewish colonizers. While their motivations were theological, they also had a clear political focus and for this reason I include them as early examples of political Christian zionism rather than simply evangelical theological movements that did not have a political agenda.

IV. Herzl and Jewish Political Zionism

Among the themes Christian zionism adopted, was the above-mentioned theme of settler colonialism and the displacement of the Palestinian majority. Herzl wrote in his diary: "We must expropriate gently the private property of the state assigned to us. We shall try to spirit the penniless population across the border by procuring employment for it in the transit countries, while denying it employment in our country."[56]

In addition, Herzl stated elsewhere that the zionist project was committed to a goal of displacing or erasing the Palestinians: "If I wish to substitute a new building for an old one, I must demolish before I construct."[57] From the outset, zionism was discreet but clear that the Palestinian population would need to be replaced, or "transferred" to neighboring countries despite the fact that it was 94 percent of the total population in Palestine when Herzl was writing these words.

One of the most important precipitating events for the success of the tiny zionist movement over the large majority Palestinian population occurred because key British colonial leaders also embraced Christian zionist ideology. The critical event was the passage of the Balfour Declaration on November 2, 1917. Christian zionism played a minor role in the British embrace of political zionism.

In 1905, Herzl's successor as the leader of the zionist movement, Chaim Weizmann, met the British politician Lord Arthur Balfour. At that point, the British government had offered the zionists the territory of Uganda. The zionist leadership rejected it as they were committed to Palestine.

Balfour had been raised in a conservative Christian family that believed in the end-times premillennial dispensationalist doctrines of Darby. While

Balfour's concerns were primarily focused on British colonial interests in the Middle East, including establishing a land bridge from the Levant (Palestine) to India, his end-times Christian beliefs predisposed him to adopt Weizmann's arguments for a Jewish state in Palestine that would be favorable to British interests. Balfour's niece, Blanche Dugdale, states as much in her biography of her uncle.[58]

The zionist lobbying campaign continued until on November 2, 1917, when Lord Balfour drafted his famous declaration after receiving approval from the British War Cabinet. The carefully phrased declaration states:

> His majesty's government view with favour the establishment in Palestine of a national home for the Jewish people, and will use their best endeavors to facilitate the achievement of this object, it being understood that nothing shall be done which may prejudice the civil and religious rights of existing non-Jewish communities in Palestine, or the rights and political status of Jews in any other country.[59]

The declaration is notable for its multiple loopholes. It fails to mention the majority population by name—the Palestinians, who were still 91 percent of the population in 1917 and owned 94 percent of the land. What did the declaration mean by "national home," when Balfour himself later admitted the intention was always for a Jewish state? And why are the Palestinians relegated to "civil and religious rights" while the zionists were granted land and as Balfour assumed a sovereign state? And couldn't the British see that enabling a tiny minority of setters to displace a 91 percent majority population was a recipe for violence?

The British bias toward the zionists and blindness toward the Palestinians have been a consistent theme of the major colonizers who have enabled the zionist project. One only need to observe the favoritism shown by the British and later the United States to the zionist movement in the decision-making during the British Mandate (1921–1948) followed by the heavy hand of the United States in manipulating the vote of the United Nations Security Council in the partition of Palestine (November 29, 1947). Middle East specialists in the US State Department and others urged President Truman to support a single democratic state in Palestine where Jews and Palestinians would be equal, but under pressure from zionist lobby Truman chose the partition option.

Instead of a single state for Palestinians and Jews, what both British and Palestinian observers warned was precisely what happened: the violent expulsion of half the Palestinian population from their homes and over 500 villages erased in what Palestinians call the Nakba (catastrophe. The United States then replaced Great Britain as the sponsor of zionist aggression and the continuing Nakba, whether through the failed Oslo process that enabled Israel to double illegal Jewish only settlements in the 1990s to financing 80 percent of the 2023–25 genocidal war on Gaza.

V. Challenging Christian and Jewish Zionism with Settler Colonial Analysis and Palestinian Liberation Theology

In January 1996, I had the privilege of addressing the Sabeel International Conference in Jerusalem alongside such luminaries as the late Jewish liberation theologian Marc Ellis, Rev. Naim Ateek, Mitri Raheb, Rev. Stephen Sizer, and the Irish theologian Michael Prior. I was impressed by Michael's political and theological critique of zionism and Christian zionism and his use of liberation theology and settler colonial analysis. Settler colonial analysis was new to me, and I was immediately attracted to it. After the conference, Michael and I spent a few days together driving around the West Bank and discussing the importance of this new field of study.

Michael died in 2004, far too young, and I still miss his joyful and radical presence in my life. He was an influential mentor for me, who set me on a path of combining settler colonial analysis and Palestinian liberation theology in my critique of zionism and Christian zionism. On my desk is a photo of Michael addressing a Palestinian rally in London, standing beside the Palestinian flag as he spoke. I still draw inspiration from him and at times I wonder if we are getting closer to his personal goal, which he shared with me in London a few months before his death: "my goal is to dismantle zionism in my lifetime." Michael did not live to accomplish his goal, but if he were alive today, I believe he would be analyzing the present genocide and fanaticism of the Netanyahu government as the unraveling of zionism before our eyes, and he would be playing a major role in helping us expose its dangerous and false doctrines.

At this point a brief introduction to settler colonial analysis is in order. It begins with Patrick Wolfe (1948–2016), the acknowledged father of settler colonial theory and the academic discipline of the same name. The following working definition summarizes the discipline:

> Settler colonialism is an ongoing system of power that perpetuates genocide and repression of indigenous peoples and cultures. Essentially hegemonic in scope, settler colonialism normalizes the continuous occupation, exploiting lands and resources to which indigenous peoples have genealogical relationships. Settler colonizers do not merely exploit indigenous peoples and lands for labor and economic interests, they displace them through settlements.[60]

Patrick Wolfe established the guiding principles of the new discipline in his groundbreaking volume *Settler Colonialism and the Transformation of Anthropology* (1999). His central argument stated that settler colonialism was a distinct field of scholarly analysis and deserved to be an independent academic discipline within the broader field of anthropology. Settler colonialism is the most lethal form of colonialism because its goal is to replace or erase the indigenous people with the colonizer's settlers. Traditional forms of colonialism are significantly different. They may occupy a population, discriminate, exploit their resources, but they eventually leave. In the case of settler colonialism, the settlers never leave. They replace and erase the indigenous, which is what the United States and Canada did to their native populations.

Wolfe was struck by how settler colonial projects utilized the myth of "empty land" (*terra nullius*, or "land belonging to no people"). Settlers are brought into the land as they were under the British Mandate in Palestine, and gradually they establish their exclusive settlements, push the natives out of their villages and homes, and eventually take over with their own nation-state.

The tragic case of the United States pushing its native Indian tribes toward the West, and eventually into isolated reservations for those who survived the genocide, is illustrative of how settler colonialism functions. Israel's campaign to annihilate Gaza's Palestinians is a contemporary case that has been televised for the world to witness in real time while Europe and the United States finance the massacres. The fact that the international courts and system of accountability have failed is a dangerous sign that in the future there will be more genocides by authoritarian regimes and empires.

Both zionism and Christian zionism are legitimate examples of settler colonialism according to Wolfe's analysis. He states that "settler zionism destroys to replace," citing the Herzl quote mentioned earlier, and that the Palestinians had to be removed for zionism and the Jewish state to succeed. Both zionism and Christian zionism used the myth of the empty land to ensure the success of their project; as the Shaftesbury inspired myth states: "a land of no people for a people with no land." In a similar vein, the zionist myth that Israel "made the desert bloom" was a variation on the same theme.

Settler colonial theory and Palestinian liberation theology provide an important counter-narrative and critique of all forms of Christian zionism as well as Jewish political zionism. A telling example is the third type of Christian zionism, what many call "Christian zionism hiding in plain sight" in our mainline Protestant and Roman Catholic churches and institutions.

Mitri Raheb is one of the leading Palestinian theologians and president of Dar al-Kalima University in Bethlehem (Palestine). His challenge to the preeminent biblical theologian Walter Brueggemann is surprising and important. Brueggemann has been a guiding light for me and thousands of Christians since the 1970s, so I had to pause and digest Rev. Raheb's critique. I will review just one challenge stated by Brueggemann in his book *Chosen?*:

> In my own thinking, which is staunchly influenced by my work as a scripture scholar, I begin with a focus on the claim of Israel as God's chosen people. That conviction is not in doubt in the Bible. It is a theological claim, moreover, that fits with compelling persuasiveness with the reality of Jews in the wake of World War II and the Shoah. Jews were indeed a vulnerable people, whose requirement of a homeland was an overriding emergency. Like so many Christians, progressive and Evangelical, I was grateful (and continue to be so) for the founding and prospering of the state of Israel as an embodiment of the chosen people.[61]

Raheb claims this statement is grounded in mainline/liberal Christian zionism and not in biblical theology. The fact that Brueggemann equates the modern state of Israel with "'the embodiment of the chosen people'" is a complete fallacy," he writes. Raheb notes that Brueggemann also confuses the Northern Kingdom of ancient Israel with the modern state of Israel. I would add that there are four different uses of the term "Israel" in the Bible, and none refer to a modern Jewish state.

Certainly the performance of Israel in the Gaza Strip, not only since

October 7, 2023, but going back to the 1950s, is a complete violation of the Torah ("Thou shalt not kill," "Thou shalt not covet," and "Thou shall have no other gods before me" all confirm the Torah has been violated). The Hebrew BIble states that Israel would lose the land if it violated the Torah, a matter that Brueggemann accepts.

Brueggemann does not seem to be aware of settler colonial analysis and how his approach to the land and chosen people enables Israel to continue to expropriate land from Palestinians and expel them because the Jewish people claim to have a sovereign right to all of historic Palestine. The Israeli government fails to abide by international law, which forbids the killing of the indigenous people and seizing their land. In fact, the militant settlers and even the secular Netanyahu's vision for Palestinians in Gaza is the complete antithesis of the Torah mandate to "love your neighbor as yourself" and to honor and care for "the sojourner in your midst."

Raheb points out that Brueggemann focuses on the dangers of antisemitism but fails to acknowledge settler colonialism, whether in his own country the United States in disenfranchising the Native Americans but also for the Palestinians. Raheb calls this flaw in Brueggemann's theology of the land a tragic inconsistency and an ethical blind spot. Raheb seems to be pleading with him when he writes, "How can somebody like Brueggemann continue to ignore the current context in which land theology is used for colonization of Palestinian land?"[62]

Unfortunately Brueggemann died on June 5, 2025, and was not able to address Raheb's challenge. Thankfully, several Palestinian theologians are raising this, and other challenges, to the mainline or liberal version of Christian Zionism that continues to dominate narratives concerning Israel, the land, and justice in Palestine. Faulty land theologies have been manipulated to justify land theft and dispossession of indigenous peoples throughout history, including those on the North American continent. Today genocide in the Gaza Strip is justified by mainline Protestant and Roman Catholic theologians, clergy, western parliamentarians, the media, and evangelical fundamentalists ranging from Rev. John Hagee to the current Speaker of the House of Representatives, Mike Johnson. Holocaust guilt or fear of being called antisemitic have led many young Christians to leave the church over this issue.

VI. Overcoming the Myth of Christian and Jewish Exceptionalism

A Palestinian laborer from Gaza reported a discussion he had with his Israeli boss about the relationship between Jews and Palestinians. The boss told him God created the Jewish people as his chosen people and blessed them with superior intelligence and the promise that they will thrive in their own land. Palestinians and all non-Jews are a lower form of creation and are closer to animals than humans. The Jewish people will dominate gentiles who are destined to serve the Jews. This perspective is not unusual among the extremist settlers in Israel and the West Bank, and I have heard similar comments from Christian zionists in the United States.

The same views have been articulated by Prime Minister Netanyahu and his Defense Minister Yoav Gallant. After the Hamas attack of October 7, 2023, Gallant said, "We are fighting human animals and are acting accordingly." He ordered a complete military assault on all the people of Gaza with no distinction between military and civilian targets, plus cutting off all food, water, and medicine to the entire population of Gaza. Israel's genocidal war was given the green light from the first week of their response to the Hamas attack on October 7th.

Israel is not alone. We find the same ethnonationalism in the United States with the white Christian nationalist movement that displaying its naked racism and settler colonialism in the 2024 national election. This is nothing new for the United States, which was founded on principles that its Black population was officially less than human and is still haunted by its "original sin" of racial superiority. When one combines false doctrines from the Bible with racism it becomes a lethal mixture that is yet to be transformed. Moreover, the genocide the United States conducted on its Black and indigenous population has yet to be reconciled, admitted, and rectified.

Whether we are discussing racism in the United States, Israel and Palestine, or anywhere else, the present focus on Israel's genocide should direct us to start the discussion with the Bible. We can begin by recognizing there are primitive and exclusivist passages in the Bible that can be considered settler colonial texts. These passages run through the Bible, especially in the books of history (Joshua, Judges, I and II Samuel, I and II Kings, I and II Chronicles, Ezra, Nehemiah, Esther).

However, if we turn to the two creation stories in Genesis 1 and 2, one example is the creation story we find in the first chapter of Genesis, where humanity is created "B'Tselem," in the very image of God. If every human being is marked with God's very image, then every life is sacred and equal to every human being. This is a foundational concept and the basis to critique any myth of exceptionalism and genocide that we find in the later texts. The Hebrew name for God in Genesis 1 is Elohim, who is the more inclusive God, whereas in the Genesis 2 creation story, Yahweh (Jehovah) is the name for God. This name also appears in historical works where there is more than a hint of exceptionalism ("chosen people") and where God directs the genocide against the Canaanites.

We see the contemporary use of the exceptionalist and genocidal texts in the present Israeli genocide against the Palestinians, which displayed itself in the first few days of Israel's response to the Hamas attacks of October 7. Prime Minister Netanyahu invoked the myth of the Amalekites being the historic enemy of the Jewish people with a call to avenge a historic grievance: "You must remember what Amalek has done to you, says our Holy Bible. And we do remember."[63]

While there is no historical record of such enmity, there are elements of it in the biblical texts, particularly in I Samuel. In the text, Yahweh commands the Prophet Samuel to test the newly anointed King Saul, tasking him with the annihilation of every man, woman, child, and livestock among the Amalekites. According to the story, Saul and his army do slaughter all the children, women, and men, but they spare the king. Samuel rebukes Saul for not finishing the job.

Israeli Prime Minister Netanyahu invoked the Amalek reference in order to justify Israel taking revenge against the Palestinians, which has become a code term for Palestinians among the extremist religious zionists. Netanyahu's so-called biblical justification for Israel's genocidal attack on every Palestinian civilian; men, women, children, including innocent civilians, has been supported by a majority of Israelis and Christian zionists who interpret the Amalekite reference as does Netanyahu. The far right Israeli rabbis then used the same texts in sermons and inspirational messages to the Israeli army prior to their assault on the Gaza Strip, granting religious legitimacy to wipe out every Palestinian in Gaza and beyond.

Mitri Raheb summarizes the tragic history of this violent and false theology:

> These settler colonial groups view themselves as a chosen people with a

> sacred claim to a promised land. They cultivate a devotion to a warrior god, a belief in an external enemy, and an exodus experience. While some countries like Canada and Australia are trying to confront their countries history of settler colonialism, the State of Israel is proudly and unapologetically pushing their settler colonial project with full power by de-facto annexing Palestinian land while excluding the Palestinian people."[64]

In early August, Friends of Sabeel–North America organized an eight-city tour of Rev. Dr. Munther Isaac, Pastor of Evangelical Lutheran Church of Hope in Ramallah, Palestine. I was honored to be part of the organizing committee in Chicago, August 2-4, 2024. Rev. Isaac lectured, preached, conducted media interviews, and answered questions on themes such as "Ending Our Complicity in Gaza's Genocide," "Wake Up the Silent Churches in America," and "The Moral Imperative of Ending the Genocide in Gaza." In a powerful lecture at Missio Dei, an Evangelical Christian community in the Uptown District of Chicago, over 300 people gave numerous ovations to his careful but direct critiques of false Christian zionist interpretations justifying genocide and remaining silent in the face of genocide.

In a heartfelt appeal, Rev. Isaac asked:

> Why does the world view us Palestinians as subhuman so as to allow a televised slaughter of over 40,000 Palestinians? If this continues our dead will number over 200,000 and continue if this madness is not stopped. Are we less than human? What does the Bible teach? Are we not created in the image of God? How can a Christian clergyman encourage Israel to wipe out all of us and another say "Nuke the Gaza Strip," and Presidential candidate Donald Trump encourage Israel to "finish the job." How can Christians and Jews forget the first chapter of Genesis where every human being is created in the image and likeness of God *[Imago Dei]*? Why does the world not care enough to stop Israel's human engineered starvation and disease campaign which on top of the bombing is clearly genocidal intent? We are now in the tenth month of this madness and there is no end in sight."[65]

Our task as people of faith or no religious beliefs is to expose, undo, and transform this dangerous ideology where ever it is bringing death and suffering to God's people. Our focus is on Palestine and Israel, where the present genocide threatens what remains of Gaza's 2.4 million Palestinians and those in the West Bank and East Jerusalem. But wherever the same racist ideologies and false biblical concepts of exceptionalism and people above the law, we must organize and resist these threats. The poet W.H. Auden summarized our challenge: "All I have is a voice to undo the folded lie." May we be inspired to build communities of equality where no one is exceptional except in loving and guarding each person's dignity.[66]

The American Jewish theologian Mark Braverman warns us about the false path of zionism (and Christian zionism):

> We must acknowledge that zionism was a mistake—an understandable but catastrophic wrong turn in our quest for safety and dignity. Until then, we will continue to build a state on top of a lie and a crime. Until then, the Palestinians will continue to resist by steadfastly refusing to relinquish their identity, their way of life, and their connection to their homeland—occupied, harassed, imprisoned, blockaded, bombarded, starved, and betrayed by their political leaders, but proud, unbowed, and refusing to disappear. Jews must recognize that our story today is not what was done to us, but what we are now doing to others. This is our tragedy, our catastrophe. This is what we must mourn.[67]

While Braverman's challenge was to the Jewish people, his words are relevant for everyone, particularly for Christians as they face the challenges from Christian zionism. The South African theologian Charles Villa-Vicencio, a veteran of the struggle against apartheid in his native land, writes "this monumental struggle for theological and political integrity is much larger than Palestine itself." He calls it "the fault line running through Western civilization, a split that dates back to the early centuries of Christianity when the followers of Jesus split with those who clung to Rome's imperial power." This is the challenge of zionism and Christian zionism—a theology of exclusivity and empire versus the message of the Hebrew prophets and Jesus of Nazareth. In this age of rising authoritarianism and a televised genocide this prophetic message is more relevant than at any point since the Nazi threat of the 1940s. It is this threat and how the question of Palestine becomes highly relevant that we turn next.

Conclusion:
Ch. 21 & Afterword

No Place Left to Go: Why Palestine Matters

"If I must die
let it bring hope
let it be a tale"
—Refaat Alareer,
If I Must Die: Poetry and Prose

"I believe in a future in which everyone is able to live freely, where Israeli Jews and Palestinians work alongside each other for a better future in a decolonized and free Palestine—and [we can] obtain it. It won't be easy but it is possible."

—Ilan Pappe, *Israel on the Brink*

Chapter 21

NO PLACE LEFT TO GO! WHY PALESTINE MATTERS

"To be Palestinian means to be infected with incurable hope."

—Mahmoud Darwish, Palestinian Poet Laureate

For decades, I have been inspired by the popular statement attributed to Martin Luther King, Jr.: "The arc of the moral universe is long but it bends toward justice." I used it to conclude sermons when I was a pastor. I gave speeches at anti-war rallies and quoted it. I used it in the classroom when I was a professor. About ten years ago, in the midst of my advocacy work, I came to realize the statement needed a conditional tone to introduce the necessity of grassroots advocacy: "The moral arc bends toward justice *when we stand up and work for it.*"[68]

However, the past two years have raised troubling questions about whether justice can ever be achieved when military power and financial pressure are used to manipulate the United Nations Security Council and the courts that uphold international law. The forces of injustice have proved to be too powerful in several tragic cases. Justice was denied to Native Americans, the Cambodians under the Khmer Rouge, the Tutsis in Rwanda, the Rohingya Muslims in Myanmar. And now I worry that the Palestinians of the Gaza Strip, as well as the people in the Darfur region of Sudan, and the Congo may likewise never see real justice. Noura Erakat, a Palestinian expert on international law, lays out a convincing case that Palestinians have been repeatedly denied justice since the Balfour Declaration of 1917, and the pattern continues through our present day.[69]

This concluding chapter will focus on the Palestinian case for justice in light of a live-streamed genocide. The Palestinians in Gaza struggle to survive the most sophisticated genocide of the modern era (thanks largely to the United States supplying 80 percent of the latest technology and weapons). International law has been ignored and the mechanisms of enforcement have been absent. Over 90 percent of Gaza's homes and infrastructure are destroyed, including thirty-six hospitals, and many of the physicians and nurses have been killed via targeted assassinations. Will the global community finally stand up and find a way to end the genocide? This is the question that hangs in the balance. The next question that follows is: will the United States and Israel get away with the genocide? Will this be the end of international law, and will we enter a new period of anarchy and global chaos with no restraints from systems of accountability? The recent military adventures of Benjamin Netanyahu and Donald Trump indicate they are impervious to international law and are free to take over other countries at will. Could the case of Palestine be the test case for restoring the global world order, or is it too late?

The International System of Justice Has Failed Palestinians

On October 25, 2025, international law expert Craig Mokhiber addressed the Gaza Tribunal in Istanbul, Turkey—a forum organized by the Hague Group in an effort to provide an alternative to the United Nations Security Council. Mokhiber knows the United Nations inside-out after spending thirty years working in various capacities at the UN, including serving as a legal advisor on the genocides in Cambodia, Bosnia-Herzegovina, and Sudan. In 2017, he was appointed Director of the United Nations Human Rights office in New York, a post he held until October 2023, when he resigned in protest over the UN's failure to address the Gaza genocide.

Mokhiber's presentation focused on the disproportionate influence held by various colonial powers in the critical decisions made by the UN Security Council and Secretariat. He noted the "diplomacy of fear" that crippled these bodies and led to biased decisions designed to protect Israel and colonial interests, namely those of the United States. The present genocide in Gaza represents the latest example of this syndrome. Mokhiber issued this warning: "Palestine sits directly at the fault line between those who believe the global order should be determined by a deference to peace through great power politics, aggression, colonialism, and imperialism, and those who demand the building of a reliable international law system, constructed on international cooperation, equality, self-determination, and the rule of international law." He added his concern that the entire global system of international law—its courts and institutions and enforcement mechanisms—are now at risk.[70]

Mokhiber's warnings were prescient, as three weeks later, on November 17, 2025, the UN Security Council adopted Resolution 2803 ("Comprehensive Plan to End the Gaza Conflict"; a US-backed peace plan agreed to by Israel and Hamas in October 2025), ignoring the Genocide Convention of 1948 (officially the Convention on the Prevention and Punishment of the Crime of Genocide), which obligates signatories to prevent and punish the crime of genocide. Now, despite the International Court of Justice stating Israel was committing "a plausible genocide" in January of 2024, and Israel ignoring the court's ruling that it must stop the killing and end its mass starvation campaign, UNSC 2803 gives the United States and Israel jurisdiction over the Gaza Strip, allowing the violence to continue without accountability.

I. Palestine Matters to Restore Legitimacy to the United Nations

As Mokhiber said, the flaws in the United Nations can be traced back to its origins. The UN Charter was finalized on June 26, 1945, and ratified by twenty-nine nations on October 24, 1945. Within a year, the young Security Council was informed the British Foreign Office would end its Mandate in Palestine by May, 1948, an admission of twenty-five years of its failed policies in Palestine. Thus the new UN was handed one of the most thorny political issues in modern history. Serious problems within the UN system surfaced immediately as the colonial powers weighed in to influence the deliberations on the future of Palestine.

There were two primary options proposed concerning a resolution to the Palestine question: a single democratic state where every citizen would be equal, and a partition of Palestine into a Jewish and a Palestinian state. The zionist lobby and the Truman administration supported the latter. Initially a slight majority of nations favored the one democratic state option—including countries that had recently emerged from colonial control. However, the colonial powers, consisting of England, the United States, France, and the Soviet Union, supported the partition plan, and through economic and various pressure tactics they were able to secure the vote to partition Palestine, which was adopted on November 29, 1947. The Palestinians and Arab states (and global south) rejected the partition, as it offered the new Jewish state 55 percent of the best land at the expense of the Palestinians, who were two-thirds of the population and had owned 91 percent of the land prior to the partition plan.

Another systemic problem built into the United Nations Security Council was the power of the veto, allowing the major powers to reject resolutions they disliked. Initially, the Soviet Union and China used this to their advantage by vetoing resolutions put forward by the West during the Cold War era. Following Israel's victory in the June 1967 war and the occupation of most of the Palestinian territories, the Sinai Peninsula, and Syrian Golan Heights, the US exercised the veto at a record-setting pace (over fifty vetoes) to protect Israel from accountability to international law, especially its land confiscation and construction of exclusive Jewish settlements. These procedures provided Israel immunity and allowed Israel to accelerate its strategy of ethnic cleansing and land theft at the expense of the Palestinians.

Despite these weaknesses, the UN remains the primary international body with the potential to return to the primacy of international law if these systemic flaws can be corrected. The institution is in desperate need of reform and there are several strategies under discussion. One option is for the member nations to utilize the General Assembly more effectively, as it is not subject to the veto which plagues the Security Council. In the General Assembly every nation has one vote. Based on recent General Assembly votes, the Palestinian case for statehood has support from the majority of UN member nations (155 of 193 countries as of November, 2025). This majority can invoke a mechanism called Uniting For Peace, which provides an alternative procedure to hold nations accountable. This instrument was used in November, 1950, to bypass a Soviet veto and place a UN peace force between North and South Korea. It was used again in 1956 when England, France, and Israel invaded Egypt, threatening a major war in the region. The three nations ultimately withdrew, and the UN international peace force was brought in to stabilize the region. The problem today is that the power of the United States and Europe may be too significant for smaller and more vulnerable nations to stand up to the pressure and support Palestine.

If UNSC Resolution 2803 fails to bring peace to the Gaza Strip, which seems likely, there will be an opportunity to adopt a more robust resolution based on international law. If the majority of nations agree, they can convene the General Assembly and invoke the Uniting For Peace instrument. Ideally, one of its first demands will be for Israel to withdraw from the entirety of the Gaza Strip. This proposal will be resisted by the US and several EU nations, but the majority could have the votes to overrule them. The next provision will be to insert an international protective force to stabilize the Gaza Strip and enable massive levels of humanitarian aid to enter with the desperately needed food, water, medicine, tents and building materials—all of which Israel has blocked. At that point the reconstruction of Gaza can begin, with the provision that it will be for the people of Gaza, not for Israeli settlers or for Trump´s vision of a "Riviera" for his wealthy friends. Then, the International Criminal Court and International Court of Justice could begin legal procedures to litigate the present Gaza genocide and prevent future genocides.

There are two other ideas that are currently under consideration by several member states in the UN. One is to move the United Nations headquarters out of New York City to remove it from direct US control. Another proposal under discussion is to censure Israel and expel it from the United Nations until it honors international law. Finally, many believe the UN Security Council veto can be removed or revised so no single country can block accountability under international law. If international law and the global order is not restored with the accountability instruments in place, I fear we will be plagued by an extended period where the authoritarian models of Trump´s US and Netanyahu´s Israel will dominate.

II. Palestine Matters for Churches to Overcome their Silence in the Face of Genocide

US Senators and Representatives have no excuse for echoing Israel´s talking points: rejecting a permanent ceasefire, limiting humanitarian aid to a starving population, and allowing genocide to continue in efforts disguised as a "peace plan." While Congress remains silent, the religious community could be the prophetic alternative to unhinged violence and global disorder. In this section I am especially concerned about the failure of the global church to rise to the challenge we find in the ethics of Jesus and the Hebrew prophets to stand up for the victims of a genocide in the Gaza Strip.

Thankfully, there are several examples of prophetic courage. One is the Lutheran Bishop of the Evangelical Lutheran Church in Jordan and the Holy Land. Bishops are often under pressure from the Israeli government, making it rare to see a Palestinian bishop take a stand for justice in the Holy Land. The example of Lutheran Bishop Ibrahim Azar offers a model, thanks to the prophetic and courageous stand he took on Reformation Sunday, October 30, 2025, stating:

> But what does Reformation look like after two years of genocide? What does the Reformation mean when we look at a world, a country, that is so broken? What does Reformation look like when children are separated from schools, worshippers from churches, families from each other by military checkpoints and barricades? When people are falsely imprisoned? When families are still searching for their loved ones under rubble?[71]

After Bishop Azar raised these questions, Abraham Lehrer, Vice President of the Central Bureau of Jews in Germany, joined by a German Lutheran church leader, walked out of the church in protest. When the delegation returned to Germany, they issued a statement denouncing the bishop′s use of the term genocide. A group of Israeli scholars called the sermon a "blood libel against Jews." Bishop Azar was aware of possible consequences, but the mandates of the Gospel and two full years of genocide demanded a courageous response.

A similar pattern of intimidation exists in religious circles across Europe and North America, where the religious landscape has allowed similar strategies of bullying and fear to dominate the discourse. The late Jewish theologian Marc Ellis called this syndrome "the ecumenical deal"; Christian clergy are told to refrain from criticizing Israel and zionism, or they will face accusations of antisemitism and rebuke. Those who abide by "the deal" can enjoy interfaith relations in relative peace, but the minute they step out of line and demand justice for Palestinians they will pay a price.

Thankfully, the tide is slowly turning as we are blessed by the support of a growing number of prophetic Jewish organizations, including Rabbis who will not only stand with us but set an example of what it means to follow their prophets and demand justice for Palestinians. A growing number of Palestinians, both Muslim and Christian, from the American Muslims for Palestine and the Kairos Palestine movement are at the forefront of articulating a theology of liberating justice and an uncompromising message of truth-telling. As previously cited, Bishop Azar is such an example: a Christian leader willing to face the consequences while knowing he was surrounded by a company of prophetic sisters and brothers. The Kairos Palestine movement in particular, as a Palestinian Christian group focused on community and justice, reinforced Bishop Azar's message. They issued their Kairos Palestine II document a few days after his sermon:

> More than ever, now is a time for costly solidarity. By its very nature, true

> solidarity is costly. It has a price. It is a faith-based stance, a human commitment and a moral responsibility. True solidarity is also the embodiment of our shared humanity and fraternity. Either we live together—or we perish together. Today it is Palestine. Tomorrow it will be other marginalized and oppressed peoples.

The statement concluded with this appeal:

> From the heart of pain, genocide and displacement, we raise this cry, a prophetic cry of steadfastness. We declare our commitment to work for the good of this land and of all humanity on the basis of our shared humanity until the day we live free in our land together with all the inhabitants of the land in true peace and reconciliation founded on justice and equality for all God's creation, where mercy and truth meet, and righteousness and peace kiss each other (Psalm 85:10).[72]

We can all take courage and guidance from our friends in the Kairos Palestine movement and join them in the journey of "costly solidarity" with those suffering at the margins of society. It means we follow the model set forth by the Hebrew Prophets, the life and teachings of Jesus, and the Prophetic example of the Prophet Muhammed (PBUH) who continue to be models of costly solidarity. Following in their footsteps will lead us to see the wisdom in Jesus' parable of the Last Judgment, which tells us: "When I was hungry did you feed me? When I was thirsty did you give me a drink?" You might extend this thinking and say, "When I was under bombardment in a televised genocide, did you block the bombs? Even though you do it to the least of these, my sisters and brothers, you do to me." (Matthew 25:35-36). If we have the courage and stay the course, we will build the movement that will surely bend the arc of history toward justice in Palestine and Israel.

III. Palestine Matters in Liberating Christian Theology from Christian Zionism

Christian zionism has been defined above as Christian political, economic, and theological support for Israel and the zionist movement. Its influence has grown from being a marginal movement in the fundamentalist wing of evangelical Christianity to a global phenomenon with significant political power in the United States Congress. What is often overlooked is the growing political role of Christian zionism in Central and South America, Africa, and Southeast Asia. Christian zionists revere Israeli Prime Minister Netanyahu and his militant agenda, even to the extent of supporting Israel´s genocide in the Gaza Strip, claiming God gave all the land of Palestine to the Jewish people and Israel has a right to defend itself and declare sovereignty over all of it.

In mid-December, 2025, Netanyahu brought 1,000 Evangelical Christian leaders from the United States to Israel for a training program on how to be an "ambassador for Israel." Israeli officials are well aware they have lost considerable support on a global level since October, 2023, including young evangelicals in the United States. The new initiative is designed to shore up support for Israel in the United States, which is Israel's primary source of political and economic support. Prior to the genocide in Gaza, Israel could count on the conservative evangelicals for unconditional support, but younger evangelicals aren´t buying into the propaganda. Support for Israel among young evangelicals declined 40 percent between 2018 and 2021.[73]

Christian zionist influence in US politics and culture has increased steadily since the early 1980s when conservative evangelicals played a prominent role in the Reagan administration. Their influence secured a significant victory during the first Trump administration (2016-20) when the US Congress voted to move the US Embassy from Tel Aviv to East Jerusalem, a project the pro-Israel lobby had been pursuing unsuccessfully since the 1970s. Both Republican and Democratic administrations avoided the pro-Israel lobby´s campaigns to move the Embassy, as it was seen as a flagrant breach of international law. Everything changed under Trump and Netanyahu after 2016, as both leaders knew Christian zionist influence could tip the scales in the US Congress. Trump admitted as much during his 2020 election campaign when he said he moved the embassy "for the evangelicals.[74]

Palestinian Christians have rejected Christian zionism for decades and have consistently called upon evangelicals and all Christian denominations worldwide to take stronger positions by rejecting this dangerous theology. As the political sway of lobbies like AIPAC and other zionist groups has increased in recent years, Christians in the US need to make this issue a priority and should cooperate with groups like Kairos Palestine and Friends of Sabeel.

The Kairos II document is both a statement straight from Palestinian

Christians and a resource for Christians worldwide to confront Christian zionism directly:

> We reject the oppression and injustice produced by the theology of racism, colonialism and ethnic supremacy embodied in Christian Zionism, a theology that has produced apartheid, ethnic cleansing and genocide of indigenous people. Christian Zionism calls on a tribal, racist god of war and ethnic cleansing, teachings utterly alien to the core of Christian faith and ethics. Christian zionism must therefore be named for what it is—a theological distortion and a moral corruption. After all efforts to invite Christian zionists to genuine repentance have been exhausted, moral, ecclesial and theological responsibility requires that they be held accountable and that their ideology be rejected and boycotted. The time has come for the churches of the world to repudiate Zionist theology and to state clearly their position on Palestine. This is a case of settler colonialism and ethnic cleansing of an indigenous people.[75]

One of the key theological issues in challenging Christian zionism is to raise its tendency to support the false gods of racism, militarism, and tribalism, while creating an idol out of the modern zionist state of Israel and zionism's concept of the "land of Israel." Christian zionists give Israel unconditional support in whatever policies the state pursues: seizing land for illegal settlements, or committing ethnic cleansing, and even genocide, all in God's name. In doing so, Christian zionism is guilty of the most grievous sin in the Bible: idolatry. "Thou shalt have no other gods before Me." Most Christian zionists defend the Israeli military campaigns and even settler pogroms against Palestinian villages, both Christian and Muslim, in the West Bank. Numerous attacks on the Christian village of Taybeh in 2025 destroyed churches and Christian monuments, and Christian zionists have remained silent. When the US Senate and House of Representatives tried to pass resolutions calling for an end to military aid to Israel or even a limited blockage of major weapons, the Christian zionist lobby joined AIPAC and the major pro-Israel lobbies to defeat those resolutions.

Throughout history, idolatry has been the litmus test for false theologies and an indication of heresy. It was the primary critique theologians Barth and Bonhoeffer registered against the Nazi-influenced theology the German church adopted in the 1930s. It was the central theme the anti-Apartheid theologians like Allen Boesak, John deGruchy, and Frank Chikane in South Africa utilized to reject the white racist theology of the Dutch Reformed Church and the racist Apartheid system imposed by the South African state. For decades the Palestinian theologians Mitri Raheb, Naim Ateek, Munther Isaac, Daniel Banoura, John and Samuel Munayer, Nadera Shalhoub-Kevorkian, and others have played a similar role in dismantling the false theology of Christian zionism. The next step is for the global church to take action at the highest levels and declare Christian zionism a heresy. The three major global bodies of Christianity are the World Council of Churches, the World Communion of Reformed Churches, and the Lausanne Committee for World Evangelization.

There have been several initiatives by the Kairos Palestine movement to secure a clear and unambiguous rejection of Christian zionism at the global level, but to date the three bodies have not delivered a clear statement on the issue of heresy. In 2025, the Palestinian theologians have been joined by South African theologians, such as Dr. Allan Boesak, to challenge the World Communion of Reformed Churches to make a definitive statement rejecting Christian zionism as a heretical theology. Boesak is remembered as the leader of the Black theologians who challenged what was then called the World Alliance of Reformed Churches in 1982 to declare Apartheid a heresy.

Linda and I were privileged to hear Dr. Boesak address our travel group at the Desmond and Leah Tutu Legacy Foundation on October 7, 2025, in Cape Town, South Africa. In his lecture Dr. Boesak reviewed the dangers of global Christian zionism, which is a distortion of Christian theology, and the need to declare it a heresy. He had recently submitted a resolution to the World Communion of Reformed Churches and hoped the Communion would adopt an unambiguous resolution declaring Christian Zionism a "status confessionis," or a heresy that was inconsistent with historic Christian theology. He reminded us that this was the basis of the argument German theologian Dietrich Bonhoeffer used in his critique of Nazi theology, and the South Africans used the same argument in their campaign to have white Apartheid theology declared a heresy in 1982.

When we returned home I contacted Dr. Boesak to see if the WCRC had adopted the South African resolution, and unfortunately they did not. They chose to issue a mild statement that avoided the "status confessionis" and heresy critique. The campaign must continue and will hopefully become a global movement to challenge Christian zionism as a heresy.[76] In addition to the Protestant global bodies cited above, it would also be important to develop a strategy to influence the Vatican and the Eastern Orthodox churches, where there is already significant support to reject Christian zionism.

IV. Palestine Matters as Jews Liberate Themselves from Zionism

The respected journalist and critic Peter Beinart has argued that Palestine matters to Jews, and, in the midst of genocide in Gaza, it should matter to everyone. Beinart is a regular contributor to the *New York Times*, a professor and activist who has gained mainstream media visibility in the United States. He made a dramatic ideological shift from liberal zionism to anti-zionism, as he could no longer defend Israel as an exclusively Jewish Apartheid state.

Beinart is an Orthodox Jew who keeps the sabbath, maintains a kosher diet, and studies the Torah religiously. His argument goes to the heart of Judaism and focuses on a single verse found in the Book of Leviticus 21:22. The passage says, "Do not profane my holy name that I may be sanctified in the midst of the Israelites." He believes the verse warns about the misuse of God´s name, but much more is at stake in this case. He believes this verse is exceedingly relevant for the present Israeli genocide in Gaza. The verse is a warning against the crime of an intentional mass slaughter of civilians and the deliberate starvation of two million people. This war crime profanes God's sacred name by the mass murder of human beings who are created in the very image of God ("*B´tselem*" in Hebrew and "*Imago Dei*" in Latin: Genesis 1:27).

Beinart cites the Babylonian Talmud where Rabbi Eleazar ben Azariah made the same argument, and asks "how could what's happening in Gaza not be a *chillul hashem*, a desecration of God's name on a scale that I simply struggle every day to comprehend, to get my mind around."[77]

Beinart concludes:

> This is going to be, I think for the Jewish people, for us, a spiritual crisis, not just a moral crisis. But if we take Judaism seriously, a spiritual crisis that will be the greatest spiritual crisis of most of our lives. It will be the greatest spiritual crisis that the Jewish people have faced since the Holocaust. It will be, of course, a spiritual crisis of a massively different order, and that's not to say that what's happening in Gaza is

> the equivalent of the Nazi Holocaust. Of course not. But it will be a radically different kind of spiritual crisis, because the question will not be, where was God when Jews were being slaughtered—6 million of them—but where were we when we desecrated God's name by allowing in our name—and in the United States, with our weapons—this kind of horror to take place day after day after day after day. And the band played on. We will not move past this as a people. We will not move past this. This will shadow us for the rest of our lives.[78]

Peter Beinart is saying that until Jews recognize this genocide and take action to end it, they will be burdened by this crime. In making this point he is fully aware that Israel does not represent all Jews and is implying Israel´s actions in Gaza do not represent him. However, it is necessary for true believers of the Jewish faith to clarify this distinction and be clear that Israel does not represent them in its intentional violations of international law. Like the Hebrew prophets, he believes Jews must stand up and oppose the genocide in Gaza and in some cases take the lead, particularly when their political leaders and mainstream Jewish organizations are refusing to be prophetic. Thankfully, a large number of Jews are doing just that, leading the opposition to the genocide.

The fastest growing Jewish organization in the United States, Jewish Voice for Peace, has taken strong positions against the genocide in Gaza, as has another Jewish group, If Not Now. They have stood together for more than two years in public protest to demand from Congress an end to genocide, a permanent ceasefire, and an end to the sale of US weapons to Israel. They work intersectionally with Christian and Muslim organizations to end the genocide and cut military aid to Israel. Their bearing witness during this time of genocide in Gaza has inspired thousands of US citizens to join them in staying vigilant until these Israeli and US war crimes have ended and Gaza is free from genocide and Israel's occupation.[79]

V. Palestine Matters to Save Academic Freedom and Free Speech at Universities

In the spring of 2024, the Gaza Solidarity Encampment began at Columbia University in New York City. The movement quickly spread to universities across the United States, Canada, Europe, Africa, and beyond. The media compared it to the anti-Vietnam war movement of the 1960s-70s, which forced a sitting President (L. B. Johnson) to step down and not run for a second term. Concerned that the movement on campuses was a threat to his MAGA agenda, Donald J. Trump and several pro-Israel organizations decided to quash the Columbia University campus movement with an immediate and aggressive response. They also decided to make an example out of two other schools: the University of Pennsylvania and Harvard University.

Universities across the country took note of the problems at these three Ivy League universities. As similar movements branched out and developed on college campuses nationwide, administrators gave orders to local and campus police to dismantle encampments and, in some cases, arrest the student leaders. University administrators threatened students with discipline, such as revoking foreign students' visas and refusing diplomas to graduating seniors. In some cases, faculty were dismissed or placed on probation for simply advising the students involved in the encampments.

Linda and I were in California during this period, and I spoke at Cal Poly State University at San Luis Obispo, where several student leaders from their encampment were present. I encouraged the students to continue with their meetings and their boycott and divestment efforts, but to be vigilant about how the administration at the university was behaving. I advised them to get legal counsel immediately in case the administration sent ICE agents and police after them. I suggested they contact Palestine Legal, ACLU, CAIR, and the Center for Constitutional Rights to see who was available to counsel them immediately.

Two of the leaders told me they were extremely worried about the response of their university. Both were Palestinian—one born in the US, the other in the Middle East. They said they needed to go underground for a month or more and assess how their university would respond. Linda and I stayed in touch with them through our local host. About five days later, we learned that the student from the Middle East was warned by a faculty advisor that his name was listed in the local newspaper as someone whose visa had been revoked, and he was in danger of being arrested. With that development, they were able to secure a plane ticket with the help of the community, and the foreign student flew home before ICE could locate him.

Another act of suppressing student dissent at Columbia University drew national attention: Mahmoud Khalil was a leader of the encampment movement and the lead student negotiator interacting with the Columbia administration. On March 8, 2025, Mahmoud and his wife were returning to their apartment when they were surrounded by ICE agents who told Khalil his student visa had been revoked by the State Department and he was under arrest. He was handcuffed and eventually sent to the Lasalle Detention Center in Louisiana. This action violated Khalil's legal status as he is a permanent resident, and his wife (who was eight months pregnant) is a US citizen.

Mahmoud Khalil's case was represented by several legal organizations including Palestine Legal, the ACLU, and the Center for Constitutional Rights. After several months of negotiations his case was dismissed by a Federal Judge. Mahmoud was released on June 20, 2025, and returned to New York where he reunited with his wife and greeted his newborn son for the first time. On November 20, 2025, the Center for Constitutional Rights and five legal organizations filed a lawsuit against the Trump Administration alleging they used biased, foreign (Israeli) organizations to target Khalil, which may have rendered his arrest and imprisonment illegal. ICE and Homeland Security were using data generated by the far-right anti-Palestinian organization Bitar, which is an Israeli organization that uses artificial intelligence with facial recognition technology to target Palestinians in Gaza and the West Bank. If Mahmoud Khalil's case confirms the use of Bitar and/or other Israeli generated surveillance technology, the illegality of his arrest and imprisonment could set the legal precedent for similar cases.[80]

I had the opportunity to meet Mahmoud Khalil via Zoom when our organization, Americans for Middle East Understanding (AMEU), honored him with the Mahoney Service Award. My colleague Nick Griffen, Director of AMEU, and I were impressed by Mahmoud's humility and his steadfast commitment to advocate for justice in Palestine without hesitation despite his precarious legal status.

Investigative reporting revealed the Trump administration was following the agenda recommended by Project Esther, a centerpiece of "Project 2025" written by the Heritage Foundation with input from various pro-Israel lobby organizations.[81] Project Esther advised the Trump administration to use the narrow definition of antisemitism developed by the International Holocaust Remembrance Alliance (IHRA), which claims criticism of the state of Israel and zionism are forms of antisemitism. The author of the IHRA definition has since declared his opposition to the political use of the definition as it constitutes a violation of the First Amendment of the Constitution. Nevertheless, the Trump administration was aware of this fact but continued to use the narrow definition in its campaign to limit academic freedom. This action enabled the US Education Department to recommend severe punishment for students, faculty and university administrations who are critical of Israel and zionism. Their goal is to eliminate any pro-Palestinian language, activities, and academic courses in universities across the United States.

The case of Trump vs. Harvard University became a national media spectacle with mixed results. On the surface, the optics indicated Harvard was a champion of free speech and academic freedom. Upon closer inspection this was not the case. Before its public showdown with the Trump Administration, Harvard made a series of decisions that flew below the media radar in which they eliminated academic programs involving the Palestinian issue. First, Harvard silenced the student organizations that led the encampments: Jewish Voice for Peace and Students for Justice in Palestine. Second, Harvard eliminated an academic program with Birzeit University, the preeminent Palestinian university in the occupied Palestinian territories. Third, Harvard Divinity School was forced to cancel a popular academic seminar that involved international faculty who were experts on Christian zionism. The monthly seminars examined the global expansion of Christian zionism in Central and South America, Africa, the Middle East, and Asia. It was abruptly shut down and its May 2025 conference cancelled. Two faculty members of Harvard Divinity School were terminated in 2025, including Hilary Rantisi, who was the assistant director of the Religion, Conflict and Peace Initiative and the only Palestinian employed by the Divinity School. Apparently, the Harvard administrators decided Palestine could be sacrificed with minimal consequences, despite the fact that each of the incidents cited above may have violated the first amendment of the Constitution.

Given the current hostility toward Palestinians in academic circles, it is important to find ways to challenge universities and urge them to uphold academic freedom and free speech at their institutions. Universities have been at the forefront of social and political change throughout US history, and in spite of the Trump administration's efforts to limit free speech at major American universities, the movement to end the genocide in Gaza continues that tradition.

VI. Palestine Matters and Needs a Global Solidarity and Advocacy Network

As the genocide in Gaza enters its third year, Israel is more isolated as we begin 2026 than it was prior to October 7, 2023. Its reputation has received a lethal blow at the popular level across the world. Despite these losses, Israel still exerts its influence over presidents, heads of state, and mainstream media corporations in the West. The US and Israel can still impose their will on the United Nations and delay decisions by the international courts to sway favor. But Israel has lost the streets and the young generation under forty years of age. Israel's power and influence is concentrated at the upper echelon of ownership of mainstream media, politics, academia, and many religious organizations. The obvious lesson before us is the Palestine case needs a well-organized grass-roots advocacy movement on a global level to take advantage of this political moment.

There is a highly successful model for global advocacy, which is the boycott, divestment, and sanctions (BDS) movement, initiated by Palestinian civil society in 2005. It has grown in popularity and efficacy by targeting businesses, pension funds, and other economic centers with well-organized grassroots campaigns. This movement has demonstrated its value through the years, and it is essential to the long-range success of the Palestinian justice movement.

However, a broader and different grassroots political movement is urgently needed to bring pressure on governments to stop the genocide in Gaza and support a political solution to the Palestine question based in international law. The essential components of this new movement exist in parts of Europe, Africa, North and South America, and Asia, but a highly efficient level of global coordination will be necessary.

There is a model for such an advocacy network of non-governmental organizations (NGOs) that was highly effective and active on every continent in the 1983-1995 era. The movement is still remembered fondly by former activists who were active during that period. It could be useful for today's activists and organizers, and a model that could be reimagined for the decades ahead. The movement was called the International Coordinating Committee on Palestine (ICCP) and it was affiliated with the United Nations Division for Palestinian Rights and the UN Committee for the Inalienable Rights of the

Palestinian People. The movement maintained a high degree of independence in its programs and the UN affiliation was a significant asset. Any future consideration of reinventing the ICCP will need to assess the role of the United Nations as it has been tarnished in recent years, as noted above. Despite these serious concerns, there may still be value in exploring UN affiliation.

The goal of the ICCP was to mobilize grassroots efforts to support Palestinian rights and international law, including educating the public and putting pressure on parliaments, the media, and religious institutions. Student associations and the justice networks in the major religions will be natural allies. The ICCP's organizational model involved an international board of directors and regional steering committees on every continent. One example was the North American steering committee where US and Canadian leaders worked in unison. The steering committees met monthly to organize their advocacy and educational strategies. In addition to the monthly strategy meetings, leadership from the steering committees were involved in planning the annual convention, which was often held at UN headquarters.

Similar steering committees existed on every continent and were composed of representatives from NGOs active in that region, developing programming that served the needs of their constituents. They included representatives from legal, academic, religious, and peace and justice organizations. Separate steering committees were formed in Israel and Palestine. In the Israel-Palestine case, Israelis and Palestinians worked separately to organize their constituency, but there was significant cooperation and some joint programming.

A highlight of the movement were the international conventions held either in Geneva, Switzerland, or Vienna, Austria, where delegates from all the regional networks gathered to hear plenary lectures. The keynoters were leading political figures in Europe and popular Palestinian or Israeli experts on peace and justice issues. Networking between regional groups was often the focus of these international meetings. Important political discussions were held in smaller workshops or strategy sessions. One of the unexpected outcomes of the international meetings were the side meetings between Israeli politicians and PLO leadership, which were illegal according to Israeli policy. Matti Peled, a former Israeli General turned peacemaker, was both a popular speaker and a member of the ICCP international steering committee.

A small working group of leaders from the early ICCP years has been meeting for the past three years to recover the history of the movement and consider whether a group of young and visionary activists might reimagine a new global solidarity network for the future. The working group includes Dr. Don Betz, who was the original visionary and leader of the ICCP; Kathy Bergen, who directed the ICCP office in Geneva for several years; Larry Ekin, who led the North American coordinating committee in the 1990s; and myself, who served on the International Committee and was active in the North American coordinating committee throughout the ICCP's tenure.

Our modest working group of ICCP elders has interviewed over twenty leaders who were active during ICCP years. The overwhelming majority of them support a reimagined ICCP and recognize it could fill a much-needed global function. While some believe the United Nations has lost its credibility since the 1980s-90s, others believe there may still be value in exploring a carefully prescribed relationship. We all agree that the new movement should be led by young Palestinian organizers, but also include leadership from other parts of the world, such as Africa, North America, Europe, Asia, and South America. The new movement should maximize the use of social media to prioritize an intersectional approach with a focus on decolonizing Palestine and de-zionizing Israel. The ultimate goal would be to highlight international law as the central organizing framework with an emphasis on self-determination for Palestinians in an independent state with full equality for all the citizens and the right of return.[82]

VII. Palestine Matters: Building a Case for Reparations

The hellish conditions Gazans find themselves in at the end of 2025 defy words and leave those familiar with daily news angry, frustrated, and grieving. With over 72,000 dead and as many as 50,000 missing and likely dead under the rubble, winter has arrived with cold and brutal rains, leaving the people of Gaza living in flimsy tents, often in or near flooded areas mixed with sewage, spreading disease. The tents are worn out and no longer water resistant. Food and clean water are scarce as Israel severely restricts the agreed upon 600 trucks per day to an average of around 100-150 trucks, refusing to allow most medicine, tents and building supplies from entering. Israel's designed campaign of starvation continues daily, as do the bombing raids, albeit at a slower pace, enabling a perception to spread in the mainstream media that a ceasefire has taken hold. In reality, Gaza is facing genocide at a slower but steady pace.

We are witnessing an advanced stage of what Palestinian analyst Nadera Shalhoub-Kevorkian calls the ultimate goal of settler colonial regimes, "necropolitics." Israel's continuing military strategy has culminated in a textbook case of twenty-first century genocide. Shalhoub-Kevorkian reminds us of the familiar words of Yosef Weitz, a leader of the Jewish National Fund, where he was head of the land acquisition department. Weitz's version of zionism includes an extreme form of settler colonial ideology with the aim to erase the Palestinian population in historic Palestine:

> It must be clear that there is no room in the country for both peoples ... If the Arabs leave it, the country will become wide and spacious for us ... The only solution is the land of Israel, without Arabs. There is no way but to transfer the Arabs from here to the neighboring countries, to transfer all of them, perhaps with the exception of Bethlehem, Nazareth, and the Old Jerusalem. Not one village, not one tribe should be left.[83]

Today's zionist military leaders and several Knesset (including parliamentarians Ben-Gvir and Smotrich) are a more extreme brand of militant zionism than Weitz. The Netanyahu government is implementing settler colonialism through a high-tech genocide in Gaza and the West Bank, where settlers kidnap Palestinian youth, burn houses and crops, and scream racist remarks about expelling or killing all the Palestinians.

In this context it may seem out of place to raise the concept of reparations, but I do so to present an alternative narrative with specific recommendations that could resist the triumph of Israeli necropolitics. The road to reparations will be long and nothing is guaranteed, but there are clear programmatic possibilities that will hopefully rise above the present malaise. Some of these steps can begin immediately while others will need to await a post-Trump administration in the United States and a more favorable political climate in Europe.

The first step is to end the genocide as soon as possible and enforce a viable, permanent ceasefire in Gaza. The Trump-Netanyahu peace plan is failing miserably, with Palestinians dying daily and too few humanitarian trucks entering the enclave. The UN General Assembly needs to take action and convene an emergency session, starting with a demand for a permanent ceasefire. A temporary pause is useless, as it leaves Israel in the driver's seat ready to resume the killing at any point. Nothing will advance, thanks to the UNSC 2803 that adopted the flawed "Trump-Netanyahu Peace Plan."

Once the decision to restore international law is in place, there should be decisions by the UNSC or General Assembly to demand that Israel must withdraw from the entire Gaza Strip and open multiple entry points for a massive infusion of humanitarian relief, including food, water, tents medicine, physicians, and building materials for the Gaza Strip. A UN Peacekeeping Force will need to take control of Gaza and provide security for the Palestinians and begin disarming Hamas and other militias. These will be delicate negotiations, and Hamas will need to be ensured that Palestinians will be at the heart of the international group responsible for governing Gaza, which will lead to self-determination, an independent state, and the right of return. Hamas should be charged with war crimes before the international courts and prosecuted the same way Israel will be.

The ICC and ICJ will be encouraged to begin proceedings regarding the genocide in Gaza and who is liable. The case for massive reparations can be pursued in the ICC, determining the Palestinians of the Gaza Strip are clearly the victims of an intentional genocide that meets all the standards of the Convention on the Prevention and Punishment of the Crime of Genocide. Considering the amount of evidence that has been submitted to both bodies since the ICJ's probable genocide ruling in January, 2024, there is likely to be considerable evidence for a conviction.

Given the urgency of the medical crises of most of the 2.2 million Gazans, the international humanitarian agencies that Israel had banned from the Gaza Strip will need to urgently be revived so the victims of diseases, wounds, and severe psychological trauma can begin to be addressed. Gaza′s networks of thirty-six hospitals and clinics will need to be rebuilt and refurnished in stages so they can be utilized as soon as possible. A restored and well-funded UNRWA will be essential to the healing process, as it has the strongest capacity for delivering wide-ranging humanitarian support and would be run by Palestinians trusted by the local population. At this point an international reparations agency will have been established to assess the total cost of the entire reconstruction and rehabilitation of the Gazans. The agency will also need to determine what countries are responsible for the genocide of Gaza and what their specific reparation portion will be, starting with Israel. Prominent among the others will be the United States, which provided over 80 percent of the weapons, followed by England, Germany, France, the Netherlands, and other nations worldwide.

There are at least two models for collection and distribution that can be reviewed, including the Claims Conference for Israel's reparations from West Germany that were established by the 1952 Luxembourg Agreement, which provided goods and funds to Israel for infrastructure, with total payments exceeding €80 billion by 2022.[84] The other model is The Iraq-Kuwait reparations model, managed by the UN Compensation Commission (UNCC) after Iraq's 1990 invasion, involving a unique, UN-mandated system.

While the above processes are victim-centered reparations models, due to the design and implementation of Israel's military strategy of total annihilation there is also the need for Israel to publicly admit its guilt and its intent to rebuild Gaza, East Jerusalem, and the West Bank. While important, it is far too early to speculate on how Israel and Palestine will heal and be able to live side by side in the future. Eventually a "Truth and Reconciliation Commission" modeled on the South African case may be the next phase of healing, but that discussion is in the distant future.

Hope on a Dark and Depressing Stage

The evidence on the ground in Gaza is beyond hopeless given the current genocide, leaving many analysts with a sense the cause of Palestine could be reaching a dead end. But don't tell that to Palestinians. This is not the Palestinian perspective. For Palestinians, hope knows darkness, and they are well acquainted with threats to their existence, including the Nakba of 1948, the massacre of Sabra-Shatila, and today's genocide in Gaza. They have survived over a century under military occupation and colonialism, and they are still alive, albeit severely wounded. Their view of hope on a darkened stage is far from a romantic sentiment, as Palestinians have had to choose life and figure out how to survive against overwhelming odds. They are also aware that hundreds of thousands, perhaps millions, did not survive. But their memory lives on and drives Palestinians toward justice.

One example of hopeful justice is the story of a remarkable Palestinian farmer and his family on a farm less than fifteen kilometers from Bethlehem. They call their farm the "Tent of Nations." Daoud Nassar, his brother Daher, and his sister Amal run a remarkable hundred-acre farm on a hilltop surrounded by Israeli settlements vying for their land. During the years Linda and I were leading solidarity tours, Daoud and his family were an important part of our itinerary. The Nassars know something about hope and darkness. Israel has been trying to seize his family's land through a variety of illegal, violent intrusions and applying political pressure to deny them what is rightfully theirs. The Nassars have the original deed to their property, purchased by their grandfather in 1916 during the Ottoman Empire, some thirty-three years before Israel existed. Yet the Israeli military and extremist settlers have attacked and destroyed as many as 3,100 of the family's olive and almond trees. They have physically attacked Daoud and Daher while they were tilling their soil, beating them severely, requiring their hospitalization.

Israel has issued military orders preventing the Nassars from building housing or a community center on their property, so the family dug caves and lived underground. After twenty years of legal maneuvers, physical attacks, and significant legal fees, the Nassar family refuses to surrender. Daoud Nassar's Christmas message of 2025 reflected their stubborn hope and sumud:

> We dare to speak of hope—not the thin hope of wishful thinking, but the deep, living hope that God breathes into all who refuse to surrender to despair. It is the hope that rises like dawn after a long night, the hope that stands its ground even where possibility seems to have run dry. Here at the Tent of Nations, hope is not merely something we feel—it is a discipline we choose each day. It is the courage to rise when circumstances press us low, the faithfulness to tend the soil, to plant trees, and to bear witness through simple, steady acts that darkness will never have the final word.[85]

The Nassar family has turned the Tent of Nations into an international peace camp, and part of their hope includes networks for friends across Europe, Canada, the United States, and Australia who stand by to help work the farm and to resist the next punitive measures Israel tries to impose on them. The fate of Tent of Nations is unknown, but they will never surrender to the unjust system of zionist settler colonialism.

The Israeli historian Ilan Pappe published a remarkable volume in 2025 titled *Israel on the Brink*. He examines eight revolutions that could lead to the decolonization of Palestine and the defeat of zionism, both inside Israel and globally. There is hope in the midst of the historical struggle underway, as Israel faces serious problems that raise questions about its long-term sustainability as a zionist state. Pappe states:

> At the time of this writing (2025), Palestine is at the center of global attention. It is difficult to know how long such concern will last. However, what's at stake this time is not just the future of Palestine and Palestinians. The events of October 2023, exposed cracks in the foundations of Israel. These cracks are widening all the time, threatening the very stability of Israel. A question mark has opened over Israel's future. What will happen to the Zionist project in the coming decades remains to be seen, but it is clear it cannot go on like it is.[86]

Pappe sees three historical and political dynamics that are already underway, and they will be the factors that transport Israel and Palestine into a new era of peaceful coexistence. He calls them the three mini-revolutions that will guide the historical process: a dramatic revolution in the definition of Judaism in the world at large, which includes the collapse of zionist ideology; the emergence of a clear Palestinian perception of the Jewish collective in a decolonized Palestine; and the deconstruction of islamophobia as an institutionalized bias among Jews. Just as Jewish immigrants to the state of Israel after 1948 were propagandized to support zionism, Pappe believes they can also be dezionized. If these mini-revolutions take place, they could facilitate Israeli-Palestinian coexistence as equal citizens in post-Israel Palestine.[87]

I am writing during this cold, snowy, and dark Advent of 2025, the liturgical season that precedes Christmas in the Christian churches. As I read my morning scripture references, they reflect ancient Israel's exile and gloomy passages of judgment and loss from the Hebrew prophets. During the season of Lent, we will read similar passages leading up to Jesus' crucifixion and the dark and foreboding themes captured in Jesus' cry from the cross: "My God, my God, why have you forsaken me?" (Psalm 22:1; Matthew 27:46). Jesus experienced total abandonment by God the Father as he was dying after forty-eight hours of interrogation, sleepless, beaten, and carrying a one-hundred-pound cross through the streets of Jerusalem, where he was finally nailed with spikes through his hands and feet.

With these thoughts in mind, I have turned to the German theologian

Jurgen Moltmann's *The Crucified God* to supplement my Advent reflections. In the introduction, Moltmann reflects on the devastation he and other young German soldiers felt as they returned from prison camps or exile in 1945. They were demoralized after Germany's defeat and the extensive destruction of their country. Even worse was their guilt after serving in Hitler's army and death machine that murdered millions of people.

Moltmann reflected on the depth of his depression and hopelessness that began to shift when he heard a lecture on theology that urged the audience to go to the depths of their guilt and loss by concentrating on Jesus' suffering, rejection, and agony on the cross. The technical term is "the theology of the cross." In this theology, suffering and death are not the end of the story. Moltmann explains:

> The whole of theology was drawn as if by a magnifying glass into a single focus: the cross. I began to see things with the eyes of Christ dying on the cross. For me the crucified Christ became more and more the foundation and criticism of Christian theology...Christ died on the cross with a loud cry, which Mark interprets with the words of the twenty-second Psalm: "My God, my God, why have you forsaken me?" This cry of abandonment is either the end of theology and every religion, or it is the beginning of a truly Christian theology—and that means a liberation theology.[88]

Moltmann goes on to interpret liberation theology as the call to the poor and marginalized, the forgotten and depressed, the homeless and the victims of evil. It is at the intersection of the total abandonment by God and the utter devastation that can lead to finding hope. Hope slowly emerges in the mysterious light of the resurrection where death and darkness are not the final word. It is what Jewish theologian Abraham Joshua Heschel discovered in the Hebrew prophets ("divine pathos"), or what St. John of the Cross identified as "the dark night of the soul." It is what the Prophet Muhammad experienced as he meditated on Mt. Hira before the Qur'an was revealed and he became the vehicle of Allah's revelation of hope and justice to humanity. For Moltmann, the descent into the darkness of death on the cross and the subsequent call to identify with and serve the poor and disinherited is where healing and hope begin. He says this is the journey of theology after Auschwitz. It enabled him to process his guilt as a former soldier for Nazi Germany and find healing by serving the poor and rebuilding his country. These actions were reciprocal, for in serving others he began to rehabilitate himself.

Whether we are Jews, Muslims, Christians, Hindus, Buddhists, Confucian, Marxists, atheists or secular humanists, we must come to terms with the moral and ethical mandate to honor the dead and maimed in Gaza and consider how we will practice theology and ethics after the Gaza genocide. As I write, the genocide continues, and it has already begun in the West Bank. As during the Holocaust under the Nazi regime, most of the world is silent, and in this case many of the countries that have gone silent are complicit in supporting the genocide in Gaza.

Just before Christmas, my wife and I watched a remarkable video of a young boy about ten years old being interviewed by a reporter in a rain-drenched tent in Gaza. The boy led the reporter inside his tent and showed him what it was like to live with the mattresses soaking wet, the tent shaking from the strong gusts of wind, pots and pans and clothing floating in the ankle-deep water. It was cold; the boy was soaking wet and began to cry. Then he screamed through his tears: "We are drowning. Where are the people? Where is Allah? We're all drowning. Where is the Umma [the Muslim world]?" He continued to scream, repeating the phrases like mantras. He waved his hands in the air to emphasize his plea: "We are drowning here. Where is the Umma? The world has abandoned us."

The reporter walked out of the tent and filmed a long row of tents blown over by the powerful wind gusts and drenching rain. The winter storm was relentless, and the tents were blown over, scattering the meagre belongings of the Gazans in the water. Everything was ruined—blankets, coats, sweaters, tents. I could not help but think the boy was uttering the same plea Jesus cried from the cross: "My God, my God, why have you forsaken me?" Then, a middle aged man appeared outside the destroyed tents, one of which may have been his temporary home. He was standing in the brown, polluted water, soaking wet and shaking from the cold. Like the boy, he had a pained look of grief and desperation as he lifted his hands to the heavens, crying out, "Why O Allah why, why, why?" Tears were flowing down his cheeks as he continued to lift his arms to the sky, screaming out to the heavens: "Why Allah? Why has this happened to us?"[89]

Now it is up to us. We have all failed Gaza. The world has abandoned Gaza, once again. Much of the western world has not only abandoned Gaza, but financed or participated directly in the genocide. The United Nations and the international courts have failed Gaza. Most of Gaza's tents are no longer water repellant, and the winter rains are relentless. The humanitarian relief organizations have hundreds of thousands of tents sitting in warehouses in Amman and Cairo because Israelis refuse to allow them to enter Gaza, as new tents might undermine their strategies of medical necropolitics. That young boy and the man, crying to the heavens, represent the Palestinians of Gaza, both the living and the dead, the wounded and maimed, the orphans and the traumatized babies, as the world continues to send Israel weapons and do nothing to demand an end to this live-streamed genocide.

The cry, "Why have you abandoned us, O God?" Where is God? God is in the destroyed tents, the rain-soaked beds and blankets. God is there, in Gaza, in the West Bank, as the beleaguered Palestinians rise each day to survive and cry out to a world where a growing movement stands with them. This is where we must be: through the relief and reconstruction workers, the physicians, nurses, and mothers and fathers. We must facilitate and enable the political solution that will free Gaza and rebuild Palestine. Now the choice is ours. Let us rise up and take a stand for justice for the Palestinian people. Let it be a new day of truth and justice for the people of Israel, and for the world. Amen.

AFTERWORD

by Rev. Dr. William J. Barber II and Phyllis Bennis

The text that follows was included as a foreword to the original edition of this book, titled Glory to God in the Lowest: Journeys to an Unholy Land.

In a recent article, the Israeli daily *Jerusalem Post* quoted Prime Minister Naftali Bennett welcoming a group of international visitors. "Your love for Israel is legendary," he said. "Your passion for Israel is an uncompromising statement of support for the Jewish state, for its people, and for our destiny. Your devotion to Israel is not only a blessing for us, but it has helped us sustain our situation during the most trying times, including wars. You rejoice in Israel's many triumphs, and you stand with us side-by-side when we most need it."

One might have reasonably assumed Bennett was welcoming Jewish visitors, appreciating their expected support for Israel. But these were Christians, coming to Israel from around the world to celebrate their support for Israel as an exclusive Jewish state. At a time when Israel's 2018 Nation-State Law asserts that only Jews, no one else in the State of Israel including the 20 percent of Israeli citizens who are Palestinians, have the right of self-determination in their own country, international support is weakening. At a time when Israeli violations of international law and human rights are leading to more and more public criticism from around the world, the uncompromising Christian support for Israel's exclusive Jewish identity is important indeed. No wonder Prime Minister Bennett was so effusive in his thanks.

Don Wagner's remarkable memoir tracks his own history and his own transition as he moved from life as a young, conservative white evangelical Christian in rural upstate New York to become a committed activist for Palestinian rights. All the while he interrogates and challenges the theological origins and the political consequences of Christian zionism for Palestinians in the occupied territory, inside Israel, and in far-flung exile.

Wagner's transformation didn't happen all at once. He came to oppose the Vietnam War as a seminary student, and to understand the primacy of racism in US society while working as an assistant pastor in a Black church. He began to grasp the reality of colonialism while meeting with Palestinians living—and dying—under Israeli occupation, and those facing dispossession and massacres in the refugee camps of Lebanon and beyond. Over time, he examined, confronted, and finally came to staunchly oppose what he eventually recognized as Christian zionism.

Wagner describes the movement's importance in helping the Jewish campaign to colonize pre-state Israel, in what was then Palestine. "In the Christian West," he writes, "Christian Zionists were invaluable as they provided Christian theological images and language for the Zionists that adopted the settler colonial goals of replacing the local population. When it came time for Zionism to market their ideas in the churches, or the British Parliament and the United States, they borrowed from the Christian Zionist narratives, such as 'God gave the entirety of Palestine to the Jewish people.' There was no place for the Palestinian Arab population. Again, the Zionist lobby borrowed from Christian Zionists, claiming the Palestinians were the 'Canaanites' or the Philistines of the Bible and had to be destroyed just as the Israelites did in the Book of Joshua."

But despite that history, until three or four decades ago, the existence of Christian zionism as a movement in the United States would have been surprising to most people. Its influence beyond theological discussions within various evangelical denominations, and behind the scenes within the Jewish zionist movement, was minimal. But as Wagner notes, that began to change during the Reagan administration of the 1980s, and the movement today counts millions of adherents and often determinative influence in the Republican Party. According to Ron Dermer, former Israeli ambassador to the US, "the backbone of Israel's support in the United States is the evangelical Christians."

Just for comparison sake, there are about 82 million evangelical Protestants in the United States, about a quarter of the US population. Eighty percent of evangelicals believe that "the creation of Israel in 1948 was a fulfillment of biblical prophecy that would bring about Christ's return." Jews, on the other hand, make up only about 7.5 million people in the United States. And while Jews have historically been the main backers of Israel, these days fewer and fewer US Jews, especially young Jews, support Israel. In fact, as Dermer noted with some dismay, American Jews are found "disproportionately among [Israel's] critics."

What dismayed Ambassador Dermer, however, is bringing new hope to supporters of human rights, international law, and equality for all across the Middle East, and specifically in Israel-Palestine. The rise of organizations like Jewish Voice for Peace, which joins human rights organizations such as Amnesty International, Human Rights Watch, and the leading Israeli human rights group B'tselem, in calling out Israeli apartheid and standing clearly against zionism and colonialism, provides a powerful challenge to Christian zionism.

Certainly it will take more work—education, mobilization, advocacy, and more—to successfully confront that movement. We come to Don Wagner's story from disparate vantage points—that of a Christian pastor and bishop with decades of mobilizing for social justice even before cofounding the Poor People's Campaign: A National Call for Moral Revival in 2017, and that of a secular Jew steeped in internationalism and organizing for Palestinian rights. Rev. Barber has collaborated for years with local and national Jewish communities across the United States, whose Jewish activists, leaders, and rabbis have shared with him their own diverse critiques of the Israeli government's long-standing oppression of Palestinians. Phyllis Bennis works with Jewish organizations as well as Muslim, Christian, and of course a wide range of secular groups committed to justice and Palestinian rights, with years of learning and writing throughout the Middle East behind her. Both of us read and engage with Israeli Jewish supporters of Palestinian rights, as well as with Palestinian analysts and civil society activists around the world.

But while we come from different starting points, we come together based on the call of the Rev. Dr. Martin Luther King, Jr., who demanded that we challenge the evil triplets of racism, poverty, and militarism. If Dr. King were alive today, he would certainly include ecological devastation as well as the toxic brew of religious [white] nationalism in the United States, which are part of the call as well. And all of that leads to the demand for international human rights, keeping the pressure on the US government to stop providing more than $3.8 billion every year directly to the Israeli military, and to stop protecting Israel from being held accountable in the United Nations or the International Criminal Court for its violations of international law.

Referencing research regarding Jewish settlement in Palestine as a colonial project, Wagner quotes the founder of modern zionism, Theodore Herzl saying, "If I wish to substitute a new building for an old one, I must demolish before I construct." That understanding continues today, as the modern government of Israel maintains a policy of dispossessing the indigenous Palestinian population and replacing them with Jewish settlers. And support for that explicit policy of dispossession-replacement comes most powerfully from organizations like CUFI, Christians United for Israel. CUFI's leader, Rev. John Hagee, spoke in May 2021 at the height of Israel's assault on Gaza. He reminded his followers that God gave the land of Israel to the Jewish people, and that the Jews are "the apple of God's eye." He also warned that if the United States did not continue to support Israel, God would not support the United States.

Rev. Barber, as a Christian theologian deeply rooted in the ancient Jewish prophets' critique of and challenge to violence, poverty, and injustice, recognizes that such acts are unacceptable. We share a commitment to opposing such actions, regardless of whether they are committed by state authorities or by the privileged against the marginalized. And as Rev. Barber recognizes, there is nothing antisemitic about such a challenge to injustice—rather, challenging exactly those acts of injustice is in fact an obligation of all religions, and indeed a requirement of prophetic authority.

As long as leaders of CUFI and similar organizations continue to distort Biblical references to win support for Israel's dispossession, occupation, and apartheid, and as long as they wield the fear of God's wrath to gain their followers' embrace of unlimited US military and political support for Israel, the movement for Palestinian rights will have to work even harder. Don Wagner's compelling story will help make that happen. We are grateful to him for sharing and glad for the chance to introduce this important story.

May 2022

Rev. William J. Barber II is president of Repairers of the Breach and co-chair of the Poor People's Campaign: A National Call for Moral Revival.

Phyllis Bennis is a fellow of the Institute for Policy Studies and serves on the board of Jewish Voice for Peace.

FAMILY, MENTORS, AND FRIENDS

My parents Donald E. Wagner, Sr., and Thelma "Pat" Wagner

Grandpa Nelson and me (around 4 years old)

My dear wife Linda Kateeb and me

My sister Karen and her husband Ken Beck, sons Matt and Jay, daughter Anna, and me at mom's funeral service

My eldest son, Jay, and his wife, Tracy, and grandkids Ashley (now 19) and Aiden (now 12)

My middle son, Matt, and his wife, Kristy, grandchildren Luke (now 10), Colin (now 8), and Claire (now 3)

My daughter Anna on the right. To her left is Lucy (5), then-husband Dave Jalensky, and Nora (10).

Rev. Dr. Joseph L. Roberts Sr., Pastor, Ebenezer Baptist Church, Atlanta, GA. (photo courtesy of Dr. Ralph Basui Watkins, Columbia Theological Seminary)

Rabbi Brant Rosen (photo courtesy of Tzedek Chicago.)

Rev. Dr. Bud Ogle, Founding Director, Good News, North of Howard Street in Chicago

Don Betz, ICCP Chair and visionary of the global advocacy network

Dr. Ghada and Ayoub Talhami; Palestinian activists and scholars

Dr. Ibrahim Abu Lughod, a Palestinian scholar (photo courtesy of Birzeit University)

Dr. Pauline Coffman, Presbyterian Church USA activist, Chair of CMES

Rev. Dr. Munther Isaac, Palestinian pastor and author of "Christ in the Rubble"

Hon. Rev. Wendell Griffen, retired judge, pastor, and Black liberation theologian

Rev. Darrel Meyers, close friend and activist, Friends of Sabeel, Southern California

(left to right) Omar Haramy, Director of Sabeel; me; and Rev. Dr. Naim Ateek, founder of Sabeel

Kathy Bergen, Friends of Sabeel Canada and former ICCP Director

Gaby Habib, General Secretary, Middle East Council of Churches

Fr. Michael Prior; Irish liberation theologian and Palestinian activist.

ENDNOTES

1 Jewish Voice for Peace, *On Antisemitism: Jewish Voice for Peace* (Chicago: Haymarket Books, 2017), xv.

2 Sam Bahour, at a Meeting with the Palestine Justice Network Solidarity Delegation, Ramallah, Palestine; February 20, 2024, https://paxchristiusa.org/2024/03/06/the-stones-cry-out-delegation-report/

3 www.hrw.org/news/2024/07/19/world-court-finds-israel-responsible-apartheid

4 "No one fully survived: Shocking statistics expose the devastating scope of Israel's genocide in Gaza" Euro-Med Human Rights Monitor, https://euromedmonitor.org/en/article/6897/No-one-fully-survived:-Shocking-statistics-expose-the-devastating-scope-of-Israel%E2%80%99s-genocide-in-Gaza/

5 "History Will Record that Israel Committed a holocaust), Electronic Intifada, March 6, 2024, electronicintifada.net/content/history-will-record-israel-committed-holocaust/45006.

6 Theologian Richard Rohr says fear is like Velcro wrapped around the brain, reshaping how we think, how we feel, and how we act; that is until the Velcro is unwrapped. Brain science tells us fear triggers the "reptilian part of the brain" and dominates our behavior often as a survival instinct until we learn how to manage the emotion. We observe effective alternatives to the traditional fear-based response. See James Massey, "Taming the Reptilian Brain," ndnr.com/mindbody/taming-the-reptilian-brain.

7 Dowey was nationally known theologian and leader of the controversial new Presbyterian "Confession of 1967," which emphasized reconciliation, justice, and peaceful approaches to conflict. For the text, see: www.pcusa.org/site_media/media/uploads/theologyandworship/pdfs/confess67.pdf

8 Several liberation theologians and priests were censured by the Vatican. These included Fathers Miguel d'Escoto and Ernesto and Fernando Cardenal, who held positions in the revolutionary Sandinista Party in Nicaragua. Archbishop Oscar Romero in El Salvador and theologians Gustavo Gutiérrez in Peru and Jon Sabrino in Brazil continued their teaching and ministries despite the Vatican opposition. Archbishop Romero challenged the right-wing government and militias in El Salvador, who were trained and underwritten by Israel and the United States. Romero was assassinated by the militias on March 24, 1980, while serving the Eucharist in the San Salvador Cathedral.

9 Most historians cite King's speech at New York City's Riverside Church, on April 4, 1967, as his first public announcement uniting the anti-war and civil rights movements. But Dr. King first linked the civil rights movement to the anti-war movement three weeks earlier, at the Washington conference of March 1967, and I was honored to witness it. The decision was difficult for Dr. King as several of his lieutenants opposed the idea. Dr. King's decision led to a significant increase in interfaith support for both movements and had a seismic impact on my political development. Some analysts believe it was the turning point for the country's support of the war.

10 Les and Tamara Payne, *The Dead Are Arising* (New York: Liveright Publications, 2020).

11 Ronald Sullivan, "Newark's White Vigilante Group, Opposed by Governor, Sees Itself as an Antidote to Riots," *New York Times,* January 24, 1968.

12 Alice George, "In 1968 The Kerner Commission Got It Right, But Nobody Listened," *Smithsonian Magazine*, March 1, 2018, www.smithsonianmag.com/smithsonian-institution/1968-kerner-commission-got-it-right-nobody-listened-180968318/

13 Matthew 25:35–40; gender-inclusive language added.

14 *Diana L. Hayes,* "A Great Cloud of Witnesses: Martin Luther King Jr.'s Roots in the African American Religious and Spiritual Traditions," *Revives My Soul Again: The Spirituality of Martin Luther King Jr., eds. Lewis V. Baldwin and Victor Anderson* (Fortress Press: 2018), 43, 44–46. Quoted in "Community," May 9, 2020; Fr. Richard Rohr's Daily Meditation, cac.org/community-weekly-summary-2020-05-09/

15 Vincent Harding, Preface to *Jesus and the Disinherited*, (Boston: Beacon Press, 1945),viii.

16 Howard Thurman, *Jesus and the Disinherited*, (Boston: Beacon Press, 1945), 1–2.

17 John 4:1-42.

18 Mark 1:35-37, Luke 5:16; Matthew 14:23.

19 After completing his assignment with the Presbyterian Church, Joe was handpicked by Dr. Martin Luther King Sr. to replace him as the senior pastor at the renowned Ebenezer Baptist Church in Atlanta, Georgia. Joe served as senior pastor there from 1975–2005.

20 In *Our Jerusalem*, Bertha Spafford Vester recounts the story of the Spafford family and the American Colony, initially an evangelical Christian group, later a luxury hotel. The manuscript was first published in Beirut and included a section on the Deir Yassin massacre and the panic created by the zionist's truck-mounted loudspeakers. Another version—published in New York and later in Israel, and sold at bookstores in both countries—omits the section about Deir Yassin.

21 Minutes of Chicago Presbytery, November 1974.

22 Adapted from "A Theological Reflection on the Middle East," Report to Presbytery from the Middle East Task Force, Chicago Presbytery, January 1977, 5–6.

23 Conference Report, ibid., 6–7.

24 Conference Report, ibid., 13–14. (Luke 9:62).

25 "Lebanon Profile—Timeline," BBC News, April 25, 2018, www.bbc.com/news/world-middle-east-14649284

26 Marion Kawas, "Searching for Palestine in Lebanon," *Mondoweiss*, December 27, 2018, mondoweiss.net/2018/12/searching-palestine-lebanon/

27 The intricate Palestinian embroidery varied from village to village and was a true art form, passed down from mother to daughter, often serving as the wedding dress worn by the new bride. The design identifies the woman as part of a Palestinian village; thus, her identity is both communal and individual.

28 Rabbi Eckstein later founded the International Fellowship of Christians and Jews, one of the leading Jewish philanthropic organizations raising funds primarily from

evangelical Christians. The group supported poor Jewish immigrants as well as Israel's illegal settlements in East Jerusalem and the West Bank.

29 Find the complete document in Donald Wagner, *Anxious for Armageddon* (Scottsdale: Herald Press, 1995), Appendix E, 215–17.

30 Georgie Anne Geyer, "Challenging the Biblical Claim to West Bank," *Chicago Sun-Times*, June 29, 1979.

31 Wesley Granberg-Michaelson, *Without Oars* (Minneapolis: Broadleaf Books, 2020), 104.

32 Hussein Agha and Robert Malley, *Tomorrow is Yesderday* (New York: Farrar, Straus, and Giroux: 2025), 219-220.

33 William Farrell, "123 Reported Dead, 550 Injured as Israelis Bomb PLO Targets in Beirut and South Lebanon," *New York Times*, July 18, 1981

34 Seymour Hersh, "The Iran Pipeline: A Hidden Chapter," *New York Times*, December 8, 1991; confirmed by Benjamin Weiser, "Behind Israel-Iran Sales," *Washington Post,* August 16, 1987.

35 Oded Yinon, "A Strategy for Israel in the Nineteen Eighties," *Kivunim: A Journal of Judaism and Zionism,* February 1982.

36 In 2017, a small Syrian faction in Lebanon, the Syrian Socialist Nationalist Party, was tried in absentia and convicted as the group responsible for the assassination of Bachir Gemayel; "Lebanese court issues death sentence over 1982 Gemayel assassination," *Reuters*, October 20, 2017.

37 Donald Wagner, Special Report: "A morning in Shatila Camp," *Palestine Human Rights Campaign*; September/October 1982.

38 Estimates of the dead ranged from 400–3,500 according to the Red Cross.

39 Article 7 (1) of the Rome Statute, Crimes against humanity, legal.un.org/icc/statute/99_corr/cstatute.htm .

40 Bernard Avishai, "Ariel Sharon's Dark Greatness," *The New Yorker*, January 13, 2014, www.newyorker.com/news/news-desk/ariel-sharons-dark-greatness.

41 Robert Fisk, *This Is Not a Movie*, directed by Yung Chang, (Brooklyn: KimStim, 2020), streaming.

42 I am using the term "evangelical" as an umbrella category encompassing various Protestant revivalist movements emerging from the first and second "Great Awakenings" in the United States. Today, US evangelicals may number between 100–125 million people, the most visible being the evangelical right or fundamentalists—about 18 percent of all evangelicals. The evangelical "center" includes evangelical denominations and evangelicals who are members of mainstream Protestant denominations. The evangelical left represents approximately 10 percent of all evangelicals such as Sojourners. In the Middle East and Europe, the term evangelical implies churches that emerged from the first wave of the sixteenth-century Protestant Reformation including Lutherans, Calvinist and Reformed churches, Presbyterian, Congregational, and the progressive Baptist denominations.

43 Vanunu's backstory is based on my personal meetings with Mordechai and my 1986 article, "Searching for Vanunu," *Middle East International*, November 7, 1986, 11.
44 "No one fully survived: Shocking statistics expose the devastating scope of Israel's genocide in Gaza" Euro-Med Human Rights Monitor, https://euromedmonitor.org/en/article/6897/No-one-fully-survived:-Shocking-statistics-expose-the-devastating-scope-of-Israel%E2%80%99s-genocide-in-Gaza.
45 When I returned to Jerusalem in April 1987, my visit coincided with a lecture by Gene Sharp, the world's leading authority on nonviolent direct action. Gene was director of the Einstein Institute at Harvard University, where they studied and documented non-violent campaigns around the globe. In his Jerusalem lecture he stated the Palestinian Intifada was 85–90 percent nonviolent in its methods. He cited the raw brutality of the Israeli military response and pointed to Defense Minister Rabin's call for the military to increase Palestinian beatings and breaking of bones. Rabin later denied giving the order but an Israeli colonel confirmed that the orders came from Rabin according to my notes from Gene Sharp's lecture; see also Amitabh Pal, "Gene Sharp's Nonviolent Impact," *The Progressive*, February 17, 2011, progressive.org/dispatches/gene-sharp-s-nonviolent-impact/.
46 Mazin Qumsiyeh, *Popular Resistance in Palestine* (New York: Pluto Press, 2011).
47 Donald E. Wagner, "The Programme of the Christian Zionists," *Middle East International*, May 1988, 19–20.
48 Peri Stone, "Persecution Reports Unfounded", *Christianity Today*, July 13, 1998.
49 Democracy Now, "Robert Fisk Recounts His Interviews with Osama bin Laden, as Well as Father of Alleged Hijacker," September 17, 2001; democracynow.org/2001/9/17/robert_fisk_recounts_his_interviews_with.
50 Sir Henry Finch, "The World's Great Restauration of Calling of the Jews," (London: Edward Griffin for William Bladen, 1621); page 6; cited in Donald Wagner, *Anxious for Armageddon* (Scottsdale, Pennsylvania) Herald Press, 1995; page 87.
51 Robert O. Smith, "Toward a Lutheran Response to Christian Zionism," ELCA Conference of Bishops gathering in San Mateo, Calif., March 2008. A relatively new type of Christian Zionism has emerged in the second Trump administration called the New Apostolic Reformation (NAR) which is a variation on part of the CUFI dispensationalist political model. It is neo-Pentecostal and borrows from dispensationalism (Battle of Armageddon and necessity of a revived Israel to prepare for Jesus' return). Secretary of Defense (War) Pete Hegseth is an example calling for a revived Messianic Kingdom in the Middle East with the United States partnering with Israel in military victories (Palestine, Iran, Lebanon and other countries) to usher in Jesus' return and dominance. See Beb Lorber's essay "Actualizing America's Christian Zionist Agenda: The New Apostolic Reformation", Institute for the Study of Christian Zionism; Volume 1, number 2, https://studychristianzionism.org/iscz-journal-vol-1-no-2-christian-zionism-and-nationalism-in-the-era-of-trump/
52 Donald M. Lewis, A Short History of Christian Zionism (Downers Grove, Illinois: Intervarsity Press, 2021); See pages 132-185.

53 For a well researched analysis of this period see Ussama Makdisi, *The Age of Coexistence* (Oakland, California: University of California Press, 2019; see pages 189-240.

54 balfourproject.org/shaftesbury/.

55 Robert Smith, Ibid.

56 *Herzl's Diary,* 1895.

57 Herzl in his novel *The Old New Land.*

58 Kenneth Young, *Arthur James Balfour*, (London: G. Bell and Sons, Ltd., 1963); p. 256.

59 The Question of Palestine, (New York, The United Nations Press, 1979); page 3.

60 Alicia Cox, "Settler Colonialism," *Oxford Bibliographies*, last modified July 26, 2017, https://www.oxfordbibliographies.com/view/document/obo-9780190221911/obo-9780190221911-0029.xml.

61 Brueggemann, *Chosen?*, xlv.

62 Raheb, *Decolonizing Palestine*, page 76; see Brueggemann, *Chosen?*, pp. 8-12.

63 Noah Lanard, "The Dangerous History Behind Netanyahu's Amalek Rhetoric," Mother Jones, www.motherjones.com/politics/2023/11/benjamin-netanyahu-amalek-israel-palestine-gaza-saul-samuel-old-testament/.

64 Raheb, *Decolonizing Palestine*, p.112–113.

65 Rev. Dr. Munther Isaac, lecture at Missio Dei, Chicago, Illinois, August 3, 2024.

66 W.H.Auden, "September 1, 1939," *Another Time*, (New York, Random House); 1940.

67 Mark Braverman, "The Torrmented Dance of the Colonizer: Peter Beinart, Liberal Zionism and the Battle for Palestine," Mondoweiss, April 6, 2021, mondoweiss.net/2021/04/the-tormented-dance-of-the-colonizer-peter-beinart-liberal-zionism-and-the-battle-for-palestine/

68 The famous quote "The arc of the moral universe…" is usually attributed to Rev Martin Luther King Jr., but was first stated by the Unitarian minister and abolitionist Theodore Parker in an 1853 sermon. www.npr.org/2010/09/02/129609461/theodore-parker-and-the-moral-universe.

69 Noura Erakat, *Justice for Some; Law and the Question of Palestine*; (Stanford, California: Stanford University Press, 2018.

70 Craig Mokhiber, Testimony at the Gaza Tribuna, https://youtu.be/xnAGrUWL8zA?si=fVXjLctfTBjFeSZO.

71 Evangelical Lutheran Bishop of Jordan and the Holy Land Dr. Sani Azar´s 2025 Reformation Day Sermon at the Church of the Redeemer in Jerusalem: www.facebook.com/naimateek/posts/during-the-recent-reformation-day-service-at-the-lutheran-church-of-the-redeemer/1291095549719634/.

72 Kairos Palestine: A Moment of Truth in a Time of Genocide; November, 2025; This is the most comprehensive theological, political, and pragmatic appeal from the Christians in Palestine to the crisis and they are facing including their very existence. Sections 1.1-1.18 describe the reality of genocide, settler colonialism and annihilation that all Palestinians are facing, both Christians and Muslims, and the sense of abandonment they feel from the silence of western governments and church leadership in the face of an ongoing genocide. https://www.kairospalestine.ps.

73 religionnews.com/2025/02/11/why-younger-evangelical-christians-are-losing-their-faith-in-israel/.
74 "Trump Says he Moved the US Embassy to Jerusalem for the Evangelicals"; www.timesofisrael.com/trump-says-he-moved-us-embassy-to-jerusalem-for-the-evangelicals/.
75 Kairos Palestine II; Section 3.7, is a categorical rejection of Christian Zionism as a false religion that provides a dangerous justification for some Christians to embrace the modern zionist state of Israel unconditionally while ignoring the clear message of Jesus and the Hebrew prophets. https://www.kairospalestine.ps/index.php/about-kairos/kairos-palestine-ii.
76 Dr. Allan Boesak, Lecture in Cape Town, October 7, 2025; summary from my notes.
77 Peter Beinart, "Desecrating God´s Name," May 26, 2925; The Beinart Notebook, peterbeinart.substack.com/p/desecrating-gods-name.
78 Beinart, Ibid.
79 The Wire: "We Shut Down Grand Central Station to Demand a Ceasefire," https://www.jewishvoiceforpeace.org/2023/10/30/wire-grand-central-action/.
80 https://www.timesofisrael.com/groups-using-facial-recognition-to-unmask-anti-israel-campus-Protesters.
81 "What Is Project Esther? The Playbook Against Pro-Palestinian USA,Al-Jazeera: May 31, 2024; https://www.aljazeera.com/news/2025/5/31/what-is-project-esther-the-playbook-against-pro-palestine-movement-in-us.
82 "When Past Advocacy Meets Present Needs: Don Betz, Kathy Bergen, Larry Ekin, and Don Wagner;" https://electron.icintifada.net/content/when-past-activism-meets-present/44411.
83 Nadera Shalhoub-Kevorkian, Security Theology, Surveillance, and Politics of Fear, Cambridige, England; Cambridge University Press, 2015; page 3.
84 "Reconsidering Reparations," Review Lecture; Arithi Sriprakash; British Journal of Educational Studies Volume 71, 2023 - Issue 2.
85 Daoud Nassar, Friends of the Tent of Nations Christmas Letter, December, 2025; https://fotonna.org/category/current-newsletter/.
86 Ilan Pappe, *Israel on the Brink*: Boston, MA.: Beacon Press, 2025; page 8.
87 Pappe, Ibid., pages 15-36.
88 Jurgen Moltmann, *The Crucified God*. Minneapolis, MN. Fortress Press, 1993; page x.
89 "We are drowning in Gaza. Where is everyone? Why O God why? why?" Facebook, Hope For Gaza Foundation, https://www.facebook.com/HopeForGazaRelief/videos/871376042469432/.

ACKNOWLEDGMENTS

Without a doubt, the Palestinians in the Gaza Strip have demonstrated remarkable determination, resilience, and courage amid Israel´s entire military arsenal of daily carpet bombing, near total destruction of Gaza's infrastructure, and severe life-threatening blockades of food and medicine. Despite Israel's intent to commit genocide, the Palestinian spirit of survival continues to inspire me, from the martyrs including the mothers, the children, and babies, the elderly, physicians, ambulance drivers, journalists, teachers, aid workers, cemetery workers, and entire families. Their will to live in the midst of a genocide is a powerful form of resistance to Israel's policy of erasure and reminds me that giving up is never an option.

In 2022, I published my memoir, *Glory to God in the Lowest: Journeys to an Unholy Land*, which chronicles my religious and political transformation from Christian zionism to advocacy for Palestinian rights. The memoir describes several formative events that I experienced firsthand, such as being caught in Israel's 1982 invasion of Lebanon, then entering the Sabra and Shatila refugee camps one day after the massacre, or living in the West Bank during the First Intifada. Over the years, I witnessed the severity of Israel's repeated military assaults and the courageous Palestinian resistance. However, nothing prepared me for the current genocide in Gaza. Medical agencies now estimate between 195,000 and 250,000 dead, which includes the missing bodies still under the rubble and the martyrs who were literally evaporated by the 2,000-pound bombs dropped on their apartment buildings. I came to realize the least I could do to honor the dead and the living in Gaza was to write a second edition of my memoir in light of the Gaza genocide.

I called my publisher, Michel Moushabeck, president of Interlink Publishing, who supported the idea and offered concrete suggestions, such as a new title that reflected the Gaza genocide. With Michel´s encouragement, I started to reimagine the memoir with the Gaza genocide at the forefront of my thinking. I thank the Palestine Justice Network of the Presbyterian Church

USA for permission to use the subtitle of the memoir, "Why Palestine Matters," the title of one of their publications.

My other major source of inspiration for this new project was my wife, Linda Kateeb, a second-generation Palestinian and an incredible source of ideas, emotional support, and editing skills. She gently and sometimes aggressively debated me on content, organization, sentence structure, grammar, and style to strengthen the clarity, coherence, and quality of my writing. Not only is she my partner in marriage, but she is my partner in advocacy—brainstorming ways to encourage our callous legislators, media, and religious leaders to take principled action to end the genocide. While we had little impact on the decision-makers of these institutions, we did find receptive audiences at the grassroots level in churches, university campuses, and informal gatherings in homes. As the genocide extended into the West Bank, the grim reality of Israel's escalating violence hit home when Linda's cousin walked out of a coffee shop in Ramallah and was shot in the back by an Israeli soldier, who stood over his body with his rifle drawn forbidding his friends from calling an ambulance. Her cousin never recovered from the shooting. He lost a great deal of blood and died two days later, leaving behind his twenty-one-year-old widow and a one-year-old son. He was but one of thousands killed by the Israeli military and militant settlers in the West Bank, not to mention the hundreds of thousands massacred in the Gaza Strip.

The enormity of this continuous genocide and the impunity that both Israeli and US officials maintain can at times immobilize us, and I am no exception. Some mornings I could not write, troubled by the latest news of massacres. The indifference of our legislators left me frustrated and angry. Linda and I would vent our frustration and then brainstorm advocacy strategies, realizing we did not have the luxury of giving up, particularly when the Palestinians in Gaza or the West Bank and East Jerusalem have no choice but to resist and stay on their land.

This volume would not have been possible without the indispensable staff members at Interlink Publishing—especially David Klein and Pam Fontes-May, whose thoughtful editing guided the final text. I am deeply indebted to my friend Rev. Dr. Munther Isaac, a Palestinian pastor and theologian who wrote the foreword. In 2023, his "Christ in the Rubble" Christmas Eve sermon went viral, reminding the world that Jesus calls for us to stand with those in greatest need. I am equally grateful for Judge Wendell Griffen, the author of the preface. He is an African American federal judge from the Deep South and both a pastor and co-director of the Samuel DeWitt Proctor Conference movement of black liberation theology. These two giants in their respective communities represent the long and parallel struggles for justice and liberation of Palestinians and African Americans in the prophetic and often radical spirit of Jesus of Nazareth.

I dedicate this memoir to the present and future generations of Palestinian children, including the martyrs and survivors of this genocide, hoping and praying that the survivors will find healing and peace in a new and restored Gaza where their families will live in security with their full rights guaranteed by a just and lasting political solution. I hope my seven grandchildren and all children around the world—especially the surviving children of Israel and Palestine—will one day witness a just and lasting peace. May this 117-year Palestinian-Israeli struggle be resolved with justice, equality, and true liberation for every citizen. While this vision seems out of reach today, we must all rise in sacrificial solidarity until these killing fields are transformed into communities of mutual care, with justice and security for every Palestinian and Israeli. Let this be our vision, for "where there is no vision, the people will perish." Change is going to come. Yes, it will.

Rev. Dr. Don Wagner, 2026, Orland Hills, Illinois